A-Z BERKSHIRE STREET ATLAS

CONTENTS

Key to Map Pages	2-3	Index to Streets	121-142
Map Pages	4-119	Index to Places	143-147
Administrative Boundaries	120		

REFERENCE

Motorway	M4	Posttown Boundary By arrangement with the Post Office	
A Road	A4	Postcode Boundary Within Posttowns	
Under Construction		Map Continuation	62
Proposed		Built Up Area	MILL ST
B Road	B471	Car Park Selected	P
Dual Carriageway		Church or Chapel	†
One Way Street Traffic flow on A Roads is indicated by a heavy line on the driver's left.	→	Fire Station	■
Pedestrianized Road		Hospital	H
Restricted Access		House Numbers A and B Roads only	113 98
Track		Information Centre	i
Footpath		National Grid Reference	¹75
Railway	Level Crossing ✕ Station ■	Police Station	▲
County Boundary		Post Office	★
District Boundary		Toilet with disabled facilities	▽ ♿

SCALE

3⅓ inches to 1 mile

0   ¼   ½   ¾   1 mile

0   250   500   750   1 kilometre

1:19,000

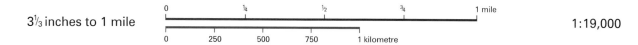

Geographers' A-Z Map Company Ltd.

Head Office:
Fairfield Road, Borough Green, Sevenoaks, Kent, TN15 8PP
Telephone 01732 781000

Showrooms:
44 Gray's Inn Road, London, WC1X 8HX
Telephone 0171 242 9246

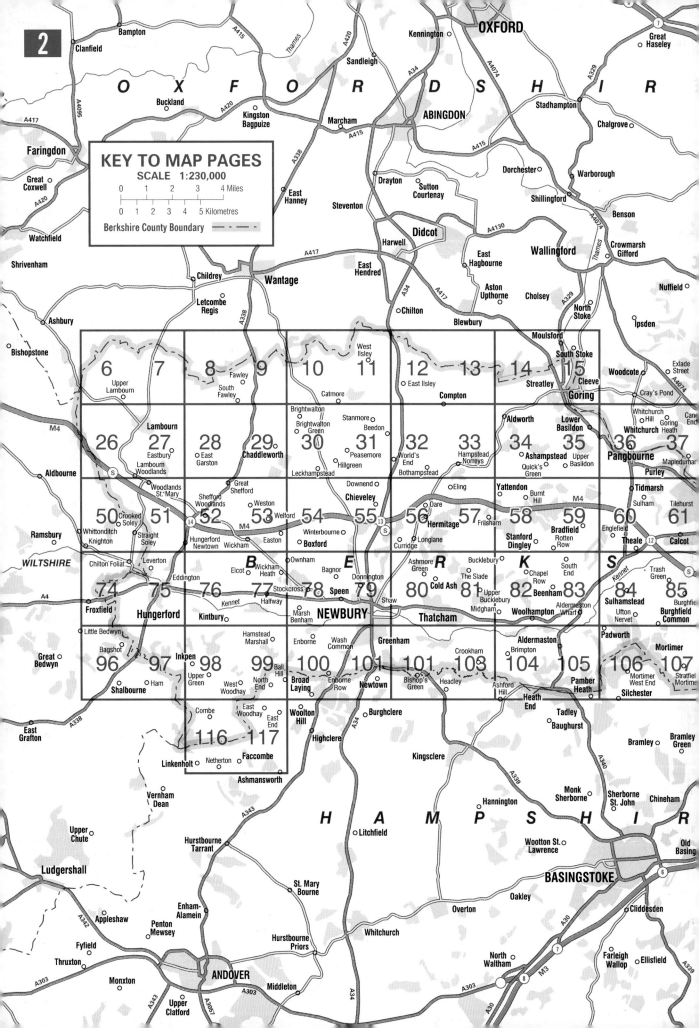

2

KEY TO MAP PAGES
SCALE 1:230,000

0   1   2   3   4 Miles
0 1 2 3 4 5 Kilometres

Berkshire County Boundary — · — · — · —

OXFORDSHIRE

Faringdon
Great Coxwell
Watchfield
Shrivenham
Ashbury
Bishopstone

Bampton
Clanfield
Buckland
Kingston Bagpuize
Marcham
East Hanney
Steventon
Childrey
Letcombe Regis
Wantage

Sandleigh
OXFORD
Kennington
Great Haseley
ABINGDON
Stadhampton
Chalgrove
Drayton
Sutton Courtenay
Dorchester
Warborough
Shillingford
Benson
Didcot
Harwell
East Hagbourne
Wallingford
Crowmarsh Gifford
East Hendred
Aston Upthorne
Cholsey
North Stoke
Nuffield
Chilton
Blewbury
Ipsden

WILTSHIRE

6	7	8	9	10	11	12	13	14	15
26	27	28	29	30	31	32	33	34	35	36	37
50	51	52	53	54	55	56	57	58	59	60	61
74	75	76	77	78	79	80	81	82	83	84	85
96	97	98	99	100	101	101	103	104	105	106	107
116	117									

Upper Lambourn
Fawley
South Fawley
Catmore
West Ilsley
East Ilsley
Compton
Moulsford
South Stoke
Streatley
Cleeve
Goring
Woodcote
Exlade Street
Cray's Pond

Lambourn
Eastbury
Lambourn Woodlands
East Garston
Chaddleworth
Brightwalton
Brightwalton Green
Stanmore
Beedon
World's End
Bothampstead
Hampstead Norreys
Aldworth
Lower Basildon
Whitchurch Hill
Goring Heath
Whitchurch
Cane
Leckhampstead
Hillgreen
Peasemore
Ashampstead
Quick's Green
Upper Basildon
Pangbourne
Mapledurham
Purley

Aldbourne
Woodlands St. Mary
Shefford Woodlands
Great Shefford
Weston
Welford
Downend
Chieveley
Eling
Oare
Yattendon
Burnt Hill
Stanford Dingley
Bradfield
Rotten Row
Tidmarsh
Sulham
Tilehurst

Ramsbury
Crooked Soley
Whittonditch
Knighton
Straight Soley
Hungerford Newtown
Wickham
Easton
Winterbourne
Boxford
Hermitage
Frilsham
Longlane
Curridge
Theale
Englefield
Calcot

Chilton Foliat
Leverton
Eddington
Elcot
Ownham
Bagnor
Donnington
Speen
Shaw
Ashmore Green
Cold Ash
Buckelbury
The Slade
Upper Bucklebury
Midgham
Chapel Row
South End
Beenham
Aldermaston Wharf
Woolhampton
Trash Green
Sulhamstead
Burghfield
Ufton Nervet
Burghfield Common

Froxfield
Hungerford
Kintbury
Stockcross
Marsh Benham
Halfway
NEWBURY
Thatcham

Little Bedwyn
Bagshot
Inkpen
Hamstead Marshall
Enborne
Wash Common
Greenham
Crookham
Brimpton
Aldermaston
Padworth
Mortimer

Great Bedwyn
Shalbourne
Ham
Upper Green
West Woodhay
North End
Ball Hill
Broad Laying
Enborne Row
Newtown
Bishop's Green
Headley
Ashford Hill
Heath End
Pamber Heath
Silchester
Mortimer West End
Stratfiel Mortime

East Grafton
Combe
East Woodhay
East End
Woolton Hill
Highclere
Burghclere
Kingsclere
Tadley
Baughurst
Bramley
Bramley Green

HAMPSHIRE

Vernham Dean
Linkenholt
Netherton
Faccombe
Ashmansworth
Hannington
Monk Sherborne
Sherborne St. John
Chineham

Upper Chute
Litchfield
Wootton St. Lawrence
Old Basing

Ludgershall
Hurstbourne Tarrant
St. Mary Bourne
BASINGSTOKE
Oakley
Cliddesden

Appleshaw
Enham-Alamein
Penton Mewsey
Hurstbourne Priors
Whitchurch
Overton
North Waltham
Farleigh Wallop
Ellisfield

Fyfield
Thruxton
Monxton
ANDOVER
Middleton
Upper Clatford

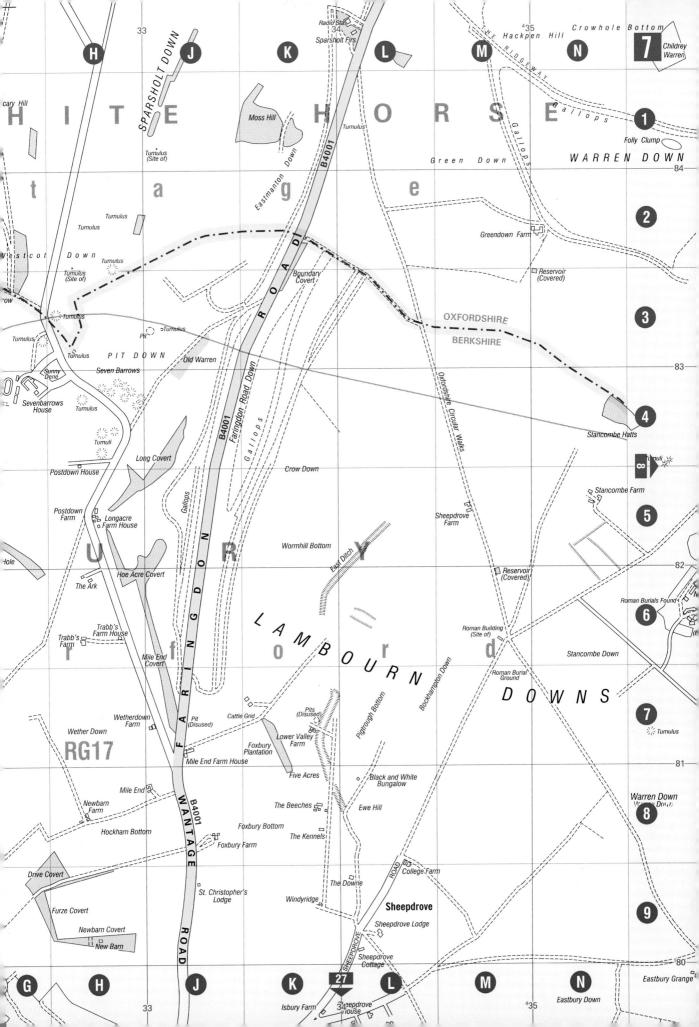

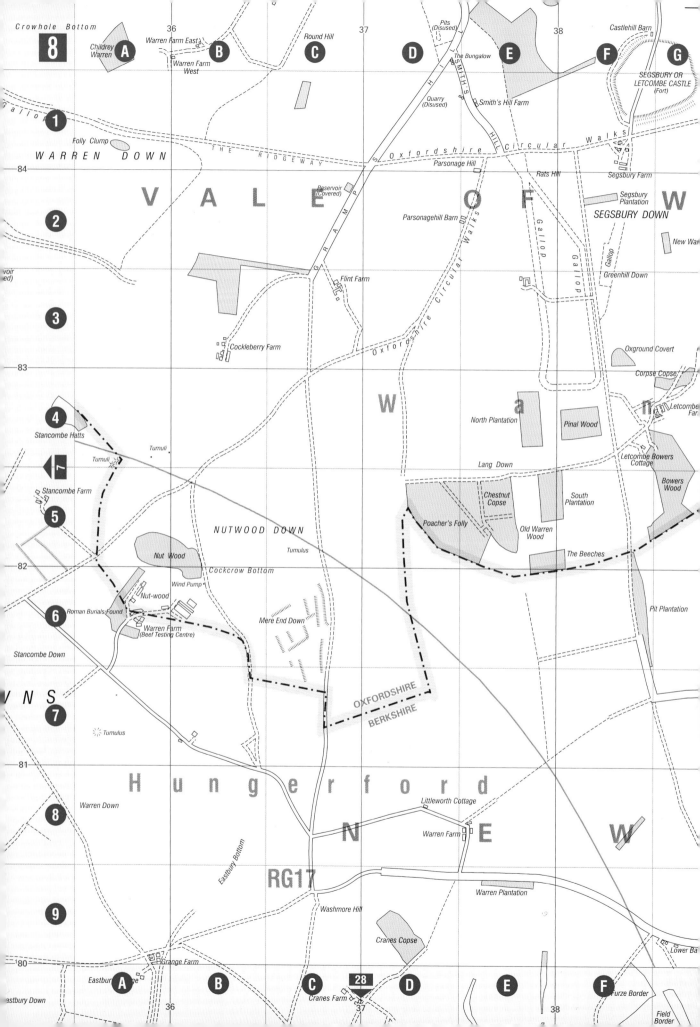

Crowhole Bottom

8

8 A Childrey Warren

Warren Farm East **B**

Round Hill **C**

D

The Bungalow **E**

Castlehill Barn **F**

G

36   37   38

Warren Farm West

SEGSBURY OR LETCOMBE CASTLE (Fort)

Pits (Disused)

Smith's Hill Farm

1 Folly Clump

Galloa

WARREN DOWN

THE RIDGEWAY

Quarry (Disused)

Parsonage Hill

Oxfordshire Circular Walks

Rats Hill

Segsbury Farm

84

VALE OF W

2

Reservoir (Covered)

Parsonagehill Barn

Gallop

Segsbury Plantation

SEGSBURY DOWN

New Wa

voir ed)

Flint Farm

Greenhill Down

Gallop

Gallop

3

Cockleberry Farm

Oxfordshire Circular Walks

83

W

a

n

Oxground Covert

Corpse Copse

North Plantation

Pinal Wood

Letcombe Far

4 Stancombe Hatts

Tumuli

Lang Down

Letcombe Bowers Cottage

Stancombe Hatts

7

Tumuli

Chestnut Copse

South Plantation

Bowers Wood

Stancombe Farm

Poacher's Folly

Old Warren Wood

5

NUTWOOD DOWN

Tumulus

The Beeches

82

Nut Wood

Cockcrow Bottom

Pit Plantation

Wind Pump

Nut-wood

6 Roman Burials Found

Warren Farm (Beef Testing Centre)

Mere End Down

Stancombe Down

OXFORDSHIRE

VNS

BERKSHIRE

7

81

Tumulus

H u n g e r f o r d

8 Warren Down

Littleworth Cottage

N

Warren Farm

E

W

Eastbury Bottom

9

RG17

Warren Plantation

Washmore Hill

Cranes Copse

Grange Farm

Eastbur ge

A Eastbur

B

Cranes Farm

C

28

D

E

F Furze Border

stbury Down

36   37   38

Lower Ba

Field Border

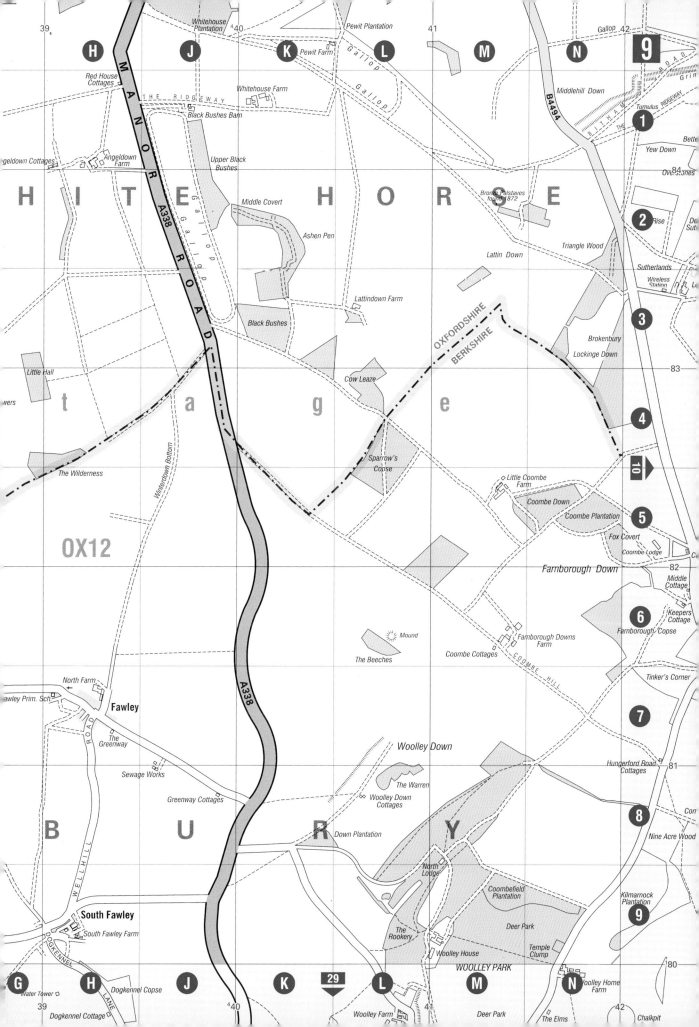

H · J · K · L · M · N

9

1

2

3

4

▶ **10**

5

6

7

8

9

G · H · J · K · **29** · L · M · N

Whitehouse Plantation
Pewit Plantation
Gallop
Gallop
Gallop 42
ROAD
Middlehill Down
Pewit Farm
B4494
THE RIDGEWAY
Red House Cottages
MANOR
Whitehouse Farm
Black Bushes Barn
Tumulus
Bette
Yew Down
84
Ove Stones
A338
geldown Cottages
Angeldown Farm
Upper Black Bushes
Gallop
Gallop
HITE
HORSE
Rise
De Sut
Middle Covert
Bronze Palstaves found 1872
Triangle Wood
Sutherlands
Ashen Pen
Lattin Down
Wireless Station
Le
Black Bushes
ROAD
Lattindown Farm
OXFORDSHIRE
BERKSHIRE
Brokenbury
Lockinge Down
83
Little Hall
t
a
g
Cow Leaze
e
wers
The Wilderness
Winterdown Bottom
Sparrow's Copse
Little Coombe Farm
Coombe Down
OX12
Coombe Plantation
Fox Covert
Coombe Lodge
C
82
Farnborough Down
Middle Cottage
Mound
Farnborough Downs Farm
Keepers Cottage
The Beeches
Coombe Cottages
Farnborough Copse
COOMBE HILL
Tinker's Corner
A338
Woolley Down
Hungerford Road Cottages
81
B
U
The Warren
Woolley Down Cottages
R
Down Plantation
Y
North Farm
Fawley Prim. Sch.
Fawley
The Greenway
Nine Acre Wood
ROAD
Sewage Works
North Lodge
Coombefield Plantation
Kilmarnock Plantation
Greenway Cottages
Deer Park
WELLHILL
The Rookery
South Fawley
South Fawley Farm
Woolley House
Temple Clump
DOGKENNEL LANE
Water Tower
Dogkennel Copse
Woolley Home Farm
80
WOOLLEY PARK
Dogkennel Cottage
39
40
Woolley Farm
41
Deer Park
42
The Elms
Chalkpit

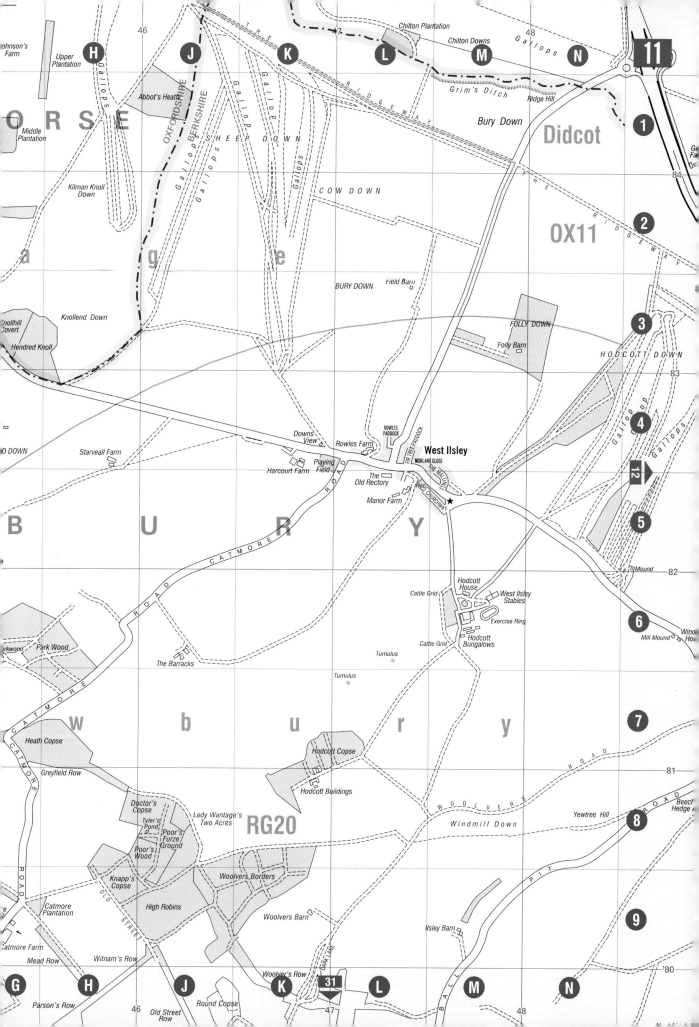

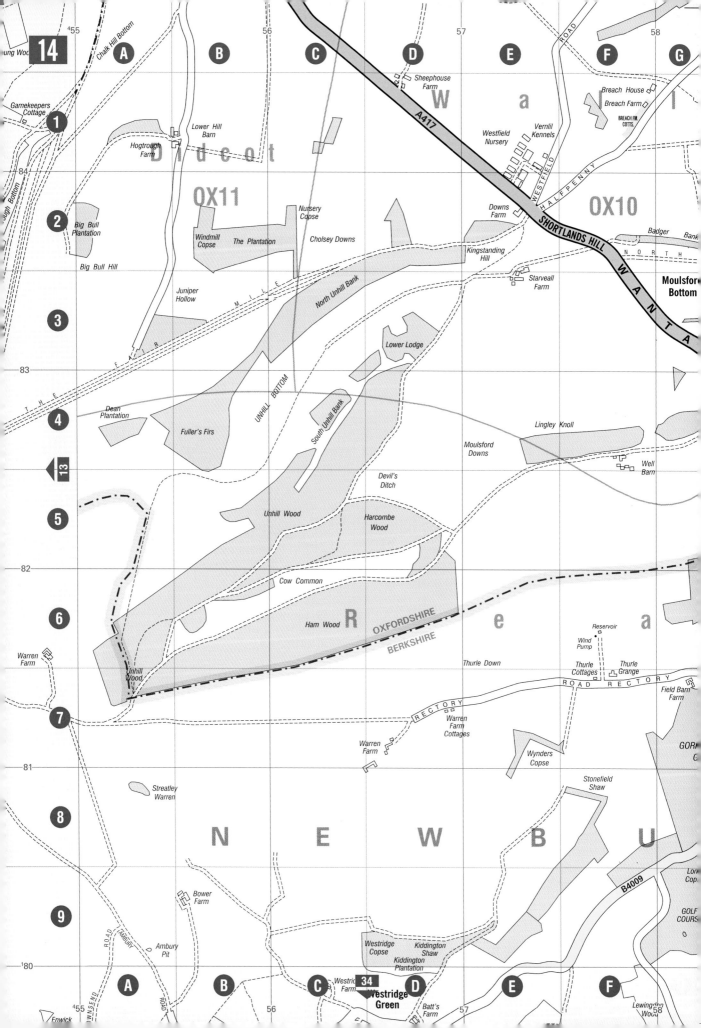

14

A B C D E F G

1
Gamekeepers
Cottage

Chalk Hill Bottom

Lower Hill Barn

Hogtrough Farm

Didcot

W a I

Sheephouse Farm

A417

Breach House
Breach Farm

BREACH FM. COTTS.

Westfield Nursery

Vernlil Kennels

2
Big Bull Plantation

OX11

Windmill Copse

The Plantation

Nursery Copse

Cholsey Downs

Downs Farm

Kingstanding Hill

Westfield

HALFPENNY

SHORTLANDS HILL

OX10

Badger Bank

Moulsford Bottom

Big Bull Hill

Starveall Farm

3
Juniper Hollow

North Unhill Bank

Lower Lodge

THE FAIR MILE

83

4
Dean Plantation

Fuller's Firs

UNHILL BOTTOM

South Unhill Bank

Moulsford Downs

Lingley Knoll

Well Barn

◄13

Devil's Ditch

5
Unhill Wood

Harcombe Wood

82

6
Warren Farm

Cow Common

Ham Wood

R

OXFORDSHIRE

BERKSHIRE

e

a

Reservoir

Wind Pump

Thurle Cottages

Thurle Grange

Thurle Down

ROAD

RECTORY

Field Barn Farm

GOR

7
Unhill Wood

RECTORY

Warren Farm Cottages

Wynders Copse

81

Warren Farm

Streatley Warren

Stonefield Shaw

8
N

E

W

B

U

B4009

Lon Cop.

9
Bower Farm

Ambury Pit

Westridge Copse

Kiddington Shaw

Kiddington Plantation

GOLF COURSE

ROAD

BANBURY

A B C D E F

Fnwick

455

56

Westridge Farm

34

Westridge Green

Batt's Farm

57

Lewingon Wood

58

455

84

Jugh Bottom

ung Woo

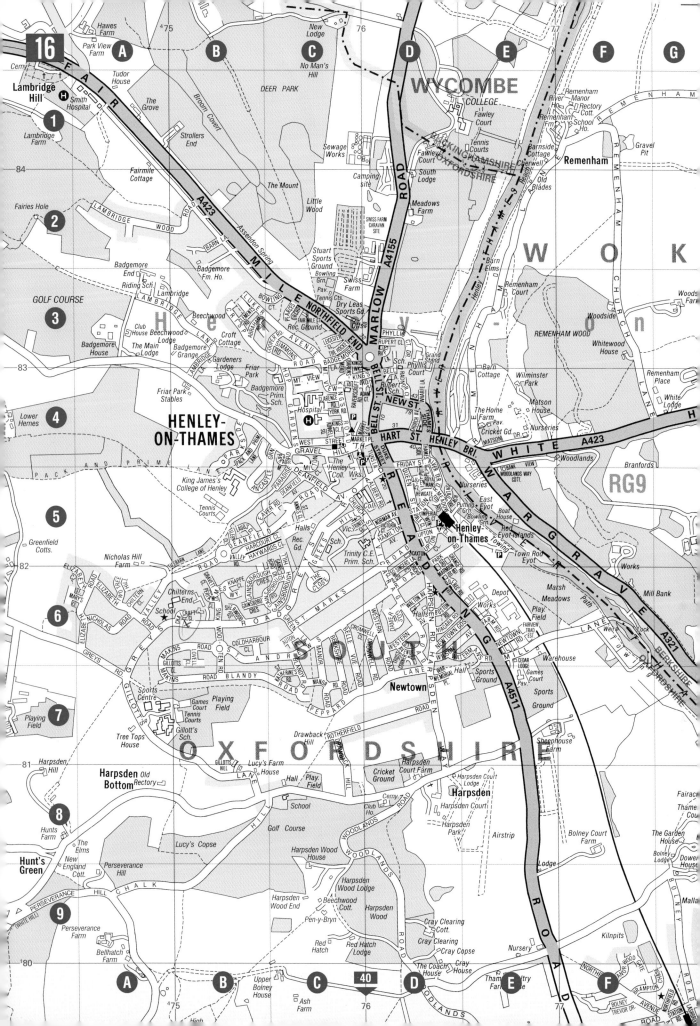

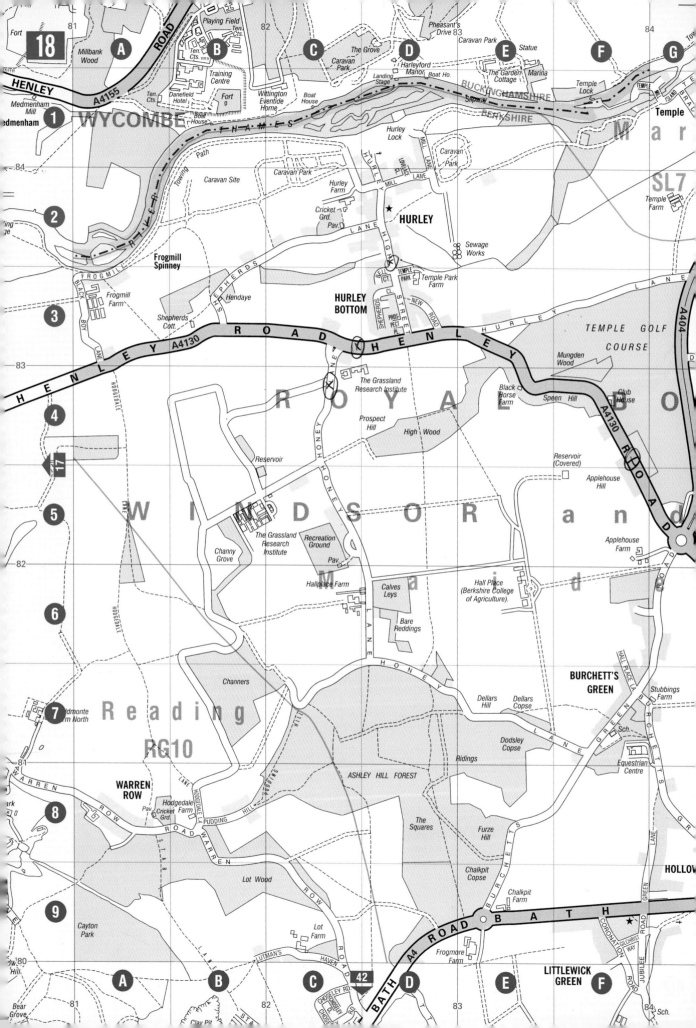

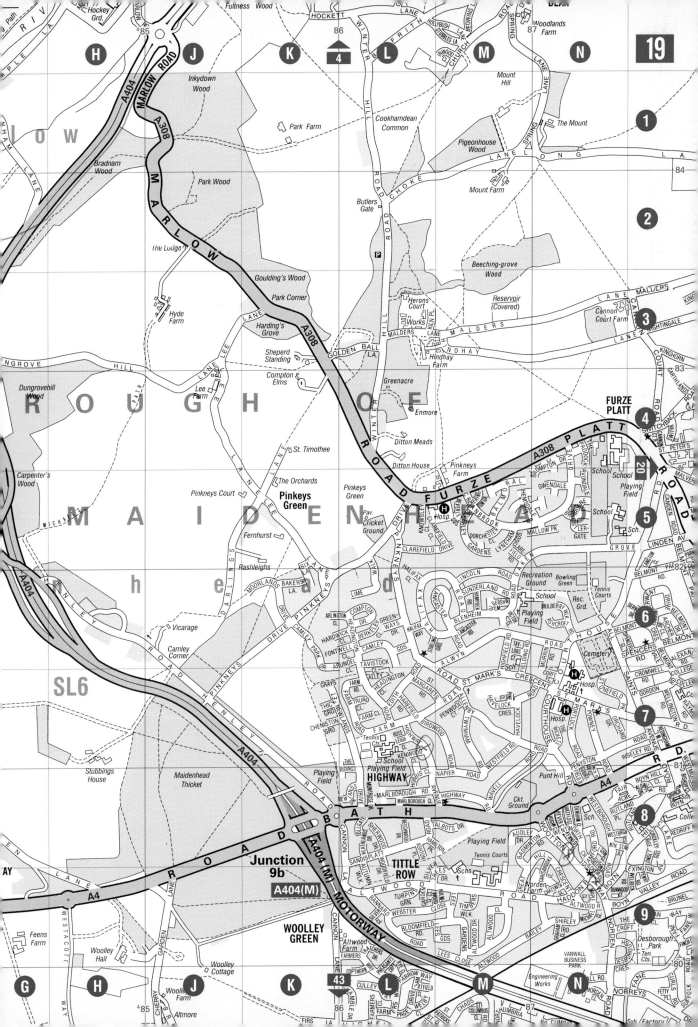

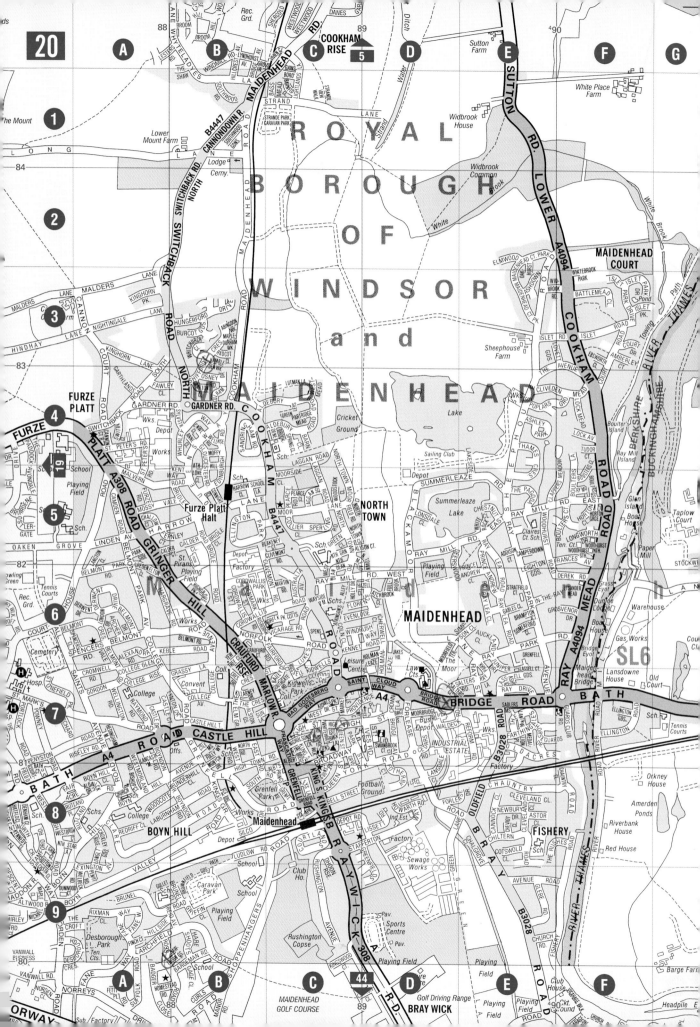

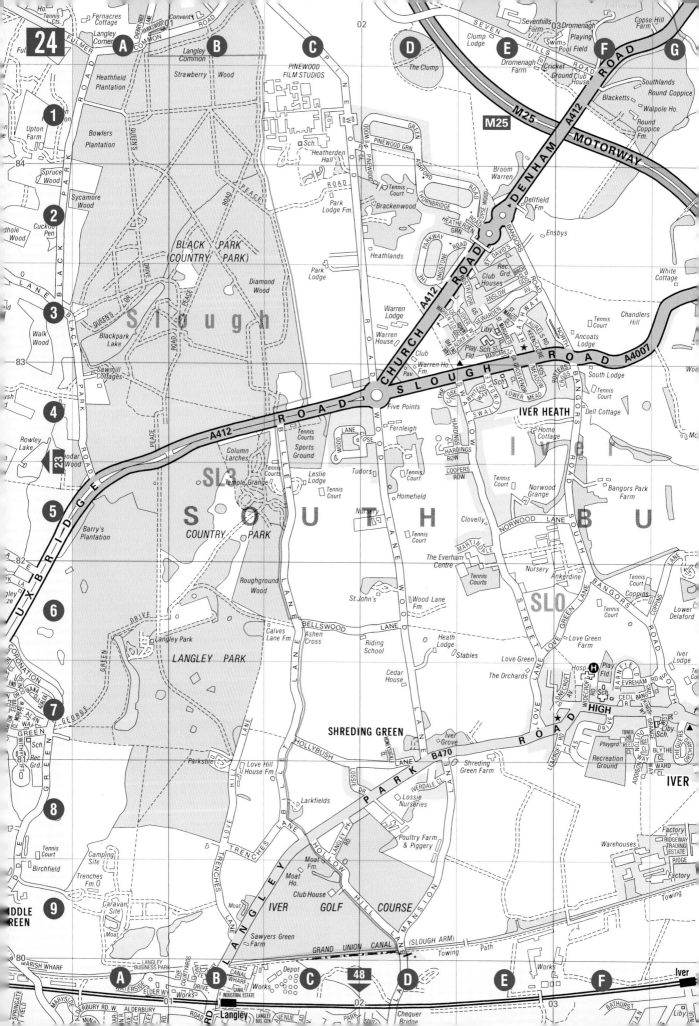

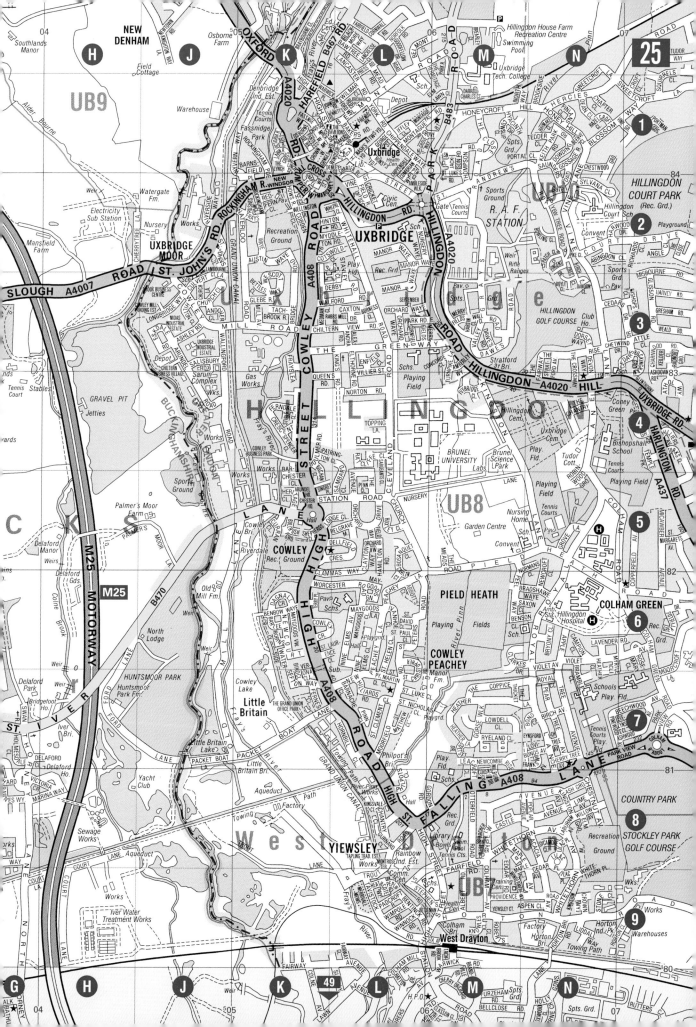

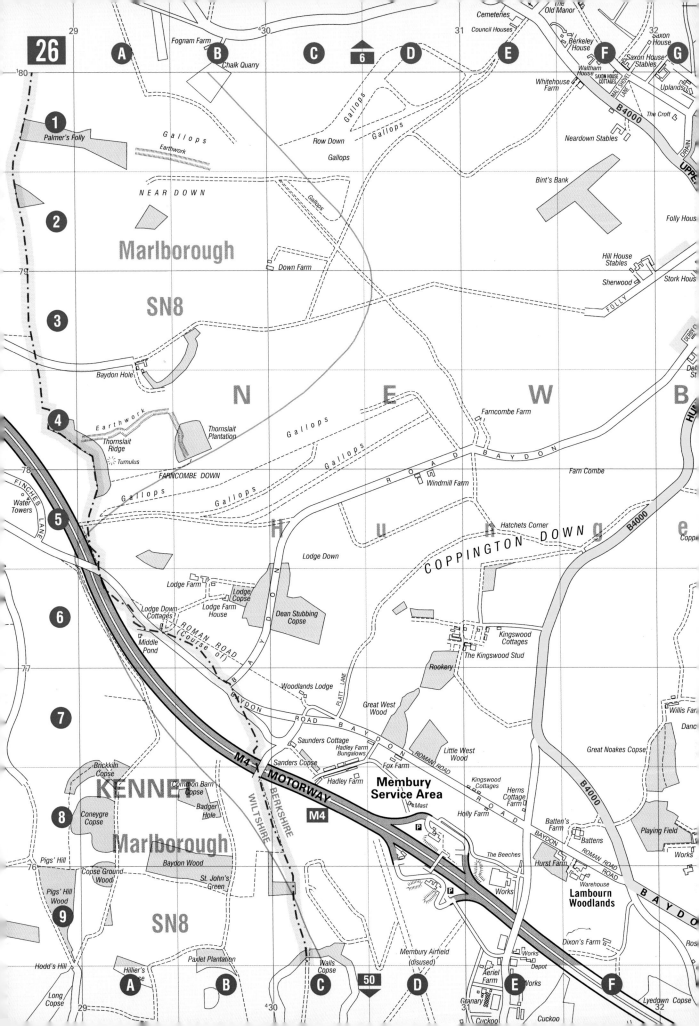

29

A   B   C   ↑6   D   E   F   G

180

1 Palmer's Folly

Gallops
Earthwork

Fognam Farm

Chalk Quarry

Row Down
Gallops

Gallops
Gallops

Cemeteries
Council Houses

Old Manor

Berkeley House

Saxon House

32

Waltham House

SAXON HOUSE COTTAGES

Saxon House Stables

Uplands

B4000

The Croft

2

NEAR DOWN

Marlborough

Neardown Stables

Bint's Bank

Folly Hous

UPPE

DRAIN

3

SN8

Baydon Hole

79

Hill House Stables

Sherwood

FOLLY

Stork Hous

Del St

4

Earthwork

Thornslait Ridge

Thornslait Plantation

Tumulus

N   E   W   B

Farncombe Farm

Farn Combe

HU

78

FARNCOMBE DOWN

Gallops

Gallops

Gallops

R O A D

B A Y D O N

Windmill Farm

Coppi

5

FINCHES LANE

Water Towers

Gallops

Gallops

Gallops

H   u   n   Hatchets Corner

g   e

B4000

COPPINGTON DOWN

Copp

Lodge Down

6

Lodge Farm

Lodge Down Cottages

Lodge Farm House

Lodge Copse

ROMAN ROAD (Course of)

Middle Pond

Dean Stubbing Copse

B A Y D O N

77

Kingswood Cottages

The Kingswood Stud

Rookery

Willis Far

Danc

7

Woodlands Lodge

PLATT LANE

ROAD

BAYDON

Great West Wood

Little West Wood

ROMAN ROAD

Great Noakes Copse

Brickkiln Copse

Saunders Cottage

Hadley Farm Bungalows

Sanders Copse

Fox Farm

Kingswood Cottages

Herns Cottage Farm

8

KENNE

Common Barn Copse

Badger Hole

Coneygre Copse

M4 MOTORWAY

WILTSHIRE

BERKSHIRE

M4

Hadley Farm

Membury Service Area

Mast

Holly Farm

Batten's Farm

Battens

Playing Field

Works

Pigs' Hill

76

Copse Ground Wood

Baydon Wood

St. John's Green

The Beeches

BAYDON

Hurst Farm

ROMAN ROAD

9

Pigs' Hill Wood

SN8

Marlborough

P

P

Works

Warehouse

Lambourn Woodlands

BAYDO

Hodd's Hill

Long Copse

Hillier's

Paxlet Plantation

Walls Copse

50

Membury Airfield (disused)

Dixon's Farm

Aeriel Farm

Works

Depot

Works

Granary

Lyedown Copse

Ros

29

A   30   B   C   D   31   E   F   32

Cuckoo   Cuckoo

A B C 8 D E F G

Washmore Hill

Cranes C

1

80

Eastbury Grange

Grange Farm

Eastbury Down

Tumulus

Cranes Farm

2

Poors' Furze

Pound's Farm

79

E a s t

G a r s t o n

D o w n

3

N E W B

Eastbury   Fields

Oakhedge Copse

Galops

Winterdown Bottom

Earthwork

Hasham Copse

Lady Copse

4

78

27

Winterdown Barn

H u n g e r f o

5

COLDBOROUGH   HILL

Jimmy's Farm

Lone Barn Farm

Lodge Copse

Furze Border

RG17

6

Manor Farm

Colett

Glebe House

East Garston

The Old Vicarage

77

Ford

ROGER'S   LANE

STATION RD

BURFORD'S

BACK   LANE

FRONT   STREE

College Farm

Hall

7

Oldborough Farm

Westfield Farm

Westfield Well

STREE

8

Parsonage Farm

Gallops

76

Thistlyclose Border

Plake's Border

se Border

GOLD HILL

Alms Copse

Maidencourt Farm

use Hill

Woodclose Border

Woodclose Copse

9

Coneyclose Copse

River Mead

Sheff Prim.

Bottom Copse

GREAT SHEFFORD

DOWNSHIRE

HAWTHORNE

Goodings

Gardener's Cottage

Chaplains House

Swimming Pool

A Dore's Border

Dore's B

Dore's Copse

C 52 D

36 37

E Manor Farm

Manor Farm Cottages

38

F Hall

STATION

CHURCH   STREET

MILLERS LA

THE MEAD

RIVERWAY

W A N

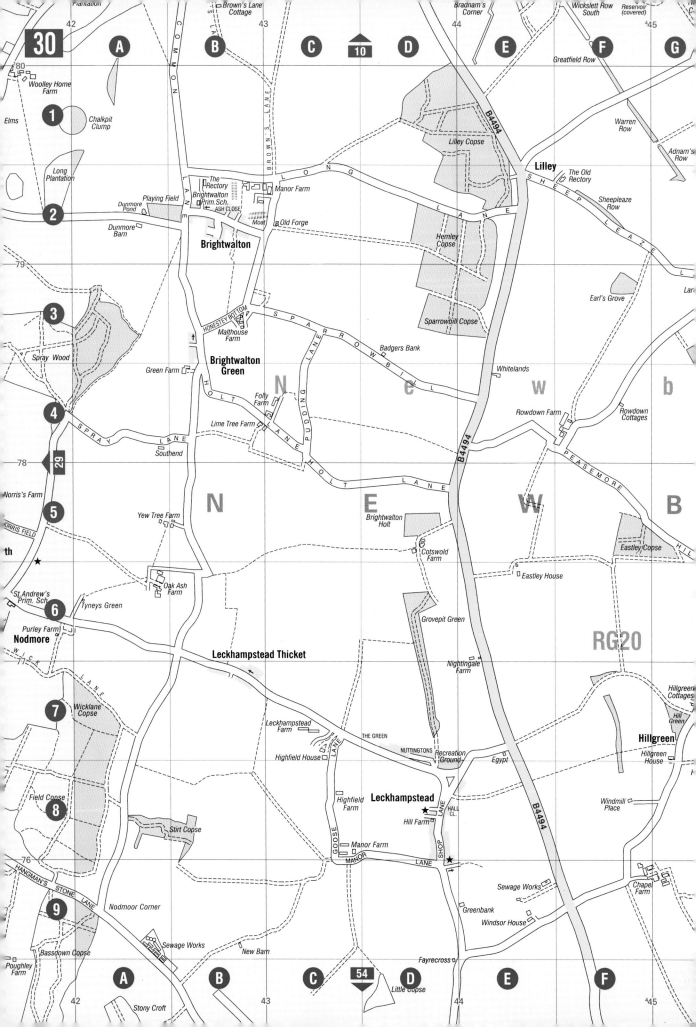

A **B** **C** ⌂ 10 **D** **E** **F** **G**

42 43 44 45

Plantation

Brown's Lane Cottage

Bradnam's Corner

Wickslett Row South

Reservoir (covered)

Greatfield Row

80

Woolley Home Farm

Elms

1 Chalkpit Clump

Warren Row

Lilley Copse

Adnam's Row

Long Plantation

The Old Rectory

Lilley

2 Dunmore Pond

The Rectory
Brightwalton Prim. Sch.
Manor Farm
ASH CLOSE
Moat
Old Forge

Sheepleaze Row

Dunmore Barn

Brightwalton

Hemley Copse

79

Sparrowbill Copse

Earl's Grove Lar

3 Spray Wood

Malthouse Farm

Badgers Bank

Brightwalton Green

Whitelands

Green Farm

Rowdown Farm

Rowdown Cottages

4 Lime Tree Farm

Folly Farm

29 78 Southend

PEASEMORE

Norris's Farm

5 NORRIS FIELD

Yew Tree Farm

Brightwalton Holt

Eastley Copse

th

St Andrew's Prim. Sch.

Oak Ash Farm

Cotswold Farm

Eastley House

6 Tyneys Green

Nodmore Purley Farm

RG20

Leckhampstead Thicket

Grovepit Green

Hillgreen Cottages

Nightingale Farm

Hill Green

77

7 Wicklane Copse

Leckhampstead Farm

THE GREEN

Hillgreen

Highfield House

NUTTINGTONS

Recreation Ground

Egypt

Hillgreen House

8 Field Copse

Highfield Farm

Leckhampstead

Windmill Place

Stirt Copse

Hill Farm

HALL CL.

76 HANGMAN'S STONE LANE

Manor Farm

SHOP

Chapel Farm

9 Nodmoor Corner

Sewage Works

Greenbank

Windsor House

Sewage Works

Bassdown Copse

New Barn

Fayrecross

Poughley Farm

Stony Croft

Little Copse

A **B** **C** 54 **D** **E** **F**

42 43 44 45

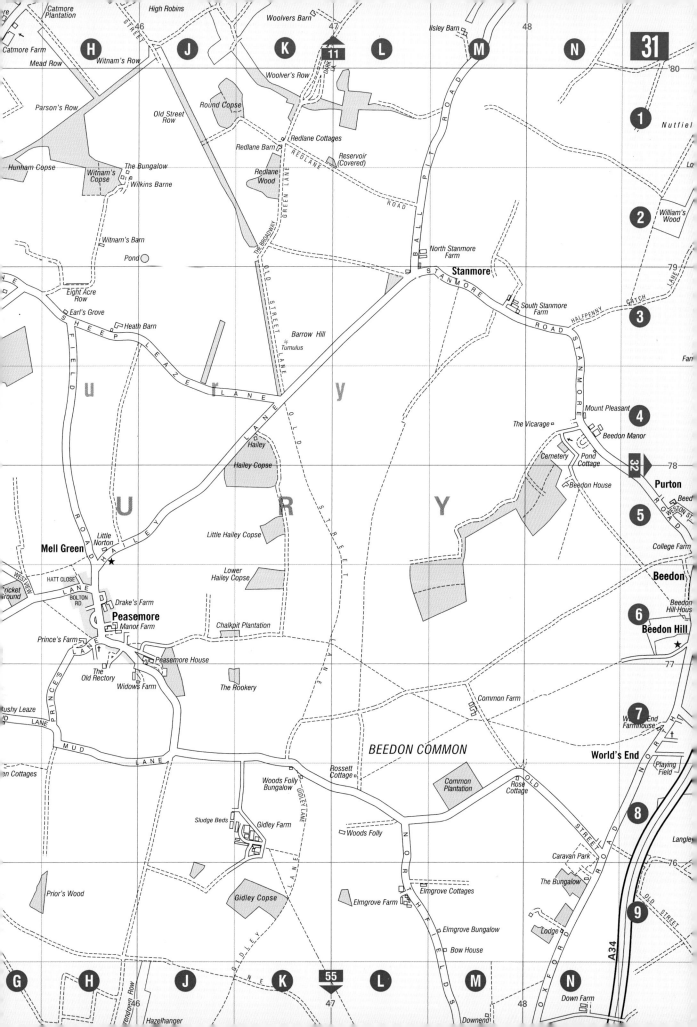

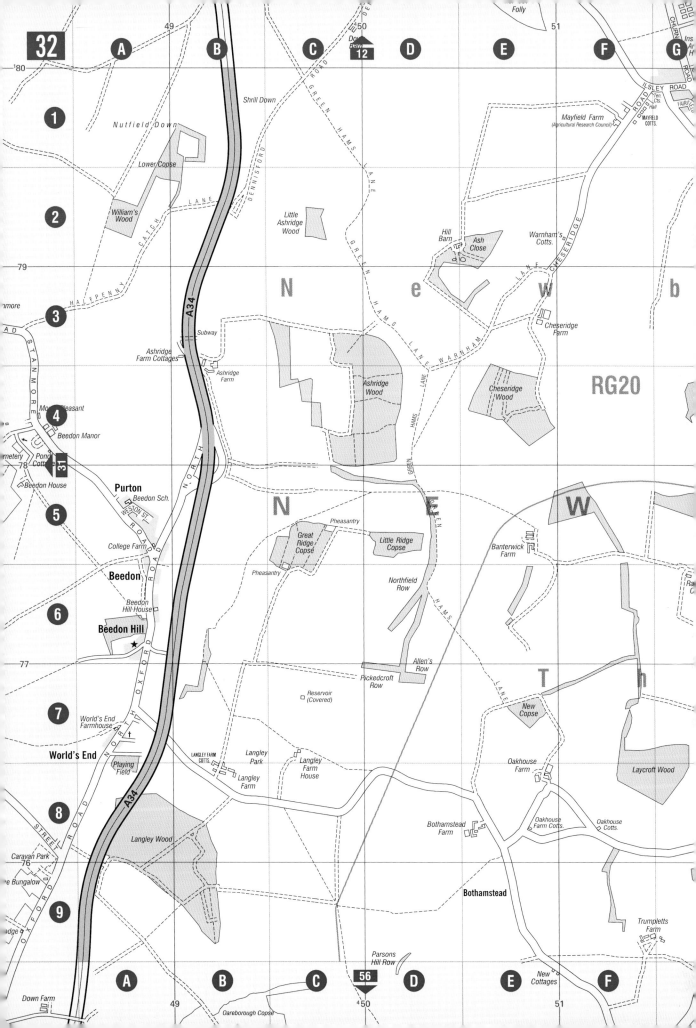

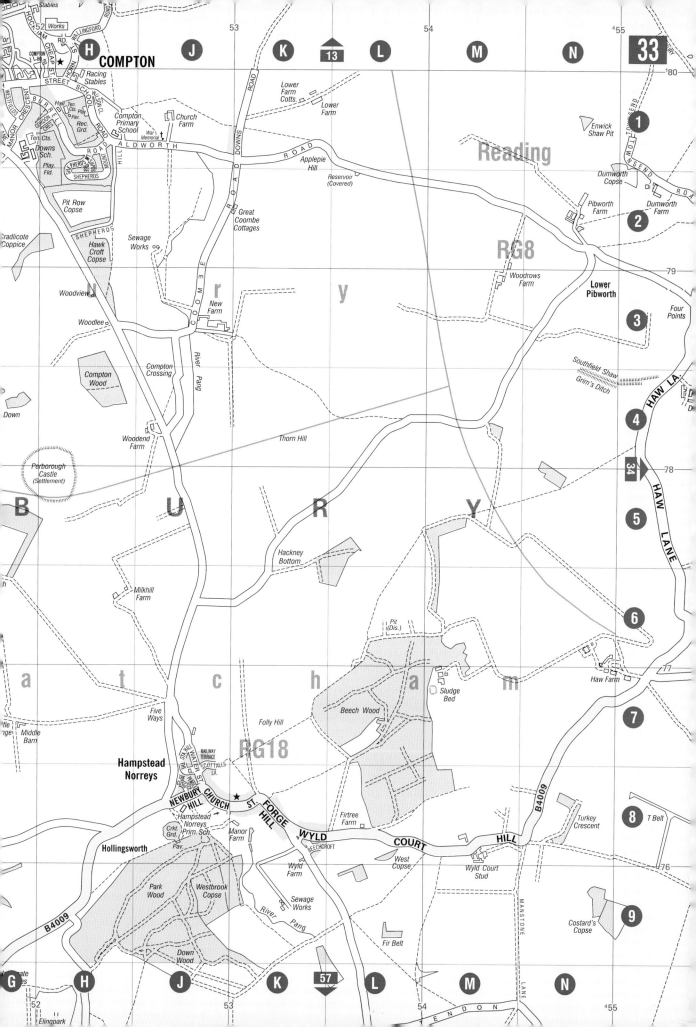

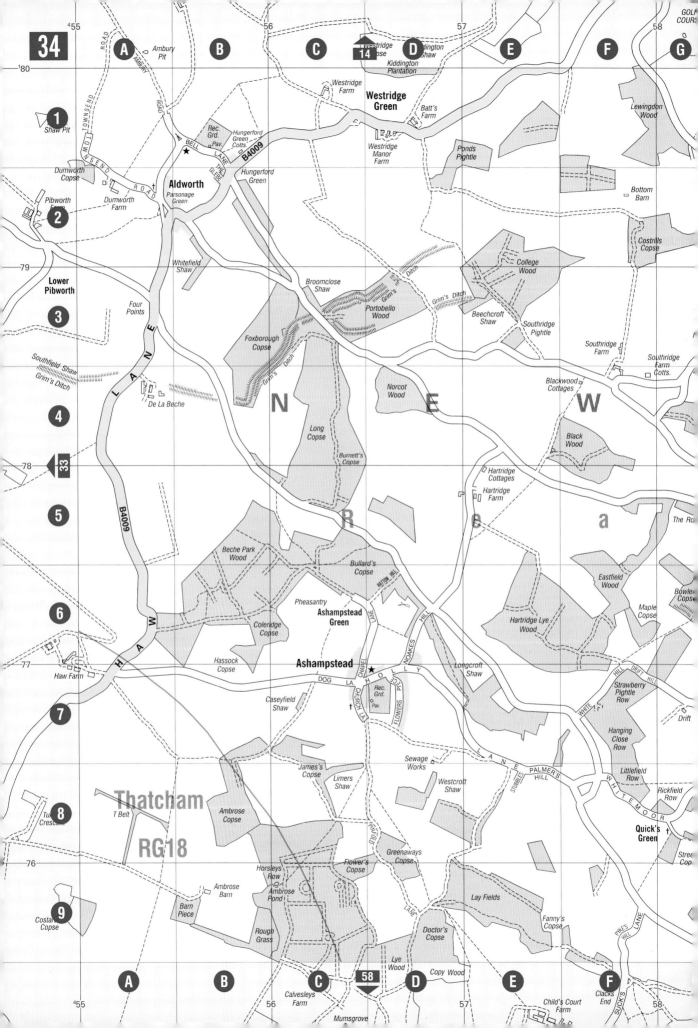

A B C D E F G

Shaw Pit
Ambury Pit
Westridge Close
14
Kiddington Shaw
Kiddington Plantation
Lewingdon Wood

Westridge Farm
Westridge Green
Batt's Farm

Dumworth Copse
Rec. Grd. Pav.
Hungerford Green Cotts.
B4009
Westridge Manor Farm
Ponds Pightle
Bottom Barn

Pibworth Farm
Aldworth
BELL
Parsonage Green
THE GLEBE LANE
Hungerford Green
Costrills Copse

Dumworth Farm
Whitefield Shaw
College Wood

Lower Pibworth
Broomclose Shaw
Grim's Ditch
Portobello Wood
Grim's Ditch
Beechcroft Shaw
Southridge Pightle

Four Points
LANE
Foxborough Copse
Grim's Ditch
Norcot Wood
Southridge Farm
Southridge Farm Cotts.

Southfield Shaw
Grim's Ditch
De La Beche
N
E
Blackwood Cottages
W
Black Wood

Long Copse
Burnett's Copse
R
Hartridge Cottages
Hartridge Farm
e
a
The Ro

33
B4009
Beche Park Wood
Bullard's Copse
Eastfield Wood
Bowler Copse

Pheasantry
HATTON HILL
Hartridge Lye Wood
Maple Copse

Coleridge Copse
Ashampstead Green
NOAKES HILL
W
HAW
Hassock Copse
Ashampstead
CHAPEL LANE
HOLLY
Rec. Grd. Pav.
FLOWERS PIECE
Longcroft Shaw
Strawberry Pightle Row
HILL DRIFT HILL

Haw Farm
Caseyfield Shaw
DOG LA.
CHURCH LA.
†
Hanging Close Row
Drift

James's Copse
Limers Shaw
Sewage Works
Westcroft Shaw
LANE
STUBBLES HILL
PALMERS HILL
WHITEMOOR
WHITE HILL
Littlefield Row
Rickfield Row

Thatcham
T Belt
Ambrose Copse
Greenaways Copse
Quick's Green
Stree Cop

RG18
Horsleys Row
Flower's Copse
Lay Fields
PIKE'S HILL LANE

Ambrose Barn
Ambrose Pond
Fanny's Copse
SUCKS

Barn Piece
Rough Grass
Doctor's Copse
Costan Copse

Lye Wood
58
Copy Wood
Clacks End

A B C Calvesleys Farm Mumsgrove D E Child's Court Farm F

55 56 57 58

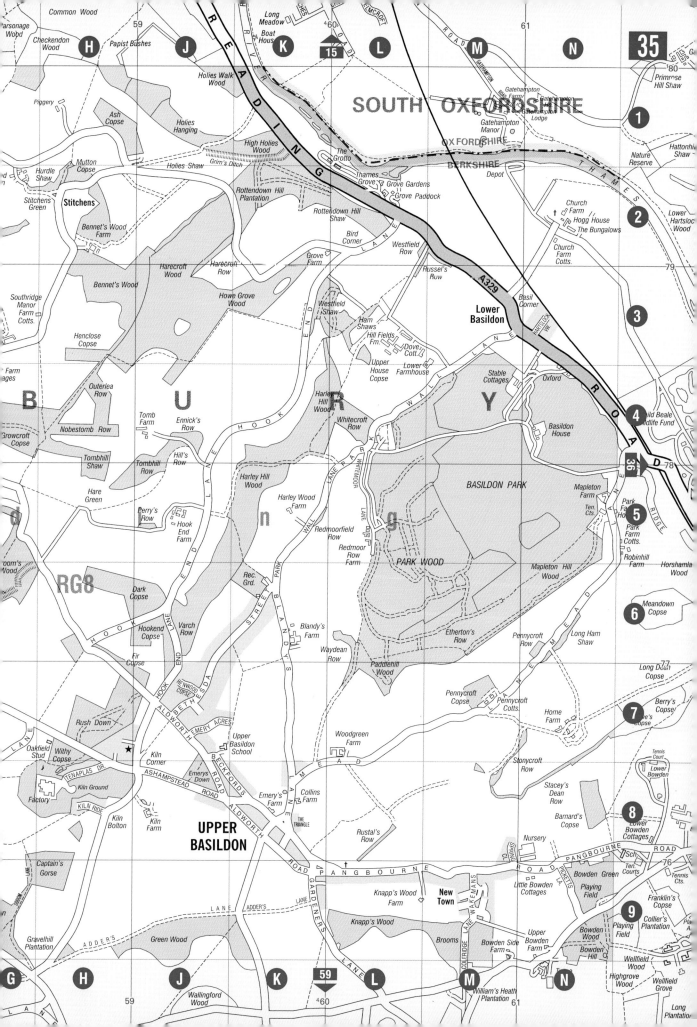

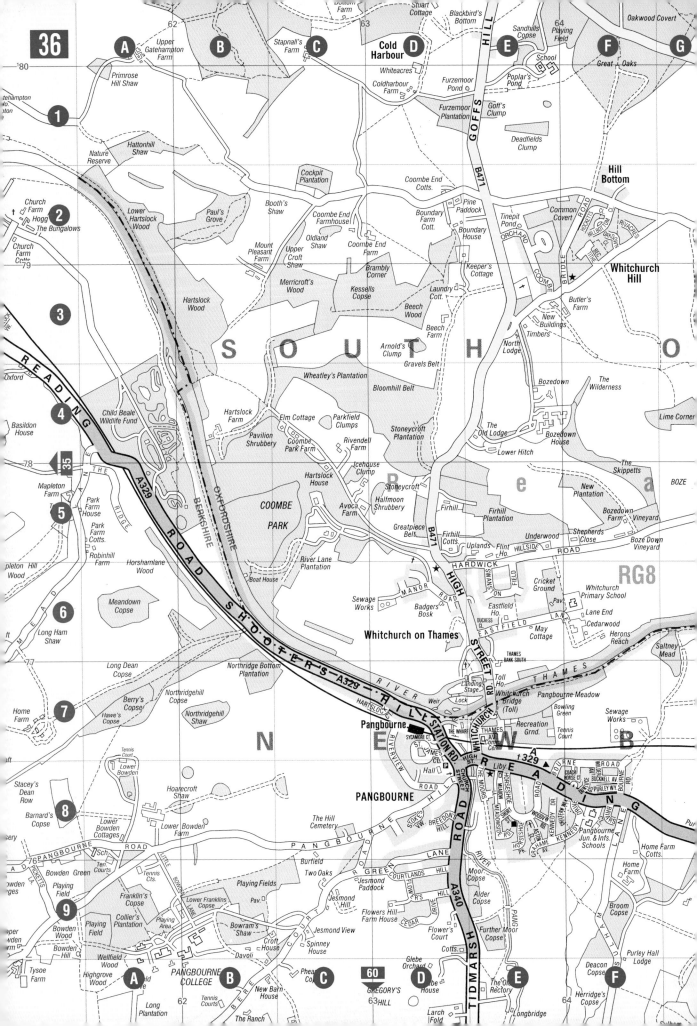

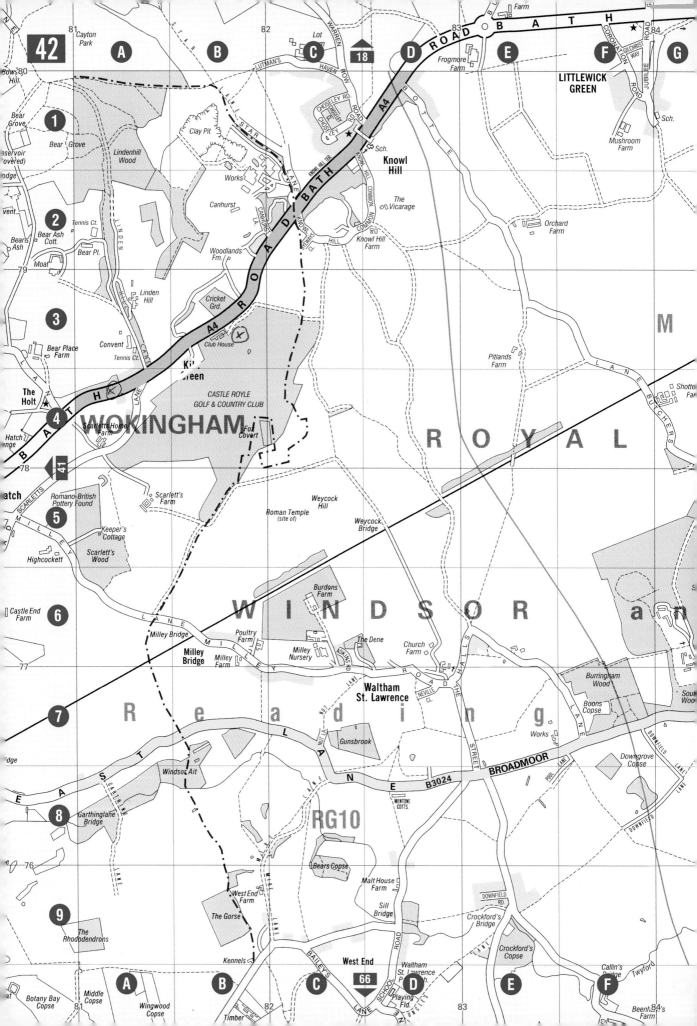

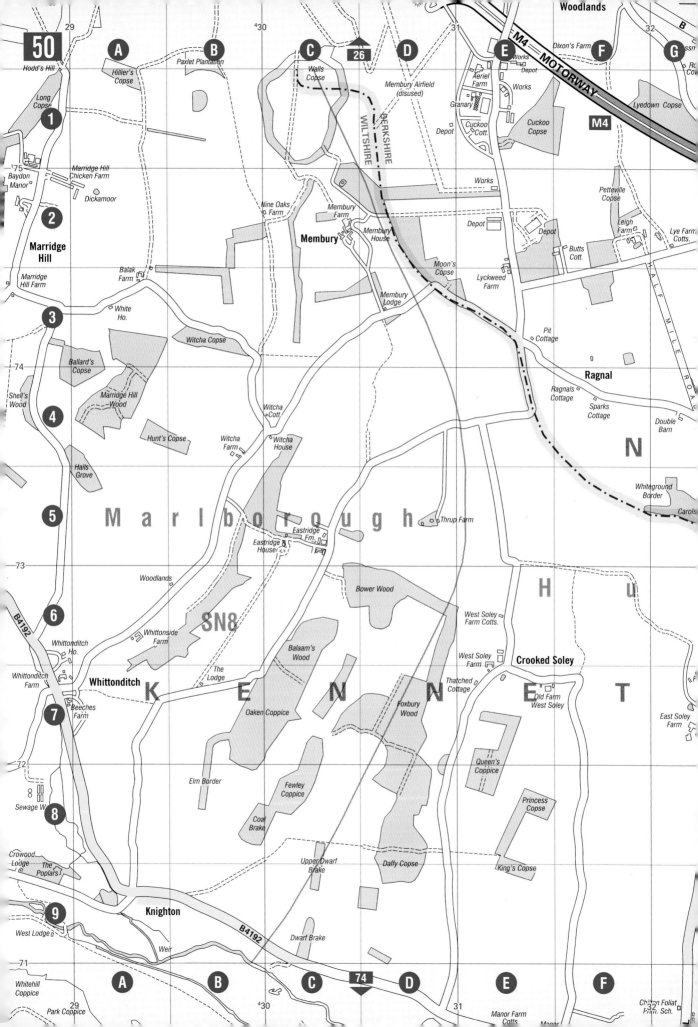

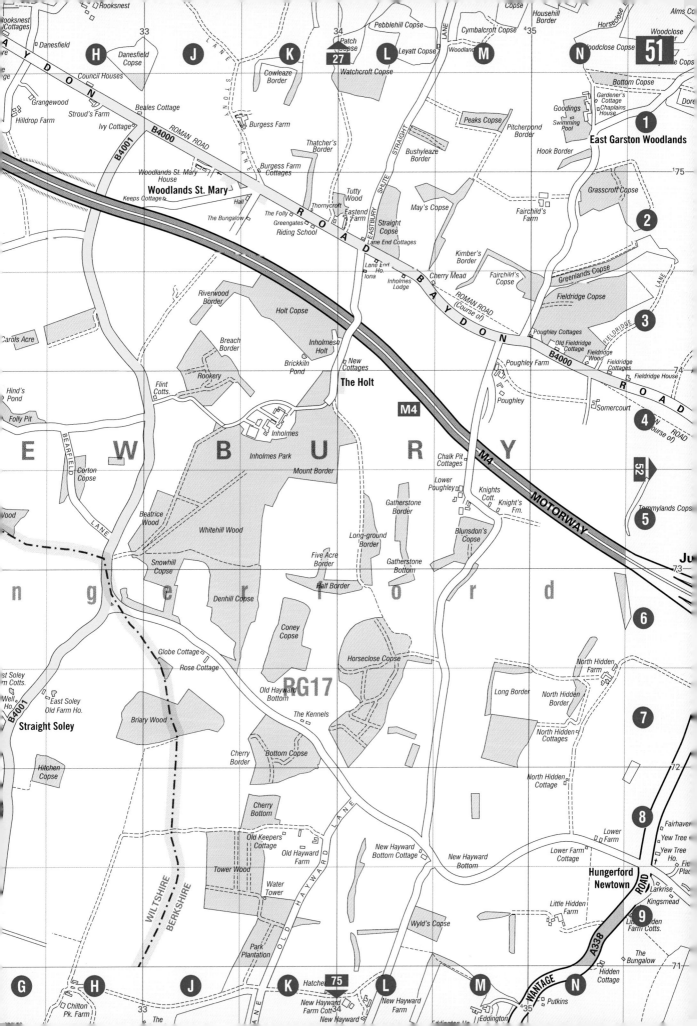

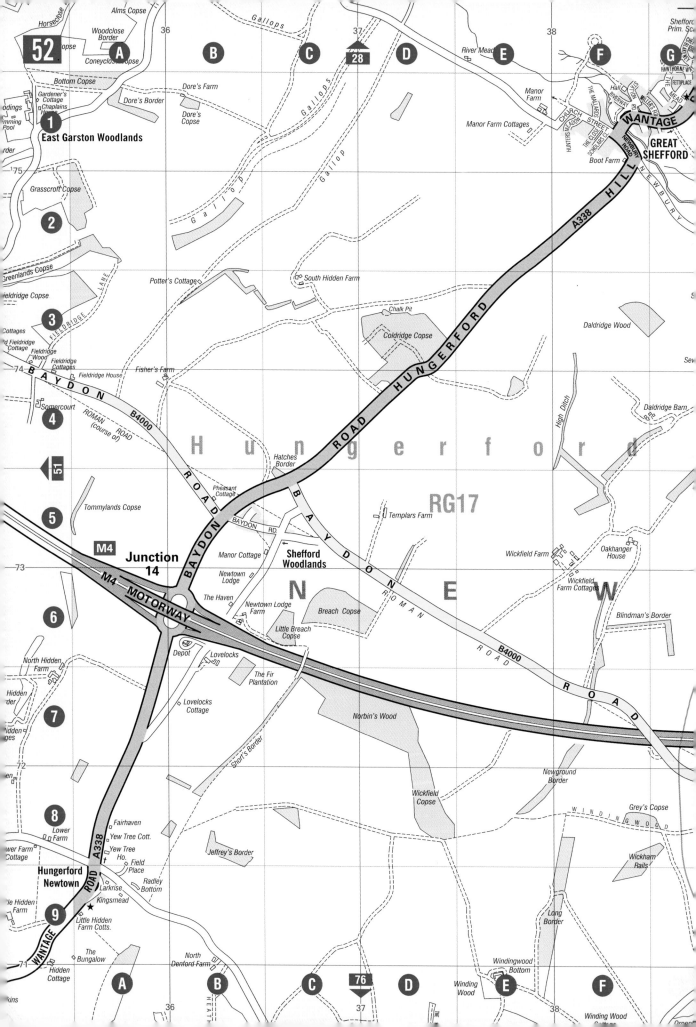

52

A B C 28 D River Mead E F G

1 East Garston Woodlands

WANTAGE

GREAT SHEFFORD

36 37 38

Horseclose
Alms Copse
Woodclose Border
Coneyclose Copse
Bottom Copse
Gardener's Cottage
Chaplains House
odings
mming Pool

Dore's Farm
Dore's Border
Dore's Copse

Gallops
Gallops
Gallop

Manor Farm
Manor Farm Cottages

Shefford Prim. Sc.
Hawthorne Way
THE MEAD
FETTIPLACE
MILLERS CLO
STATION RD
RIVERWAY
Hall
THE MALLARDS
CHURCH STREET
HUNTERS MEADOW
THE CLOSE
SCHOLARS CL
NEWBURY ROAD
Boot Farm

2 Grasscroft Copse

75

3 Greenlands Copse
Fieldridge Copse
Cottages
d Fieldridge Cottage
Fieldridge Wood
Fieldridge Cottages

Potter's Cottage
South Hidden Farm
Chalk Pit
Coldridge Copse
Daldridge Wood
Sev

74 BAYDON

4 Somercourt
Fieldridge House
Fisher's Farm
ROMAN ROAD (course of)
B4000

HUNGERFORD ROAD

A338 HILL

High Ditch
Daldridge Barn

◄ 51

5 Tommylands Copse
BAYDON RD.
Hatches Border
Pheasant Cottage

RG17

Templars Farm
Wickfield Farm
Oakhanger House

73 M4 Junction 14
M4 MOTORWAY
BAYDON ROAD
Manor Cottage
Newtown Lodge
The Haven
Shefford Woodlands
N
Newtown Lodge Farm
Breach Copse
Little Breach Copse
E
ROMAN ROAD
B4000
W
Wickfield Farm Cottages
Blindman's Border

6 North Hidden Farm

Hidden der

Depot
Lovelocks
The Fir Plantation
Lovelocks Cottage
Norbin's Wood

7

72

Short's Border
Wickfield Copse
Newground Border
Grey's Copse
WINDING WOOD

8 Lower Farm
Fairhaven
Yew Tree Cott.
Yew Tree Ho.
Field Place
Jeffrey's Border
A338 ROAD
Larkrise
Kingsmead
Hungerford Newtown
Radley Bottom
Wickham Rails

le Hidden Farm
Long Border

9 WANTAGE ROAD
Little Hidden Farm Cotts.
The Bungalow
Hidden Cottage
North Denford Farm
Windingwood Bottom
Winding Wood
Winding Wood

71

A B C 76 D E F

36 HEATH 37 THE 38

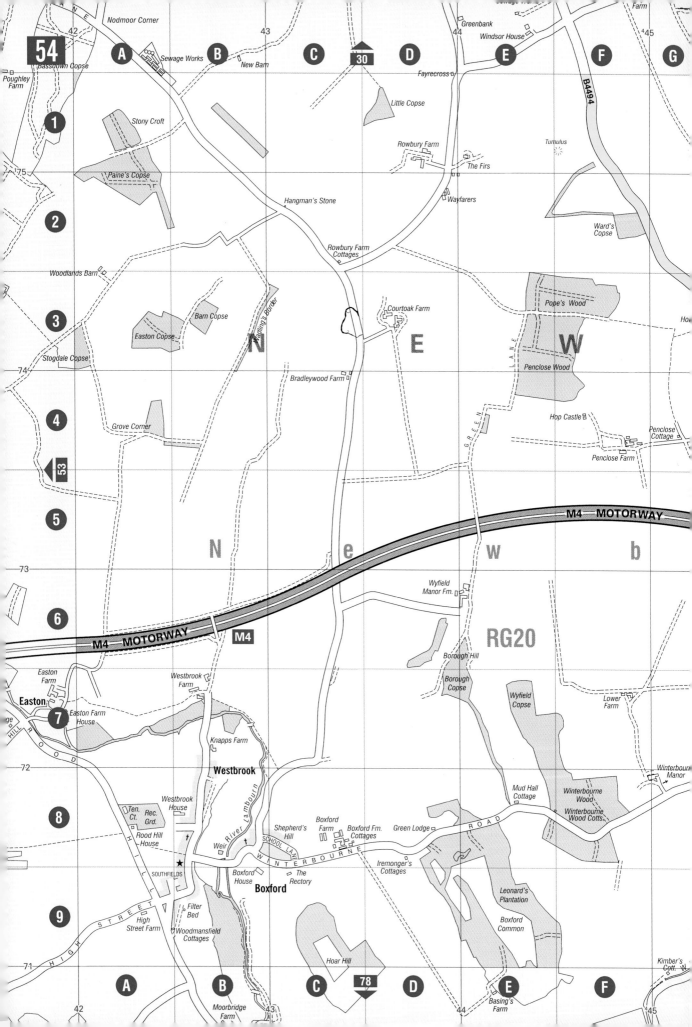

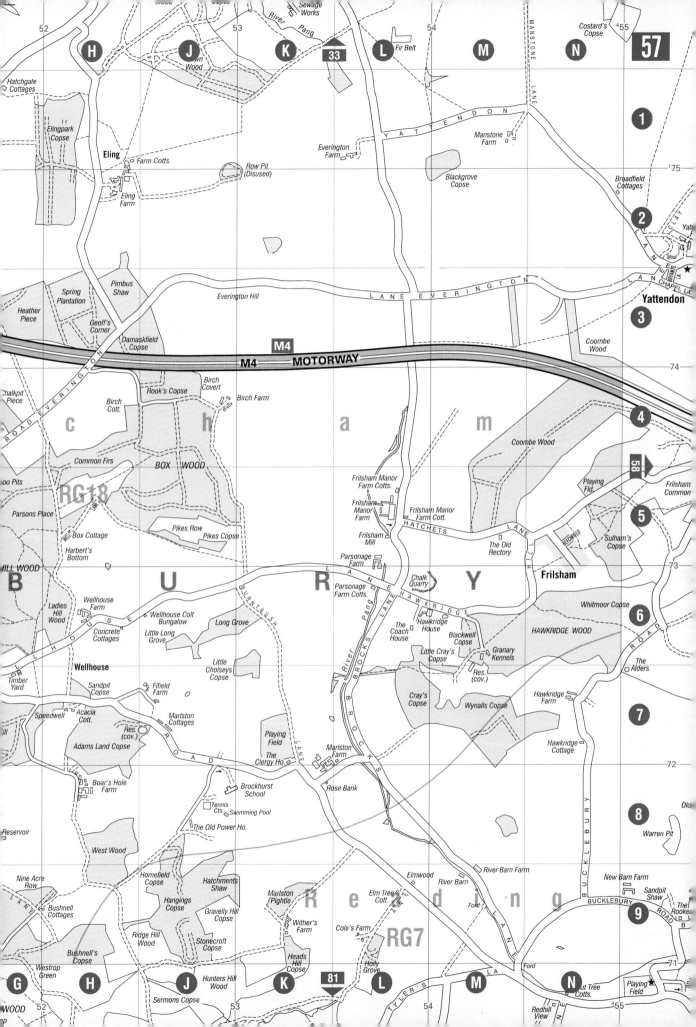

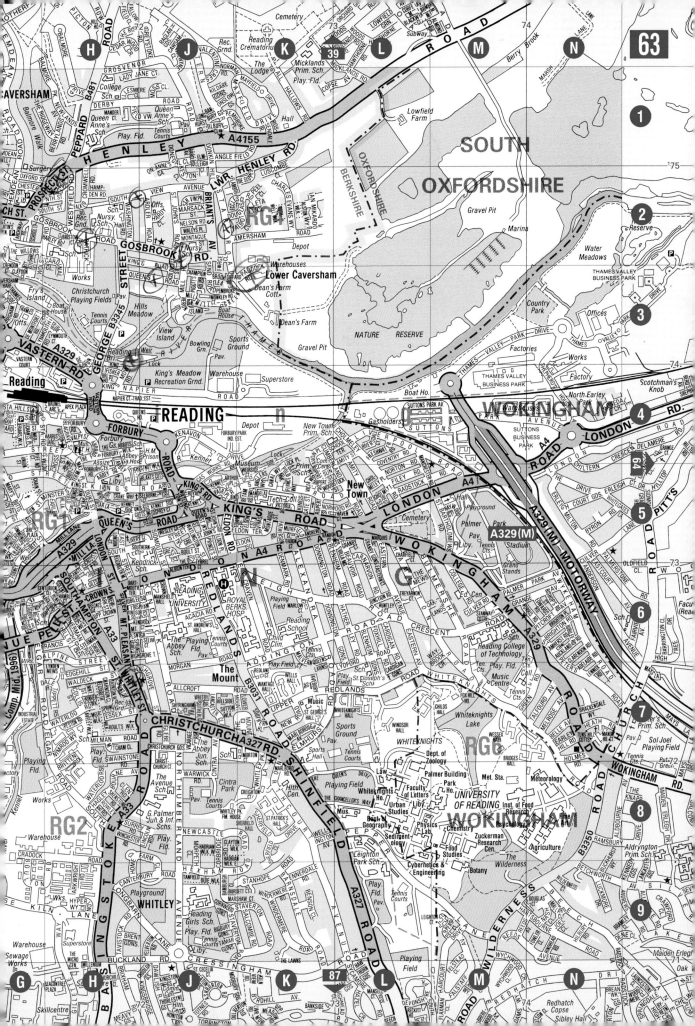

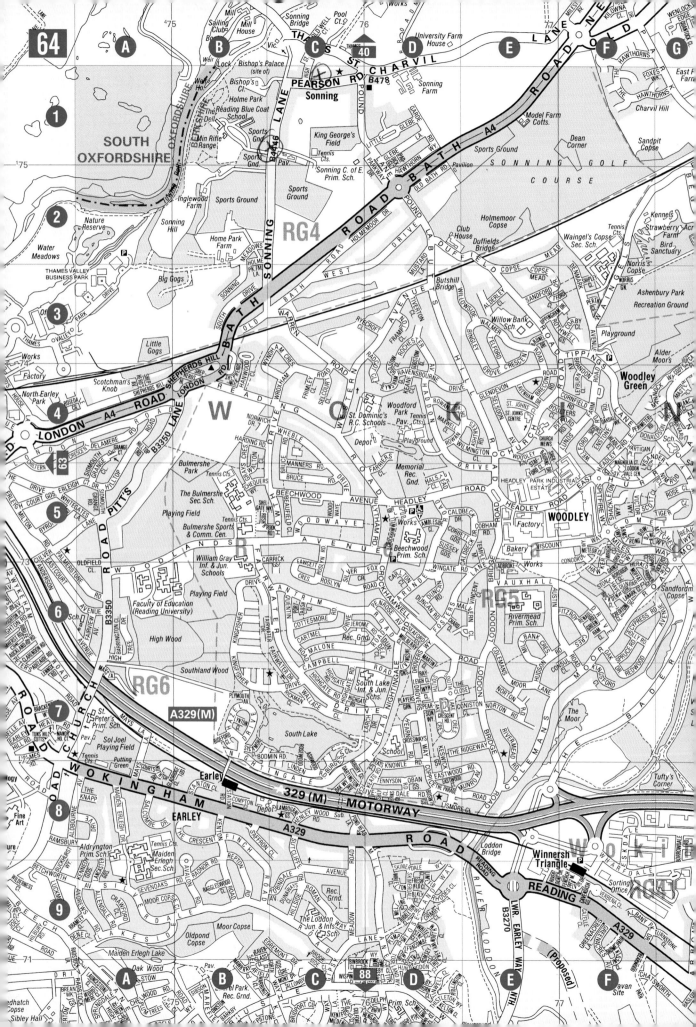

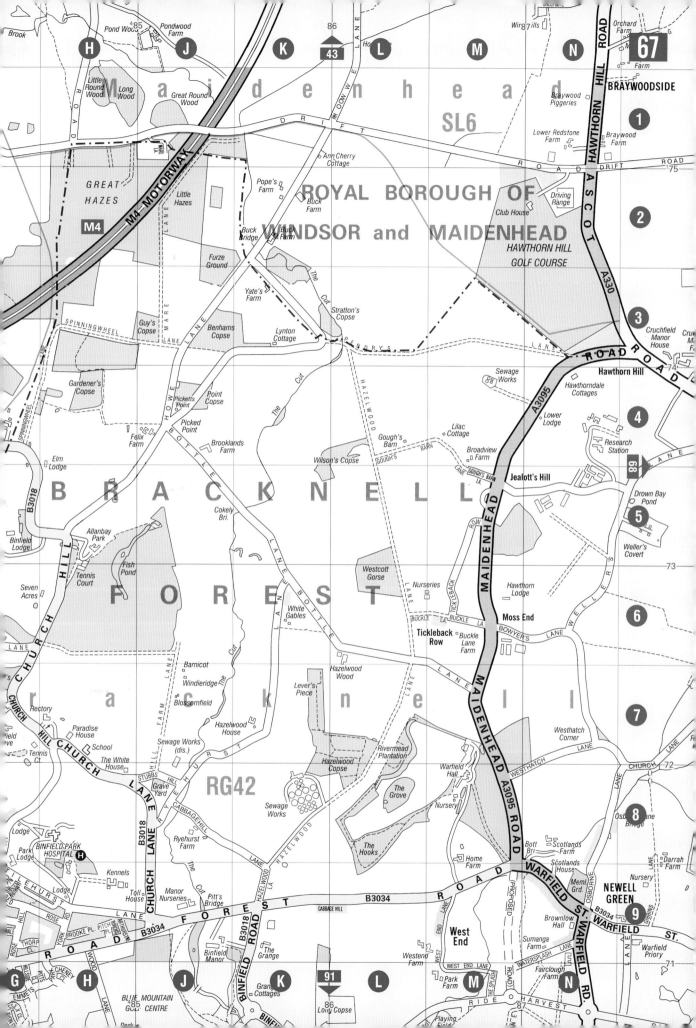

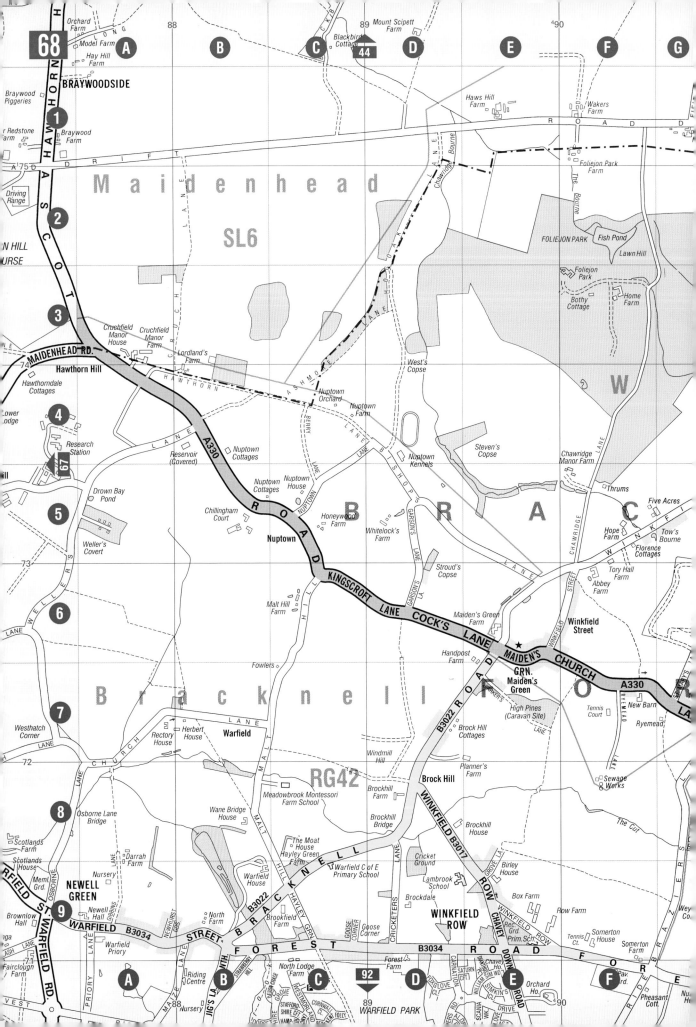

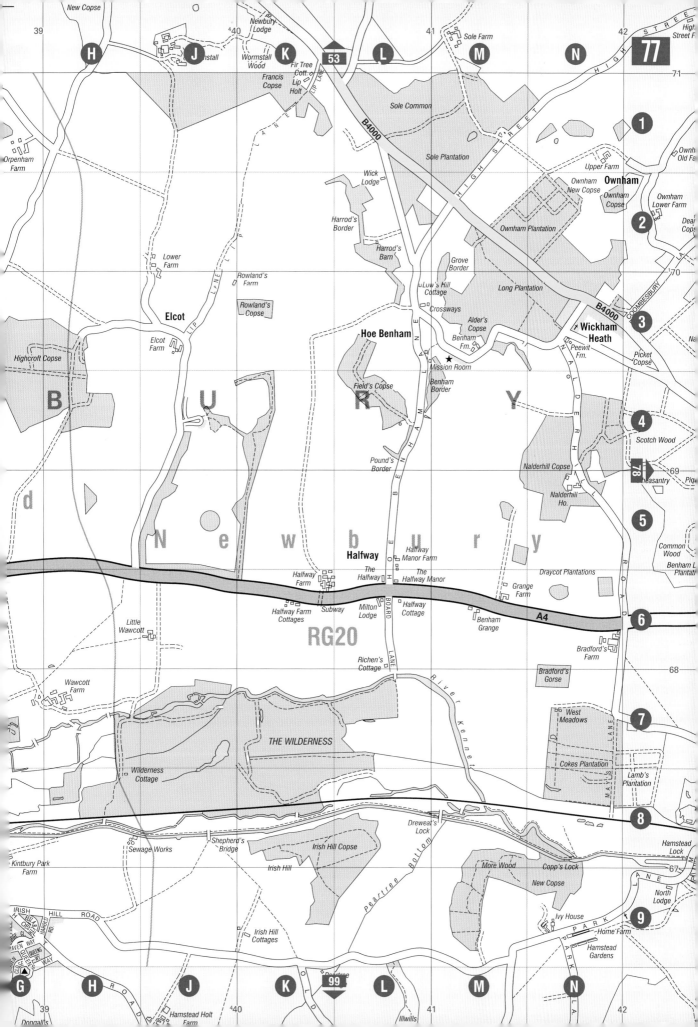

6 horewood close
Newbury
RG14 1PY

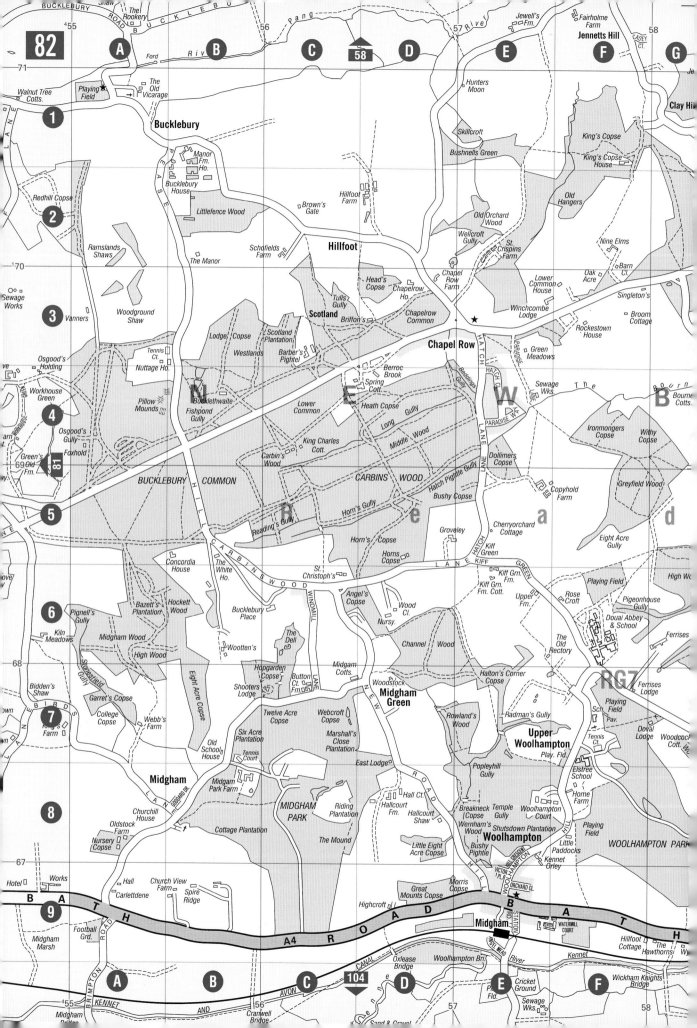

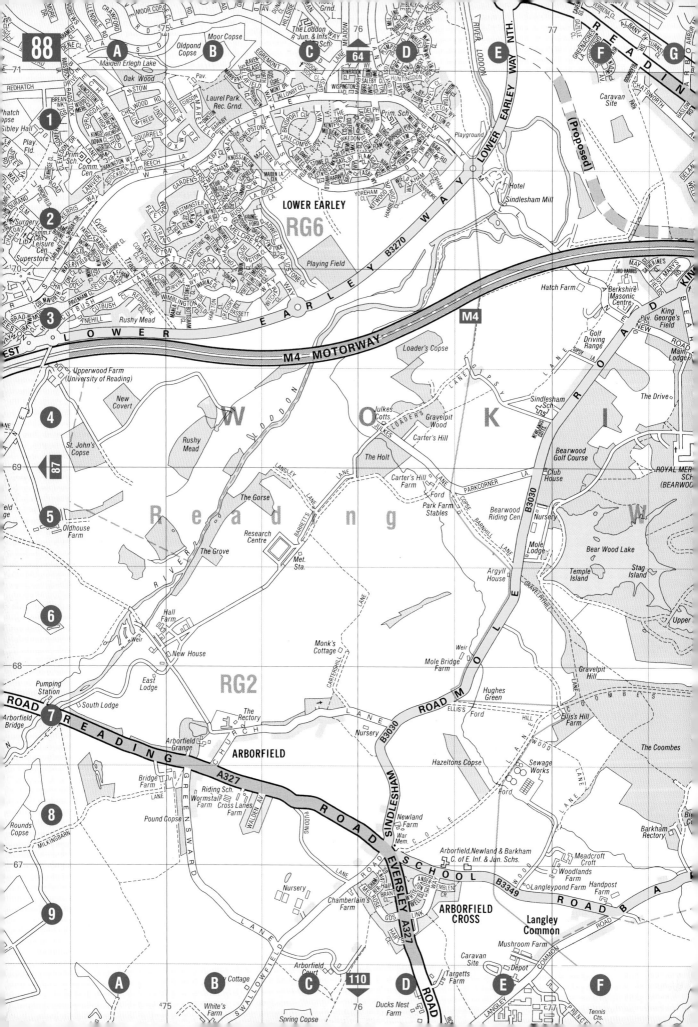

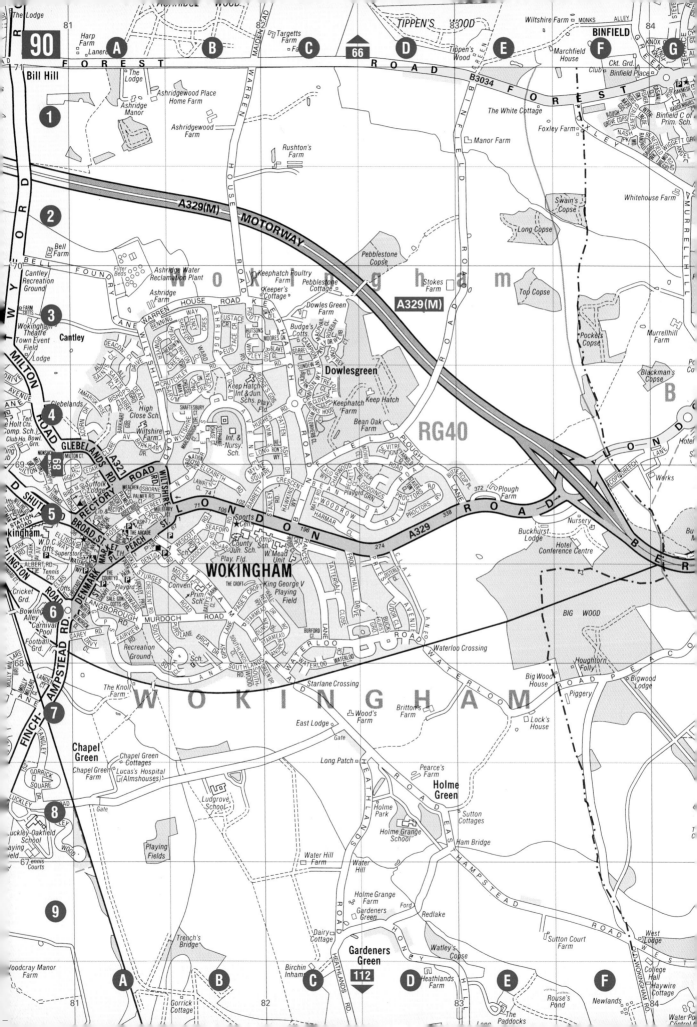

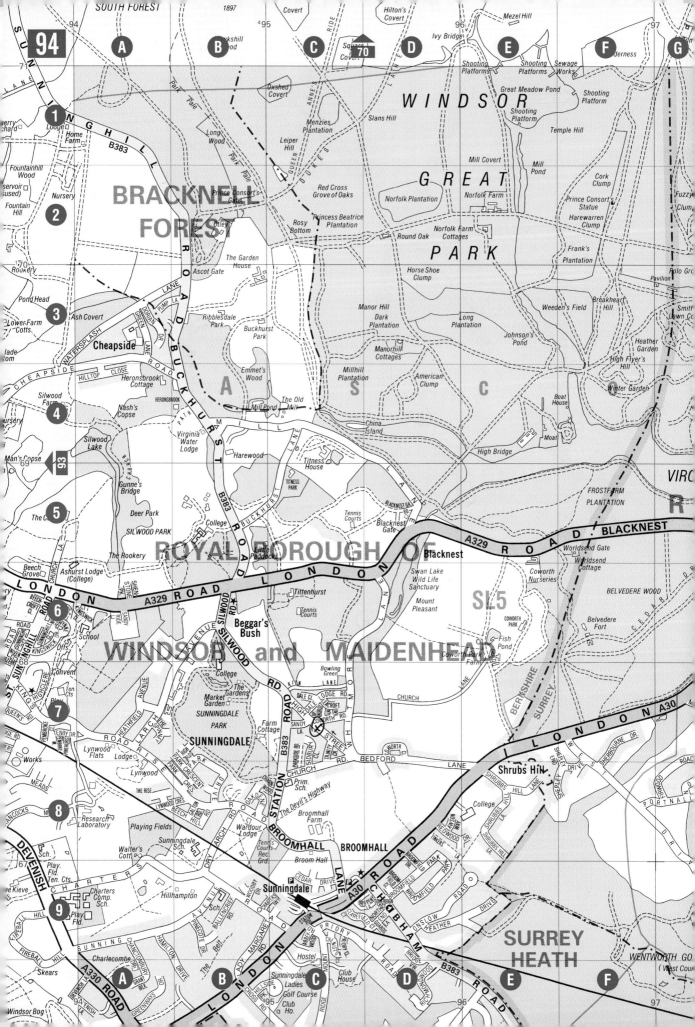

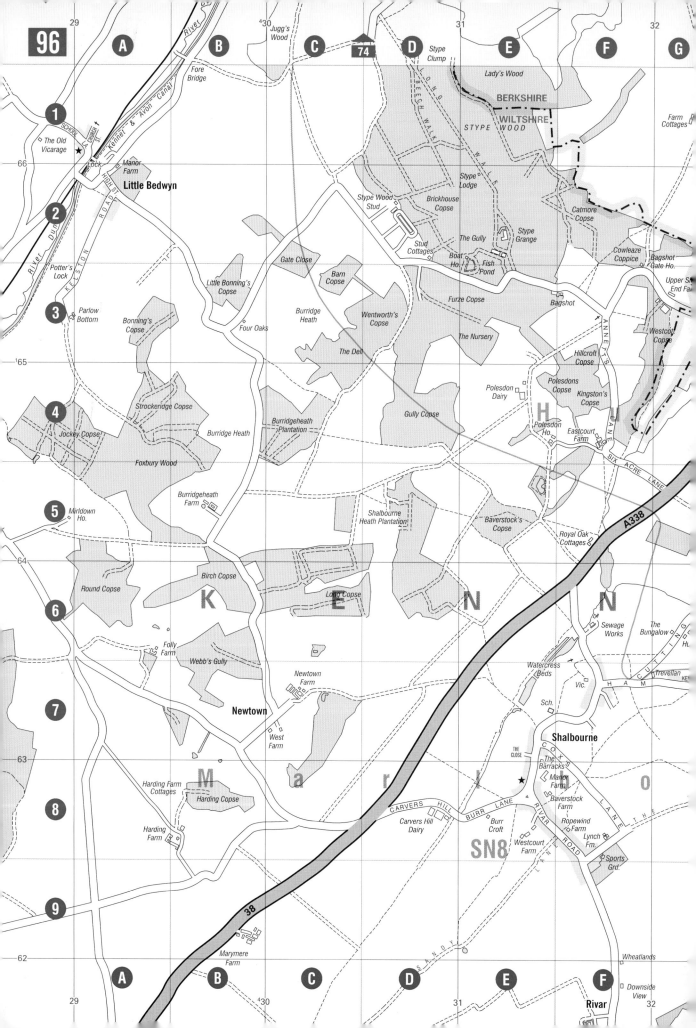

29 | A | B | 430 Jugg's Wood | C | 74 | D | Stype Clump | E | 31 | F | G | 32

1
The Old Vicarage
SCHOOL
Kennet & Avon Canal
Fore Bridge
Lady's Wood
BERKSHIRE
WILTSHIRE
STYPE WOOD
Farm Cottages

66

2
Lock
Manor Farm
Little Bedwyn
HIGH ST
Stype Lodge
Stype Wood Stud
Brickhouse Copse
Stud Cottages
The Gully
Stype Grange
Catmore Copse
Cowleaze Coppice
Bagshot Gate Ho.
Upper St End Fa

River Dun
Potter's Lock
KELSTON ROAD
Gate Close
Barn Copse
Boat Ho.
Fish Pond
Bagshot
Westcott Copse

3
Parlow Bottom
Little Bonning's Copse
Burridge Heath
Wentworth's Copse
Furze Copse
The Nursery
Hillcroft Copse
ANNETT'S

65
Bonning's Copse
Four Oaks
The Dell
Gully Copse
Polesdon Dairy
Polesdons Copse
Kingston's Copse
H
U

4
Strockeridge Copse
Burridge Heath
Burridgeheath Plantation
Polesdon Ho.
Eastcourt Farm
SIX ACRE LANE

Jockey Copse
Foxbury Wood
Burridgeheath Farm
Shalbourne Heath Plantation
Baverstock's Copse
A338

5
Mirldown Ho.
Royal Oak Cottages

64
Round Copse
Birch Copse
K
Long Copse
E
N
Sewage Works
N
The Bungalow
Trevellan
CUTTING

6
Folly Farm
Webb's Gully
Newtown Farm
Watercress Beds
Vic.
HAM

7
Newtown
West Farm
Sch.
Shalbourne
THE CLOSE
Cox's
The Barracks

63
M
a
r
l
Manor Farm
Baverstock Farm
O

8
Harding Farm Cottages
Harding Copse
CARVERS HILL
BURR LANE
Burr Croft
Ropewind Fm.
Lynch Fm.
RIVAR ROAD
LANE
THE

Harding Farm
Carvers Hill Dairy
Westcourt Farm
SN8
Sports Grd.

9
38
Wheatlands

62
Marymere Farm
Downside View

29 | A | B | 430 | C | 31 | D | E | F | **Rivar** | 32

SANDY

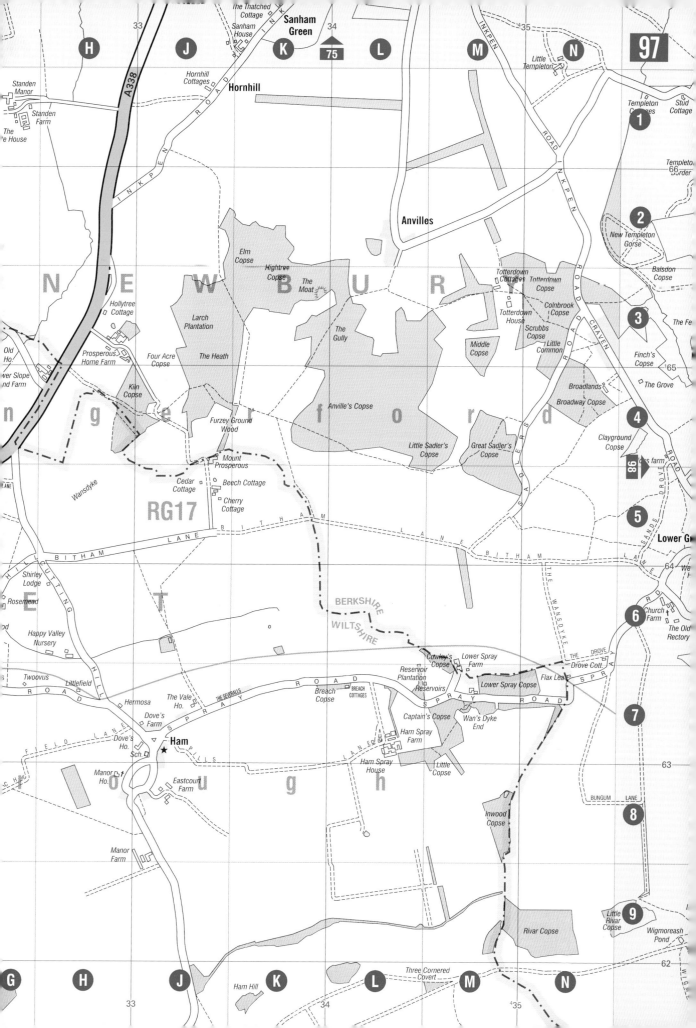

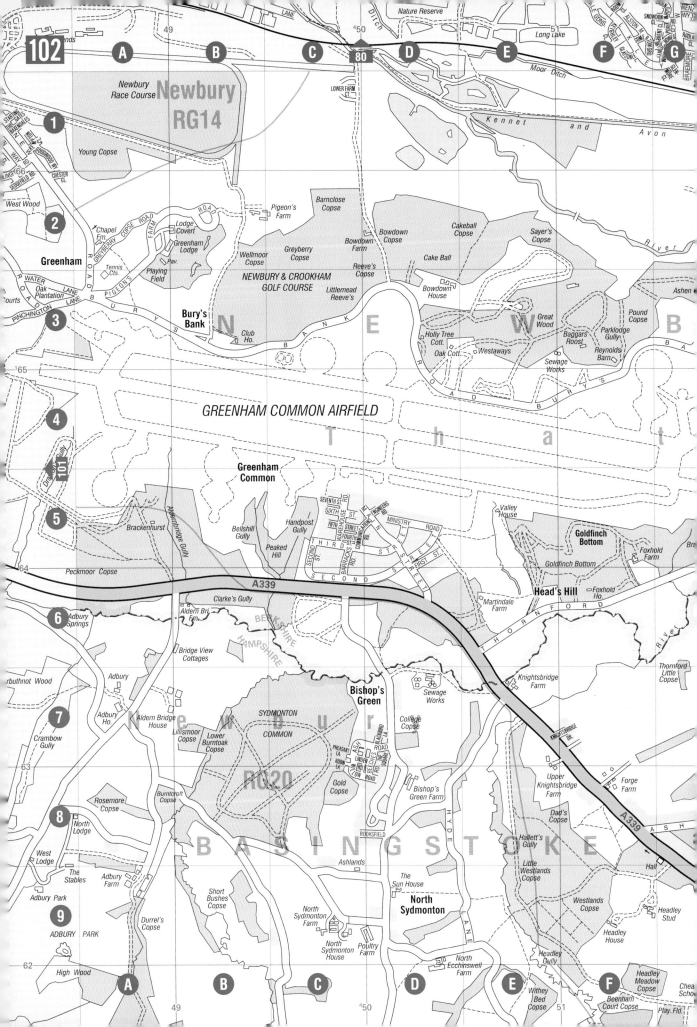

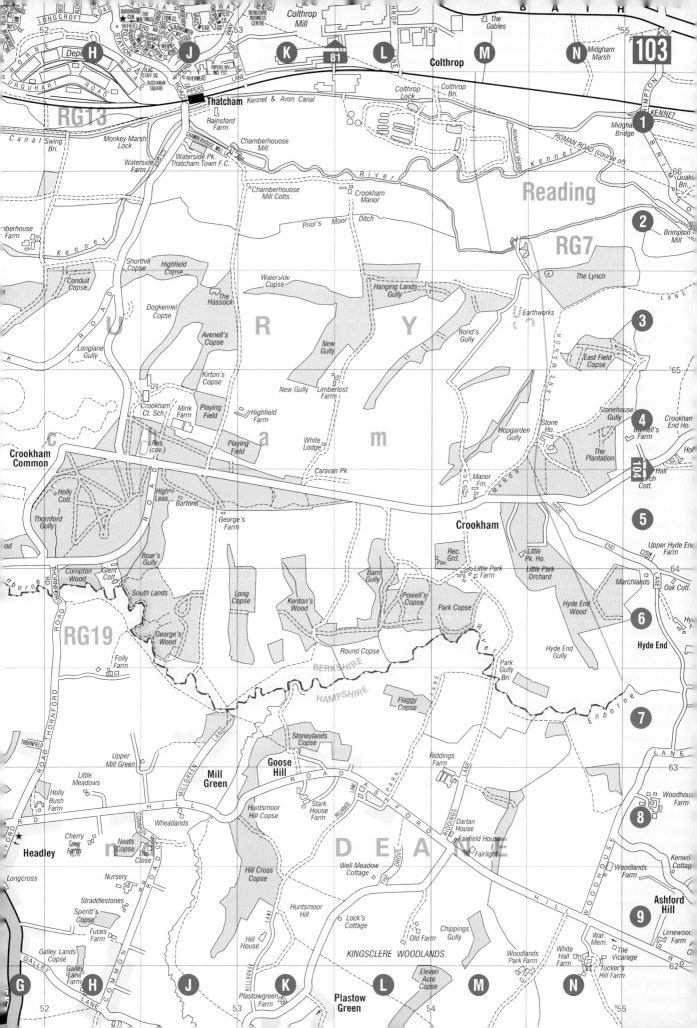

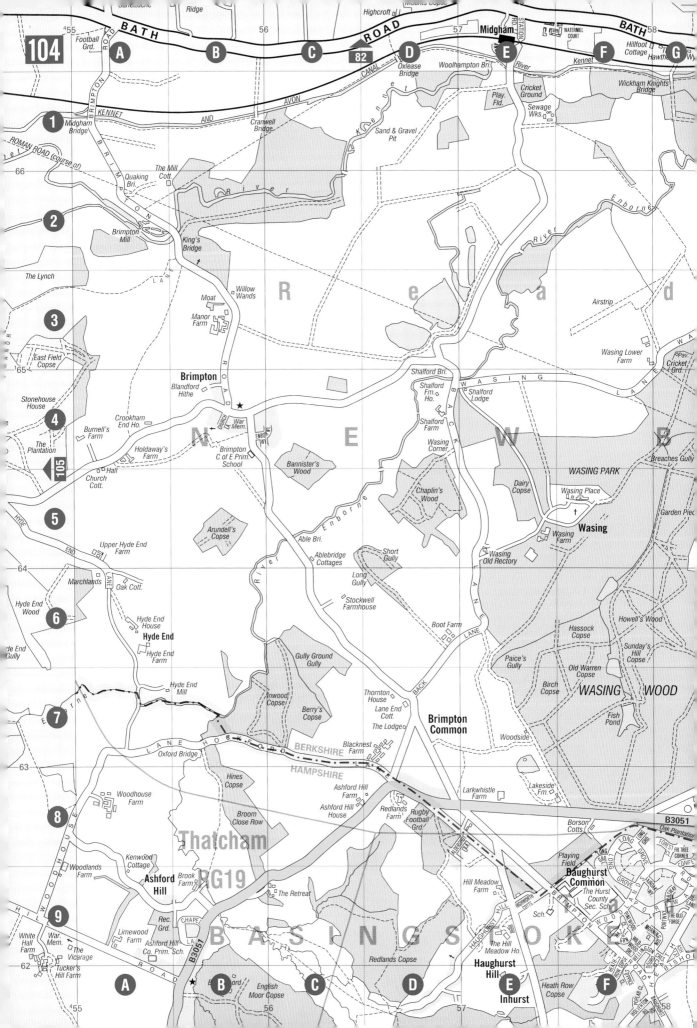

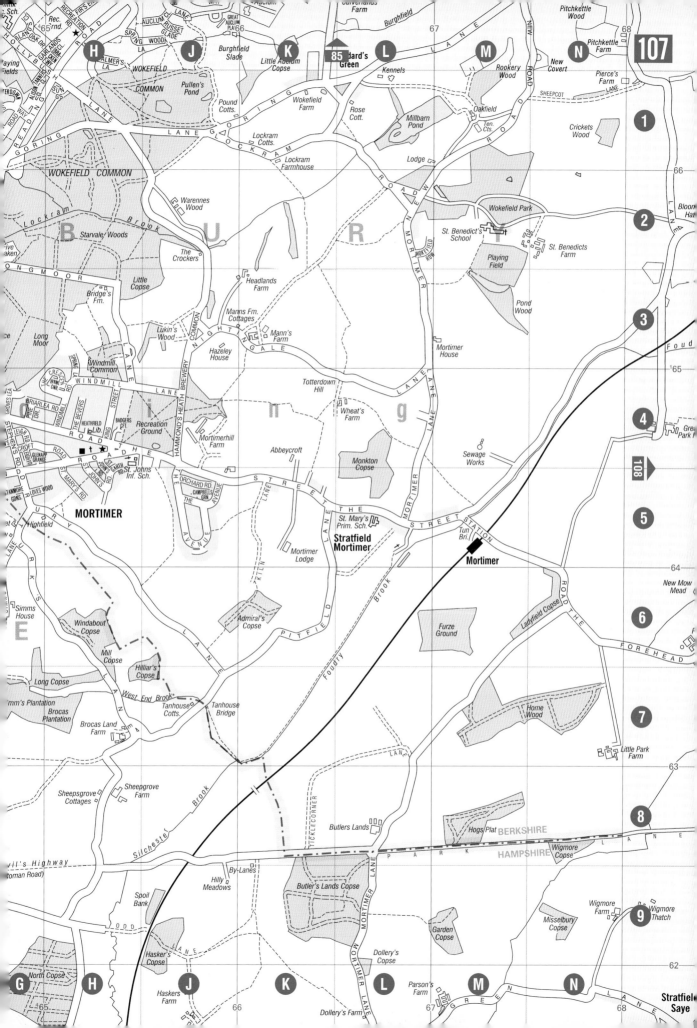

109

SPENCERS WOOD

RG2

Kenney's Farm

Great Wood

Tanners Farm Dairy

Old Dunnings

New Plantation

Pheasantry

Kiln Copse

GREAT

Emms Copse

Farle

Badgers Wood

Drayton Beauchamp

Kilnclose Pond

Cocksetters

Cuckoo Pen

Farleyhill Place Gardens

Rowe's Farm

Raggett's Farm

Nutbean

Fir Grove

Chill Hill

Cemetery

The Broadwater

Sandpit Farm

Wheelers Fm.

Blackwater

Wheeler's Copse

River

Ford

Bodys Farm

Prim. Sch.

Playing Field

Riding Stables

Lamb's Farm

Parkside

Sheepbridge Court Farm

Moat

Sheepbridge Ct.

The Island Ho.

Mill House

Sheep Bridge

Girdlers

Playing Fld.

Tennis Ct.

Hall

Oakhaven

Swallowfield Park

River

Poultry Houses

Wyvols Court

Bowyer's Farm

Brookside

Salter's Bridge

King's Bridge

Handpost Farm

Swallowfield

Oakleigh House

Goddard's Farm

Deep Water

Springalls Farm

Riseley Farm

Yew Tree Farm

The Lodge

Glasspool Farm

Riseley Gorse Farm

Collins Copse

Noah's Ark

St. Leger's Copse

Riseley

Chapel

Rec. Grd.

Hall

The Devil's Highway

(Roman Road)

BERKSHIRE

HAMPSHIRE

Cordery's Farm

Coldharbour Wood

Park Corner

New Inn Copse

Ham's Wood

WELLINGTON COUNTRY PARK

Birchen Copse

Caravan Park

Riseley Wood

Mill Wood

Hall's Farm

Top Hill Copse

Heckfield Heath

Heckfield Heath House

Pound Copse

Hook

RG27

River Whitewater

Springwater Farm

WOKINGHAM

HART

BASINGSTOKE ROAD

A33

B3349

ODIHAM ROAD

110

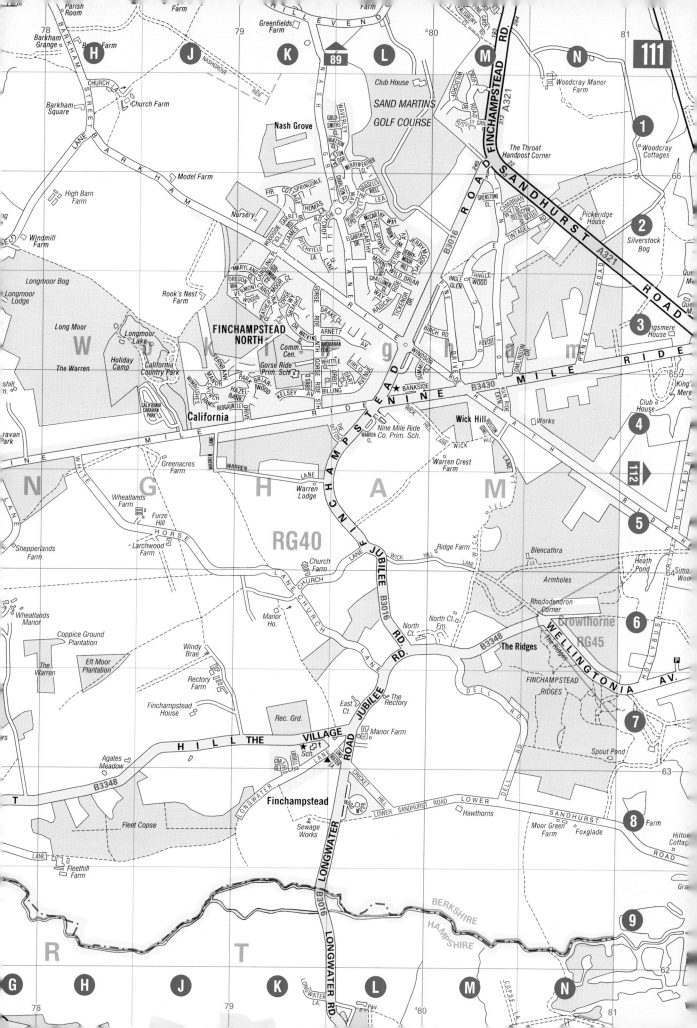

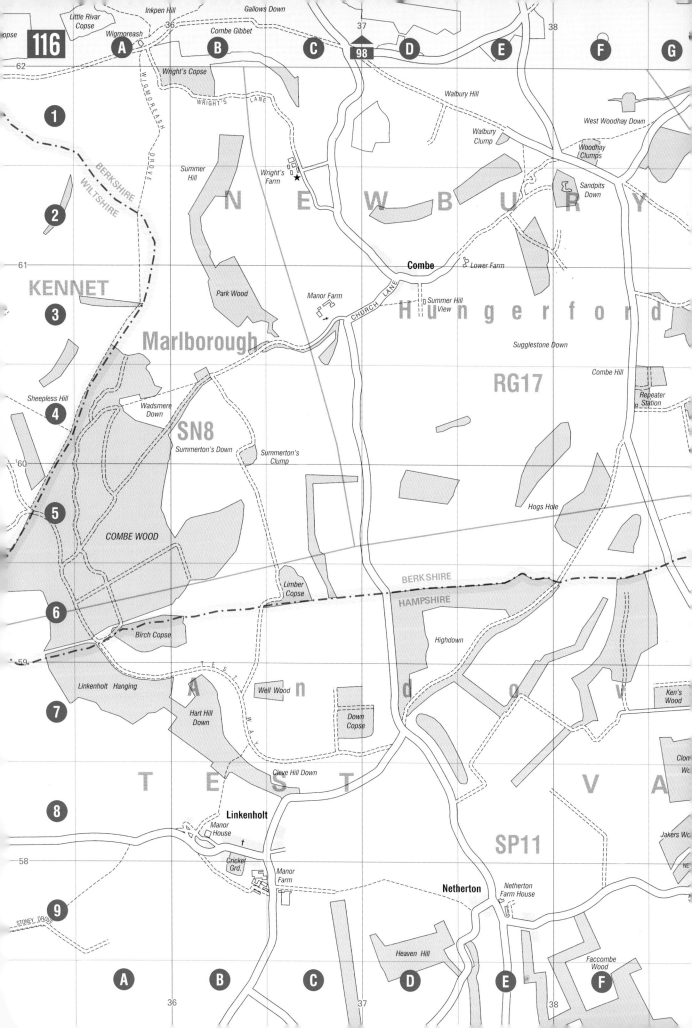

A   B   C   98   D   E   F   G

Little Rivar Copse

opse

Inkpen Hill

Gallows Down

Wigmoreash

Combe Gibbet

62

36

37

38

Wright's Copse

WRIGHT'S LANE

1

BERKSHIRE

WILTSHIRE

WIGMOREASH DROVE

Summer Hill

Wright's Farm

★

N   E   W   B   U   R   Y

Walbury Hill

West Woodhay Down

Walbury Clump

Woodhay Clumps

2

Sandpits Down

61

KENNET

Combe

Lower Farm

3

Park Wood

Manor Farm

CHURCH LANE

Summer Hill View

H u n g e r f o r d

Sugglestone Down

Marlborough

RG17

Combe Hill

Sheepless Hill

Wadsmere Down

SN8

Summerton's Down

Summerton's Clump

Repeater Station

4

60

5

COMBE WOOD

Hogs Hole

Limber Copse

BERKSHIRE

HAMPSHIRE

6

Birch Copse

Highdown

59

Linkenholt Hanging

T E S T   W A Y

Well Wood

A n d o v e r

Ken's Wood

7

Hart Hill Down

Down Copse

T E S T   V A L

Cleve Hill Down

Clon Wo

8

Linkenholt

Manor House

†

SP11

Jakers Wo

58

Cricket Grd.

Manor Farm

Netherton

Netherton Farm House

NE

STONEY DROVE

9

Heaven Hill

Faccombe Wood

A   B   C   D   E   F

36

37

38

117

H | Mannings

J

K | Berries Fm

99

L | Fish Pond | Park Copse

M | Ten. Cts. | Village Hall | **Heath End** | Barn Croft

N | Farm Copse | Copse Farm

Woo Hou

Well House

Highwood Far. 39

Bottomstead Farm

Rectory Farm

East Woodhay

Church Farm

Malverleys

1 | Garvards Copse

2 | Penton's Copse

Sch.

East End Farm

East End

Stargrove

Rabbit Pit Farm

Blacklands Copse

3 | Fern Close Copse | Tower House | Hollington Copse

B A S I N G S T O K E

HAMPSHIRE

BERKSHIRE

and

N e w b u r y

Lower Eastwick Copse

Upper Eastwick Copse

Eastwick

Dean Hill

Brick Kiln Farm

Solomon's Copse

Brickkiln Copse

Jones Farm

4 | Collarmakers Copse | Long Copse

Yews Farm

Hollington

'60

Ruffian's Copse

Apsley Farm

Pilot Hill

Home's Pond

Charldown Bungalow

Charldown Top Down

D E A N

RG20

Jones' Copse

Killah Copse

5

Kinghams Farm

6 | Grove Copse

West Down Copse

Ruffian's Copse

Apsley Copse

The Oaks

The Rods

The Plantation

Charldown Bottom Copse

Kydd's Copse

Buckhanger Copse

59

7

The Clump

Iron's Hill

Hitchen

8

Faccombe

Roe Wood

MANOR COTTS.

Northerwood

Brown's Copse

Curzon Street Farm

Faccombe Manor

Robins Croft Copse

Privet Copse

58

The Isle

Manor Farm

Ashmansworth Manor

9

Ashmansworth

Chapel Cotts.

War Mem.

Highfield

Fieldway

CROSS

GRE

G | 39

H | GREEN LANE

LONDON LANE

J | Bartlettsdown Plantation | Bartlett's Down

Bartlett's Down

K

40

Woodhay Poor

L

41

M | The New Rank

★

N | 42

62

61

LANE

FULLERS

BARN GLA

LANE

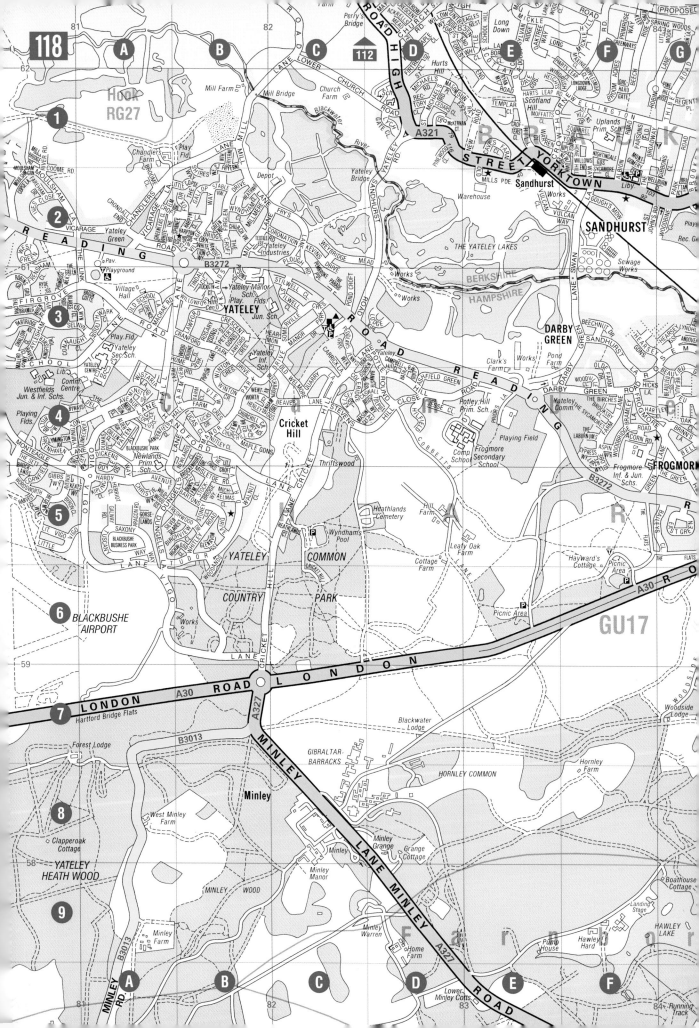

INDEX TO STREETS

HOW TO USE THIS INDEX

1. Each street name is followed by its Posttown or Postal Locality and then by its map reference; e.g. Abattoirs Rd. Read —4G **62** is in the Reading Posttown and is to be found in square 4G on page **62**. The page number being shown in bold type.
A strict alphabetical order is followed in which Av., Rd., St., etc. (though abbreviated) are read in full and as part of the street name; e.g. Ashcroft Clo. appears after Ash Ct. but before Ashcroft Ct.

2. Streets and a selection of Subsidiary names not shown on the Maps, appear in the index in *Italics* with the thoroughfare to which it is connected shown in brackets;
e.g. *Abbotsbury Ho. Read —3J **87** (off Lulworth Rd.)*

3. With the now general usage of Postcodes for addressing mail, it is not recommended that this index is used for such a purpose.

GENERAL ABBREVIATIONS

All : Alley
App : Approach
Arc : Arcade
Av : Avenue
Bk : Back
Boulevd : Boulevard
Bri : Bridge
D'way : Broadway
Bldgs : Buildings
Bus : Business
Cen : Centre
Chu : Church
Chyd : Churchyard
Circ : Circle
Cir : Circus
Clo : Close
Comn : Common
Cotts : Cottages
Ct : Court
Cres : Crescent
Dri : Drive
E : East
Embkmt : Embankment
Est : Estate
Gdns : Gardens
Ga : Gate
Gt : Great
Grn : Green
Gro : Grove
Ho : House
Ind : Industrial
Junct : Junction
La : Lane
Lit : Little
Lwr : Lower
Mnr : Manor
Mans : Mansions
Mkt : Market
M : Mews
Mt : Mount
N : North
Pal : Palace
Pde : Parade
Pk : Park
Pas : Passage
Pl : Place
Rd : Road
S : South
Sq : Square
Sta : Station
St : Street
Ter : Terrace
Up : Upper
Vs : Villas
Wlk : Walk
W : West
Yd : Yard

POSTTOWN AND POSTAL LOCALITY ABBREVIATIONS

Aldm : Aldermaston
Aldw : Aldworth
Arbor : Arborfield
Arbor X : Arborfield Cross
Asc : Ascot
Ash'd : Ashampstead
Ash'd C : Ashampstead Common
Ashf : Ashford
Ash H : Ashford Hill
Ashmw : Ashmansworth
Ashm G : Ashmore Green
Ast : Aston
Bagn : Bagnor
Bag : Bagshot
Bal H : Ball Hill
B'ham : Barkham
Baug : Baughurst
Bay : Baydon
B Hill : Beech Hill
Beed : Beedon
Been : Beenham
Ben H : Benham Hill
Binf : Binfield
Bin H : Binfield Heath
Bish : Bisham
Bis G : Bishops Green
B'water : Blackwater
Blew : Blewbury
Bour : Bourne End
Box : Boxford
Brack : Bracknell
Brad : Bradfield
Bray : Bray
Bright : Brightwalton
Brimp : Brimpton
Brimp C : Brimpton Common
Bckby : Bucklebury
Bur G : Burchetts Green
Burc : Burghclere
Bfld : Burghfield
Bfld C : Burghfield Common
Burn : Burnham
Calc : Calcot
Camb : Camberley
Catm : Catmore
Cav : Caversham
Chadw : Chaddleworth
Chad : Chadwell Heath
Chalk : Chalkhouse Green
Chalv : Chalvey
Chap R : Chapel Row
Charv : Charvil
Chav D : Chavey Down
Chaz H : Chazey Heath
Chvly : Chieveley
Chilt F : Chilton Foliat
Chol : Cholsey
Cipp : Cippenham
C Grn : Cockpole Green
Cold A : Cold Ash
Col T : College Town
Coln : Colnbrook
Colt : Colthrop
Combe : Combe
Comp : Compton
Cook : Cookham
Cook D : Cookham Dean
Cow : Cowley
Cray P : Crays Pond
Croc H : Crockham Heath
Crook C : Crookham Common
Crowt : Crowthorne
Cur : Curridge
Dat : Datchet
Den : Denham
Don : Donnington
Dor : Dorney
Dor R : Dorney Reach
D'den : Dunsden
Ear : Earley
E Gar : East Garston
E Ils : East Ilsley
E Wood : East Woodhay
E'bury : Eastbury
E'ton : Easton
Ecc : Ecchinswell
Edd : Eddington
Egh : Egham
Elc : Elcot
Emm G : Emmer Green
Enb : Enborne
Eng : Englefield
Eton : Eton
Eton C : Eton College
Eton W : Eton Wick
Eve : Eversley
Fac : Faccombe
Far H : Farley Hill
Farn : Farnborough (Hampshire)
Farnb : Farnborough (Oxfordshire)
Farn C : Farnham Common
Farn R : Farnham Royal
Felt : Feltham
Fif : Fifield
Finch : Finchampstead
F Hth : Flackwell Heath
Fril : Frilsham
Frim : Frimley
Frogm : Frogmore (Surrey)
Frox : Froxfield
Ful : Fulmer
Gall C : Gallowstree Common
G Grn : George Green
Gor : Goring
Gor H : Goring Heath
Graz : Grazeley
Gt Shef : Great Shefford
Green : Greeham
Half : Halfway
Ham : Ham
Hamp N : Hampstead Norreys
Ham M : Hamstead Marshall
Hare H : Hare Hatch
Harm : Harmondsworth
Harp : Harpsden
Hawl : Hawley
Hdly : Headley (Berkshire)
H'row A : London Heathrow Airport
Hedg : Hedgerley
Hen T : Henley-on-Thames
Henw : Henwick
Herm : Hermitage
Hil : Hillingdon
Holyp : Holyport
Hook : Hook
Hort : Horton
Houn : Hounslow
Hung : Hungerford
Hur : Hurley
Hurst : Hurst
Ink : Inkpen
Ink C : Inkpen Common
Iver : Iver
Kid E : Kidmore End
Kiln G : Kiln Green
Kint : Kintbury
Kint H : Kintbury Holt
Know H : Knowl Hill
L Bed : L Bedwyn
Lamb : Lambourn
Lamb W : Lambourn Woodlands
Land E : Lands End
Langl : Langley
Leck : Leckhampstead
Let B : Letcombe Bassett
Light : Lightwater
Link : Linkenholt
L Mar : Little Marlow
L Sand : Little Sandhurst
L Grn : Littlewick Green
Lock : Lockinge
Lwr B : Lower Basildon
Lwr Ear : Lower Earley
Lwr P : Lower Padworth
Lwr S : Lower Shiplake
M'head : Maidenhead
Map : Mapledurham
Mar : Marlow
Medm : Medmenham
Mid : Middlegreen
Midg : Midgham
Mort : Mortimer
Mort C : Mortimer Common
Mort W : Mortimer West End
Moul : Moulsford
Newb : Newbury
Newt : Newtown
Newt C : Newtown Common
N Asc : North Ascot
N End : North End
Nup : Nuptown
Oak G : Oakley Green
Old Win : Old Windsor
Owl : Owlsmoor
Pad : Padworth
Pad C : Padworth Common
Pam H : Pamber Heath
Pang : Pangbourne
P'mre : Peasemore
Pen : Penwood
Ping : Pingewood
Play : Playhatch
Pur T : Purley on Thames
Read : Reading
Rem : Remenham
Rise : Riseley
Rusc : Ruscombe
Sand : Sandhurst
Shalb : Shalbourne
Shaw : Shaw
Shef W : Shefford Woodlands
Shin : Shinfield
S'lake : Shiplake
S'lake X : Shiplake Cross
Shur R : Shurlock Row
Sil : Silchester
Sind : Sindlesham
Slou : Slough
Son : Sonning
Son C : Sonning Common
S Asc : South Ascot
S Faw : South Fawley
S Sto : South Stoke
South : Southend
Speen : Speen
Spen W : Spencers Wood
Stai : Staines
Stan D : Stanford Dingley
Stanw : Stanwell
Stcks : Stockcross
Stoke P : Stoke Poges
Strat S : Stratfield Saye
Streat : Streatley
Sul : Sulham
Sul'd : Sulhamstead
S'dale : Sunningdale
S'hill : Sunninghill
Swal : Swallowfield
Tadl : Tadley
Tap : Taplow
That : Thatcham
Thea : Theale
Three M : Three Mile Cross
Tid : Tidmarsh
Tile : Tilehurst
Tok G : Tokers Green
Tut C : Tutts Clump
Twy : Twyford
Uft N : Ufton Nervet
Up Bas : Upper Basildon
Up Buck : Upper Bucklebury
Up Cul : Upper Culham
Up Lamb : Upper Lambourn
Up Wool : Upper Woolhampton
Uxb : Uxbridge
Vir W : Virginia Water
Wal L : Waltham St Lawrence
Want : Wantage
Warf : Warfield
Warf P : Warfield Park
Warg : Wargrave
War R : Warren Row
Wash W : Wash Water
Water : Water Oakley
Wel C : Wellington College
W Dray : West Drayton
W Ils : West Ilsley
W Wood : West Woodhay
W'ton : Weston
Wex : Wexham
Whis G : Whistley Green
Whit H : Whitchurch Hill
Whit T : Whitchurch on Thames
White : White Waltham
Wick : Wickham
W'sham : Windlesham
Wind : Windsor
Wink : Winkfield
Wink R : Winkfield Row
Winn : Winnersh
Wint : Winterbourne
Wokgm : Wokingham
Wbrn G : Wooburn Green
Woodc : Woodcote
Wood M : Woodlands St Mary
Wdly : Woodley
Woods : Woodspeen
Woolh : Woolhampton
Wool H : Woolton Hill
Woos : Woosehill
Wray : Wraysbury
Yat : Yateley
Yatt : Yattendon
Yiew : Yiewsley

INDEX TO STREETS

Abattoirs Rd. Read —4G **62**
Abberbury Clo. Don —5J **79**
Abbetts La. Camb —6M **119**
Abbey Clo. Brack —7A **92**
Abbey Clo. Newb —2L **101**
Abbey Clo. Slou —8A **22**
Abbey Clo. Wokgm —4A **90**
Abbey Ct. Camb —4N **119**
Abbey Pk. Bfld C —8G **84**
Abbey Rd. Bour —2K **5**
Abbey Rd. Vir W —7M **95**
Abbey Sq. Read —5H **63**
Abbey St. Read —4H **63**
Abbey Way. Mar —9B **4**
Abbey Wood. S'dale —9C **94**
Abbotsbury. Brack —7K **91**
*Abbotsbury Ho. Read —3J **87***
(off Lulworth Rd.)
Abbots Dri. Vir W —7K **95**
*Abbots Ho. Read —4H **63***
(off Abbey St.)
Abbot's Rd. Bfld C —9G **84**
Abbots Rd. Newb —1L **101**
Abbots Wlk. Read —4H **63**
Abbots Wlk. Wind —8A **46**
Abbott's Clo. Uxb —6L **25**
Abbotts Way. Slou —9N **21**
Aberaman. Cav —7F **38**
Abercorn Ho. Hawl —8J **119**
Aberdeen Av. Slou —8C **22**
Aberford Clo. Read —5C **62**
Abex Rd. Newb —8L **79**
Abingdon Clo. Brack —7B **92**
Abingdon Clo. Uxb —2N **25**
Abingdon Dri. Cav —7J **39**
Abingdon Rd. E Ils —7B **12**
Abingdon Rd. Sand —1G **119**
Abingdon Wlk. M'head —3B **20**
Abney Ct. Dri. Bour —5L **5**
Abrahams Rd. Hen T —3B **16**
Abury La. Brack —8D **92**
Acacia Av. Owl —9H **113**
Acacia Av. W Dray —8N **25**
Acacia Av. Wray —1N **71**
Acacia Ct. Brack —6M **91**
Acacia Ho. Slou —9H **23**
Acacia M. W Dray —5L **49**
Acacia Rd. Read —6J **63**
Acacia Rd. Stai —9J **73**
Accommodation La. W Dray —7H **49**
Ackrells Mead. Sand —9D **112**
Acorn Dri. Wokgm —4A **90**
Acorn M. Farn —9L **119**
Acorn Rd. B'water —4F **118**
Acorn Wlk. Calc —7K **61**
Acre Bus. Pk. Read —3H **87**
Acre Pas. Wind —7F **46**
Acre Rd. Read —3G **86**
Acre, The. Mar —5D **4**
Adam Clo. Baug —9G **105**
Adam Clo. Slou —9C **22**
Adam Ct. Hen T —4D **16**
Adams Way. Ear —1M **87**
Adder's La. Up Bas —9H **35**
Addington Clo. Wind —9C **46**
Addington Rd. Read —6K **63**
Addiscombe Chase. Tile —1J **61**
Addiscombe Rd. Crowt —6G **112**
Addison Clo. Iver —8F **24**
Addison Ct. M'head —5E **20**
Addison Rd. Read —3G **62**
Adelaide Clo. Slou —1C **46**
Adelaide Rd. Ashf —9L **73**
Adelaide Rd. Read —7N **63**
Adelaide Sq. Wind —8F **46**
Adelphi Gdns. Slou —1G **46**
Adey's Clo. Newb —1M **101**
Adkins Rd. Wal L —6C **42**
Admiral Kepple Ct. Asc —2H **93**
Admiral's Ct. Read —7G **62**
Admiralty Way. Camb —5K **119**
Admoor La. South —1K **83**
Adwell Dri. Lwr Ear —2B **88**
Adwell Sq. Hen T —4C **16**
Adwood Ct. That —8H **81**
Agar Cres. Brack —2M **91**
Agars Pl. Dat —5J **47**
Agate Clo. Wokgm —4K **89**
Aggisters La. Wokgm —8H **89**
Agincourt. Asc —5M **93**
Agincourt Clo. Wokgm —5K **89**
Agricola Way. That —9H **81**
Ainsdale Cres. Read —8A **62**
Aintree. Lamb —3H **27**
Aintree Clo. Coln —7F **48**
Aintree Clo. Green —1N **101**
Aird Clo. Wool H —9C **100**
Airport Way. Stai —1H **73**
Ajax Av. Slou —8D **22**
Alandale Clo. Read —3K **87**
Alan Pl. Read —7A **62**
Alan Way. G Grn —7N **23**
Albain Cres. Ashf —6M **73**
Albany Pk. Coln —6E **48**
Albany Pk. Frim —8N **119**
Albany Pk. Dri. Winn —9F **64**
Albany Pl. Egh —8C **72**
Albany Rd. Old Win —2J **71**
Albany Rd. Read —5D **62**
Albany Rd. Wind —8F **46**
Alben Rd. Binf —9G **66**
Albert Clo. Slou —2H **47**
Albert Pl. Eton W —4C **46**
Albert Rd. Ashf —9N **73**
Albert Rd. Bag —9H **115**
Albert Rd. Brack —3M **91**
Albert Rd. Cav —9E **38**
Albert Rd. Crowt —5F **112**
Albert Rd. Egh —1M **95**
Albert Rd. Hen T —5D **16**
Albert Rd. Newb —7L **79**
Albert Rd. Old Win —9F **46**
Albert Rd. W Dray —9M **25**
Albert Rd. Wokgm —5N **89**
Albert St. M'head —8C **20**
(in two parts)
Albert St. Slou —2H **47**
Albert St. Wind —7D **46**
Albion Clo. Slou —9J **23**
Albion Ho. Langl —4C **48**
Albion Rd. Sand —1F **118**
Albion Ter. Read —6J **63**
Albury Clo. Read —3C **62**
Albury Gdns. Calc —9M **61**
Alcot Clo. Crowt —6F **112**
Aldborough Spur. Slou —7G **22**
Aldbourne Av. Ear —8N **63**
Aldbourne Rd. Burn —6L **21**
Aldeburgh Clo. Cav —5J **39**
Aldebury Rd. M'head —4B **20**
Aldenham Clo. Cav —7J **39**
Aldenham Ter. Brack —8N **91**
Alden View. Wind —7N **45**
Alderbrook Clo. Crowt —6C **112**
Alderbury Rd. Slou —1A **48**
Alderbury Rd. W. Slou —1A **48**
Alder Clo. Egh —9N **71**
Alder Clo. Slou —9B **22**
Alder Dri. Bfld C —8G **84**
Alder Dri. Tile —6K **61**
Alderfield Clo. Thea —8G **60**
Alder Gro. Yat —4A **118**
Alderley Clo. Wdly —3E **64**
Alderman Willey Clo. Wokgm —5N **89**
Alder Rd. Den —1K **25**
Alder Rd. Iver —3E **24**
Aldershot La. Baug —8D **104**
Alderside Wlk. Egh —9N **71**
Alders, The. That —7G **80**
Aldin Av. N. Slou —1J **47**
Aldin Av. S. Slou —1J **47**
Aldridge Pk. Wink R —1D **92**
Aldridge Rd. Slou —5C **22**
Aldwick Dri. M'head —8A **20**
Aldworth Clo. Brack —6L **91**
Aldworth Clo. Read —7C **62**
Aldworth Gdns. Crowt —5E **112**
Aldworth Rd. Comp —1H **33**
Aldworth Rd. Up Bas —7J **35**
Alexander Ct. Read —5F **62**
Alexander Rd. Egh —9D **72**
Alexander Rd. That —9H **81**
Alexander Wlk. Brack —7M **91**
Alexandra Av. Camb —4L **119**
Alexandra Clo. Stai —9L **73**
Alexandra Rd. Egh —1L **95**
Alexandra Rd. M'head —6A **20**
Alexandra Rd. Read —5K **63**
Alexandra Rd. Slou —2F **46**
Alexandra Rd. Uxb —3L **25**
Alexandra Rd. Wind —8F **46**
Alford Clo. Tile —4L **61**
Alfred St. Read —5F **62**
Alice Gough Homes. Brack —5M **91**
Alice La. Burn —5L **21**
Alison Clo. Bfld C —9G **85**
Alison Wlk. Cav —2K **63**
Allanson Rd. Mar —4D **4**
Allcroft Rd. Read —7J **63**
Allenby Rd. Camb —3L **119**
Allenby Rd. M'head —7M **19**
Allendale Clo. Sand —8E **112**
Allendale Rd. Ear —9A **64**
Allerds Rd. Farn R —2B **22**
Alleyns La. Cook —7H **5**
All Hallows Rd. Cav —1K **63**
Allington Ct. Slou —7H **23**
Allison Ct. Read —5F **62**
Allison Gdns. Pur T —8K **37**
Allnatt Av. Winn —2H **89**
Allonby Clo. Lwr Ear —1C **88**
All Saints Av. M'head —6N **19**
All Saints Clo. Wokgm —4A **90**
All Saints Cres. Farn —8J **119**
All Saints Rise. Warf —1A **92**
All Saints Rd. Light —9M **115**
Allsmore La. Brack —5C **92**
All Soul's Rd. Asc —6K **93**
Alma Ct. Burn —4M **21**
Alma Rd. Eton W —3B **46**
Alma Rd. Wind —8E **46**
Alma St. Read —4C **62**

Almond Av. Newb —6L 79
Almond Av. W Dray —2N 49
Almond Clo. Egh —1K 95
Almond Clo. Farn —9M 119
Almond Clo. Wind —8D 46
Almond Clo. Wokgm —7H 89
Almond Dri. Cav —9M 39
Almond Rd. Burn —3L 21
Almond Ville. Burn —4M 21
Almons Way. Slou —6K 23
Almshouses. Read —5G 62
(off Castle St.)
Almswood Rd. Tadl —8J 105
Alpha St. N. Slou —1J 47
Alpha St. S. Slou —2H 47
Alpine St. Read —6H 63
Alsace Wlk. Camb —8M 119
Alston Gdns. M'head —7B 20
Alston M. That —9F 80
Alston Wlk. Cav —2K 63
Altona Way. Slou —7D 22
Alton Ride. B'water —3G 119
Altwood Bailey. M'head —9M 19
Altwood Clo. M'head —9M 19
Altwood Clo. Slou —6A 22
Altwood Dri. M'head —9M 19
Altwood Rd. M'head —9L 19
Alvista Av. Tap —7L 21
Alwyn Rd. M'head —6M 19
Alyson Ct. M'head —5C 20
Amanda Ct. Slou —2M 47
Ambarrow Cres. Sand —9D 112
Ambarrow La. Sand —8B 112
Ambassador. Brack —7K 91
Amberley Clo. Newb —7K 79
Amberley Ct. M'head —3F 20
Amberley Dri. Twy —7J 41
Amberley Rd. Slou —6A 22
Amberley Way. Uxb —3M 25
Amblecote Rd. Tile —5B 62
Ambleside Clo. Wdly —5D 64
Ambleside Rd. Light —9K 115
Ambleside Wlk. Uxb —2L 25
(off Cumbrian Way)
Ambrook Rd. Read —3H 87
Ambrose Pl. Read —5F 62
Ambrose Rd. Tadl —9K 105
Ambury Rd. Aldw —9A 14
Amen Corner Bus. Pk. Binf —4J 91
Amerden Clo. Tap —7G 21
Amerden La. Bray —1H 45
Amerden La. Tap —7G 21
Amerden Way. Slou —1C 46
Amersham Clo. Calc —8K 61
Amersham Rd. Cav —2K 63
Amethyst Clo. Wokgm —4J 89
Amethyst La. Read —6C 62
Amherst Rd. Read —6N 63
Amity Rd. Read —5L 63
Amity St. Read —4L 63
Ammanford. Cav —8F 38
Ampere Rd. Newb —8M 79
Ancaster Dri. Asc —3H 93
Ancastle Grn. Hen T —5B 16
Andermans. Wind —7N 45
Anderson Av. Ear —6N 63
Anderson Cres. Arbor X —9D 88
Anderson Pl. Bag —6H 115
Andover Clo. Tile —3L 61
Andover Clo. Uxb —3J 25
Andover Drove. Wash W —6F 100
Andover Rd. B'water —3G 118
Andover Rd. Newb —5H 101
Andover Rd. Pen —8F 100
Andrew Clo. Wokgm —6C 90
Andrew's Clo. Thea —9F 60
Andrews Rd. Ear —9A 64
Angel Ct. Newb —7L 79
Angel Mead. Woolh —9E 82
Angel Pl. Binf —1G 90
Angle Clo. Uxb —2N 25
Angle Field Rd. Cav —1J 63
Anglers Way. Read —5K 63
Anglesey Av. Farn —9K 119
Angus Clo. Calc —8M 61
Anne Clo. M'head —4B 20
Anneforde Pl. Brack —2L 91
Annerdale. Cold A —2F 80
Annesley Gdns. Winn —1H 89
Annett's La. Hung —3F 96
Ansculf Rd. Slou —4C 22
Anslow Gdns. Iver —3E 24
Anslow Pl. Slou —6M 21
Anson Cres. Read —4K 87
Anson Wlk. Read —4K 87
Anstey Pl. Bfld C —8H 85
Anstey Rd. Read —5F 62
Anston Clo. Lwr Ear —3N 87
Antares Clo. Wokgm —5L 89
Anthian Clo. Wdly —4G 65
Anthony Way. Slou —8N 21
Antrim Rd. Wdly —6C 64
Anvil Ct. Langl —3B 48
Apex Plaza. Read —4H 63
Aplin Way. Light —9K 115
Appleby End. Read —5B 62
Apple Clo. Tile —9J 37
Apple Clo. Wokgm —6L 89
Apple Croft. M'head —2N 43
Appledore. Brack —8K 91
Appledore M. Farn —9L 119
Appleford Clo. That —9G 81
Appleford Rd. Read —8A 62
Apple Tree Av. Uxb & W Dray —6N 25
Appletree Clo. Brack —3L 91
Appletree La. Slou —2L 47
Appletree La. Spen W —9H 87
Appletree Pl. Brack —3L 91
Apple Tree Way. Owl —9H 113
Appley Ct. Camb —4M 119
Appley Dri. Camb —3M 119
Approach Rd. Tap —7H 21
April Clo. Camb —7N 119
Apsey Ct. Binf —2J 91
Aquila Clo. Wokgm —5K 89
Aragon Ct. Brack —6N 91
Aragon Rd. Yat —5A 118
Arborfield Clo. Slou —2G 47
Arborfield Rd. Shin —7M 87
Arbor La. Winn —9G 64
Arbor Meadows. Winn —9G 64
Arbour Clo. Read —7F 62
Arcade, The. Newb —8L 79
Arcade, The. Wokgm —5A 90
Archangel Way. That —7J 81
Archer Clo. M'head —6A 20
Archers Ct. Mar —6C 4
Archer Ter. W Dray —8M 25
Arch Hill. Bin H —3N 39
Archway Rd. Cav —2G 63
Arden Clo. Brack —4C 92
Ardingly. Brack —7L 91
Ardler Rd. Cav —2J 63
Ardwell Clo. Crowt —5C 112
Arenal Dri. Crowt —7F 112
Argosy La. Stai —4L 73
Argyle Rd. Newb —9K 79
Argyle Rd. Read —5E 62
Argyle St. Read —5E 62
Argyll Av. Slou —8C 22
Arix Ho. Twy —8J 41
Arkle Av. That —8C 80
Arkley Ct. M'head —4F 44
Arkwright Dri. Brack —4H 91
Arkwright Rd. Coln —8F 48
Arkwright Rd. Read —9H 63
Arlington Bus. Pk. Thea —9H 61
Arlington Clo. Brack —3L 91
Arlington Clo. M'head —6K 19
Arlington La. Newb —9J 55
Arlington Rd. Ashf —9N 73
Arlington Sq. Brack —4L 91
Armadale Ct. Read —6D 62
Armitage Ct. Asc —8M 93
Armour Hill. Tile —2L 61
Armour Rd. Tile —3L 61
Armour Wlk. Tile —3L 61
Armstrong Rd. Egh —1L 95
Armstrong Way. Wdly —5F 64
Arncliffe. Brack —7L 91
Arndale Way. Egh —9B 72
Arnett Av. Wokgm —3K 111
Arnhem Rd. Newb —8M 79
Arnside Clo. Twy —6J 41
Arrowhead Rd. Thea —1F 84
Arrowsmith Way. That —9J 81
Arthur Clark Home, The. Cav —1F 62
Arthur Clo. Bag —9H 115
Arthur Pl. Read —5J 63
Arthur Rd. Newb —9J 79
Arthur Rd. Slou —1F 46
Arthur Rd. Wind —7E 46
Arthur Rd. Wokgm —5M 89
Arthurstone Birches. Binf —9H 67
Arun Clo. Winn —2G 89
Arundel Clo. M'head —6L 19
Arundel Ct. Slou —3M 47
Arundel Ho. Uxb —5K 25
Arundel Rd. Uxb —3J 25
Arundel Rd. Wdly —6D 64
Ascot Clo. Green —2N 101
Ascot Rd. M'head & Brack —2N 67
Ascot Wood Pl. Asc —5K 93
Ashampstead Rd. Read —8A 62
Ashampstead Rd. Up Bas —8J 35
Ashbourne. Brack —8K 91
Ashbourne Gro. M'head —2N 43
Ashbourne Ho. Chalv —1G 47
Ashbourne Way. That —8E 80
Ashbrook Rd. Old Win —4K 71
Ashburton Rd. Read —1J 87
Ashbury Dri. B'water —8L 119
Ashbury Dri. Tile —5K 61
Ashby Ct. Read —4H 87
Ash Clo. B'water —4G 119
Ash Clo. Bright —2B 30
Ash Clo. Slou —2C 48
Ash Ct. Newb —7L 79
Ash Ct. Wokgm —5A 90
Ashcroft Clo. Cav —8E 38
Ashcroft Ct. Burn —3L 21
Ashcroft Rd. M'head —6N 19
Ashdale Clo. Stai —6M 73
Ashdale Pk. Wokgm —4A 112
Ashdown. M'head —3E 20
Ashdown Clo. Brack —4D 92
Ashdown Rd. Uxb —3N 25
Asher Dri. Asc —3F 92
Ashfield Grn. Yat —4D 118
Ashford Av. Son C —1E 38
Ashford Clo. Ashf —8M 73
Ashford Cres. Ashf —7M 73
Ashford Hill Rd. Hdly —8G 102
Ashford La. Dor —1L 45
Ashford Rd. Iver —1D 24
Ash Ga. That —7J 81
Ash Grn. Read —3K 87
Ash Gro. Stai —9K 73
Ash Gro. Stoke P —1H 23
Ash Gro. W Dray —8N 25
Ash La. Baug —9G 104
Ash La. Bfld C —7H 85
Ash La. Wind —8N 45
Ashley Clo. Ear —1A 88
Ashley Ct. M'head —7E 20
Ashley Dri. B'water —5G 119
Ashley Hill Pl. C Grn —6L 17
Ashley Pk. M'head —4E 20
Ashley Rd. Read —7E 62
Ashley Rd. Uxb —3J 25
Ashman Rd. That —8K 81
Ashmere Clo. Calc —8K 61
Ashmere Ter. Read —4E 62
Ashmore Grn. Rd. Cold A —4E 80
Ashmore La. Wind —4C 68
Ashmore Rd. Read —2J 87
Ashridge. Farn —9K 119
Ashridge Ct. Newb —9L 79
Ashridge Grn. Brack —3M 91
Ashridge Rd. Wokgm —3B 90
Ash Rd. Bis G —7C 102
Ash Rd. Tile —5M 61
Ash Ter. Ashm G —3E 80
Ashton Clo. Tile —4K 61
Ashton Pl. Kint —9G 76
Ashton Pl. M'head —8L 19
Ashton Rd. Wokgm —2L 89
Ash Tree Gro. Ham M —3N 99
Ashtrees Rd. Wdly —4E 64
Ash View Clo. Ashf —9M 73
Ash View Gdns. Ashf —9M 73
Ashville Way. Wokgm —6N 89
Ash Way. Wokgm —8H 89
Ashwood. Wdly —7C 64
Ashwood Av. Uxb —7N 25
Ashwood Clo. Tile —6J 61
Ashwood Dri. Newb —7A 80
Ashwood Rd. Egh —1K 95
Ashworth Dri. That —9F 80
Askew Dri. Spen W —8H 87
Aspen Clo. Slou —6D 22
Aspen Clo. Stai —7G 73
Aspen Clo. W Dray —9N 25
Aspin Way. B'water —4F 118
Astley Clo. Wokgm —4L 89
Aston Av. Tile —4J 61
Aston Clo. Pang —7B 36
Aston Ct. Read —7B 62
Aston Ferry La. Ast —1H 17
Aston La. Rem —4H 17
Aston Mead. Wind —6A 46
Astor Clo. M'head —8E 20
Astor Clo. Winn —9J 65
Astra Mead. Wink R —1E 92
Atfield Gro. W'sham —6N 115
Atherton Clo. Stai —3L 73
Atherton Clo. Tile —4N 61
Atherton Ct. Wind —6F 46
Atherton Cres. Hung —6K 75
Atherton Pl. Lamb —2H 27
Atherton Rd. Hung —6K 75
Athlone Clo. M'head —5B 20
Athlone Sq. Wind —7E 46
Athol Way. Uxb —4N 25
Atkinson's All. M'head —6C 20
Atlantic Ho. Read —3G 87
Atrebatti Rd. Sand —9G 113
Attle Clo. Uxb —3N 25
Auburn Ct. Cav —2G 62
Auckland Clo. M'head —6E 20
Auckland Rd. Read —6N 63
Auclum Clo. Bfld C —9J 85
Auclum La. Bfld C —9J 85
Audley Clo. Newb —6A 80
Audley Dri. M'head —8M 19
Audley St. Read —4D 62
Audley Way. Asc —5G 92
Augur Clo. Stai —9G 73
August End. G Grn —7N 23
August End. Read —4C 62
Augustine Clo. Coln —9F 48
Augustine Wlk. Warf —2B 92
Austen Gdns. Newb —2M 101
Austin Rd. Wdly —6E 64
Austin Waye. Uxb —2K 25
Australia Av. M'head —6C 20
Australia Rd. Slou —1K 47
Auton Pl. Hen T —6C 16
Autumn Clo. Cav —6K 39
Autumn Clo. Slou —9B 22
Autumn Wlk. M'head —9L 19
Autumn Wlk. Warg —3J 41
Avalon Rd. Bour —2M 5
Avalon Rd. Ear —9B 64
Avebury. Brack —8L 91
Avebury. Slou —8C 22
Avebury Sq. Read —7K 63
Aveley Wlk. Read —7H 63
Avenue Clo. W Dray —2L 49
Avenue Rd. M'head —9E 20
Avenue Rd. Stai —9E 72
Avenue Sucy. Camb —5M 119
Avenue, The. Asc —1K 93
Avenue, The. Bour —3K 5
Avenue, The. Camb —4M 119
Avenue, The. Cow —5L 25
Avenue, The. Crowt —5F 112
Avenue, The. Dat —7K 47
Avenue, The. Egh —6C 72
Avenue, The. Light —9K 115
Avenue, The. M'head —3F 20
Avenue, The. Mort —5J 107
Avenue, The. Old Win —2K 71
Avenue, The. Wokgm —1J 113
Avenue, The. Wray —1N 71
Averil Ct. Tap —7M 21
Avington Clo. Tile —4J 61
Avocet Cres. Col T —1H 119
Avon Clo. Calc —7N 61
Avon Clo. Slou —8A 22
Avon Ct. Binf —1G 91
Avondale. M'head —5N 19
Avondale Rd. Ashf —7L 73
Avon Gro. Brack —2N 91
Avon Pl. Read —4K 63
Avon Way. Newb —7A 80
Avon Way. Pad —5N 83
Axbridge. Brack —7B 92
Axbridge Rd. Read —1J 87
Aylesbury Cres. Slou —7F 22
Aylesford Vs. Whis G —3K 65
Aylesworth Av. Slou —4D 22
Aylesworth Spur. Old Win —4K 71
Aylsham Clo. Tile —4M 61
Ayrton Senna Rd. Tile —5K 61
Aysgarth. Brack —8K 91
Aysgarth Pk. M'head —4E 44
Azalea Way. G Grn —7N 23

Bachelors Acre. Wind —7F 46
Back La. Been —5J 83
Back La. Brimp C —7D 104
Back La. Kint —2E 98
Back La. Spen W —2G 109
Back La. Stan D —8F 58
Back La. Tile —3J 61
Backsideans. Warg —3J 41
Back St. E Gar —7B 28
Bacon Clo. Col T —2H 119
Bader Ct. Farn —9K 119
Bader Gdns. Slou —1E 46
Bader Way. Wdly —7F 64
Badgebury Rise. Mar —1A 4
Badgemore La. Hen T —3C 16
Badger Clo. M'head —1A 44
Badger Dri. Light —9K 115
Badger Dri. Twy —6J 41
Badgersbridge Ride. Wind —4L 69
Badgers Clo. Ashf —9N 73
Badgers Croft. Mort C —4H 107
Badgers Glade. Bfld C —9H 85
Badgers Hill. Vir W —7L 95
Badgers Rise. Cav —8G 38
Badgers Sett. Crowt —5D 112
Badgers Wlk. S'lake —2F 40
Badgers Way. Brack —3C 92
Bad Goodesberg Way. M'head —7C 20
Badminton Rd. M'head —8M 19
Bagley Clo. W Dray —1M 49
Bagnols Way. Newb —9J 79
Bagshot Grn. Bag —7H 115
Bagshot Rd. Asc —2L 115
Bagshot Rd. Brack & Crowt —5M 91
Bagshot Rd. Egh —2L 95
Baigents La. W'sham —6N 115
Bailey Clo. M'head —7C 20
Bailey Clo. Wind —8C 46
Baileys Clo. B'water —5G 118
Bailey's La. Wal L —9C 42
Baily Av. That —7E 80
Bain Av. Camb —7M 119
Bainbridge Rd. Calc —8J 61
Baird Clo. Slou —1D 46
Baird Rd. Arbor X —2D 110
Bakeham La. Egh —2M 95
Bakers La. M'head —6K 19
Bakers Rd. Uxb —1L 25
Baker St. Read —5F 62
Bakers Yd. Uxb —1L 25
Baldwin Rd. Burn —4M 21
Baldwins Shore. Eton —5F 46
Balfour Cres. Brack —7M 91
Balfour Cres. Newb —5G 100
Balfour Dri. Calc —8J 61
Balfour Pl. Mar —3B 4
Balintore Ct. Col T —1H 119
Ballamoor Clo. Calc —9H 61
Ballard Grn. Wind —6A 46
Ballard Rd. Camb —9D 114
Ballencrief Rd. S'dale —9B 94
Balliol Rd. Cav —1D 62
Balliol Way. Owl —9J 113
Ball Pit Rd. E Ils —2L 31
Ball Pit Rd. W Ils —9M 11
Balmoral. M'head —5M 19
Balmoral Clo. Slou —7A 22
Balmoral Gdns. Wind —9F 46
Balmore Dri. Cav —9H 39
Balmore Pk. Cav —9H 39
Bamburgh Clo. Read —9J 63
Bamford Pl. Calc —8J 61
Banbury. Brack —9B 92
Banbury Av. Slou —6B 22
Banbury Gdns. Cav —1J 63
Band La. Egh —9A 72
Bandon Clo. Uxb —3N 25
Bangors Clo. Iver —7F 24
Bangors Rd. N. Iver —2E 24
Bangors Rd. S. Iver —4F 24
Bankside. Wokgm —4L 111
Bankside Clo. Read —1K 87
Banks Spur. Chalv —1D 46
Bank View. Hen T —4E 16
Bannard Rd. M'head —9L 19
Bannister Clo. Slou —1N 47
Bannister Gdns. Yat —4D 118
Bannister Rd. Bfld C —9G 84
Barbara's Meadow. Tile —2J 61
Barber Clo. Hurst —5K 65
Barberry Way. B'water —7K 119
Barbrook Clo. Tile —1L 61
Barchester Clo. Uxb —4K 25
Barchester Rd. Slou —1A 48
Barclay Rd. Calc —8K 61
Barclose Av. Cav —1J 63
Bardney Clo. M'head —2A 44
Bardolph's Clo. Tok G —5D 38
Bardown. Chvly —1L 55
Barfield Rd. That —7D 80
Barge La. Swal —7F 108
Bargeman Rd. M'head —1B 44
Bargeway, The. Blew —1B 12
Barholme Clo. Lwr Ear —1D 88
Barkby. Lwr Ear —1B 88
Barker Ct. Hurst —4L 65
Barker Grn. Brack —7M 91
Barkham Ride. Wokgm —1H 111
Barkham Rd. B'ham & Wokgm —9G 89
Barkham St. B'ham —9H 89
Barkhart Dri. Wokgm —4A 90
Barkhart Gdns. Wokgm —4A 90
Barkis Mead. Owl —8J 113
Barkwith Clo. Lwr Ear —1D 88
Barlee Cres. Uxb —6K 25
Barley Clo. That —9J 81
Barley Mead. Warf —2B 92
Barley Mow Rd. Egh —9L 71
Barley Wlk. Tile —6J 61
Barnacre Clo. Uxb —7L 25
Barnard Clo. Cav —8J 39
Barnards Hill. Mar —5A 4
Barn Clo. Brack —4A 92
Barn Clo. Kint —9G 76
Barn Clo. M'head —4C 20
Barn Clo. Read —8D 62
Barn Clo. La. Ashmw —9M 117
Barn Cres. Newb —3H 101
Barn Dri. M'head —1L 43
Barnes Way. Iver —8G 25
Barnett Ct. Brack —4A 92
Barnett Grn. Brack —8M 91
Barnfield. Iver —7F 24
Barnfield. Slou —9N 21
Barn Field. Yat —4B 118
Barnfield Clo. Cook —1C 20
Barnhill Clo. Mar —3B 4
Barnhill Gdns. Mar —3B 4
Barnhill Rd. Mar —3B 4
Barn La. Hen T —5B 16
Barn Owl Way. Bfld C —8J 85
Barnsdale Rd. Read —9K 63
Barnsfield Pl. Uxb —1K 25
Barnway. Egh —9L 71
Barnwood Clo. Read —4E 62
Baron Ct. Read —5D 62
Baronsmead. Hen T —4C 16
Barons Way. Egh —9E 72
Barony Ho. Brack —3J 91
Barossa Rd. Camb —2N 119
Barracane Dri. Crowt —5F 112
Barrack La. Wind —7F 46
Barracks La. Spen W —9H 87
Barracks Rd. Green —5C 102
Barrett Cres. Wokgm —5B 90
Barrett's La. Arbor —5C 88
Barrington Clo. Ear —6A 64
Barrington Ho. Read —4H 87
Barrow Lodge. Slou —5E 22
Barr's Rd. Tap —7L 21
Barry Av. Wind —6E 46
Barry Pl. Read —4G 62
Bartelotts Rd. Slou —5N 21
Bartholomew Pl. Warf —2A 92
Bartholomew St. Newb —9K 79
Bartlemy Clo. Newb —2J 101
Bartlemy Rd. Newb —2J 101
Bartletts La. Holyp —6C 44
Barton Rd. Slou —1A 48
Barton Rd. Tile —6J 61
Bartons Dri. Yat —5B 118
Bartons Way. Farn —9G 119
Barwell Clo. Crowt —5D 112
Basemoors. Brack —4B 92
Basford Way. Wind —9N 45
Basil Clo. Ear —2M 87
Basingstoke Rd. Aldm —2H 105
Basingstoke Rd. Hook —9H 109
Basingstoke Rd. Read —5H 87
Basingstoke Rd. Rise —8H 109
Basingstoke Rd. Spen W & Swal —1G 109
Basingstoke Rd. Three M —6G 87
Baskerville La. S'lake —2F 40
Baskerville Rd. Son C —1E 38
Baslow Rd. Winn —1G 88
Basmore Av. Lwr S —1G 40
Bassett Clo. Lwr Ear —3B 88
Bassett Rd. Uxb —1K 25
Bassett Way. Slou —5B 22
Bass Mead. Cook —1C 20
Batcombe Mead. Brack —9B 92
Bates Clo. G Grn —7N 23
Bath Ct. M'head —8N 19
Bath Rd. Calc & Read —8H 61
Bath Rd. Camb —3N 119
Bath Rd. Coln —5C 48
(Brands Hill)
Bath Rd. Coln —7F 48
(Poyle)
Bath Rd. Colt —8J 81
Bath Rd. Edd —5L 75
Bath Rd. Frox —7A 74
Bath Rd. Hare H —5M 41
Bath Rd. Hung —6E 74
Bath Rd. M'head —8J 19
Bath Rd. Newb —6D 78
Bath Rd. Slou —7L 21
Bath Rd. Son —3B 64
Bath Rd. Tap —7F 20
Bath Rd. That —7C 80
Bath Rd. Thea —1D 84
Bath Rd. W Dray & Hay —7J 49
Bathurst Clo. Iver —1G 49
Bathurst Rd. Winn —1G 89
Bathurst Wlk. Iver —1F 48
Battery End. Newb —4H 101
Battle Clo. Speen —7H 79
Battlemead Clo. M'head —3F 20
Battle Rd. Gor —7N 15
Battle Rd. Newb —4G 101
Battle St. Read —4F 62
Batty's Barn Clo. Wokgm —6B 90
Baughurst Rd. Aldm —4A 106
Baughurst Rd. Baug —9F 104
Bawtree Rd. Uxb —1L 25
Baxendales, The. Green —1N 101
Bay Clo. Ear —2M 87
Baydon Dri. Read —7E 62
Baydon Rd. Lamb W —7B 26
Baydon Rd. Shef W —5B 52
Bay Dri. Brack —4B 92
Bayer Ho. Newb —7K 79
Bayford Clo. B'water —8L 119
Bayford Dri. Calc —8N 61
Bay Ho. Brack —4B 92
Bayley Ct. Winn —2G 89
Bayley Cres. Burn —6K 21
Baylis Pde. Slou —7G 22
Baylis Rd. Slou —8F 22
Bayliss Rd. Warg —4J 41
Bay Rd. Brack —3B 92
Baysfarm Ct. W Dray —7K 49
Baytree Ct. Burn —4M 21
Bay Tree Rise. Calc —7K 61
Beacon Ct. Read —5D 62
Beaconsfield Rd. Farn R —3E 22
Beaconsfield Way. Ear —1N 87
Beacontree Plaza. Read —1H 87
Beales Farm Rd. Lamb —3H 27
Beals La. Tile —5H 61
Beancroft Rd. That —9G 81
Bean Oak Rd. Wokgm —5C 90
Bearfield La. Hung —4H 51
Bear La. Newb —8L 79
Bearwood Path. Winn —9F 64
Bearwood Rd. Sind —3G 88
Beatty Dri. Read —4M 61
Beauchief Clo. Lwr Ear —3M 87
Beaudesert Rd. W Dray —1M 49
Beaufield Clo. Wdly —5C 64
Beaufort Clo. Mar —5C 4
Beaufort Gdns. Asc —3H 93
Beaufort Gdns. Mar —5C 4
Beaufort Pl. Bray —1G 44
Beauforts. Egh —9L 71
Beaulieu Clo. Brack —5C 92
Beaulieu Clo. Dat —7K 47
Beaulieu Gdns. B'water —4G 118
Beaumaris Ct. Slou —6D 22
Beaumont Clo. M'head —2L 43
Beaumont Gdns. Brack —7B 92
Beaumont Rise. Mar —5C 4
Beaumont Rd. Slou —5F 22
Beaumont Rd. Wind —8E 46
Beaver La. Yat —4C 118
Beavers Clo. Tadl —9J 105
Beaver Way. Wdly —5G 64
Beckett Clo. Wokgm —5C 90
Beckford Av. Brack —8M 91
Beckfords. Up Bas —7J 35
Beckings Way. F Hth —1N 5
Bec Tithe. Whit H —2F 36
Bede Wlk. Read —9J 63
Bedfont Ct. Stai —9H 49
Bedfont Rd. Stai —3M 73
Bedford Av. Slou —7B 22
Bedford Clo. M'head —2L 43
Bedford Clo. Newb —5G 100
Bedford Gdns. Wokgm —4L 89
Bedford La. Asc —7D 94

Bedford Rd. Read —4F 62
(in two parts)
Bedfordshire Down. Warf —1C 92
Bedfordshire Way. Wokgm —5J 89
Bedwins La. Cook —9F 4
Beecham Rd. Read —5C 62
Beechbrook Av. Yat —4C 118
Beech Clo. Bfld —7J 85
Beech Clo. Stai —4L 73
Beech Clo. W Dray —2N 49
Beechcroft. Hamp N —8K 33
Beechcroft Clo. Asc —6N 93
Beechcroft Ct. Brack —5M 91
Beech Dri. B'water —5H 119
Beeches Rd. Bis G —7D 102
Beeches, The. Gor —9K 15
Beeches, The. Tile —1L 61
Beechfield. Fril —5N 57
Beech Glen. Brack —6M 91
Beech Hill Rd. Asc —8B 94
Beech Hill Rd. B Hill —5D 108
Beechingstoke. Mar —4D 4
Beech La. Ear —9N 63
Beech La. Woodc —5N 15
Beech Lodge. Stai —9F 72
Beechmont Av. Vir W —7M 95
Beechnut Clo. Wokgm —6L 89
Beechnut Dri. B'water —3F 118
Beech Ride. Sand —1F 118
Beech Rd. Farn —9L 119
Beech Rd. Pur T —8H 37
Beech Rd. Read —1L 87
Beech Rd. Slou —1N 47
Beech Rd. Tok G —6D 38
Beechtree Av. Egh —1K 95
Beechtree Av. Mar —2B 4
Beech Wlk. Hung —1D 96
Beech Wlk. That —9H 81
Beech Wlk. W'sham —6N 115
Beechwood Av. Tile —4L 61
Beechwood Av. Uxb —7N 25
Beechwood Av. Wdly —5C 64
Beechwood Clo. Asc —2H 93
Beechwood Dri. M'head —8L 19
Beechwood Rd. Slou —6F 22
Beechwood Rd. Vir W —9J 95
Beedon Dri. Brack —8H 91
Beehive Clo. Uxb —1N 25
Beehive La. Binf —4G 91
Beehive Rd. Binf —4H 91
Beehive Rd. Stai —9G 73
Beggars Hill Rd. Land E —2G 64
Beighton Clo. Lwr Ear —3M 87
Belfast Av. Slou —7E 22
Belgrave Ct. B'water —6H 119
Belgrave M. Uxb —5L 25
Belgrave Pl. Slou —1J 47
Belgrave Rd. Slou —8G 23
Belgravia Ct. Read —6D 62
Bell Av. W Dray —3N 49
Bell Clo. Slou —6K 23
Bellclose Rd. W Dray —1M 49
Bell Ct. Hur —3D 18
Bell Ct. Twy —8J 41
Belle Av. Read —7N 63
Belleisle. Pur T —8J 37
Belleisle Ct. Pur T —8J 37
(off Trenthams Clo.)
Belle Vue Rd. Hen T —6C 16
Belle Vue Rd. Read —5F 62
Belle Vue Ter. Read —5E 62
Bell Foundry La. Wokgm —2N 89
Bell Hill. Newb —5G 100
Bell Holt. Newb —5G 100
Bell Ho. Gdns. Wokgm —5N 89
Bellingham Wlk. Cav —8G 39
Bell La. Aldw —1B 34
Bell La. B'water —4G 118
Bell La. Eton W —3B 46
Bell La. Hen T —4D 16
Bell La. Ink —7C 98
Bell Pde. Wind —8B 46
Bell Pl. Bag —7J 115
Bells Hill. Stoke P —2J 23
Bells Hill Grn. Stoke P —1J 23
Bells La. Hort —9C 48
Bell St. Hen T —4D 16
Bell St. M'head —8C 20
Bellswood La. Iver —6C 24
Bell View. Wind —9B 46
Bell View Clo. Wind —8B 46
Bellvue Pl. Slou —2H 47
Bellweir Clo. Stai —6C 72
Belmont. Slou —6C 22
Belmont Clo. Uxb —1L 25
Belmont Cres. M'head —6N 19
Belmont Dri. M'head —6A 20
Belmont M. Camb —6N 119
Belmont Pk. Av. M'head —5A 20
Belmont Pk. Rd. M'head —6A 20
Belmont Rd. Camb —5N 119
Belmont Rd. Crowt —4F 112
Belmont Rd. M'head —6A 20
Belmont Rd. Read —5D 62
Belmont Rd. Uxb —1L 25
Belmont Vale. M'head —6A 20
Belvedere Ct. B'water —6H 119
Belvedere Dri. Newb —2L 101
Belvedere Dri. Winn —9F 64
Belvedere Mans. Chalv —1F 46
Bembridge Ct. Slou —2H 47
Bembridge Pl. Read —5J 63
Benbow Waye. Uxb —6K 25
Benbricke Grn. Brack —2L 91
Bencombe Rd. Mar —2C 4
Benedict Grn. Warf —2B 92
Benen-Stock Rd. Stai —2H 73
Benetfield Rd. Binf —1F 90
Benham La. Rise —7K 109
Bennet Ct. Camb —4N 119
Bennet Ct. Read —2G 87
Bennet Rd. Read —2G 86
Bennet's Hill. Bfld —4J 85
Bennett Clo. Newb —6K 79
Bennett Clo. Gdns. Newb —6K 79
Bennetts Clo. Slou —9C 22
Bennett's Yd. Uxb —1K 25
Benning Clo. Wind —9N 45
Bennings Clo. Brack —2L 91
Benning Way. Wokgm —3A 90
Benson Clo. Read —9K 63
Benson Clo. Slou —9J 23
Benson Clo. Uxb —6M 25
Bensonholme. Pad —8L 83
Benson Rd. Crowt —5D 112
Bentinck Rd. W Dray —9L 25
Bentley Pk. Burn —3N 21
Bentley Rd. Slou —9C 22
Benyon Ct. Read —6E 62
(in two parts)
Benyon M. Read —6E 62
Berberis Wlk. W Dray —3M 49
Bere Ct. Rd. Pang —2A 60
Bere Rd. Brack —8B 92
Beresford Av. Slou —8L 23
Beresford Rd. Read —4E 62
Berkeley Av. Read —6E 62
Berkeley Clo. M'head —6L 19
Berkeley Ct. Read —6F 62
Berkeley Dri. Wink —5K 69
Berkeley M. Burn —7N 21
Berkeley Rd. Newb —9K 79
Berkley Clo. Stai —6E 72
Berkshire Av. Slou —7D 22
Berkshire Bus. Cen. That —9K 81
Berkshire Ct. Brack —4K 91
Berkshire Dri. That —9K 81
Berkshire Dri. Tile —5K 61
Berkshire Rd. Camb —9C 114
Berkshire Rd. Hen T —6C 16
Berkshire Way. Wokgm & Brack —5F 90
Bernadine Clo. Warf —2B 92
Bernard Ct. Camb —5M 119
Berners Clo. Slou —8A 22
Bernersh Clo. Sand —9G 113
Berries Rd. Cook —8L 5
Berrybank. Col T —3J 119
Berrycroft. Brack —3A 92
Berryfield. Slou —7L 23
Berry Hill. Tap —7G 21
Berrylands Rd. Cav —1H 63
Berry La. Brack —4C 68
Berrys La. Read —2N 85
Berrys Rd. Up Buck —5M 81
Berstead Clo. Lwr Ear —2A 88
Berwick Av. Slou —7D 22
Berwick La. Mar —4B 4
Berwick Rd. Mar —4A 4
Beryl Clo. Wokgm —4K 89
Bestobell Rd. Slou —7E 22
Beswick Gdns. Brack —3C 92
Betam Rd. Read —5K 63
Betchworth Av. Ear —9N 63
Bethesda St. Up Bas —7J 35
Betjeman Ct. W Dray —9L 25
Betjeman Wlk. Yat —5A 118
Betteridge Rd. That —9J 81
Bettles Clo. Uxb —3K 25
Bettoney Vere. Bray —1F 44
Beverley Clo. Mar —5A 4
Beverley Clo. That —7F 80
Beverley Ct. Slou —1K 47
Beverley Gdns. M'head —5M 19
Beverley Gdns. Warg —4K 41
Beverley Rd. Tile —3K 61
Bevers, The. Mort C —4H 107
Bexley Ct. Read —6D 62
Bexley St. Wind —7E 46
Bibury Clo. Wdly —8C 64
Bideford Clo. Farn —9K 119
Bideford Clo. Wdly —7B 64
Bideford Spur. Slou —4D 22
Bietigheim Way. Camb —3N 119
Big Barn Gro. Warf —2B 92
Bigbury Gdns. Read —9J 63
Bigfrith La. Cook —9E 4
Biggs La. Arbor & Finch —1E 110
Big La. Lamb —2H 27
Biko Clo. Uxb —6K 25
Biko Ct. Read —5J 63
Billet La. Iver & Slou —4C 24
Billet Rd. Stai —7H 73
Billing Av. Finch —4K 111
Billingbear La. Binf —7F 66
Bilton Clo. Coln —8F 48
Bilton Ind. Est. Brack —6J 91
Binbrook Clo. Lwr Ear —1C 88
Binfield Rd. Brack —1K 91
Binfield Rd. Wokgm —1E 90
Bingham Rd. Burn —6K 21
Binghams, The. M'head —2E 44
Bingley Gro. Wdly —3E 64
Binstead Dri. B'water —4H 119
Birch Av. Tile —4A 62
Birch Av. W Dray —7N 25
Birch Clo. Camb —9B 114
Birch Clo. Iver —3E 24
Birch Clo. Son C —1F 38
Birch Cres. Uxb —2N 25
Birch Dri. B'water —6H 119
Birches, The. B'water —4F 118
Birches, The. Gor —8K 15
Birchetts Clo. Brack —3M 91
Birchfields. Camb —5N 119
Birch Grn. Stai —8H 73
Birch Gro. Brack —6N 91
Birch Gro. Slou —6D 22
Birch Gro. Wind —7N 45
Birch Hill Rd. Brack —9M 91
Birchington Rd. Wind —8C 46
Birchland Clo. Mort W —4F 106
Birchlands Ct. Owl —8J 113
Birch La. Asc —3D 92
Birch La. Mort C —5G 106
Birchmead. Winn —1J 89
Birch Rd. Bfld C —8G 85
Birch Rd. Tadl —8G 105
Birch Rd. W'sham —6N 115
Birch Rd. Wokgm —3L 111
Birch Side. Crowt —4D 112
Birch Tree View. Light —9K 115
Birch View. Read —1K 87
Birchview Clo. Yat —5A 118
Birchwood Clo. Cav —7J 39
Birchwood Dri. Light —9M 115
Birchwood Rd. Newb —7A 80
Birchwoods, The. Tile —4J 61
Birdhill Av. Read —1K 87
Bird M. Wokgm —5N 89
Birds La. Midg —7N 81
Bird Wood Ct. Son C —1G 39
Birdwood Rd. Col T —2K 119
Birdwood Rd. M'head —7L 19
Birkbeck Pl. Owl —9J 113
Birkdale. Brack —9J 91
Birkhall Clo. Calc —7K 61
Birley Rd. Slou —7F 22
Bisham Ct. Bish —9C 4
Bisham Ct. Slou —1H 47
Bishop Ct. M'head —8A 20
Bishopdale. Brack —6L 91
Bishops Clo. Uxb —3N 25
Bishop's Dri. Wokgm —4A 90
Bishops Farm Clo. Oak G —8L 45
Bishopsgate Rd. Egh —7J 71
Bishops Gro. W'sham —6M 115
Bishop's La. Brack —4D 68
Bishops Orchard. Farn R —4D 22
Bishop's Rd. Read —6N 63
Bishops Rd. Slou —1J 47
Bishops Rd. Tut C —1G 83
Bishops Way. Egh —9E 72
Bishopswood Ct. Baug —9H 105
Bishopswood La. Baug —9G 104
Bishopswood Rd. Tadl —9H 105
Bispham Ct. Read —6J 63
Bissley Dri. M'head —2K 43
Bitham La. Hung —5H 97
Bitham Rd. Lock —1N 9
Bittern Clo. Col T —1H 119
Bitterne Av. Tile —6J 61
Bix La. M'head —5K 19
Blackamoor La. M'head —5D 20
Blackbird Clo. Bfld C —8J 85
Blackbird Clo. Col T —1H 119
Blackbird La. Bis G —7D 102
Blackbird La. M'head —9C 44
Black Boy La. Hur —3A 18
Blackbushe Airport. B'water —6A 118
Blackbushe Bus. Pk. Yat —5A 118
Blackbushe Pk. Yat —4A 118
Blackcap Pl. Col T —1J 119
Blackdown Way. That —9F 80
Black Horse Clo. Wind —8N 45
Blacklands Rd. Up Buck —6M 81
Blackley Clo. Ear —9D 64
Blackmeadows. Brack —8N 91
Blackmoor Clo. Asc —4G 92
Blackmoor Wood. Asc —4G 92
Blackmore La. Son C —1G 38
Blackmore Way. Uxb —1L 25
Blacknest Ga. Rd. Asc —5D 94
Blacknest Rd. S'dale & Vir W —5F 94
Black Pk. Rd. Wex —3N 23
Blackpond La. Farn C —1D 22
Blacksmith Row. Slou —3B 48
Blackstroud La. E. Light —9N 115
Blackstroud La. W. Light —9N 115
Blackthorn Av. W Dray —3N 49
Blackthorn Clo. Tile —3J 61
Blackthorn Cres. Farn —9K 119
Blackthorn Dell. Slou —2L 47
Blackthorne Cres. Coln —8F 48
Blackthorne Ind. Est. Coln —9F 48
Blackthorne Rd. Coln —9F 48
Blackwater Clo. Cav —9L 39
Blackwater Clo. Spen W —9H 87
Blackwater Ind. Est. B'water —4J 119
Blackwater Rise. Calc —8H 61
Blackwater Valley Relief Rd. Camb —5K 119
Blackwater Valley Route. Farn —9N 119
Blaenant. Cav —8F 38
Blaenavon. Cav —8F 38
Blagdon Rd. Read —1J 87
Blagrave Farm La. Cav —8C 38
Blagrave La. Cav —1C 62
Blagrave Rise. Tile —6K 61
Blagrave St. Read —4H 63
Blagrove Dri. Wokgm —7L 89
Blagrove La. Wokgm —7L 89
Blair Rd. Slou —9G 22
Blake Clo. Crowt —6G 112
Blake Clo. Wokgm —3C 90
Blakeney Ct. M'head —5C 20
Blakeney Fields. Gt Shef —9G 28
Blakes Cotts. Read —5J 63
Blakes La. Hare H —3L 41
Blake's La. Tadl —9K 105
Blakes Ride. Yat —3A 118
Blakes Rd. Warg —3J 41
Blanchard Clo. Wdly —4G 64
Blandford Clo. Slou —2M 47
Blandford Ct. Slou —2M 47
Blandford Rd. Read —3J 87
Blandford Rd. N. Slou —2M 47
Blandford Rd. S. Slou —2M 47
Bland's Clo. Bfld C —9G 85
Blandy Rd. Hen T —7B 16
Blandys Hill. Kint —2G 98
Blandy's La. Up Bas —6K 35
Blane's La. Brack & Asc —1C 114
Blatches Clo. Thea —9E 60
Blay's Clo. Egh —1L 95
Blay's La. Egh —2K 95
Bledlow Clo. Newb —5H 101
Blenheim Clo. Wokgm —5K 89
Blenheim Gdns. Read —6L 63
Blenheim Pl. Read —6G 62
(off Castle St.)
Blenheim Rd. Cav —9G 38
Blenheim Rd. M'head —6M 19
Blenheim Rd. Newb —9K 79
Blenheim Rd. Read —5K 63
Blenheim Rd. Slou —3M 47
Blenheim Ter. Read —6G 62
(off Castle St.)
Blewburton Wlk. Brack —6B 92
Blewbury Dri. Tile —5J 61
Blinco La. G Grn —7N 23
Blind La. Bour & F Hth —3L 5
Blind La. Holyp —5D 44
Blind La. Lamb —3H 27
Blomfield Dale. Brack —4H 91
Blondell Clo. W Dray —5L 49
Bloomfield Dri. Brack —2A 92
Bloomfieldhatch La. Graz —2B 108
Bloomfield Rd. M'head —9L 19
Bloomsbury Way. B'water —6G 119
Blossom Av. Thea —9F 60
Blossom La. Thea —9F 60
Blossom Way. Uxb —1N 25
Blossom Way. W Dray —3N 49
Blount Cres. Binf —2J 91
Blount's Ct. Rd. Son C —1H 39
Bloxworth Clo. Brack —6C 92
Blue Ball La. Egh —9A 72
Bluebell Dri. Bfld C —8G 84
Bluebell Hill. Brack —3B 92
Bluebell Meadow. Winn —9H 65
Bluecoats. That —7G 80
Blue Coat Wlk. Brack —7A 92
Bluethroat Clo. Col T —1J 119
Blumfield Ct. Slou —5N 21
Blumfield Cres. Slou —6N 21
Blundell's Rd. Tile —4M 61
Blunts Av. W Dray —6N 49
Blyth Av. That —9H 81
Blythe Clo. Iver —7G 24
Blythewood La. Asc —5H 93
Blyth Wlk. Read —7H 63
(off Charndon Clo.)
Boames La. Enb —4D 100
Board La. Half —6L 77
Boarlands Clo. Slou —8B 22
Boarlands Path. Cipp —8B 22
Boathouse Reach. Hen T —5D 16
Bobgreen Ct. Read —5J 87
Bobmore La. Mar —3C 4
Bockhampton Rd. Lamb —3H 27
Bockmer La. Medm —1N 17
Boden's Ride. Asc —2G 115
Bodmin Av. Slou —6C 22
Bodmin Clo. That —9F 80
Bodmin Rd. Wdly —7B 64
Body Rd. Read —5G 62
Bog La. Brack —7C 92
Bolderwood. Bfld C —8G 85
Boleyn Clo. Stai —9F 72
Bolingbroke Way. That —8J 81
Bolney Rd. Lwr S —9G 16
Bolney Trevor Dri. Lwr S —1F 40
Bolton Av. Wind —9F 46
Bolton Cres. Wind —9E 46
Bolton Pl. Newb —8L 79
Bolton Rd. P'mre —6H 31
Bolton Rd. Wind —9E 46
Boltons La. Binf —1J 91
Bolwell Clo. Twy —9L 41
Bomer Clo. W Dray —6N 49
Bomford Clo. Herm —6C 56
Bond Clo. W Dray —7N 25
Bond St. Egh —9K 71
Bone La. Newb —8M 79
Bonemill La. Enb —9H 79
Bones La. Bin H —2N 39
Bonsey's Yd. Uxb —1L 25
Borderside. Slou —7J 23
Borrowdale Rd. Winn —8G 64
Bosanquet Clo. Uxb —5L 25
Boscawen Way. That —8K 81
Bosham Clo. Ear —3A 88
Bosman Dri. W'sham —3L 115
Bostock La. Thea —1C 84
Boston Av. Read —7F 62
Boston Dri. Bour —4M 5
Boston Gro. Slou —7E 22
Boston Rd. Hen T —6D 16
Bosworth Gdns. Wdly —8D 64
Botany Clo. That —8J 81
Bothy, The. Warg —3J 41
Botmoor Way. Chad —7K 29
Bottisham Clo. Lwr Ear —3B 88
Bottle La. L Grn —1D 42
Bottle La. Warf —4J 67
Bottom Ho. Son C —1F 38
Bottom La. Sul'd —4D 84
Bouldish Farm Rd. Asc —7J 93
Boulmer Rd. Uxb —4K 25
Boulters Clo. M'head —5F 20
Boulters Clo. Slou —1C 46
Boulters Clo. Wdly —4E 64
Boulters Ct. M'head —5F 20
Boulters Gdns. M'head —5F 20
Boulters Ho. Brack —6B 92
Boulters La. M'head —5F 20
Boulton Rd. Read —9G 63
Boult St. Read —5J 63
Boult's Wlk. Read —7H 63
Boundary Clo. Tile —6K 61
Boundary La. Cav —1E 62
Boundary Rd. Ashf —9K 73
Boundary Rd. Newb —8M 79
Boundary Rd. Tap —5H 21
Boundary Vs. B'water —5J 119
Bourn Clo. Lwr Ear —2B 88
Bourne Arch. That —7E 80
Bourne Av. Read —8H 63
Bourne Av. Wind —9E 46
Bourne Clo. Bour —2M 5
Bourne Clo. Calc —8J 61
Bourne Cotts. Wool H —7D 100
Bourne End Bus. Cen. Bour
(off Cores End Rd.) —4M 5
Bourne Rd. Pang —8E 36
Bourne Rd. Slou —1F 46
Bourne Rd. That —7E 80
Bourne Rd. Vir W —7M 95
Bourneside. Vir W —9J 95
Bourne Vale. Hung —6J 75
Bourton Clo. Tile —5N 61
Bouverie Way. Slou —4N 47
Boveney Clo. Slou —1C 46
Boveney New Rd. Eton W —3A 46
Boveney Rd. Dor —4M 45
Bowden Rd. Asc —7M 93
Bower Cres. Wokgm —3A 90
Bower Way. Slou —8A 22
Bowes-Lyon Clo. Wind —7E 46
(off Alma Rd.)
Bowes Rd. Stai —9F 72
Bowes Rd. That —9G 80
Bowfell Clo. Tile —2K 61
Bowland Dri. Brack —9B 92
Bowling Clo. Uxb —2N 25
Bowling Ct. Hen T —3C 16
Bowling Grn. La. Pur T —8J 37
Bowling Grn. Rd. That —6D 80
Bowlings, The. Camb —3N 119
Bowman Ct. Wel C —6D 112
Bowmans Clo. Burn —3L 21
Bowry Dri. Wray —3A 72
Bowyer Cres. Wokgm —3A 90
Bowyer Dri. Slou —9A 22
Bowyer's La. Brack —6M 67
Boxford Ridge. Brack —5M 91
Boxwood Clo. W Dray —1N 49
Boyd Ct. Brack —3L 91
Boyle Clo. Uxb —3N 25
Boyndon Rd. M'head —7A 20
Boyn Hill Av. M'head —8A 20
Boyn Hill Clo. M'head —8A 20
Boyn Hill Rd. M'head —9N 19
Boyn Valley Rd. M'head —9N 19
Bracebridge. Camb —4L 119
Bracken Bank. Asc —3F 92
Bracken Clo. Tile —3K 61
Bracken Copse. Ink —5D 98
Brackendale Rd. Camb —4N 119
Brackendale Way. Read —7N 63
Brackenforde. Slou —1L 47
Bracken Rd. M'head —1N 43
Brackens, The. Crowt —3E 112
Bracken Way. Bfld C —9H 85
Bracken Way. F Hth —1M 5
Brackenwood Dri. Tadl —9J 105
Bracknell Beeches. Brack —5M 91
Bracknell Clo. Camb —9C 114
Bracknell Enterprise Cen. Brack —4L 91
Bracknell Rd. Bag —4G 115
Bracknell Rd. Camb —8D 114
Bracknell Rd. Crowt —5G 113
Bracknell Rd. Crowt —1C 114
(Penny Hill)
Bracknell Rd. Warf —9B 68
Bradcutts La. Cook —6H 5
Bradenham La. Mar —1G 18
Bradfields. Brack —7A 92
Bradford Rd. Slou —7C 22
Brading Way. Pur T —8L 37
Bradley Clo. Kint —1G 98
Bradley Rd. Slou —8F 22
Bradmore Way. Lwr Ear —3N 87
Bradshaw Clo. Wind —7A 46
Bradshawe Waye. Uxb —6N 25
Bradwell Rd. Tile —1K 61
Braemar Gdns. Slou —1C 46
Braemore Clo. That —1G 102
Bramber Ct. Slou —9C 22
Bramber M. Cav —9L 39
Bramble Clo. Uxb —7N 25
Bramble Cres. Tile —4M 61
Bramble Dri. M'head —1L 43
Bramblegate. Crowt —4E 112
Brambles, The. Crowt —4B 112
Brambles, The. Newb —2J 101
Brambles, The. W Dray —3M 49
Bramblings. Cav —7E 38
Bramley Clo. Ear —9N 63
Bramley Clo. M'head —2N 43
Bramley Clo. Stai —9K 73
Bramley Ct. Crowt —6C 112
Bramley Gro. Crowt —5B 112
Bramley La. B'water —4F 118
Bramley Rd. Camb —7M 119
Bramley Rd. Sil —9C 106
Bramling Av. Yat —3A 118
Brammas Clo. Slou —2E 46
Brampton Chase. Lwr S —1F 40
Brampton Ct. M'head —6E 20
Brampton M. Mar —6B 4
Bramshaw Rd. Read —3A 62
Bramshill Clo. Arbor —2D 110
Bramwell Clo. That —9J 81
Bran Clo. Tile —4M 61
Brandon Av. Wdly —3F 64
Brands Rd. Slou —5C 48
Brandville Rd. W Dray —1M 49
Branksome Ct. Read —5F 62
Branksome Hill Rd. Col T —2J 119
Brant Clo. Arbor X —9D 88
Brants Bri. Brack —4B 92
Braunfels Wlk. Newb —9J 79
Braybank. Bray —1F 44
Braybourne Clo. Uxb —1K 25
Braybrook Dri. Hurst —4L 65
Braybrooke Gdns. Warg —4J 41
Braybrooke Rd. Brack —2M 91
Braybrook Rd. Warg —4J 41
Bray Clo. Bray —2F 44
Bray Ct. M'head —3F 44
Braye Clo. Sand —9G 113
Brayfield Rd. Bray —1F 44
Brayford Rd. Read —3J 87
Bray Rd. M'head —8E 20
Bray Rd. Read —8B 62
Braywick Rd. M'head —8C 20
Braywood Av. Egh —9A 72
Braziers La. Wink R —9G 68
Breach Cotts. Ham —7L 97
Breach Sq. Hung —7K 75
Breadcroft La. M'head —1J 43
Breadcroft Rd. M'head —2K 43
Bream Clo. Mar —7A 4
Brean Wlk. Ear —1N 87
Brearley Clo. Uxb —1M 25
Brechin Ct. Read —6J 63
(off Kendrick Rd.)
Brecon Ct. Chalv —1E 46
Brecon Rd. Wdly —4E 64
Bredon Rd. Wokgm —2L 89
Bredward Clo. Burn —4L 21
Breech, The. Col T —2J 119
Breedon's Hill. Pang —8D 36
Bremer Rd. Stai —7H 73
Brendon Clo. Tile —3M 61
Brent Clo. That —9G 80
Brent Gdns. Read —9H 63
Brent Rd. Bour —3L 5
Brerewood. Ear —1M 87
Brewery Comn. Mort —4J 107
Brewhouse Hill. Frox —7B 74
Briant's Av. Cav —2J 63
Briants Piece. Herm —6E 56
Briar Clo. Cav —8G 38
Briar Clo. Tap —7L 21
Briardene. M'head —5N 19
Briar Glen. Cook —9J 5
Briarlea Rd. Mort C —4G 107
Briars Clo. Pang —8F 36

Briars, The. Slou —4A 48
Briars, The. Stai —3H 73
Briar Way. Slou —6D 22
Briar Way. Tadl —9L 105
Briar Way. W Dray —1N 49
Briarwood. Finch —4K 111
Brickfield Cotts. Crowt —7D 112
Brickfield La. Burn —2K 21
Brickiln Ind. Est. Tadl —9L 105
Bridge Av. Cook —1B 20
Bridge Av. M'head —7D 20
Bridge Clo. Slou —8B 22
Bridge Clo. Stai —8F 72
Bridge End. Camb —5M 119
Bridge Ho. Read —4H 63
Bridge La. Vir W —7N 95
Bridgeman Dri. Wind —8C 46
Bridgemead. Frim —9N 119
Bridge Rd. Asc —7N 93
Bridge Rd. Bag —7H 115
Bridge Rd. Camb —6M 119
Bridge Rd. M'head —7D 20
Bridge Rd. Uxb —3K 25
Bridges Clo. Wokgm —4L 89
Bridges Hall. Read —7M 63
Bridges, The. Mort W —5D 106
Bridgestone Dri. Bour —4M 5
Bridge St. Cav —2G 62
Bridge St. Coln —6E 48
Bridge St. Hung —5K 75
Bridge St. M'head —7D 20
Bridge St. Newb —8L 79
Bridge St. Read —5G 63
Bridge St. Stai —8F 72
Bridge St. Plaza. Read —5G 63
Bridge View. S'dale —9D 94
Bridge Wlk. Yat —2B 118
Bridgewater Clo. Read —3C 62
Bridgewater Ct. Slou —3B 48
Bridgewater Ter. Wind —7F 46
Bridle Clo. M'head —5B 20
Bridle Rd. M'head —5B 20
Bridle Rd. Whit H —3F 36
Bridlington Spur. Slou —2D 46
Bridport Clo. Lwr Ear —1C 88
Bridport Way. Slou —5D 22
Brierly Pl. Tile —9K 37
Briff La. Been —5L 81
Briff La. Up Buck —5L 81
Brigham Rd. Read —3G 63
Brighton Pl. Read —6N 63
Brighton Rd. Read —6N 63
Brighton Spur. Slou —5D 22
Brill Clo. Cav —9G 38
Brill Clo. M'head —1A 44
Brill Clo. Mar —5A 4
Brimblecombe Clo. Wokgm —2M 89
Brimpton Rd. Baug —9F 104
Brimpton Rd. Brimp —1A 104
Brimpton Rd. Read —8B 62
Brinn's La. B'water —4G 118
Briony Ho. Read —4H 87
Brisbane Rd. Read —4B 62
Bristol Clo. Stai —3M 73
Bristol Ct. Stanw —3M 73
Bristol Way. Slou —9H 23
Bristow Ct. Cav —2H 63
Bristow Rd. Camb —6M 119
Britannia Ct. W Dray —2L 49 (off Green, The)
Britannia Ind. Est. Coln —8F 48
Britannia Way. Stai —4L 73
Brittain Ct. Sand —2G 118
Britten Rd. Read —8H 63
Britwell Rd. Burn —4M 21
Brixham Rd. Read —1H 87
Broadacre. Stai —9H 73
Broadcommon Rd. Hurst —4M 65
Broadhalfpenny La. Tadl —9L 105
Broad Hinton. Twy —1L 65
Broadlands Clo. Calc —7L 61
Broadlands Ct. Brack —3J 91
Broadlands Dri. S Asc —9M 93
Broad La. Brack —5N 91
Broad La. Up Buck —5M 81
Broadley Grn. W'sham —7N 115
Broadmark Rd. Slou —8K 23
Broadmeadow End. That —7J 81
Broadmoor Est. Crowt —6H 113
Broadmoor La. Son —9D 40
Broadmoor La. Wal L & White —8E 42
Broad Oak. Slou —5E 22
Broadoak. Tadl —9M 105
Broadoak Ct. Slou —5E 22
Broad Platts. Slou —2M 47
Broadpool Cotts. Asc —2K 93
Broadrick Heath. Warf —2A 92
Broad St. E Ils —7B 12
Broad St. Read —5G 62
Broad St. Wokgm —5A 90
Broad St. Mall, The. Read —5G 62
Broad St. Wlk. Wokgm —5A 90
Broadwater Clo. Wray —4N 71
Broadwater La. Twy —2K 65
Broadwater Pk. M'head —4H 45
Broadwater Rd. Twy —1K 65
Broadway. Brack —4M 91
Broadway. M'head —7C 20
Broadway. Stai —9J 73
Broadway. That —8G 80
Broadway. Wink —5L 69
Broadway Courtyard. That —8G 81
Broadway Rd. Light & W'sham —9M 115
Broadway, The. Lamb —2H 27
Broadway, The. P'mre —2K 31
Broadway, The. Sand —1F 118
Brocas Rd. Bfld C —1G 106
Brocas St. Eton —6F 46
Brockenhurst Dri. Yat —5B 118
Brockenhurst Rd. Asc —6K 93
Brockenhurst Rd. Brack —5C 92
Brock Gdns. Read —4C 62
Brocklands. Yat —5A 118
Brock La. M'head —7C 20
Brockley Clo. Tile —4A 62
Brockmer La. Medm —1N 17
Brocks La. Fril & Bckby —7L 57
Brocks Way. S'lake —2F 40
Brock Way. Vir W —7L 95
Brockway Ho. Langl —4C 48
Broken Furlong. Eton —4D 46
Broken Way. Newt —8N 101
Bromley Wlk. Tile —5N 61
Brompton Clo. Lwr Ear —2C 88
Brompton Dri. M'head —5N 19
Bromycroft Rd. Slou —4C 22
Bronte Rise. Green —2M 101
Brookbank. Wbrn G —4N 5
Brook Bus. Cen. Cow —3J 25
Brook Clo. Owl —9J 113
Brook Clo. Stai —4N 73
Brook Clo. Wokgm —3M 89
Brook Cotts. Yat —3A 118
Brook Cres. Slou —7A 22
Brookdene Clo. M'head —4C 20
Brook Dri. Brack —6B 92
Brooke Pl. Binf —9H 67
Brookers Corner. Crowt —5G 113
Brooker's Hill. Shin —5K 87
Brookers Row. Crowt —4G 113
Brookfield Rd. Wbrn G —4N 5
Brook Grn. Brack —3K 91 (in two parts)
Brookhouse Dri. Wbrn G —4N 5
Brook La. Wal L —2C 66
Brook Lea. Cav —3J 63
Brooklyn Dri. Emm G —6H 39
Brooklyn Way. W Dray —2L 49
Brookmill, The. Read —8E 62
Brook Path. Slou —8B 22 (in two parts)
Brook Rd. Bag —8H 115
Brook Rd. Camb —5M 119
Brooksby Clo. B'water —4F 118
Brooksby Rd. Tile —2L 61
Brookside. Calc —8N 61 (off Millers Gro.)
Brookside. Cook —6D 48
Brookside. Sand —2G 118
Brookside. Uxb —1N 25
Brookside. Wokgm —4L 89
Brookside Av. Ashf —9K 73
Brookside Av. Wray —9N 47
Brookside Clo. Ear —9C 64
Brookside Pk. Farn —8L 119
Brooks Rd. That —7H 81
Brook St. Twy —9J 41
Brook St. Wind —8F 46
Brook St. W. Read —6G 62
Brookway. Newb —9B 80
Broom Acres. Sand —1F 118
Broom Clo. Calc —7K 61
Broome Clo. Yat —2A 118
Broomfield Clo. Asc —9D 94
Broomfield Dri. Asc —8D 94
Broomfield Pk. Asc —9D 94
Broomfield Rd. Tile —4N 61
Broom Gro. Wokgm —7J 89
Broomhall La. Asc —8C 94
Broom Hill. Cook —9J 5
Broom Hill. Stoke P —1J 23
Broom Ho. Langl —3A 48
Broomsquires Rd. Bag —8J 115
Broom Way. B'water —5J 119
Broughton Clo. Read —3C 62
Brownfield Gdns. M'head —9B 20
Browning Clo. That —7F 80
Brownlow Dri. Brack —2N 91
Brownlow Rd. Read —5E 62
Brownrigg Cres. Brack —3B 92
Brownrigg Rd. Ashf —8N 73
Brownsfield Rd. That —7F 80
Brown's La. Bright —9B 10
Bruan Rd. Newb —2K 101
Bruce Clo. Slou —9C 22
Bruce Rd. Wdly —5C 64
Bruce Wlk. Wind —8N 45
Brucewood Pde. Mar —2C 4
Brudenell. Wind —9B 46
Brummell Rd. Newb —7J 79
Brunel Arc. Read —4H 63
Brunel Clo. M'head —9B 20
Brunel Dri. Crowt —2G 113
Brunel Dri. Wdly —3E 64
Brunel Rd. M'head —9A 20
Brunel Rd. Read —8A 62
Brunel Rd. Thea —1F 84
Brunel Way. Slou —9H 23
Brunswick. Brack —9L 91
Brunswick Hill. Read —5E 62
Brunswick Lodge. Read —5E 62 (off Brunswick Hill)
Brunswick St. Read —5E 62
Bruton Way. Brack —9B 92
Bryant Av. Slou —6F 22
Bryants La. Yatt —3A 58
Brybur Clo. Read —2K 87
Bryer Pl. Wind —9N 45
Bryony Clo. Uxb —6N 25
Bryony Ho. Brack —3J 91
Buccaneer Clo. Wdly —4G 64
Buccleuch Rd. Dat —6J 47
Buchanan Sq. That —1J 103
Buchan Clo. Uxb —4K 25
Buchannan Dri. Wokgm —3K 111
Buckden Clo. Wdly —6F 64
Buckham Hill. Gt Shef & Chadw —7H 29
Buckhurst Gro. Wokgm —6D 90
Buckhurst Hill. Brack —6C 92
Buckhurst La. Asc —5B 94
Buckhurst Rd. Asc —4B 94
Buckhurst Way. Ear —9N 63
Buckingham Av. Slou —7A 22
Buckingham Av. E. Slou —7E 22
Buckingham Dri. Emm G —9H 39 (in three parts)
Buckingham Gdns. Slou —1H 47
Buckingham Gro. Uxb —3N 25
Buckingham Rd. Newb —1J 101
Buckland Av. Slou —3K 47
Buckland Clo. Farn —9N 119
Buckland Cres. Wind —7B 46
Buckland Rd. Read —9H 63
Bucklebury. Brack —9L 91
Bucklebury Clo. Holyp —4F 44
Bucklebury Rd. Bckby —9N 57
Buckle La. Warf —6L 67 (in two parts)
Bucknell Av. Pang —8F 36
Bucknell Clo. Read —8N 61
Buckside. Cav —2G 62
Buckthorn Clo. Wokgm —4C 90
Buckthorns. Brack —2J 91
Budebury Rd. Stai —9H 73
Budge's Gdns. Wokgm —4B 90
Budge's Rd. Wokgm —4B 90
Buffins. Tap —5H 21
Bulkeley Av. Wind —9D 46
Bulkeley Clo. Egh —9L 71
Bullbrook Dri. Brack —3B 92
Bullbrook Row. Brack —4B 92
Bullfinch Clo. Col T —1J 119
Bull La. Brack —3M 91
Bull La. Rise —7F 108 (in two parts)
Bull Meadow, The. Streat —8H 15
Bullrusgh Gro. Uxb —5K 25
Bulmershe Rd. Read —5L 63
Bulpit La. Hung —7K 75
Bunby Rd. Stoke P —1H 23
Bunce's Clo. Eton W —4D 46
Bunces La. Bfld C —9H 85
Bunce's La. Gor H —3H 37
Bundy's Way. Stai —9G 72
Bungalow Dri. Tile —4L 61
Bungler's Hill. Far H —4A 110
Bungum La. Ham —8N 97
Bunkers Hill. Newb —5G 101
Bunten Meade. Slou —9D 22
Burbage Grn. Brack —7C 92
Burbidge Clo. Calc —9N 61
Burchell Rd. Newb —6J 79
Burchett Coppice. Wokgm —2L 111
Burchetts Grn. La. Bur G —7F 18
Burchetts Grn. Rd. L Grn —9E 18
Burcombe Way. Emm G —9H 39
Burcot Gdns. M'head —3B 20
Burdett Ct. Read —9J 63
Burdock Clo. Bfld C —9J 85
Burdwood Cen. That —9H 81
Burfield Rd. Old Win —3J 71
Burford Clo. Mar —2A 4
Burford Ct. Read —4F 62
Burford Ct. Wokgm —6C 90
Burford Gdns. Slou —6M 21
Burford Rd. Camb —5M 119
Burford's. E Gar —7B 28
Burgess Clo. Wdly —8C 64
Burgess La. Kint H —5H 99
Burges Way. Stai —9H 73
Burgett Rd. Slou —2D 46
Burghead Clo. Col T —2H 119
Burghfield Rd. Read —2N 85
Burleigh La. Asc —3H 93
Burleigh M. Cav —7J 39
Burleigh Rd. Asc —4H 93
Burleigh Rd. Frim —9N 119
Burley Way. B'water —3G 119
Burlingham Clo. Read —5J 87
Burlings, The. Asc —3H 93
Burlington Av. Slou —1G 46
Burlington Ct. B'water —6H 119
Burlington Ct. Slou —1G 47
Burlington Rd. Burn —5L 21
Burlington Rd. Slou —1G 47
Burlington Rd. Tile —5L 61
Burlsdon Way. Brack —3B 92
Burne-Jones Dri. Col T —3H 119
Burness Clo. Uxb —3L 25
Burnetts Rd. Wind —7A 46
Burney Bit. Pam H —9N 105
Burney Bit Rd. Tadl —9N 105
Burnham Clo. Bour —3L 5
Burnham Clo. Wind —8N 45
Burnham Gro. Brack —2N 91
Burnham La. Slou —6N 21
Burnham Rise. Emm G —6J 39
Burnham Rd. Tadl —8H 105
Burnistone Clo. Lwr Ear —1D 88
Burn Moor Chase. Brack —9B 92
Burns Clo. Wdly —8D 64
Burns Wlk. That —7F 80
Burntbush La. Fril —6K 57
Burnt Ho. Gdns. Warf —2B 92
Burnthouse La. Ping —6B 86
Burnthouse Ride. Brack —6H 91
Burnt Oak. Cook —8K 5
Burnt Oak. Wokgm —2L 111
Burnt Pollard La. Light —9N 115
Burn Wlk. Burn —4L 21
Burrcroft Ct. Read —7A 62
Burrcroft Rd. Read —7A 62
Burrell Rd. Comp —1H 33
Burrell Rd. Frim —9N 119
Burr La. Shalb —8E 96
Burroughs Cres. Bour —3L 5
Burroway Rd. Slou —2C 48
Burrows Hill Clo. Houn —9K 49
Burrows Hill La. Houn —1J 73
Burton Clo. W'sham —6N 115
Burtons Hill. Kint —9G 77
Burton Way. Wind —9A 46
Burwell Clo. Lwr Ear —2B 88
Bury's Bank Rd. Green —3A 102
Bush Wlk. Wokgm —5A 90
Business Cen., The. Wokgm —7N 89
Business Village, The. Slou —9K 23
Butchers La. White —4F 42
Bute St. Read —7B 62
Butler Rd. Bag —8J 115
Butler Rd. Crowt —4F 112
Butlers Clo. Wind —7N 45
Butler's Orchard. Kid E —2D 38
Butson Clo. Newb —8J 79
Buttenshaw Av. Arbor —2E 110
Buttenshaw Clo. Arbor —2F 110
Buttercup Clo. Wokgm —5D 90
Buttercup Sq. Stai —5L 73
Butter Mkt. Read —5H 63
Buttermere Av. Slou —6M 21
Buttermere Gdns. Brack —5N 91
Buttersteep Rise. Asc —1F 114
Butts Cen. Read —5G 62 (off Castle St.)
Buttsfield Rd. Chad —4K 29
Butts Hill Rd. Son & Wdly —2D 64
Buxton Av. Cav —9F 38
Buxton Rd. Ashf —9L 73
Bybend Clo. Farn R —2D 22
Byefield Rd. Read —8B 62
Byeways Clo. Know H —2C 42
Byland Dri. M'head —4E 44
Byreton Clo. Ear —1A 88
Byron Clo. Mar —4D 4
Byron Clo. Newb —3K 101
Byron Clo. Twy —9K 41
Byron Clo. Yat —5A 118
Byron Ct. Wind —9C 46
Byron Dri. Crowt —7F 112
Byron Ho. Langl —4C 48
Byron Rd. Ear —5N 63
Byron Rd. Twy —9K 41
Byron Way. W Dray —3N 49
Bythorn Clo. Lwr Ear —1D 88
Byways. Burn —6K 21
Byways. Yat —4A 118
Bywood. Brack —9K 91
Byworth Clo. Read —4H 87
Cabbage Hill. Warf —9K 67
Cabbagehill La. Warf —8J 67
Cabin Moss. Brack —9B 92
Cabrera Av. Vir W —8L 95
Cabrera Clo. Vir W —8M 95
Caddy Clo. Egh —9B 72
Cadogan Clo. Cav —9K 39
Cadogan Clo. Holyp —5D 44
Cadogan Clo. Tile —5M 61
Cadwell Dri. M'head —2A 44
Caesars Camp Rd. Camb —9D 114
Caesars Ga. Warf —3B 92
Cain Rd. Brack —4H 91
Cairngorm Pl. Slou —5F 22
Cairngorm Rd. That —9G 80
Caistor Clo. Calc —8J 61
Calard Dri. That —6D 80
Calbourne Dri. Calc —8L 61
Calbroke Rd. Slou —5B 22
Calbrooke Rd. Slou —4B 22
Calcot Pl. Dri. Calc —8M 61
Caldbeck Dri. Wdly —5D 64
Calder Clo. M'head —5B 20
Calder Clo. Tile —4N 61
Calder Ct. Langl —4A 48
Calder Ct. M'head —5A 20
Calder Way. Coln —9F 48
Caldwell Rd. W'sham —5N 115
Caledonia Rd. Stai —5M 73
Caleta Clo. Cav —2K 63
Calfridus Way. Brack —5B 92
California Caravan Pk. Finch —4J 111
Calleva Ind. Pk. Aldm —8G 105
Callington Rd. Read —2H 87
Callin's La. Been —1F 66
Callis Farm Clo. Stai —3M 73
Callow Hill. Vir W —5L 95
Calshot Pl. Calc —8L 61
Camberley Rd. Houn —9N 49
Cambourne Clo. Lwr Ear —2N 87
Cambourne Rd. Houn —9N 49
Cambria Ct. Slou —1L 47
Cambria Ct. Stai —8F 72
Cambria Gdns. Stai —4M 73
Cambrian Clo. Camb —4M 119
Cambrian Way. Calc —8L 61
Cambrian Way. Wokgm —2M 111
Cambridge Av. Burn —3L 21
Cambridge Av. Slou —7C 22
Cambridge Clo. W Dray —5L 49
Cambridge Ho. Wind —7E 46
Cambridge Rd. Crowt —6G 112
Cambridge Rd. Mar —5B 4
Cambridge Rd. Owl —9J 113
Cambridge Rd. Uxb —1L 25
Cambridgeshire Clo. Warf —2C 92
Cambridgeshire Clo. Wokgm —5K 89
Cambridge St. Read —4E 62
Cambridge Wlk. Camb —3N 119
Camden Pl. Bour —4L 5
Camden Pl. Calc —8J 61
Camden Rd. M'head —5A 20
Camellia Way. Wokgm —4J 89
Camley Gdns. M'head —6L 19
Camley Pk. Dri. M'head —6K 19
Camm Av. Wind —9A 46
Campbell Clo. Yat —3D 118
Campbell Rd. Wdly —7C 64
Campbells Grn. Mort C —5J 107
Camperdown. M'head —5E 20
Campion Clo. B'water —6K 119
Campion Clo. Uxb —6N 25
Campion Ho. Brack —3J 91
Campion Way. Wokgm —3C 90
Camp Rd. Uft N —8D 84
Canada Rd. Slou —1K 47
Canadian Memorial Av. Asc —4H 95
Canal Ind. Est. Langl —1B 48
Canal Wlk. Hung —5K 75
Canal Way. Read —5K 63
Canal Wharf. Langl —1B 48
Canberra Rd. Houn —9N 49
Candleford Clo. Brack —2N 91
Candover Clo. W Dray —6L 49
Canford Ct. Read —5D 62
Canhurst La. Know H —2B 42
Cannock Clo. M'head —8E 20
Cannock Way. Lwr Ear —2B 88
Cannon Clo. Col T —1K 119
Cannon Ct. Rd. M'head —3A 20 (in two parts)
Cannondown Rd. Cook —1B 20
Cannon Hill. Brack —8N 91
Cannon Hill Clo. M'head —3F 44
Cannon La. M'head —8L 19
Cannon St. Read —4E 62
Canon Hill Dri. M'head —2D 44
Canon Hill Est. M'head —2E 44
Canon Hill Way. M'head —3E 44
Canopus Way. Stai —4M 73
Cansfield End. Newb —8K 79
Canterbury Av. Slou —5E 22
Canterbury Rd. Read —9H 63
Cantley Cres. Wokgm —3M 89
Caraway Rd. Ear —2N 87
Carbery La. Asc —5L 93
Carbinswood La. Woolh —5B 82
Cardiff M. Read —3F 62
Cardiff Rd. Read —3E 62
Cardigan Gdns. Read —7L 63
Cardigan Rd. Read —6L 63
Cardinal Clo. Cav —2H 63
Cardinals, The. Brack —6M 91
Cardinals Wlk. Tap —7M 21
Cardwell Cres. Asc —7M 93
Carew Clo. Tile —9J 37
Carey Clo. Wind —9D 46
Carey Rd. Wokgm —6A 90
Carey St. Read —5F 62
Cariad Ct. Gor —7K 15
Carisbrooke Clo. Cav —7J 39
Carisbrooke Clo. M'head —9N 19
Carisbrooke Ct. Slou —8H 23
Carland Clo. Lwr Ear —2N 87
Carlile Gdns. Twy —6J 41
Carlisle Rd. Slou —8F 22
Carlisle Rd. Tile —2M 61 (in two parts)
Carlton Clo. Wdly —6D 64
Carlton Ct. Stai —9H 73
Carlton Ct. Uxb —6L 25
Carlton Rd. Cav —8D 38
Carlton Rd. Slou —8K 23
Carlyle Ct. Crowt —6G 112
Carmarthen Rd. Slou —8G 22
Carnarvon Rd. Read —5L 63
Carnation Clo. Crowt —2F 112
Carnation Dri. Wink R —1D 92
Carnegie Rd. Newb —9L 79
Carnoustie. Brack —9J 91
Carnoustie Ct. Read —5K 63 (off Muirfield Clo.)
Carolina Pl. Wokgm —3K 111
Caroline Clo. W Dray —1L 49
Caroline Ct. Mar —4C 4
Caroline Ct. Read —6E 62
Caroline Dri. Wokgm —4M 89
Caroline St. Read —4F 62
Carrick Gdns. Wdly —5B 64
Carrick La. Yat —3C 118
Carrington Rd. Slou —8G 23
Carroll Cres. Asc —7J 93
Carron Clo. Tile —5A 62
Carsdale Clo. Read —7F 62
Carshalton Rd. Camb —9D 114
Carshalton Way. Lwr Ear —2B 88
Carston Gro. Calc —8N 61
Carter Clo. Wind —8C 46
Carter's Hill. Wokgm & Brack —8C 66
Cartershill La. Arbor —7C 88
Carters Rise. Calc —8M 61
Cartmel Dri. Wdly —6C 64
Carvers Hill. Shalb —8D 96
Cary Clo. Newb —4H 101
Casey Ct. South —9F 58
Cassia Dri. Ear —2M 87
Castle Av. Dat —5J 47
Castle Av. W Dray —8M 25
Castle Cotts. Newt —7M 101
Castle Ct. M'head —7A 20
Castlecraig Ct. Col T —2H 119
Castle Cres. Read —6F 62
Castle Dri. M'head —7A 20
Castle End Rd. Rusc —7L 41
Castle Farm Caravan Site. Wind (off White Horse Rd.) —8N 45
Castle Gro. Newb —6K 79
Castle Hill. Far H —3A 110
Castle Hill. M'head —7B 20
Castle Hill. Read —6F 62
Castle Hill. Wind —7F 46
Castle Hill Rd. Egh —7K 71
Castle Hill Ter. M'head —7B 20
Castle La. Don —5J 79
Castle M. M'head —7B 20
Castle St. Read —5G 62
Castle St. Slou —2H 47
Castleton Ct. Mar —5C 4
Castleview Pde. Slou —3M 47
Castleview Rd. Slou —3L 47
Caswall Clo. Binf —1G 90
Caswall Ride. Yat —4D 118
Catalina Clo. Wdly —5G 65
Catcliffe Way. Lwr Ear —3M 87
Catena Rise. Light —9K 115
Catherine Rd. Newb —9L 79
Catherines Clo. W Dray —1L 49
Catherine's Hill. Mort —5F 106
Catherine St. Read —4D 62
Catmore Rd. W Ils —7G 11
Caunter Rd. Speen —7H 79
Causeway. Cook —8L 5
Causeway Est. Stai —8C 72
Causeway, The. Bray —1E 44 (in two parts)
Causeway, The. Mar —6C 4
Causeway, The. Stai —8E 72
Causmans Way. Tile —3K 61
Cavalier Clo. Thea —9E 60
Cavalry Cres. Wind —9E 46
Cavendish Clo. Tap —7K 21
Cavendish Ct. B'water —6H 119
Cavendish Ct. Coln —7F 48
Cavendish Ct. Mar —5C 4
Cavendish Ct. Newb —6B 80
Cavendish Gdns. Winn —9F 64
Cavendish Meads. Asc —8N 93
Cavendish Pk. Col T —3J 119
Cavendish Rd. Cav —7J 39
Caversham Pk. Dri. Cav —8J 39
Caversham Pk. Rd. Cav —7J 39
Caversham Rd. Read —4G 62
Caversham Wharf. Read —3G 63
Caves Farm Clo. Sand —1E 118
Cawcott Dri. Wind —7A 46
Cawsam Gdns. Cav —9J 39
Caxton Clo. Read —3C 62
Caxton Ct. Hen T —5D 16
Caxton Dri. Uxb —3L 25
Cecil Aldin Dri. Tile —8K 37
Cecil Rd. Iver —7F 24
Cecil Way. Slou —5B 22
Cedar Av. B'water —4H 119
Cedar Av. W Dray —8N 25
Cedar Chase. Tap —5G 21
Cedar Clo. Bag —7H 115
Cedar Clo. Burn —5N 21
Cedar Clo. Wokgm —5A 90
Cedar Ct. Egh —8B 72
Cedar Ct. Mar —5C 4

Cedar Ct. Wind —8C 46
Cedar Dri. Asc —9C 94
Cedar Dri. Brack —2N 91
Cedar Dri. Cook —8K 5
Cedar Dri. Mar —1A 4
Cedar Dri. Pang —9D 36
Cedar Dri. S'hill —6F 94
Cedar Gro. That —8F 80
Cedar La. Frim —9N 119
Cedar Lodge. Hen T —6E 16
Cedar Mt. Newb —2K 101
Cedar Rd. Read —2L 87
Cedars. Brack —6C 92
Cedars Clo. Sand —1D 118
Cedars Dri. Uxb —3N 25
Cedars Rd. M'head —7D 20
Cedars, The. Tile —2L 61
Cedar Way. Slou —4N 47
Cedar Wood Cres. Cav —9H 39
Celandine Clo. Crowt —4G 113
Celandine Gro. That —7J 81
Celia Cres. Ashf —9L 73
Cell Farm Av. Old Win —2K 71
Centennial Ct. Brack —4L 91
Central Dri. Slou —8B 22
Central La. Wink —5L 69
Central Wlk. Wokgm —5A 90
Central Way. Wink —5L 69
Centre Rd. Wind —6M 45
Centurion Clo. Col T —1H 119
Centurion Clo. Read —6G 63
Century Rd. Stai —9D 72
Chaffinch Clo. Col T —1H 119
Chaffinch Clo. Tile —5J 61
Chaffinch Clo. Wokgm —6K 89
Chagford Rd. Read —2H 87
Chain St. Read —5G 63
Chalcott. Chalv —2G 46
Chalcraft Clo. Hen T —6B 16
Chalfont Clo. Ear —2N 87
Chalfont Way. Ear —2N 87
Chalford Rd. Newb —9J 79
Chalgrove Clo. M'head —8E 20
Chalgrove Way. Emm G —7J 39
Chalk Hill. Harp —9A 16
Chalkhouse Grn. La. Chalk (in two parts) —4G 38
Chalkhouse Grn. Rd. Kid E —2D 38
Chalklands. Bour —3L 5
Chalkpit Cotts. Hung —4M 51
Chalk Pit La. Burn —1L 21
Chalkpit La. Mar —4A 4
Chalky La. Cur —7M 55
Challis Pl. Brack —4J 91
Challoner Clo. Wokgm —3L 111
Challow Ct. M'head —5A 20
Chalvey Gdns. Slou —1G 46
Chalvey Gro. Slou —2D 46
Chalvey Pk. Slou —1G 47
Chalvey Rd. E. Slou —1G 46
Chalvey Rd. W. Slou —1F 46
Chamberhouse Mill La. That —1J 103
Chamberlains Gdns. Arbor X —9D 88
Chambers, The. Read —5H 63 (off East St.)
Champion Rd. Cav —3J 63
Chancellor's Way, The. Ear —8L 63
Chancery M. Read —5F 62
Chanctonbury Dri. Asc —9A 94
Chandlers La. Yat —2A 118
Chandos Mall. Chalv —1H 47
Chandos Rd. Newb —2K 101
Chandos Rd. Stai —9E 72
Chantry Clo. W Dray —8L 25
Chantry Clo. Wind —7C 46
Chantry Mead. Hung —6J 75
Chantry Rd. Bag —8G 115
Chantry, The. Uxb —4N 25
Chapel Clo. S Sto —3L 15
Chapel Ct. Hung —5L 75
Chapel Dri. B Hill —5D 108
Chapel Hill. Tile —4K 61
Chapel La. Ash H —9B 104
Chapel La. Ash'd —7C 34
Chapel La. Bag —8G 115
Chapel La. Binf —2G 91
Chapel La. Cur —8B 56
Chapel La. Farn & B'water —9K 119
Chapel La. Herm —4F 56
Chapel La. Lamb —2H 27
Chapel La. Mort —5A 106
Chapel La. Rise —7J 109
Chapel La. Spen W —9H 87
Chapel La. Stoke P —1K 23
Chapel La. Yatt —3A 58
Chapel Rd. Camb —4M 119
Chapel Row. Twy —9J 41
Chapel St. Mar —5B 4
Chapel St. Slou —1H 47
Chapel St. That —8G 81
Chapel St. Uxb —2K 25
Chapel View. Lamb —3H 27
Chaplain's Hill. Crowt —6H 113
Chapman Clo. W Dray —2N 49
Chapman La. Bour & F Hth —2L 5
Chapman Wlk. That —7E 80
Chapter Clo. Uxb —1N 25
Chapter M. Wind —6F 46
Chard Clo. Wdly —6D 64
Charfield Ct. Read —5L 63
Chariots Pl. Wind —7F 46
Charlbury Clo. Brack —6C 92
Charles Clore Ct. Read —8A 62
Charles Evans Way. Cav —2K 63
Charles Gdns. Slou —7K 23
Charles Ho. Wind —7E 46
Charles Sq. Brack —4N 91
Charles St. Newb —4H 101
Charles St. Read —4F 62
Charles St. Wind —7E 46
Charlock Clo. That —6H 81
Charlotte Clo. Herm —6D 56
Charlton. Wind —8M 45
Charlton Clo. Slou —1D 46
Charlton Clo. Wokgm —2L 111
Charlton Ct. Owl —9H 113
Charlton La. Swal —4J 109
Charlton Pl. Newb —7L 79
Charlton Sq. Wind —8M 45
Charlton Wlk. Wind —8M 45
Charmwood Clo. Newb —6K 79
Charndon Clo. Read —7H 63
Charnham La. Hung —4K 75
Charnham Pk. Hung —4K 75
Charnham St. Hung —5K 75
Charnwood. Asc —8B 94
Charnwood Rd. Uxb —3N 25
Charrington Rd. Calc —8J 61
Charta Rd. Egh —9D 72
Charter Clo. Slou —2H 47
Charterhouse Clo. Brack —7B 92
Charter Pl. Uxb —1L 25
Charter Rd. Newb —3K 101
Charter Rd. Slou —8A 22
Charters Clo. Asc —7N 93
Charters La. Asc —7N 93
Charters Rd. Asc —9N 93
Charters Way. Asc —9B 94
Charvil Ho. Rd. Charv —8F 40
Charvil La. Son —1D 64
Charville Dri. Calc —8J 61
Charwood Rd. Wokgm —5C 90
Chase Gdns. Binf —9G 66
Chaseside Av. Twy —6J 41
Chase, The. Calc —8L 61
Chase, The. Crowt —4E 112
Chase, The. Don —4K 79
Chase, The. Mar —4E 4
Chatfield. Slou —6C 22
Chatham St. Read —4F 62
Chatsworth Av. Winn —1F 88
Chatsworth Clo. Cav —7J 39
Chatsworth Clo. M'head —9N 19
Chatteris Way. Lwr Ear —2A 88
Chatton Clo. Lwr Ear —3N 87
Chaucer Clo. Emm G —8G 39
Chaucer Clo. Wokgm —5D 90
Chaucer Cres. Newb —6J 79
Chaucer Gro. Camb —4N 119
Chaucer Rd. Ashf —8M 73
Chaucer Rd. Crowt —6F 112
Chaucer Way. Wokgm —6K 89
Chauntry Clo. M'head —8F 20
Chauntry Rd. M'head —8E 20
Chavey Down Rd. Wink R —9E 68
Chawridge La. Wink —5F 68
Chazey Clo. Chaz H —5C 38
Chazey Rd. Cav —9D 38
Cheam Clo. Brack —7A 92
Cheapside. Read —4G 62
Cheapside Rd. Asc —5M 93
Cheap St. Comp —9H 13
Cheap St. Newb —9L 79
Cheddington Clo. Tile —6N 61
Cheeseman Clo. Wokgm —4B 90
Chelford Way. Cav —9F 38
Chelsea Clo. Tile —3N 61
Cheltenham Vs. Stai —3G 73
Chelwood Dri. Sand —9D 112
Chelwood Rd. Ear —1A 88
Cheney Clo. Binf —1H 91
Cheniston Ct. S'dale —9C 94
Cheniston Gro. M'head —7K 19
Chepstow Rd. Tile —2L 61
Chequer La. Strat S —8D 108
Chequers Orchard. Iver —7G 24
Chequers Sq. Uxb —1K 25
Chequers Way. Wdly —5B 64
Cherbury Clo. Brack —6B 92
Cherington Ga. M'head —5M 19
Cherington Way. Asc —4H 93
Cheriton Av. Twy —7J 41
Cheriton Clo. Newb —2M 101
Cheriton Ct. Read —6G 62
Cheriton Pl. Son C —1F 38
Cheriton Way. B'water —4H 119
Cherries, The. Slou —7K 23
Cherry Av. Slou —1M 47
Cherry Clo. Cav —5J 39
Cherry Clo. F Hth —1M 5
Cherry Clo. Newb —6K 79
Cherry Garden La. M'head —2J 43
Cherry Garden La. White —5J 43
Cherry Gro. Hung —6J 75
Cherry La. W Dray —3N 49
Cherry Orchard. Gt Shef —9G 28
Cherry Orchard. Stai —9H 73
Cherry Orchard. Stoke P —1K 23
Cherry Orchard. W Dray —1M 49
Cherry Tree Av. W Dray —7N 25
Cherry Tree Clo. Owl —9H 113
Cherry Tree Dri. Brack —5A 92
Cherrytree Gro. Wokgm —7H 89
Cherry Tree La. Ful —1A 24
Cherrytree La. Iver —2H 25
Cherry Tree Rd. Farn R —1E 22
Cherry Way. Hort —9D 48
Cherrywood Av. Egh —2K 95
Cherrywood Rd. Farn —9L 119
Chertsey La. Stai —9F 72
Chertsey Rd. W'sham & Chob —6N 115
Chervil Way. Bfld C —9J 85
Cherwell Clo. M'head —6D 20
Cherwell Clo. Slou —5C 48
Cherwell Cres. Read —5F 62 (off Trinity Pl.)
Cherwell Rd. Bour —3M 5
Cherwell Rd. Cav —7G 38
Cheshire Ct. Slou —1K 47
Cheshire Pk. Warf —1B 92
Chesseridge Rd. Comp —2F 32
Chesterblade La. Brack —9A 92
Chester Clo. Green —2N 101
Chesterfield Rd. Ashf —8M 73
Chesterfield Rd. Newb —1L 101
Chester Ho. Uxb —5K 25
Chesterman St. Read —6H 63
Chester Rd. Slou —7F 22
Chester St. Cav —2G 63
Chester St. Read —4D 62
Chesterton Dri. Stai —5N 73
Chesterton Rd. That —6F 80
Chestnut Av. Cav —9L 39
Chestnut Av. Slou —1N 47
Chestnut Av. Vir W —6H 95
Chestnut Av. W Dray —8N 25
Chestnut Av. Wokgm —5H 89
Chestnut Clo. B'water —5J 119
Chestnut Clo. Egh —1K 95
Chestnut Clo. M'head —5E 20
Chestnut Clo. Thea —8F 60
Chestnut Cotts. Streat —8J 15
Chestnut Ct. Newb —7L 79 (off Victoria Gdns.)
Chestnut Cres. Newb —7L 79
Chestnut Cres. Shin —7L 87
Chestnut Dri. Bfld —7J 85
Chestnut Dri. Egh —1M 95
Chestnut Dri. Wind —1A 70
Chestnut Gro. Pur T —8L 37
Chestnut Gro. Stai —9K 73
Chestnut Mnr. Clo. Stai —9J 73
Chestnuts, The. S'lake —2F 40
Chestnut Wlk. Hung —7K 75
Chestnut Wlk. Read —5H 63
Chestwood Gro. Uxb —1N 25
Chetwode Clo. Wokgm —5C 90
Chetwynd Dri. Uxb —3N 25
Cheviot Clo. Farn —9J 119
Cheviot Clo. M'head —8E 20
Cheviot Clo. Newb —5G 101
Cheviot Dri. Charv —9G 40
Cheviot Rd. Sand —8D 112
Cheviot Rd. Slou —4B 48
Chevley Gdns. Burn —3M 21
Chewter Clo. Bag —7J 115
Chewter La. W'sham —4L 115
Cheyne Way. Farn —9K 119
Chichester Ct. Slou —2K 47
Chichester Rd. Tile —4M 61
Chicory Clo. Ear —2M 87
Chievley Clo. Tile —4K 61
Chilcombe Way. Lwr Ear —1C 88
Childrey Way. Tile —4J 61
Childs Hall. Read —7M 63
Child St. Lamb —2G 27
Chillingham Way. Camb —5N 119
Chiltern Bus. Village. Uxb —3J 25
Chiltern Clo. Hen T —6A 16
Chiltern Clo. Mar —5A 4
Chiltern Clo. Newb —5G 101
Chiltern Ct. Emm G —7G 39
Chiltern Cres. Ear —5N 63
Chiltern Dri. Charv —9G 40
Chiltern Rd. Burn —6L 21
Chiltern Rd. Cav —9J 39
Chiltern Rd. M'head —8E 20
Chiltern Rd. Sand —9D 112
Chilterns Pk. Bour —2M 5
Chiltern View. Pur T —8L 37
Chiltern View Rd. Uxb —3K 25
Chiltern Wlk. Pang —8E 36
Chilton Ct. Tap —7M 21
Chilton Way. Hung —6J 75
Chilwick Rd. Slou —5B 22
Chippendale All. Uxb —1L 25
Chippendale Clo. Baug —9G 105
Chippendale Clo. B'water —6J 119
Chippendale Waye. Uxb —1L 25
Chippenham Clo. Lwr Ear —3M 87
Chipstead Rd. Houn —9N 49
Chisbury Clo. Brack —8B 92
Chitterfield Ga. W Dray —6N 49
Chittering Clo. Lwr Ear —2B 88
Chive Rd. Ear —2N 87
Chivers Dri. Wokgm —3K 111
Chives Pl. Warf —2A 92
Chobham Rd. S'dale & Wok —9D 94
Choke La. M'head —2L 19
Cholmeley Pl. Read —5L 63
Cholmeley Rd. Read —4L 63
Cholmeley Ter. Read —5L 63
Cholsey Clo. That —8J 81
Choseley Clo. Know H —1C 42
Choseley Rd. Know H —1C 42
Chrislaine Clo. Stai —3L 73
Christchurch Ct. Read —7J 63
Christchurch Dri. B'water —3G 119
Christchurch Gdns. Read —7J 63
Christchurch Rd. Houn —8N 49
Christchurch Rd. Read —7J 63
Christchurch Rd. Vir W —5J 95
Christian Sq. Wind —7E 46
Christie Clo. Light —9M 115
Christie Heights. Green —2M 101
Christie Wlk. Yat —5A 118
Christopher Ct. Newb —9M 79
Chudleigh Gdns. Read —1J 87
Church App. Stanw —3L 73
Church Av. Hen T —4D 16
Church Clo. Croc H —4C 100
Church Clo. Eton —5F 46
Church Clo. Lamb —2H 27
Church Clo. M'head —8A 20
Church Clo. Uxb —3J 25
Church Clo. W Dray —2M 49
Church Clo. Winn —1H 89
Church Cotts. Read —6M 61
Church Croft. Hung —5K 75
Church Dri. Bray —1F 44
Church End La. Tile —5N 61
Churchfield M. Slou —7J 23
Church Ga. That —8G 80
Church Gro. Wex —6L 23
Church Hams. Finch —4J 111
Church Hill. Brack —7G 67
Church Hill. E Ils —8B 12
Church Hill. Hurst —6K 65
Church Hill. White —5J 43
Churchill Clo. Farn —9M 119
Churchill Clo. Read —1H 87
Churchill Ct. Stai —9J 73
Churchill Cres. Farn —9M 119
Churchill Cres. Yat —4B 118
Churchill Dri. Mar —3D 4
Churchill Dri. Winn —1G 89
Churchill Rd. Asc —4J 93
Churchill Rd. Slou —3A 48
Church Island. Stai —8E 72
Church La. Arbor —7B 88
Church La. B'ham —1H 111
Church La. Binf —9J 67
Church La. Bray —1F 44
Church La. Brimp —4B 104
Church La. Chvly —3M 55
Church La. Combe —3C 116
Church La. Croc H —4C 100
Church La. Far H —4B 110
Church La. Finch —6K 111
Church La. Hung —5K 75
Church La. Rusc —8L 41
Church La. S'lake —4E 40
Church La. Sil —9E 106
Church La. Speen —7H 79
Church La. Stoke P —5H 23
Church La. Streat —7C 34
Church La. S'dale —7D 94
Church La. S'hill —6N 93
Church La. That —8G 80
Church La. Three M & Shin —7H 87
Church La. Uft N —6C 84
Church La. Uxb —3J 25
Church La. Warf —7A 68
Church La. Wex —5K 23
Church La. Wind —7F 46
Church La. Wink —7F 68
Church La. Yatt —3A 58
Church M. Pur T —8L 37
Church M. Wdly —4E 64
Church Pde. Ashf —8N 73
Church Path. Bray —1F 44
Church Path. S'hill —5A 94
Church Rd. Aldm —3J 105
Church Rd. Asc —6K 93
Church Rd. Ashf —7N 73
Church Rd. Bag —7G 114
Church Rd. Bour —6N 5 (in two parts)
Church Rd. Brack —4N 91
Church Rd. Cav —2F 62
Church Rd. Chav D —3E 92
Church Rd. Cook D —9F 4
Church Rd. Ear —7A 64
Church Rd. Egh —9A 72
Church Rd. Farn R —4E 22
Church Rd. Frim —8N 119
Church Rd. Frox —6B 74
Church Rd. Iver —4D 24
Church Rd. M'head —9E 20
Church Rd. Mar —2G 5
Church Rd. Mort —6D 106
Church Rd. Old Win —2J 71
Church Rd. Owl —9J 113
Church Rd. Pang —8D 36
Church Rd. Sand —9D 112
Church Rd. Shaw —6L 79
Church Rd. S'dale —8C 94
Church Rd. Swal —4K 109
Church Rd. Tadl —9N 105
Church Rd. Uxb —5L 25
Church Rd. W Dray —2L 49
Church Rd. W'sham —6L 115
Church Rd. Wdly —4E 64
Church Rd. E. Crowt —5F 112
Church Rd. W. Crowt —6F 112
Church Side. E Ils —8B 12
Church St. Burn —5M 21
Church St. Cav —2G 62
Church St. Chalv —1E 46
Church St. Crowt —5F 112
Church St. Gt Shef —1F 52
Church St. Hamp N —8J 33
Church St. Hen T —5C 16
Church St. Hung —5K 75
Church St. Kint —9F 76
Church St. L Bed —1A 96
Church St. Read —6H 63
Church St. Slou —1H 47
Church St. Stai —8E 72
Church St. Thea —9E 60
Church St. Twy —9J 41
Church St. Warg —3H 41
Church St. Wind —7F 46
Church Ter. Binf —2G 91
Church Ter. Read —6G 62 (off Dover St.)
Church Ter. Wind —8A 46
Church View. Been —5J 83
Church View. White —5J 43
Church View. Yat —2B 118
Church View Cotts. Brad —6L 59
Church Wlk. Burn —5L 21
Churchward Wlk. Calc —8N 61
Church Way. Hung —6J 75
Churchway. W Ils —5M 11
Churn Rd. Comp —8G 12
Cinnamon Clo. Ear —2M 87
Cintra Av. Read —8J 63
Cippenham Clo. Slou —8B 22
Cippenham La. Slou —8B 22
Circle Hill Rd. Crowt —5G 112
Circuit La. Read —7B 62
City Rd. Tile —6J 61
Clacy Grn. Brack —2L 91
Clammas Way. Uxb —6K 25
Clanfield Cres. Tile —2K 61
Clanfield Ride. B'water —4H 119
Clappers Meadow. M'head —5E 20
Clapps Ga. Rd. Pam H —9N 105
Clare Av. Wokgm —4A 90
Clarefield Clo. M'head —5L 19
Clarefield Ct. S'dale —9C 94
Clarefield Dri. M'head —5L 19
Clarefield Rd. M'head —5M 19
Clare Gdns. Egh —9B 72
Claremont Gdns. Mar —5C 4
Claremont Rd. Mar —5C 4
Claremont Rd. Stai —9E 72
Claremont Rd. Wind —8E 46
Clarence Cres. Wind —7E 46
Clarence Dri. Egh —8L 71
Clarence Rd. Hen T —4C 16
Clarence Rd. Wind —7C 46
Clarence St. Egh —9A 72
Clarence St. Stai —8F 72
Clarence Way. Calc —8J 61
Clarendon Clo. Winn —1J 89
Clarendon Ct. B'water —6H 119
Clarendon Ct. Slou —8K 23
Clarendon Gdns. Newb —7L 79
Clarendon Rd. Ashf —8N 73
Clarendon Rd. Read —6N 63
Clare Rd. M'head —8A 20
Clare Rd. Stai —5L 73
Clare Rd. Tap —7M 21
Clares Grn. Spen W —8H 87
Clarke Cres. Col T —2J 119
Clarkes Dri. Uxb —6M 25
Clark's Gdns. Hung —6K 75
Classics, The. Lamb —4H 27
Classon Clo. W Dray —1M 49
Claverdon. Brack —9L 91
Clay Clo. Tile —3J 61
Claydon Ct. Cav —3G 63
Claydon Gdns. B'water —8L 119
Clayhall La. Old Win —2H 71
Clay Hill. Been —3F 108
Clayhill Clo. Brack —5C 92
Clay Hill Cres. Newb —6A 80
Clayhill Rd. Bfld C & Bfld —8G 85
Clay La. Been —5H 83
Clay La. Stanw —4N 73
Clay La. Wokgm —5D 90
Clayton Ct. Langl —2B 48
Clayton Gro. Brack —3B 92
Clayton Rd. Farn —8K 119
Claytons Meadow. Bour —5M 5
Clayton Wlk. Read —8J 63
Clayton Way. Uxb —5L 25
Clearsprings. Light —9K 115
Cleeve Ct. Streat —7K 15
Cleeve Down. Gor —7M 15
Cleeve Rd. Gor —7K 15
Clemants Clo. Slou —1K 47
Clements Clo. Spen W —1G 109
Clements Mead. Tile —4J 61
Clements Rd. Hen T —3B 16
Clent Rd. Read —8H 63
Cleopatra Pl. Warf —2B 92
Clevedon Dri. Ear —1N 87
Clevedon Rd. Tile —1M 61
Cleve Ho. Brack —6B 92
Cleveland. Charv —9G 41
Cleveland Clo. M'head —8E 20
Cleveland Gro. Newb —8K 79
Cleveland Pk. Stai —3M 73
Cleveland Rd. Uxb —5L 25
Clevemede. Gor —7L 15
Cleves Ct. Wind —9B 46
Clewer Av. Wind —8C 46
Clewer Ct. Rd. Wind —6D 46
Clewer Fields. Wind —7E 46
Clewer Hill Rd. Wind —8A 46
Clewer New Town. Wind —8C 46
Clewer Pk. Wind —6C 46
Clifford Gro. Ashf —8N 73
Cliffords Way. Bour —2L 5
Clifton Clo. M'head —1D 44
Clifton Ct. Stanw —3M 73
Clifton Pk. Rd. Cav —1F 62
Clifton Rise. Warg —4K 41
Clifton Rise. Wind —7N 45
Clifton Rd. Newb —9J 79
Clifton Rd. Slou —1K 47
Clifton Rd. Wokgm —3M 89
Clifton St. Read —5F 62
Clintons Grn. Brack —3L 91
Clive Ct. Slou —1F 46
Clivedale Rd. Wdly —8D 64
Cliveden Mead. M'head —4E 20
Cliveden Rd. Tap —5G 21
Clive Grn. Brack —7M 91 (in two parts)
Clivemont Rd. M'head —5C 20
Cloister M. Thea —9F 60
Cloisters, The. Cav —1G 62
Cloisters, The. Frim —8N 119
Clonmel Way. Burn —4L 21
Close End. Lamb —3H 27
Close, The. Asc —4G 92
Close, The. Bour —1L 5
Close, The. Brack —6N 91
Close, The. Bfld C —8H 85
Close, The. Col T —1J 119
Close, The. Frim —9N 119
Close, The. Gt Shef —1F 52
Close, The. Hamp N —8J 33
Close, The. Hen T —6C 16
Close, The. Iver —4D 24
Close, The. Light —9K 115
Close, The. Mar —5A 4
Close, The. Shalb —7E 96
Close, The. Slou —8N 21
Close, The. That —7E 80
Close, The. Uxb —2N 25 (Court Dri.)
Close, The. Uxb —1M 25 (Honeycroft Hill)
Close, The. Vir W —7M 95
Close, The. Wdly —7D 64
Clough Dri. Herm —6C 56
Clove Clo. Lwr Ear —2M 87
Clover Clo. Wokgm —4C 90
Club La. Crowt —5H 113
Clyde Rd. Stai —5L 73
Coach Horse Ct. Pang —8F 36
Coachmans Ct. Newb —6M 79
Coach Ride. Mar —3B 4
Coach Rd. Asc —2H 93
Coalport Way. Tile —3M 61
Cobb Clo. Dat —7M 47
Cobbett's La. Yat —4D 118
Cobblers Clo. Farn R —3D 22
Cobden Clo. Uxb —2K 25
Cobham Rd. Wdly —5E 64
Cochrane Clo. That —8H 81
Cochrane Pl. W'sham —5N 115
Cock-A-Dobby. Sand —9E 112
Cockett Rd. Slou —2N 47
Cock La. South —1G 83
Cockney Hill. Tile —6N 61
Cockpit Path. Wokgm —6A 90
Cock's La. Warf —6D 68
Cody Clo. Wdly —4G 64
Coe Spur. Slou —2D 46
Coftards. Slou —7L 23
Cold Ash Hill. Cold A —2F 80
Coldborough Rise. Brack —3K 91
Coldharbour Clo. Hen T —6B 16
Cold Harbour La. Farn —9J 119
Coldharbour Rd. Hung —7K 75
Coldicutt St. Cav —3J 63
Coldmoorholme La. Bour —4J 5
Cole La. Arbor X —8D 88
Colemans Moor La. Wdly —6E 64
Colemans Moor Rd. Wdly —8E 64
Colenorton Cres. Eton W —3A 46
Coleridge Av. Yat —4C 118
Coleridge Clo. Crowt —6G 113
Coleridge Clo. Twy —1L 65
Coleridge Cres. Coln —7F 48
Coleridge La. Pang —1M 59

Coleridge Rd. Ashf —8M **73**
Coleridge Way. W Dray —3M **49**
Coley Av. Read —7F **62**
(in two parts)
Coley Hill. Read —6F **62**
Coley Pk. Rd. Read —6F **62**
Coley Pl. Read —6G **62**
Colham Av. W Dray —9M **25**
Colham Grn. Rd. Uxb —6N **25**
Colham Mill Rd. W Dray —1L **49**
Colham Rd. Uxb —5N **25**
Colham Roundabout. Uxb —7N **25**
Colin Way. Slou —2D **46**
Collaroy Rd. Cold A —4F **80**
College Av. Egh —9C **72**
College Av. M'head —7B **20**
College Av. Slou —2G **46**
College Cres. Col T —1J **119**
College Cres. Wind —8D **46**
College Glen. M'head —7A **20**
College Piece. Mort —4G **106**
College Ride. Bag —9D **114**
College Ride. Camb —2N **119**
College Rise. M'head —7A **20**
College Rd. Brack —6N **91**
College Rd. Cipp —9B **22**
College Rd. Col T —2J **119**
College Rd. M'head —6A **20**
College Rd. Read —6M **63**
College Way. Ashf —8N **73**
Colleton Dri. Twy —9K **41**
Collier Clo. M'head —5C **20**
Colliers Way. Read —5B **62**
Collingwood Wlk. Tile —5J **61**
Collins Clo. Newb —7N **79**
Collins Dri. Herm —6C **56**
Collis St. Read —7H **63**
Colliston Wlk. Calc —9N **61**
Colmworth Clo. Lwr Ear —3N **87**
Colnbrook By-Pass. Coln & W Dray —5D **48**
Colnbrook Ct. Coln —7G **48**
Coln Clo. M'head —6C **20**
Colndale Rd. Coln —8F **48**
Colne Av. W Dray —1K **49**
Colnebridge Clo. Stai —8F **72**
Colne Orchard. Iver —7G **25**
Colne Pk. Caravan Site. W Dray —3K **49**
Colne Reach. Stai —2G **73**
Colne Way. Stai —6C **72**
Coln Trading Est. Coln —7G **48**
Colonial Rd. Slou —1J **47**
Colston Clo. Calc —8L **61**
Colthrop La. That —9L **81**
Coltsfoot Clo. Bfld C —8J **85**
Coltsfoot Dri. W Dray —7M **25**
Columbia Ct. Wokgm —2K **111**
Colwyn Clo. Yat —3A **118**
Colyer Clo. Herm —4F **56**
Colyton Way. Pur T —8K **37**
Combermere Clo. Wind —8D **46**
Combe Rd. Tile —5N **61**
Combe View. Hung —7K **75**
Comet Rd. Stai —4L **73**
Comet Way. Wdly —5F **64**
Comfrey Clo. Wokgm —3C **90**
Commercial Rd. Read —2G **86**
Commonfield La. B'ham —2G **110**
Common Hill. Eng —8A **60**
Common La. Bright & Farnb —2B **30**
Common La. Eton C —4E **46**
Common Rd. Dor —3M **45**
Common Rd. Eton W —3B **46**
Common Rd. Hdly —8H **103**
Common Rd. Slou —3B **48**
Commons Rd. Wokgm —2L **89**
Common, The. W Dray —3K **49**
Communications Rd. Green —5C **102**
Compton Av. Tile —5J **61**
Compton Clo. Brack —8J **91**
Compton Clo. Ear —8B **64**
Compton Clo. Sand —9G **113**
Compton Ct. Burn —7A **22**
Compton Dri. M'head —6L **19**
Compton Ho. Comp —9G **13**
Comsaye Wlk. Brack —7N **91**
Concleve Clo. Aldm —3J **105**
Concorde Clo. Uxb —3M **25**
Concorde Rd. M'head —1A **44**
Concorde Way. Slou —1E **46**
Concorde Way. Wdly —5F **64**
Condor Clo. Tile —1K **61**
Conduit La. Dat —5N **47**
Conegar Ct. Slou —9G **22**
Conifer Clo. Baug —9G **104**
Conifer Crest. Newb —5G **100**
Conifer Dri. Tile —2J **61**
Conifer La. Egh —9D **72**
Conifers, The. Crowt —3E **112**
Conifer Wlk. Wind —6M **45**
Coningham Rd. Read —5J **87**
Coningsby. Brack —6N **91**
Coningsby Clo. M'head —2A **44**
Coningsby La. Fif —8F **44**
Conisboro Av. Cav —8E **38**
Conisboro Way. Cav —8E **38**
Coniston Clo. Mar —5A **4**
Coniston Clo. That —8D **80**
Coniston Clo. Wdly —7E **64**
Coniston Ct. Light —9L **115**
Coniston Ct. Newb —7L **79**
Coniston Cres. Burn —6M **21**
Coniston Dri. Tile —2N **61**
Connaught Av. Ashf —8M **73**
Connaught Clo. Crowt —7D **112**
Connaught Clo. M'head —5B **20**
Connaught Clo. Read —5D **62**
Connaught Clo. Yat —3A **118**
Connaught Rd. Bag —7F **114**
Connaught Rd. Newb —8M **79**
Connaught Rd. Read —5D **62**
Connaught Rd. Slou —1K **47**
Constable Way. Col T —3J **119**
Constitution Rd. Read —4B **62**
Consul Clo. Wdly —7E **64**
Convent Rd. Wind —8C **46**
Conway Dri. That —6E **80**
Conway Rd. Calc —7K **61**
Conway Rd. Tap —7L **21**
Conygree Clo. Lwr Ear —2A **88**
Cookham Clo. Sand —9G **113**
Cookham Dean Bottom. Cook —7G **4**
Cookham Rd. Brack —4J **91**
Cookham Rd. M'head —4B **20**
Coombe Ct. That —8H **81**
Coombe Hill. Farnb —6M **9**
Coombe Hill Ct. Wind —1N **69**
Coombe La. Asc —6M **93**
Coombe Pine. Brack —8A **92**
Coombe Rd. Comp —3J **33**
Coombe Rd. Yat —2A **118**
Coombesbury La. Stcks —3A **78**
Coombes La. Wokgm —7F **88**
Coombe, The. Streat —8H **15**
Cooper Clo. Read —4J **87**
Cooper Rd. Hen T —3C **16**
Cooper Rd. W'sham —6N **115**
Coopers Clo. Stai —9F **72**
Coopers Cres. That —7F **80**
Coopers Hill La. Egh —7L **71**
(in three parts)
Coopers Pightle. Kid E —2D **38**
Coopers Row. Iver —5D **24**
Cooper Way. Slou —2D **46**
Cope Hall La. Newb —3F **100**
Copenhagen Clo. Read —4J **87**
Copenhagen Wlk. Crowt —6F **112**
Copperage Rd. Farnb —5C **10**
Copper Beech Clo. Wind —7N **45**
Copperdale Clo. Ear —9M **63**
Copperfield Av. Owl —8J **113**
Copperfield Av. Uxb —6N **25**
Coppermill Rd. Wray —3B **72**
Coppice Clo. Baug —9F **104**
Coppice Clo. Newb —2M **101**
Coppice Dri. Wray —4M **71**
Coppice Gdns. Crowt —5D **112**
Coppice Gdns. Yat —4A **118**
Coppice Grn. Brack —2K **91**
(in two parts)
Coppice Rd. Wdly —8D **64**
Coppice, The. W Dray —7M **25**
Coppidbeech La. Brack —5F **90**
Coppins La. Iver —6G **24**
Copse Av. Cav —1K **63**
Copse Barnhill La. Wokgm —5E **88**
Copse Clo. Mar —5A **4**
Copse Clo. Tile —1L **61**
Copse Clo. Up Buck —3L **81**
Copse Clo. W Dray —2L **49**
Copse Dri. Wokgm —4M **89**
Copse La. Eve —9M **111**
Copse Mead. Wdly —3E **64**
Copse, The. Tadl —9J **105**
Copse, The. Warg —2K **41**
Copse Way. Wokgm —3K **111**
Copse Wood. Iver —2E **24**
Copthorn Clo. M'head —1L **43**
Copthorne Chase. Ashf —8N **73**
Copthorne Dri. Light —9L **115**
Corbett Gdns. Wdly —5D **64**
Corbridge Rd. Read —8J **63**
Corby Clo. Egh —1L **95**
Corby Clo. Wdly —3F **64**
Corby Dri. Egh —1L **95**
Cordelia Croft. Warf —3B **92**
Cordelia Gdns. Stai —4M **73**
Cordelia Rd. Stai —4M **73**
Corderoy Clo. That —9J **81**
Cordwallis Pk. M'head —6B **20**
Cordwallis Rd. M'head —6B **20**
Cordwallis St. M'head —6B **20**
Cores End Rd. Bour —4M **5**
Corey Ho. Brack —4M **91**
Corfe Gdns. Slou —8C **22**
Corfe M. Cav —9L **39**
Corfe Pl. M'head —7N **19**
Corfield Clo. Finch —7K **111**
Coriander Way. Ear —2M **87**
Corinne Clo. Read —2H **87**
Corinthian Way. Stanw —4L **73**
Cormorant Pl. Col T —2J **119**
Cornbunting Clo. Col T —2H **119**
Corn Croft. Warf —2B **92**
Cornfield. Yat —5A **118**
Cornfield Clo. Uxb —3L **25**
Cornfield Grn. Wokgm —3L **89**
Cornfield Rd. Wdly —4F **64**
Cornflower Clo. Wokgm —4J **89**
Cornwall Av. Slou —5E **22**
Cornwall Clo. Eton W —4A **46**
Cornwall Clo. M'head —4B **20**
Cornwall Clo. Tile —9J **37**
Cornwall Clo. Warf —1C **92**
Cornwall Clo. Wokgm —5J **89**
Cornwall Rd. Uxb —1L **25**
Cornwall Way. Stai —9F **72**
Cornwell Rd. Old Win —3J **71**
Cornwood Gdns. Read —9J **63**
Coronation Av. G Grn —6N **23**
Coronation Av. Wind —8J **47**
Coronation Cotts. Hurst —8J **65**
Coronation Rd. Asc —9K **93**
Coronation Rd. L Grn —9F **18**
Coronation Rd. Yat —2C **118**
Coronation Sq. Read —8B **62**
Coronation Sq. Wokgm —4B **90**
Corporation Cottage. Newb —7K **79**
Corrie Gdns. Vir W —9L **95**
Corsair Clo. Stai —4L **73**
Corsair Rd. Stai —4M **73**
Corsham Rd. Calc —9N **61**
Corsham Way. Crowt —5F **112**
Corwen Rd. Tile —4L **61**
Costa Clo. Newb —6H **79**
Cotswold Clo. Farn —9J **119**
Cotswold Clo. M'head —8E **20**
Cotswold Clo. Slou —2E **46**
Cotswold Clo. Stai —9H **73**
Cotswold Clo. Uxb —2K **25**
Cotswold Rd. Sand —9D **112**
Cotswold Way. Tile —2J **61**
Cottage La. Ping —1C **86**
Cotterell Clo. Brack —2M **91**
Cotterell Gdns. Twy —1L **65**
Cottesbrooke Clo. Coln —7E **48**
Cottesmore. Brack —9L **91**
Cottesmore Rd. Wdly —6C **64**
Coulson Way. Burn —6L **21**
County La. Warf —1A **92**
Course Rd. Asc —5K **93**
Court Clo. M'head —3F **44**
Court Cres. Slou —7F **22**
Court Dri. M'head —3F **20**
Court Dri. Uxb —2N **25**
Courtenay Dri. Emm G —6H **39**
Courtfield Dri. M'head —8N **19**
Court Gdns. Camb —4N **119**
Courthouse Rd. M'head —7N **19**
Courtlands. M'head —8C **20**
Courtlands Av. Slou —3M **47**
Courtlands Hill. Pang —9D **36**
Courtlands Rd. Newb —1M **101**
Court La. Burn —4N **21**
Court La. Dor —2L **45**
Court La. Iver —9H **25**
(in two parts)
Courtney Rd. Houn —9N **49**
Court Rd. M'head —4F **20**
Courts Rd. Ear —8A **64**
Court, The. That —7G **81**
Courtyards, The. Langl —1B **48**
Courtyard, The. Thea —9F **60**
Courtyard, The. Wokgm —6A **90**
Cousins Clo. W Dray —8M **25**
Coventry Rd. Read —4L **63**
Coverdale Way. Slou —5A **22**
Covert La. Brack —6N **91**
Covert, The. Asc —9L **93**
Covert, The. Farn —9J **119**
Covey Clo. Farn —9L **119**
Cow La. E Ils —7B **12**
Cow La. Moul —4G **15**
Cow La. Read —2E **62**
(in two parts)
Cowley Bus. Pk. Cow —4K **25**
Cowley Cres. Uxb —6K **25**
Cowley Mill Rd. Uxb —3J **25**
Cowley Mill Trading Est. Uxb —3J **25**
Cowley Rd. Uxb —3K **25**
Coworth Clo. Asc —7D **94**
Coworth Pk. S'hill —6E **94**
Coworth Rd. Asc —7C **94**
Cowper Rd. Slou —5C **22**
Cowper Way. Read —8D **62**
Cowslade. Speen —6H **79**
Cowslip Clo. Tile —6J **61**
Cowslip Clo. Uxb —1M **25**
Cowslip Cres. That —6H **81**
Coxborrow Clo. Cook —8J **5**
Coxeter Rd. Newb —7J **79**
Cox Grn. Col T —3H **119**
Cox Grn. La. M'head —2M **43**
Cox Grn. Rd. M'head —1N **43**
Cox's La. Midg —9M **81**
Cox's La. Shalb —7E **96**
Crabtree Clo. Herm —6C **56**
Crabtree La. Cur —7B **56**
Crabtree Rd. Camb —7M **119**
Cradock Rd. Read —8G **63**
Craig Av. Read —4B **62**
Crail Clo. Wokgm —8M **89**
Crake Pl. Col T —1H **119**
Cranberry Wlk. B'water —6K **119**
Cranborne Gdns. Read —2A **62**
Cranbourne Av. Calc —8K **61**
Cranbourne Av. Wind —8B **46**
Cranbourne Clo. Slou —9E **22**
Cranbourne Cotts. Wind —7L **69**
Cranbourne Hall Cotts. Wind —5L **69**
Cranbourne Rd. Slou —9E **22**
Cranbrook Dri. M'head —5M **19**
Cranbury Rd. Read —5D **62**
Crane Ct. Col T —1H **119**
Crane Wharf. Read —5H **63**
Cranford Av. Stai —4M **73**
Cranford Clo. Hurst —4L **65**
Cranford Clo. Stai —4M **73**
Cranford Pk. Dri. Yat —3B **118**
Cranmer Clo. Tile —1J **61**
Craufurd Ct. M'head —6B **20**
Craufurd Rise. M'head —6B **20**
Craven Clo. Kint —1G **99**
Craven Dene. Newb —7M **79**
Craven Rd. Ink —3N **97**
Craven Rd. Newb —9J **79**
Craven Rd. Read —6K **63**
Craven Way. Kint —9G **77**
Crawford Clo. Ear —9A **64**
Crawford Gdns. Camb —4M **119**
Crawford Pl. Newb —8K **79**
Crawley Chase. Wink R —1E **92**
Crawshay Dri. Emm G —6H **39**
Crayle St. Slou —4C **22**
Craysleaze. Kid E —2D **38**
Crecy Clo. Wokgm —5K **89**
Creden Clo. M'head —6A **20**
Crediton Clo. Wdly —6F **64**
Cree's Meadow. W'sham —7M **115**
Creighton Ct. Read —8K **63**
Cremyll Rd. Read —3F **62**
Crendon Ct. Cav —2G **63**
Crescent Dri. M'head —7B **20**
Crescent Ho. Wdly —7D **64**
Crescent Rd. Read —6L **63**
Crescent Rd. Tile —3L **61**
Crescent Rd. Wokgm —6A **90**
Crescent, The. Ashf —9N **73**
Crescent, The. B'water —5H **119**
Crescent, The. Brack —6N **91**
Crescent, The. Ear —8B **64**
Crescent, The. Egh —1N **95**
Crescent, The. Kint —9F **76**
Crescent, The. Lwr P —7L **83**
Crescent, The. M'head —7B **20**
Crescent, The. Mort —4H **107**
Crescent, The. S'lake —1G **40**
Crescent, The. Slou —1G **46**
Crescent, The. Thea —8F **60**
Cressex Clo. Binf —1G **91**
Cressida Chase. Warf —3B **92**
Cressingham Rd. Read —9J **63**
Cressington Pl. Bour —3L **5**
Cress Rd. Slou —1D **46**
Cresswell Rd. Newb —7A **80**
Cresswells Mead. M'head —4E **44**
Crest Clo. Rusc —7K **41**
Creswell Clo. Read —5J **87**
Cricketers La. Warf —9D **68**
Cricketers La. W'sham —5N **115**
Cricket Field Gro. Crowt —6H **113**
Cricket Field Rd. Uxb —2L **25**
Cricketfield Rd. W Dray —3K **49**
Cricket Hill. Finch —8L **111**
Cricket Hill. Yat —6C **118**
Cricket Hill La. Yat —6B **118**
Crimp Hill. Old Win & Egh —4H **71**
Crisp Gdns. Binf —2J **91**
Crispin Clo. Cav —8D **38**
Crisp Rd. Hen T —3B **16**
Crocker Clo. Asc —3J **93**
Crockford Pl. Binf —2K **91**
Crockhamwell Rd. Wdly —6D **64**
Crocus Way. Wokgm —4J **89**
Croft Clo. Uxb —1N **25**
Croft Clo. Wokgm —9M **89**
Crofters Clo. Sand —1E **118**
Crofters, The. Old Win —3J **71**
Crofthill Rd. Slou —5D **22**
Croft La. Newb —7J **79**
Croft La. Yat —2A **118**
Crofton Clo. Brack —7B **92**
Croft Rd. Gor —8L **15**
Croft Rd. Hung —5K **75**
Croft Rd. Mort —4G **107**
Croft Rd. Newb —2K **101**
Croft Rd. Spen W —9J **87**
Croft Rd. Wokgm —9M **89**
Croft, The. Brack —2M **91**
Croft, The. Kint —9F **76**
Croft, The. M'head —9N **19**
Croft, The. Mar —4E **4**
Croft, The. Wokgm —6B **90**
Croft, The. Yat —2B **118**
Cromer Clo. Tile —3K **61**
Cromer Rd. W. Houn —9N **49**
Cromwell Clo. Hen T —6C **16**
Cromwell Dri. Slou —7G **23**
Cromwell Gdns. Mar —5C **4**
Cromwell Pl. Newb —8L **79**
Cromwell Rd. Asc —6L **93**
Cromwell Rd. Camb —2N **119**
Cromwell Rd. Cav —2H **63**
Cromwell Rd. Hen T —6D **16**
Cromwell Rd. M'head —7A **20**
Cromwell Rd. Mar —5C **4**
Cromwell Rd. Newb —6N **79**
Cromwell Ter. Speen —6H **79**
Crondall End. Yat —2A **118**
Crondell Ct. Camb —5M **119**
Cropper Clo. That —8K **81**
Crosfields Clo. Read —3J **87**
Cross Fell. Brack —6L **91**
Cross Gates Clo. Brack —5C **92**
Cross Keys Rd. S Sto —2L **15**
Crossland Rd. Read —5H **63**
Cross La. Ashmw —9N **117**
Cross La. Graz —2B **108**
Cross Oak. Wind —8C **46**
Cross Rd. Asc —9B **94**
Cross Rd. Uxb —1K **25**
Cross St. Read —4H **63**
Cross St. Uxb —1K **25**
Cross St. Wokgm —5A **90**
Crossway. Brack —4N **91**
Crossways. Egh —9E **72**
Crossways. Wdly —7D **64**
Crossway, The. Uxb —3N **25**
Crosthwaite Way. Slou —6N **21**
Crouch La. Wink —4H **69**
Crowfield Dri. That —8E **80**
Crowle Rd. Lamb —3G **27**
Crown Acre Clo. That —8F **80**
Crown Ct. That —8F **80**
Crown La. Farn R —3C **22**
Crown La. M'head —7D **20**
Crown La. Thea —9F **60**
Crown La. Vir W —8M **95**
Crown Mead. That —8F **80**
Crown Meadow. Coln —6C **48**
Crown Pl. Owl —9J **113**
Crown Pl. Read —6J **63**
Crown Rd. Mar —5B **4**
Crown Rd. Vir W —8L **95**
Crown Row. Brack —8A **92**
Crown St. Egh —9B **72**
Crown St. Read —6H **63**
Crown Wlk. Uxb —1K **25**
Crown Way. W Dray —9N **25**
Crow Piece La. Farn R —1B **22**
Crowsley Rd. S'lake —1F **40**
Crowsley Way. Son C —1E **38**
Crowthorne Rd. Brack —7L **91**
Crowthorne Rd. Crowt & Brack —4H **113**
Crowthorne Rd. Sand —1E **118**
Crowthorne Rd. N. Brack —5M **91**
Croxley Rise. M'head —8A **20**
Cruch La. Tap —3B **68**
Cruikshank Lea. Col T —3J **119**
Crummock Clo. Slou —7M **21**
Crutchley Rd. Wokgm —4B **90**
Culford Clo. Lwr Ear —1C **88**
Culham Dri. M'head —4B **20**
Culham Ho. Brack —6B **92**
Cullen Clo. Yat —4A **118**
Cullerns Pas. M'head —8C **20**
Culley Way. M'head —1L **43**
Culloden Way. Wokgm —5K **89**
Culvercroft. Binf —2J **91**
Culver La. Ear —5N **63**
Culver Rd. Newb —2K **101**
Culver Rd. Owl —9H **113**
Culver Rd. Read —6M **63**
Culvert La. Uxb —3J **25**
Cumberland Av. Slou —5E **22**
Cumberland Dri. Brack —3A **92**
Cumberland Rd. Ashf —7L **73**
Cumberland Rd. Read —4K **63**
Cumberland St. Stai —9E **72**
Cumberland Way. Wokgm —5J **89**
Cumbrae Clo. Slou —9J **23**
Cumbria Clo. M'head —1N **43**
Cumbrian Way. Uxb —1L **25**
Cumnor Way. Brack —6B **92**
Cunworth Ct. Brack —8K **91**
Curlew Clo. That —8F **80**
Curlew Dri. Tile —6K **61**
Curling Way. Newb —7N **79**
Curls La. M'head —1B **44**
Curls Rd. M'head —1A **44**
Curl Way. Wokgm —6M **89**
Curly Bri. Clo. Farn —9K **119**
Curnock Ct. Newb —1J **101**
Curran Clo. Uxb —5K **25**
Curridge Grn. Cur —8B **56**
Curridge Piece. Cur —7C **56**
Curridge Rd. Cur —9L **55**
Curtis Rd. Calc —7K **61**
Curzon Mall. Slou —1H **47**
Curzon St. Read —4D **62**
Cusden Wlk. Read —5G 62
(off Castle St.)
Cutbush Clo. Lwr Ear —3A **88**
Cutbush La. Lwr Ear —3N **87**
Cutbush La. Shin —5L **87**
Cutting Hill. Hung —7F **96**
Cuttings, The. Hamp N —8J **33**
Cwmcarn. Cav —7F **38**
Cygnet Clo. That —8E **80**
Cygnet Way. Hung —4K **75**
Cypress Clo. Wokgm —2M **111**
Cypress Ho. Langl —4C **48**
Cypress Rd. Wdly —6F **64**
Cypress Wlk. Egh —1K **95**
Cypress Way. B'water —4F **118**
Cyril Vokins Rd. Newb —9B **80**
Dacre Av. Cav —9L **39**
Dagmar Rd. Wind —8F **46**
Dagnall Cres. Uxb —6K **25**
Dalby Cres. Green —2M **101**
Dalcross. Brack —8B **92**
Dale Clo. Asc —7C **94**
Dale Ct. Chalv —1E **46**
Dale Gdns. Sand —1E **118**
Daleham Av. Egh —9B **72**
Dale Lodge Rd. Asc —7C **94**
Dale Rd. Read —7H **63**
Dalley Ct. Col T —2H **119**
Dalton Clo. Tile —4M **61**
Damer Gdns. Hen T —6D **16**
Danbridge Dri. Bour —4N **5**
Dandridge Clo. Slou —3M **47**
Danehill. Lwr Ear —3A **88**
Danes Gdns. Cook —9K **5**
Daniel's La. Hung —5G **96**
Danvers Clo. That —9G **81**
Danywern Dri. Winn —1H **89**
Darby Grn. La. B'water —4F **118**
Darby Grn. Rd. B'water —4E **118**
Darell Rd. Cav —1F **62**
Dark Dale. Asc —7D **92**
Darkhole Ride. Wind —1K **69**
Dark La. Brad —5L **59**
Dark La. E Ils —9K **11**
Dark La. Hung —5N **75**
Dark La. Pang —4N **59**
Dark La. Tile —2J **61**
Dark La. W'sham —6L **115**
Darleydale Clo. Owl —8H **113**
Darling's La. M'head —6J **19**
Darrel Clo. Langl —3A **48**
Darrell Charles Ct. Uxb —1M **25**
Dart Clo. Finch —4L **111**
Dart Clo. Slou —5C **48**
Dart Clo. That —8D **80**
Dartington Av. Wdly —8C **64**
Dartington Clo. Tile —4N **61**
Dartmouth Clo. Brack —5B **92**
Dartmouth Ter. Read —6H **63**
Darvills La. Read —3D **66**
Darvill's La. Slou —1F **46**
Darwall Dri. Asc —4G **93**
Darwin Clo. Read —2G **87**
Darwin Rd. Slou —1A **48**
Dashwood Clo. Brack —3A **92**
Dashwood Clo. Slou —3L **47**
Datchet Pl. Dat —7K **47**
Datchet Rd. Hort —9A **48**
Datchet Rd. Old Win —1J **71**
Datchet Rd. Slou —3H **47**
Datchet Rd. Wind —6F **46**
Dauntless Rd. Bfld C —7J **85**
Davenport Rd. Brack —3B **92**
Daventry Clo. Coln —7G **48**
Daventry Ct. Brack —3M **91**
David Smith Ct. Calc —7N **61**
Davis Clo. Mar —6C **4**
Davis Clo. Winn —2G **89**
Davis Gdns. Col T —2J **119**
Davis St. Hurst —9H **65**
Davis Way. Hurst —8J **65**
Davy Clo. Wokgm —6A **90**
Dawes E. Rd. Burn —5M **21**
Dawes Moor Clo. Slou —7L **23**
Dawe's Rd. Uxb —3M **25**
Dawley Ride. Coln —7F **48**
Dawlish Rd. Read —1J **87**
Dawnay Clo. Asc —3J **93**
Dawnay Rd. Camb —1M **119**
Dawn Redwood Clo. Hort —9B **48**
Dawson Clo. Wind —8C **46**
Deacon Clo. Wokgm —3A **90**
Deaconfield. S Sto —3L **15**
Deacon's La. Herm —5F **56**
Deacon Way. Tile —2A **62**
Deadman's La. Gor H —2J **37**
Deadmans La. Green —4M **101**
Deadman's La. Thea —8E **60**
Deadmoor La. Newt —8J **101**
Deal Av. Slou —7B **22**
Dean Clo. Uxb —1N **25**
Dean Clo. Wind —9N **45**
Deanfield Av. Hen T —5C **16**
Deanfield Clo. Mar —4B **4**
Deanfield Rd. Hen T —5B **16**
Dean Gro. Wokgm —4A **90**
Dean La. Cook —7F **4**
Dean Pde. Camb —9C **114**
Deans Clo. Stoke P —2K **23**
Deans Ct. W'sham —7N **115**
Deansgate. Brack —9M **91**
Deansgate Rd. Read —6H **63**
Dean St. Mar —5B **4**
Deanswood Rd. Tadl —9J **105**
Deanwood Ho. Stcks —6F **78**
De Beauvoir Rd. Read —5L **63**
De Bohun Rd. Read —3H **63**
Decies Way. Stoke P —2J **23**
Dedmere Ct. Mar —5D **4**
Dedmere Rise. Mar —5C **4**
Dedmere Rd. Mar —5C **4**
Dedworth Dri. Wind —7B **46**
Dedworth Rd. Wind —8M **45**
Deena Clo. Slou —8A **22**
Deepdale. Brack —6L **91**

Deepdene Clo. Read —5E 62
Deepfield. Dat —6K 47
Deepfield Rd. Brack —4A 92
Deerhurst Av. Winn —1H 89
Deerhurst Clo. Calc —8M 61
Dee Rd. Tile —6N 61
Deer Rock Hill. Brack —8N 91
Deerswood. M'head —5D 20
Defford Clo. Wokgm —2L 89
De Havilland Way. Stai —3M 73
Delafield Dri. Calc —8K 61
Delaford Clo. Iver —7H 25
Delamere Rd. Ear —4A 64
Delane Dri. Winn —2G 88
Delaney Clo. Tile —4N 61
Delft Clo. Tile —4N 61
Deller St. Binf —2K 91
Dellfield Cres. Uxb —5L 25
Dell Rd. Crowt —7M 111
Dell Rd. Finch —7M 111
Dell Rd. Tile —2K 61
Dell Rd. W Dray —3N 49
Dell, The. M'head —2K 43
Dell, The. Read —5J 63
Dell, The. Yat —4A 118
Delph, The. Lwr Ear —1D 88
De Montfort Cres. Hung —7J 75
De Montfort Rd. Read —3G 63
De Montfort Rd. Speen —6J 79
Dempsey Ho. Read —5N 61
Denbridge Ind. Est. Uxb —1K 25
Denbury Gdns. Read —3J 87
Denby Way. Tile —3N 61
Dencliffe. Ashf —9N 73
Dene Clo. Brack —2N 91
Dene Clo. Ear —9N 63
Dene Way. Don —6K 79
Denford La. Hung —3A 76
Denham Clo. M'head —8N 19
Denham Dri. Yat —4B 118
Denham Gro. Brack —8N 91
Denham Rd. Egh —8B 72
Denham Rd. Iver —2E 24
Denhose Clo. Lwr Ear —2N 87
Denley Sq. Uxb —1K 25
Denly Way. Light —9M 115
Denmark Av. Wdly —3F 64
Denmark Rd. Newb —9M 79
Denmark Rd. Read —5K 63
Denmark St. M'head —6B 20
Denmark St. Wokgm —6A 90
Denmead Ct. Brack —8B 92
Dennisford Rd. Comp —2B 32
Dennisford Rd. E Ils —9D 12
Dennis Way. Slou —8N 21
Denny Rd. Slou —3A 48
Denton Clo. That —9F 80
Denton Rd. Wokgm —5A 90
Depot Rd. M'head —8C 20
Derby Clo. Lamb —3G 26
Derby Rd. Cav —1H 63
Derby Rd. Newb —1K 101
Derby Rd. Uxb —3K 25
Derby St. Read —4F 62
Derek Horn Ct. Camb —3M 119
Derek Rd. M'head —6F 20
Deridene Clo. Stai —3M 73
De Ros Pl. Egh —9B 72
Derrick Clo. Calc —8K 61
Derry Rd. Farn —9K 119
Derwent Av. Tile —2M 61
Derwent Clo. Wokgm —5K 89
Derwent Dri. M'head —6A 20
Derwent Dri. Slou —6M 21
Derwent Rd. Light —9L 115
Derwent Rd. That —8D 80
Desborough Cres. M'head —9N 19
Desford Ct. Ashf —6N 73
Desford Way. Ashf —6N 73
Devenish Clo. S'hill —8N 93
Devenish La. Asc —1N 115
Devenish Rd. Asc —8M 93
Devereux Rd. Wind —8F 46
Deveron Dri. Tile —4A 62
Devil's Highway, The. Crowt —5C 112
De Vitre Grn. Wokgm —4D 90
Devitt Clo. Read —2M 87
Devon Av. Slou —7E 22
Devon Chase. Warf —1B 92
Devon Clo. Col T —2H 119
Devon Clo. Wokgm —5K 89
Devon Dri. Cav —9L 39
Devonshire Clo. Farn R —3D 22
Devonshire Gdns. Tile —1J 61
Devonshire Grn. Farn R —3D 22
Devonshire Pk. Read —1L 87
Devon Way. Uxb —3N 25
Dewberry Clo. That —7J 81
Dhoon Rise. M'head —8C 20
Diamedes Av. Stai —4L 73
Diamond Rd. Slou —1J 47
Diamond Way. Wokgm —4K 89
Diana Clo. G Grn —7N 23
Dianthus Pl. Wink R —1E 92
Dickens Ct. Wokgm —5N 89
Dickens Wlk. Newb —2L 101
Dickens Way. Yat —4A 118
Dieppe Clo. Wokgm —5K 89
Digby Rd. Newb —7J 79
Dines Way. Herm —5F 56
Disraeli Ct. Coln —5C 48
Ditchfield La. Wokgm —2K 111
Ditchling. Brack —9L 91
Ditton Pk. Rd. Slou —5N 47
Ditton Rd. Dat —7M 47
Ditton Rd. Langl —4A 48
Dittons, The. Finch —4L 111
Doctors La. Herm —5D 56
Doddington Clo. Lwr Ear —2B 88
Doddsfield Rd. Slou —4C 22
Dodsells Well. Wokgm —2L 111
Dogkennel La. S Faw —9H 9
Dog La. Ash'd —7C 34
Doles Hill. B'ham —8J 89
Doles La. Wokgm —7K 89
Dolman Rd. Newb —6L 79
Dolphin Clo. Aldm —3H 105
Dolphin Clo. Winn —2H 89
Dolphin Ct. Brack —6N 91
Dolphin Ct. Slou —1K 47
Dolphin Ct. Stai —7H 73
Dolphin Ct. N. Stai —7H 73
Dolphin Rd. Slou —1K 47
Doman Rd. Camb —5K 119
Donaldson Way. Wdly —4F 64
Doncastle Rd. Brack —5J 91
Don Clo. Tile —4A 62
Donegal Clo. Cav —1J 63
Donkey La. W Dray —3K 49
Donkin Hill. Cav —1J 63
Donnington Clo. Camb —5M 119
Donnington Gdns. Read —6K 63
Donnington Lodge. Don —4K 79
Donnington Pl. Winn —1J 89
Donnington Rd. Read —5K 63
Donnington Sq. Newb —6K 79
Donnybrook. Brack —9L 91
Dorcas Ct. Camb —6N 119
Dorchester Clo. M'head —5M 19
Dorchester Ct. Read —6C 62
Dorchester Ct. Stai —8H 73
Doreen Clo. Farn —9J 119
Dorian Dri. Asc —3A 94
Dorking Way. Calc —8H 61
Dormer Clo. Crowt —5E 112
Dormer Clo. Newb —4J 101
Dornels. Slou —7L 23
Dorney Reach Rd. Dor R —2J 45
Dorney Wood Rd. Burn —2M 21
Dorothy St. Read —6H 63
Dorset Rd. Ashf —7L 73
Dorset Rd. Wind —7E 46
Dorset St. Read —4C 62
Dorset Vale. Warf —1B 92
Dorset Way. Uxb —3N 25
Dorset Way. Wokgm —5K 89
Doublet Clo. That —8D 80
Douglas Ct. Ear —9N 63
Douglas Grange. Hurst —8J 65
Douglas La. Wray —2A 72
Douglas Ride. Wool H —9C 100
Douglas Rd. Cav —2K 63
Douglas Rd. Slou —6F 22
Douglas Rd. Stai —3L 73
Douro Clo. Baug —9F 104
Dove Clo. Lwr Ear —3M 87
Dovecote Rd. Read —4H 87
Dovedale Clo. Cav —1F 62
Dovedale Clo. Owl —8H 113
Dove Ho. Cres. Slou —4A 22
Dover Rd. Slou —7B 22
Dover St. Read —6G 62
Doveton Way. Newb —7M 79
Dowding Clo. Wdly —5F 64
Dowding Ct. Crowt —4G 112
Dowding Rd. Uxb —1N 25
Dower Pk. Wind —1A 70
Downend La. Chvly —1M 55
Downfield La. Wal L & White —7F 42
Downfield Rd. Wal L —9E 42
Downham Ct. Read —2L 87
Downing Path. Slou —5A 22
Downing Rd. Tile —4L 61
Downlands. E Gar —7B 28
Downmill Rd. Brack —4K 91
Down Pl. Water —5K 45
Downs Clo. E'bury —6M 27
Downshire. Gt Shef —9G 28
Downshire Sq. Read —6E 62
Downshire Way. Brack —4L 91
(in two parts)
Downside. Brack —5M 91
Downs La. Blew —1C 12
Downs Rd. Comp —1K 33
Downs Rd. Slou —1M 47
Downs Way. Tile —2K 61
Doyle Gdns. Yat —5A 118
Drain Hill. Lamb —1G 26
(in two parts)
Drake Av. Slou —3M 47
Drake Av. Stai —9G 73
Drake Clo. Brack —7M 91
Drake Clo. Wokgm —3K 111
Draper Clo. That —9G 81
Drawback Hill. Hen T —7C 16
Draycott. Brack —7B 92
Drayhorse Dri. Bag —8H 115
Drayton Clo. Brack —4A 92
Drayton Gdns. W Dray —1M 49
Drayton Rd. Read —4B 62
Dresden Way. Tile —3N 61
Drewett Clo. Read —5J 87
Drift Hill. Ash'd —7F 34
Drift Rd. M'head & Wink —1K 67
Drift Rd. Wink —4K 69
Drift Way. Coln —7D 48
Driftway Clo. Lwr Ear —2C 88
Drive, The. Bour —3K 5
Drive, The. Dat —7K 47
Drive, The. Ear —5N 63
Drive, The. Newb —2J 101
Drive, The. Slou —1N 47
Drive, The. Vir W —7N 95
Drive, The. Wray —2M 71
Droitwich Clo. Brack —5A 92
Drome Path. Winn —9F 64
Dropmore Rd. Burn —2M 21
Drove La. Cold A —1E 80
Drovers Way. Brack —5C 92
Drovers Way. Wdly —7D 64
Drove, The. Hdly —9L 103
Drove, The. Hung —6N 97
Drove, The. Sil —8E 106
Druce Way. That —8G 81
Drummond Clo. Brack —3C 92
Drury La. Mort —5G 107
Dry Arch Rd. Asc —8B 94
Dryden. Brack —9L 91
Dryden Clo. That —6G 80
Dryland Ho. Read —5N 61
Duchess Clo. Whit T —6E 36
Dudley Clo. Tile —3M 61
Dudley Ct. Slou —2J 47
Dudley M. Tile —2M 61
Dudley Rd. Ashf —8N 73
Duffield La. Stoke P —1H 23
Duffield Pk. Stoke P —4J 23
Duffield Rd. Son & Wdly —2D 64
Dugdale Ho. Egh —9D 72
(off Pooley Grn. Rd.)
Duke of Cornwall Av. Camb —9A 114
Dukesbridge Ct. Read —5H 63
(off Duke St.)
Dukes Covert. Bag —4H 115
Dukeshill Rd. Brack —3M 91
Dukes La. Asc —2C 94
Dukes Meadow Ind. Est. Bour —4M 5
Duke's Ride. Crowt —6C 112
Dukes Ride. Sil —9B 106
Duke St. Hen T —4D 16
Duke St. Read —5H 63
Duke St. Wind —6E 46
Dukes Wood. Crowt —5F 112
(in two parts)
Dulnan Clo. Tile —4A 62
Dulverton Gdns. Read —1J 87
Dumas Clo. Yat —4A 118
Dumbarton Way. Cav —8L 39
Dunaways Clo. Ear —9C 64
Dunbar Clo. Slou —7J 23
Dunbar Dri. Wdly —6F 64
Duncan Dri. Wokgm —6B 90
Duncan Gdns. Pur T —9K 37
Duncannon Cres. Wind —9N 45
Duncan Rd. Wdly —6D 64
Duncroft. Wind —9B 46
Dundas Clo. Brack —6M 91
Dundee Rd. Slou —7B 22
Dundela Clo. Wdly —6D 64
Dunford Pl. Brack —2J 91
Dungells Farm Clo. Yat —5B 118
Dungells La. Yat —5A 118
Dungrove Hill. M'head —3G 19
Dunholme Clo. Lwr Ear —1D 88
Dunholme End. M'head —2A 44
Dunkirk Clo. Wokgm —5K 89
Dunluce Gdns. Pang —8F 36
Dunn Cres. Kint —1G 98
Dunnock Way. Warg —2K 41
Dunoon Clo. Calc —8M 61
Dunromyn Caravan Pk. Bray —5H 45
Dunsden Way. Bin H —4N 39
Dunsfold Rd. Tile —5N 61
Dunstall Clo. Tile —4L 61
Dunstan Rd. That —7H 81
Dunster Clo. Cav —7J 39
Dunster Gdns. Slou —8C 22
Dunt Av. Hurst —8K 65
Dunt La. Hurst —7J 65
Dunwood Ct. M'head —9N 19
Durand Rd. Ear —2N 87
Durham Av. Slou —7C 22
Durham Clo. Read —3J 87
Durham Clo. Wokgm —5K 89
Durham Rd. Owl —8J 113
Durley Mead. Brack —7C 92
Dusseldorf Way. Read —5G 62
Dutch Barn Clo. Stai —3L 73
Dutch Elm Av. Wind —6H 47
Dutton Way. Iver —7F 24
Duval Pl. Bag —7H 115
Dwyer Rd. Read —8N 61
Dyson Clo. Wind —9D 46
Dysons Clo. Newb —8J 79
Dysonswood La. Tok G —5E 38

Eagle Clo. Crowt —3E 112
Eaglehurst Cotts. Binf —9G 67
Eagles Nest. Sand —9E 112
Earleydene. Asc —1L 115
Earley Hill Rd. Read —7N 63
Earley Pl. Read —5H 63
Earlsfield. Holyp —3F 44
Earlsfield Clo. Cav —9L 39
Earlswood. Brack —9M 91
Easington Dri. Lwr Ear —1D 88
Eastbourne Rd. Slou —7B 22
East Bri. Slou —9L 23
E. Burnham La. Farn R —2C 22
Eastbury Av. Tile —4J 61
Eastbury Ct. Brack —2K 91
Eastbury Pk. Winn —1J 89
Eastbury Shute. Hung —2L 51
Eastcourt Av. Ear —6N 63
East Cres. Wind —7B 46
Eastcroft. Slou —5D 22
East Dri. Calc —7M 61
East Dri. Stoke P —4G 22
East Dri. Vir W —9K 95
Eastern Av. Read —5L 63
Eastern Ct. Read —6L 63
Eastern Dri. Bour —3N 5
Eastern La. Crowt —6K 113
Eastern Rd. Brack —4A 92
Eastfield Clo. Slou —2J 47
Eastfield La. Whit T —6E 36
Eastfield Rd. Burn —6K 21
East Grn. B'water —5G 118
Easthampstead Rd. Brack —4L 91
Easthampstead Rd. Wokgm —5B 90
Eastheath Av. Wokgm —7N 89
Eastheath Gdns. Wokgm —8N 89
East La. Chvly —3M 55
East La. Rusc —7M 41
Eastlyn Rd. Pam H —9N 105
East Mall. Stai —8G 72
Easton Hill. E'ton —8N 53
East Ridge. Bour —3M 5
East Rd. M'head —7B 20
East Rd. W Dray —3N 49
E. Stratton Clo. Brack —7C 92
East St. Read —5H 63
E. View Clo. Warg —3K 41
E. View Rd. Warg —3K 41
Eastwood Ct. Wdly —8D 64
Eastwood Rd. Wdly —8D 64
Eaton Ct. Read —5F 62
(off Oxford Rd.)
Eaton Pl. Read —5F 62
Eaton Rd. Camb —5M 119
Ebborne Sq. Lwr Ear —2B 88
Ebsworth Clo. M'head —3F 20
Eccles Clo. Cav —2J 63
Eddington Hill. Edd —4L 75
Eddington Rd. Brack —8J 91
Eddystone Wlk. Stai —4M 73
Eden Clo. Slou —4B 48
Edenhall Clo. Tile —1L 61
Edenham Clo. Lwr Ear —2D 88
Edenham Cres. Read —7E 62
Eden Way. Winn —2G 89
Edgar Milward Clo. Tile —3A 62
Edgar Rd. W Dray —8M 25
Edgar Wallace Pl. Bour —2M 5
Edgbarrow Ct. Crowt —7E 112
Edgbarrow Rise. L Sand —8E 112
Edgcumbe Pk. Dri. Crowt —5E 112
Edgecombe La. Newb —6N 79
Edgedale Clo. Crowt —6F 112
Edgehill St. Read —7H 63
Edgell Clo. Vir W —5N 95
Edgell Rd. Stai —9G 73
Edgewood Clo. Crowt —3E 112
Edinburgh Av. Slou —6C 22
Edinburgh Dri. Stai —9L 73
Edinburgh Gdns. Wind —8F 46
Edinburgh Rd. M'head —5B 20
Edinburgh Rd. Mar —4C 4
Edinburgh Rd. Read —5E 62
Edith Rd. M'head —7L 19
Edmonds Ct. Brack —3N 91
Edmunds Way. Slou —6K 23
Edneys Hill. Wokgm —8J 89
Edward Av. Camb —4L 119
Edward Ct. Stai —9K 73
Edward Ct. Wokgm —6N 89
Edward Rd. Charv —8G 40
Edward Rd. W'sham —6N 115
Edwards Ct. Slou —1G 46
Edwards Hill. Lamb —3H 27
Edward Way. Ashf —6N 73
Edwin Clo. That —8J 81
Eeklo Pl. Newb —1M 101
Egerton Rd. Col T —3K 119
Egerton Rd. Read —2L 87
Egerton Rd. Slou —5A 22
Egham By-Pass. Egh —9A 72
Egham Hill. Egh —1M 95
Egremont Dri. Lwr Ear —9C 64
Egremont Gdns. Slou —9C 22
Eight Acres. Burn —5L 21
Eight Bells. Newb —9K 79
Elan Clo. Tile —5N 61
Elbow Meadow. Coln —7G 49
Eldart Clo. Tile —5B 62
Elder Clo. Tile —3K 61
Elder Clo. W Dray —8M 25
Elderfield Rd. Stoke P —1H 23
Elder Way. Langl —1A 48
Eldon Pl. Read —5J 63
Eldon Rd. Read —5J 63
Eldon Sq. Read —5K 63
Eldon St. Read —5K 63
Eldon Ter. Read —5K 63
Elford Clo. Lwr Ear —2B 88
Elgar Av. Crowt —3F 112
Elgar Rd. Read —6G 63
Elgar Rd. S. Read —7H 63
Elgarth Dri. Wokgm —2L 111
Eliot Clo. Cav —9G 39
Eliot Clo. That —6F 80
Eliot Dri. Mar —3D 4
Elizabethan Clo. Stai —5L 73
Elizabethan Way. Stai —5L 73
Elizabeth Av. Bag —8J 115
Elizabeth Av. Newb —3H 101
Elizabeth Clo. Brack —6N 91
Elizabeth Clo. Cook —8K 5
Elizabeth Clo. Hen T —6A 16
Elizabeth Ct. Slou —1J 47
Elizabeth Ct. Thea —9F 60
Elizabeth Ct. Tile —3L 61
Elizabeth Ct. Warg —3J 41
Elizabeth Ct. Wokgm —5N 89
Elizabeth Gdns. Asc —7L 93
Elizabeth Gdns. Kint —9G 77
Elizabeth M. Read —5H 63
Elizabeth Rd. Hen T —6A 16
Elizabeth Rd. Mar —4C 4
Elizabeth Rd. Wokgm —5B 90
Elizabeth Rout Clo. Spen W —9J 87
Elizabeth Wlk. Read —7H 63
Elizabeth Way. Stoke P —2H 23
Ellenborough Clo. Brack —3A 92
Ellerton Clo. Thea —8F 60
Ellesfield Av. Brack —6J 91
Ellesmere Clo. Cav —1H 63
Elliman Av. Slou —8G 23
Elliman Sq. Slou —1H 47
Ellington Gdns. Tap —7F 20
Ellington Pk. M'head —5B 20
Ellington Rd. Tap —7F 20
Elliott Rise. Asc —4G 93
Ellis Av. Slou —1G 46
Ellison Clo. Wind —9B 46
Ellison Way. Wokgm —5N 89
Ellis Rd. Crowt —4E 112
Ellis's Hill. Arbor —7E 88
Elmar Grn. Slou —4C 22
Elm Bank. Yat —2A 118
Elmbank Av. Egh —1K 95
Elm Clo. Farn C —1E 22
Elm Clo. Stai —5L 73
Elm Cotts. Wool H —9D 100
Elm Ct. Owl —8J 113
Elm Ct. Son C —1G 38
Elm Croft. Dat —7L 47
Elmcroft. Gor —9L 15
Elmcroft Dri. Ashf —9N 73
Elm Dri. Bfld —6J 85
Elm Dri. Wink —5K 69
Elm Gro. M'head —7B 20
Elm Gro. That —6E 80
Elm Gro. W Dray —8N 25
Elmhurst Rd. Gor —7L 15
Elmhurst Rd. Read —7K 63
Elmhurst Rd. Slou —2B 48
Elmhurst Rd. That —6D 80
Elm La. Bour —2K 5
Elm La. Lwr Ear —1M 87
(in two parts)
Elm Lawn Clo. Uxb —1M 25
Elmleigh Ct. Cav —1J 63
Elmley Clo. Wokgm —2L 89
Elm Lodge Av. Read —4D 62
Elm Pk. S'dale —1N 115
Elm Pk. Ct. Read —5D 62
Elm Pk. Rd. Read —5D 62
Elm Rd. Lwr Ear —1L 87
Elm Rd. Tok G —6D 38
Elm Rd. Wind —9D 46
Elms Av. That —8H 81
Elms Dri. Bour —4M 5
Elmshott La. Slou —8A 22
Elmsleigh Cen., The. Stai —8G 73
Elmsleigh Rd. Stai —9G 72
Elms Rd. Wokgm —6N 89
Elms, The. B'water —5H 119
Elms, The. Warf P —1D 92
Elmstone Dri. Tile —3K 61
Elmsway. Ashf —9N 73
Elmwood. M'head —2E 20
Elmwood Rd. Slou —8K 23
Elruge Clo. W Dray —2L 49
Elsinore Av. Stai —5M 73
Elsley Rd. Tile —1L 61
Elstow Av. Cav —7J 39
Elstree Clo. Tile —2L 61
Eltham Av. Cav —8L 39
Elthorne Rd. Uxb —3L 25
Elton Dri. M'head —6A 20
Elton La. W'ton —3J 53
Elvaston Way. Tile —5N 61
Elveden Clo. Lwr Ear —1D 88
Elvendon Rd. Gor —7L 15
Elwell Clo. Egh —9B 72
Ely Av. Slou —6E 22
Elyham. Pur T —8J 37
Ely Rd. Thea —1F 84
Embankment, The. Wray —5L 71
Ember Rd. Slou —2C 48
Emblen Cres. Arbor X —9D 88
Embrook Way. Calc —8H 61
Emerald Clo. Wokgm —4K 89
Emerald Ct. Slou —1G 47
Emerson Ct. Crowt —5F 112
Emery Acres. Up Bas —7J 35
Emery Down Clo. Brack —5D 92
Emma La. Warg —3K 41
Emmbrook Ct. Read —1L 87
Emmbrook Ga. Wokgm —3L 89
Emmbrook Rd. Wokgm —3L 89
Emmbrook Vale. Wokgm —2L 89
Emm Clo. Wokgm —3L 89
Emmer Grn. Ct. Cav —8J 39
Emmer Grn. Rd. Bin H —4M 39
Emmets Nest. Binf —1G 91
Emmets Pk. Binf —1G 91
Emmview Clo. Wokgm —4L 89
Empress Rd. Calc —7K 61
Enborne Clo. Tile —4K 61
Enborne Ct. Newb —1H 101
Enborne Gdns. Brack —2A 92
Enborne Gro. Newb —9J 79
Enborne Pl. Newb —9J 79
Enborne Rd. Newb —1G 100
Enborne St. Enb & Newb —6D 100
Enborne Way. Brimp —4B 104
Enfield Clo. Uxb —3L 25
Engineers Rd. Green —5D 102
Englefield Clo. Egh —1L 95
Englefield Rd. Thea —8D 60
Englehurst. Egh —1L 95
Englemere Rd. Brack —2K 91
English Gdns. Wray —2M 71
Ennerdale. Brack —6L 91
Ennerdale Cres. Slou —6M 21
Ennerdale Rd. Read —9K 63
Ennerdale Way. That —8D 80
Ensign Clo. Stai —5L 73
Ensign Way. Stai —5L 73
Enstone Rd. Wdly —4F 64
Enterprise Way. That —9K 81
Epping Clo. Read —5F 62
Epping Way. Brack —6C 92
Epsom Clo. Camb —1N 119
Epsom Ct. Read —6F 62
Epsom Cres. Green —1M 101
Erfstadt Ct. Wokgm —6A 90
Erica Clo. Slou —8A 22
Erica Dri. Wokgm —6B 90
Eric Av. Cav —7G 39
Eriswell Clo. Lwr Ear —1D 88
Erleigh Ct. Dri. Ear —5N 63
Erleigh Ct. Gdns. Ear —5N 63
Erleigh Dene. Newb —1K 101
Erleigh Rd. Read —6K 63
Ermine St. Stcks —5C 78
Ermin Wlk. That —8E 80
Errington Dri. Wind —7C 46
Erskine Clo. Pam H —9A 106
Eschle Ct. Slou —7G 23
Esher Rd. Camb —9D 114
Eskdale Gdns. M'head —3E 44
Eskdale Rd. Uxb —3J 25
Eskdale Rd. Winn —8F 64
Eskin Clo. Tile —5A 62
Essex Av. Slou —6E 22
Essex Pl. Lamb —2H 27
Essex Rise. Warf —2C 92
Essex St. Newb —3G 101
Essex St. Read —7H 63
Essex Way. Son C —2G 38
Ethel Rd. Ashf —9M 73
Eton Clo. Dat —5J 47
Eton Ct. Eton —6F 46
Eton Ct. Stai —9G 73
Eton Pl. Mar —5B 4
Eton Rd. Dat —4H 47
Eton Sq. Eton —6F 46
Eton Wick Rd. Eton W —3A 46
Eustace Cres. Wokgm —3B 90
Evedon. Brack —9M 91
Evelyns Clo. Uxb —7N 25
Evendon's Clo. Wokgm —8M 89
Evendon's La. Wokgm —9K 89
Evenlode. M'head —6C 20
Evenlode Way. Sand —1G 119
Everard Av. Slou —1G 46
Everest Rd. Camb —9A 114
Everest Rd. Crowt —4F 112
Everest Rd. Stai —4L 73
Evergreen Ct. Stai —4L 73
Evergreen Dri. Calc —8N 61
Evergreen Oak Av. Wind —9J 47
Evergreen Way. Stai —4L 73
Evergreen Way. Wokgm —6L 89
Everington La. Herm —4H 57
Everitts Corner. Slou —8A 22
Everland Rd. Hung —5K 75
(in two parts)
Eversley Rd. Arbor X —9D 88
Eversley Rd. Finch & Arbor X —5D 110
Eversley St. Eve —9F 110
Evesham Rd. Emm G —8H 39
Evesham Wlk. Owl —9H 113

Evreham Rd. Iver —7F **24**
Evreux Clo. That —9J **81**
Ewing Way. Newb —2L **101**
Exbourne Rd. Read —3J **87**
Exchange Rd. Asc —7M **93**
Exeford Av. Ashf —8N **73**
Exeter Ct. Read —3H **87**
Exeter Way. Thea —9F **60**
Exmoor Rd. That —8F **80**
Explorer Av. Stai —5M **73**
Exwick Sq. Read —3K **87**
Eynsford Clo. Cav —8L **39**
Eynsford Ter. W Dray —7N **25**
Eynsham Clo. Wdly —4D **64**
Eyre Grn. Slou —4C **22**

Factory Path. Stai —8F **72**
Fair Acre. M'head —8N **19**
Fairacre. Wool H —9D **100**
Fairacres Ind. Est. Wind —8N **45**
Fair Clo. Ho. Newb —9L **79**
Faircroft. Slou —5D **22**
Faircross. Brack —5M **91**
Faircross Quarters. Herm —6C **56**
Faircross Rd. Read —7C **62**
Fairfax. Brack —3L **91**
Fairfax Pl. Newb —6B **80**
Fairfax Rd. Farn —9M **119**
Fairfield. Comp —1G **32**
Fairfield App. Wray —3M **71**
Fairfield Av. Dat —6L **47**
Fairfield Av. Stai —8G **73**
Fairfield Clo. Dat —6M **47**
Fairfield La. Farn R —3D **22**
Fairfield Rd. Burn —4M **21**
Fairfield Rd. Gor —7M **15**
Fairfield Rd. Uxb —1L **25**
Fairfield Rd. W Dray —8M **25**
Fairfield Rd. Wray —3M **71**
Fairfields. Hung —6K **75**
Fairford Rd. M'head —6C **20**
Fairford Rd. Tile —2K **61**
Fairhaven. Egh —9A **72**
Fairhaven Ct. Egh —9A **72**
Fairholme Rd. Ashf —9M **73**
Fairlawn Pk. Wind —1A **70**
Fairlawns Clo. Stai —9J **73**
Fairlea. M'head —1L **43**
Fairlie Rd. Slou —7C **22**
Fairlight Av. Wind —8F **46**
Fairlop Clo. Calc —8L **61**
Fairmead Clo. Col T —2J **119**
Fairmead Rd. Shin —6L **87**
Fair Mile. Hen T —1A **16**
Fair Mile Ct. Hen T —3C **16**
Fair Mile, The. Blew —4A **14**
Fairoak Way. Baug —9F **104**
Fairsted Clo. Tile —4N **61**
Fairview Av. Ear —6A **64**
Fairview Ct. Ashf —9N **73**
Fairview Rd. Hung —6K **75**
Fairview Rd. Slou —5B **22**
Fairview Rd. Tap —7K **21**
Fairview Rd. Wokgm —6A **90**
Fairview Trading Est. Hen T —6E **16**
Fairwater Dri. Wdly —5B **64**
Fairway. Vir W —8L **95**
Fairway Av. Tile —6L **61**
Fairway Av. W Dray —9K **25**
Fairway Clo. W Dray —9L **25**
Fairway, The. Burn —3M **21**
Fairway, The. M'head —2M **43**
Fairway, The. Uxb —3N **25**
Fakenham Clo. Lwr Ear —3N **87**
Fakenham Way. Owl —9H **113**
Falaise. Egh —9N **71**
Falcon Av. Read —2L **87**
Falcon Bus. Pk. Finch —4F **110**
Falcon Clo. Light —9J **115**
Falcon Coppice. Wool H —9D **100**
Falcon Ct. Frim —8N **119**
Falcon Dri. Stai —3L **73**
Falcon Fields. Aldm —8K **105**
Falcon Ho. Gdns. Wool H —9C **100**
Falcon Way. Wokgm —5L **89**
Falcon Way. Yat —3A **118**
Falconwood. Egh —2N **95**
Falkland Dri. Newb —2K **101**
Falkland Garth. Newb —3H **101**
Falkland Rd. Cav —2H **63**
Falkland Rd. Newb —4H **101**
Falling La. W Dray & Uxb —8M **25**
Fallowfield Clo. Cav —9H **39**
Falmouth Rd. Read —4J **87**
Falmouth Rd. Slou —7C **22**
Falmouth Way. That —8J **81**
Falstaff Av. Ear —1M **87**
Fanes Clo. Brack —3K **91**
Fane Way. M'head —1A **44**
Faraday Clo. Arbor —3D **110**
Faraday Clo. Slou —6D **22**
Faraday Rd. Newb —8M **79**
Faraday Rd. Slou —6D **22**
Faraday Way. Arbor X —1F **110**
Farcrosse Clo. Sand —1G **119**
Fareham Dri. Yat —2A **118**
Faringdon Clo. Sand —9G **113**
Faringdon Dri. Brack —7A **92**
Faringdon Rd. Up Lamb & Let B —7J **7**
Faringdon Wlk. Read —8B **62**
Farleigh M. Cav —8L **39**
Farley Copse. Brack —3J **91**
Farman Clo. Wdly —4G **65**
Farm Clo. Asc —7M **93**
Farm Clo. Brack —3K **91**
Farm Clo. Crowt —3G **112**
Farm Clo. M'head —7L **19**
Farm Clo. Pur T —8K **37**
Farm Clo. Stai —9F **72**
Farm Clo. Yat —4B **118**
Farm Cotts. Wokgm —3N **89**
Farm Cres. Slou —6K **23**
Farm Dri. Tile —6J **61**
Farmers Clo. M'head —1L **43**
Farmers Clo. Read —5H **87**
Farmers Rd. Stai —9F **72**
Farmers Way. M'head —9L **19**
Farmiloe Clo. Pur T —9K **37**
Farm La. Cipp —8F **22**
Farm Rd. Bour —3K **5**
Farm Rd. Hen T —6E **16**
Farm Rd. M'head —7L **19**
Farm Rd. Stai —9J **73**
Farm Rd. Tap —7K **21**
Farm View. Yat —4B **118**
Farm Way. Stai —3G **73**
Farm Yd. Wind —6F **46**
Farnburn Av. Slou —6D **22**
Farnell Rd. Stai —7H **73**
Farnham Clo. Brack —4A **92**
Farnham Dri. Cav —9L **39**
Farnham La. Slou —4A **22**
Farnham Pk. La. Farn R —1E **22**
Farnham Rd. Slou —4D **22**
Farningham. Brack —8B **92**
Farnsfield Clo. Lwr Ear —3N **87**
Farrell Clo. Camb —6N **119**
Farriers Clo. Wdly —5D **64**
Farrier's La. E Ils —7B **12**
Farrowdene Rd. Read —3J **87**
Farrow Way. M'head —1L **43**
Farthingales, The. M'head —7E **20**
Farthing Grn. La. Stoke P —3J **23**
Fassnidge View. Uxb —1K **25**
Fatherson Rd. Read —5K **63**
Faulkner Pl. Bag —6H **115**
Faversham Rd. Owl —9H **113**
Fawcett Cres. Wdly —5C **64**
Fawcett Rd. Wind —7D **46**
Fawler Mead. Brack —6C **92**
Fawley Clo. M'head —4A **20**
Fawley Rd. Read —7C **62**
Fawsley Clo. Coln —6F **48**
Faygate Way. Lwr Ear —2A **88**
Feathers La. Wray —6B **72**
Fells, The. Tile —6H **61**
Felstead Clo. Ear —1M **87**
Feltham Hill Rd. Ashf —9N **73**
Felton Way. Tile —4K **61**
Fence La. Herm —8G **56**
Fenchurch M. Winn —9F **64**
Fencote. Brack —8A **92**
Fennel Clo. Ear —2M **87**
Fennel Clo. Newb —6A **80**
Fenton Av. Stai —9K **73**
Fernbank. Finch —3J **111**
Fernbank Cres. Asc —3G **93**
Fernbank Pl. Asc —3F **92**
Fernbank Rd. Asc —4G **92**
Fernbrook Rd. Cav —8E **38**
Fern Clo. Calc —7K **61**
Fern Clo. Crowt —3F **112**
Ferndale Av. Read —8A **62**
Ferndale Clo. Tile —1M **61**
Ferndale Ct. That —8G **81**
Ferndale Cres. Uxb —4K **25**
Ferndale Rd. Ashf —9L **73**
Fern Dri. Tap —7L **21**
Ferne Clo. Gor —7L **15**
Fernery, The. Stai —9F **72**
Fernes Clo. Uxb —7K **25**
Fern Glen. Tile —3K **61**
Fernhill Clo. B'water —8K **119**
Fernhill Clo. Brack —2K **91**
Fernhill La. B'water —8J **119**
Fernhill Rd. B'water & Farn —7J **119**
Fernhill Wlk. B'water —8K **119**
Fernhurst Rd. Calc —8K **61**
Fern La. Mar —2J **5**
Fernley Ct. M'head —5A **20**
Fern Wlk. Ashf —9L **73**
Fern Wlk. Calc —7K **61**
Ferrard Clo. Asc —3G **92**
Ferrer Gro. Newb —2M **101**
Ferrers Av. W Dray —1L **49**
Ferry Hill. Chol —2J **15**
Ferry La. Ast —1J **17**
Ferry La. Bour —6M **5**
Ferry La. Cook —8M **5**
Ferry La. Gor —8K **15**
Ferry La. Medm —1N **17**
Ferry La. S Sto —2J **15**
Ferry La. Stai —6C **72**
Ferry La. Warg —3H **41**
Ferry Rd. Bray —1F **44**
Ferry Rd. S Sto —2K **15**
Fettiplace. Gt Shef —1G **52**
Fetty Pl. M'head —1A **44**
Fidler's La. E Ils —7B **12**
Fidlers Wlk. Warg —3K **41**
Field Clo. Bfld C —9J **85**
Fielden Pl. Brack —4A **92**
Fieldhead Gdns. Bour —4L **5**
Field Ho. Clo. Asc —1K **115**
Fieldhouse Ind. Est. Mar —5D **4**
Fieldhouse La. Mar —5D **4**
Fieldhouse Way. Mar —5D **4**
Fieldhurst. Slou —4A **48**
Fielding Gdns. Crowt —6F **112**
Fielding Rd. Col T —3J **119**
Fielding Rd. M'head —6M **19**
Fieldings, The. Holyp —6D **44**
Field La. Ham —7G **97**
Field Pk. Brack —3A **92**
Field Path. Farn —8K **119**
Fieldridge La. Hung —3N **51**
Field Rd. Farn —8K **119**
Field Rd. P'mre —3H **31**
Field Rd. Read —6F **62**
Fields, The. Slou —1F **46**
Field View. Cav —1H **63**
Field View. Egh —9D **72**
Field Way. Uxb —5L **25**
Fieldway. Winn —1J **89**
Fife Ct. Read —4G **63**
Fifehead Clo. Ashf —9M **73**
Fifield La. Wink —1G **68**
Fifield Rd. M'head —6G **45**
Fifth Rd. Newb —1H **101**
Fifth St. Green —5C **102**
Filbert Dri. Tile —4K **61**
Filey Rd. Read —5L **63**
Filey Spur. Slou —2D **46**
Filmer Rd. Wind —8N **45**
Finbeck Way. Lwr Ear —3M **87**
Fincham End Dri. Crowt —6D **112**
Finchampstead Rd. Wokgm —2M **111**
Finch Ct. M'head —9A **20**
Finches La. Bay —5A **26**
Finch Rd. Ear —8B **64**
Finch Way. Bfld C —8J **85**
Findhorn Clo. Col T —2H **119**
Findings, The. Farn —9J **119**
Fineleigh Ct. Slou —9G **22**
Finians Clo. Uxb —1N **25**
Finmere. Brack —9N **91**
Finney Dri. W'sham —6N **115**
Finstock Clo. Lwr Ear —2C **88**
Finstock Grn. Brack —6C **92**
Firbank Pl. Egh —1K **95**
Fir Cottage Rd. Wokgm —2K **111**
Fircroft Clo. Tile —3K **61**
Fir Dri. B'water —6H **119**
Fireball Hill. Asc —9N **93**
Firglen Dri. Yat —2B **118**
Firgrove Rd. Yat —3A **118**
Firlands. Brack —7N **91**
Firlands Av. Camb —4N **119**
Firmstone Clo. Lwr Ear —2B **88**
Fir Pit La. Tile —4K **61**
Firs Av. Wind —9B **46**
Firs Clo. Finch —3L **111**
Fir's End. Bfld C —9H **85**
Firs La. M'head —1K **43**
Firs La. Read —7D **62**
Firs Rd. Tile —6K **61**
First Av. Mar —5E **4**
First Cres. Slou —6E **22**
Firs, The. Brack —7C **92**
Firs, The. Ink —5D **98**
Firs, The. Read —6F **62**
Firs, The. That —7E **80**
First St. Green —5D **102**
Fir Tree Av. Stoke P —5H **23**
Fir Tree Av. W Dray —2N **49**
Fir Tree Clo. Asc —9K **93**
Firtree Clo. Sand —9D **112**
Fir Tree Corner. Baug —8G **104**
Fir Tree La. Newb —7B **80**
Fir Tree Paddock. W Ils —4L **11**
Fir Tree Pl. Ashf —9N **73**
Firview Clo. Mar —6D **4**
Firwood Dri. Camb —4N **119**
Firwood Rd. Vir W —8G **94**
Fisher Grn. Binf —1F **90**
Fishermans La. Aldm —3J **105**
Fishermans Retreat. Mar —6C **4**
Fisherman's Way. Bour —3M **5**
Fishers Ct. Emm G —7J **39**
Fisher's La. Cold A —1C **80**
Fishery Rd. M'head —9E **20**
Fishguard Spur. Slou —1K **47**
Fishponds Clo. Wokgm —7M **89**
Fishponds Rd. Wokgm —7M **89**
Fiske Ct. Yat —3C **118**
Fitzrobert Pl. Egh —9B **72**
Fitzroy Cres. Wdly —6F **64**
Five Acre. Tile —3J **61**
Flag Staff Sq. That —9J **81**
Flambards. Cav —2J **63**
Flamborough Clo. Lwr Ear —1D **88**
Flamborough Path. Lwr Ear —1D **88**
Flamborough Spur. Slou —1C **46**
Flamingo Clo. Wokgm —6K **89**
Flanders Ct. Egh —9D **72**
Flats, The. B'water —5F **118**
Flaxman Clo. Ear —1M **87**
Flecker Clo. That —6F **80**
Fleet Clo. Wokgm —5K **89**
Fleetham Gdns. Lwr Ear —2A **88**
Fleet Hill. Finch —8G **110**
Fleet La. Finch —8G **110**
Fleetwood Ct. Stanw —3M **73**
Fleetwood Rd. Slou —9H **23**
Fleming Clo. Arbor —3D **110**
Fleming Rd. Newb —8M **79**
Fletcher Gdns. Brack —3H **91**
Flexford Grn. Brack —8J **91**
Flint Cotts. Wood M —4J **51**
Flintgrove. Brack —3A **92**
Flintlock Clo. Stai —1H **73**
Flodden Dri. Calc —8L **61**
Floral Way. That —6H **81**
Florence Av. M'head —6C **20**
Florence Clo. Yat —3A **118**
Florence Ct. Read —6D **62**
Florence Rd. Col T —2H **119**
Florence Wlk. Read —5K **63**
Florian Gdns. Read —7B **62**
(in two parts)
Florida Ct. Read —6E **62**
Florida Ct. Stai —8H **73**
Flower's Hill. Pang —9D **36**
Flowers Piece. Ash'd —7D **34**
Fobney St. Read —6G **63**
Fokerham Rd. That —9J **81**
Folder's La. Brack —2N **91**
Foliejohn Way. M'head —3K **43**
Folkestone Ct. Slou —4B **48**
Follett Clo. Old Win —3K **71**
Folly La. Bfld C —5H **85**
Folly Rd. Ink —4D **98**
Folly Rd. Lamb —3F **26**
Folly, The. Newb —1M **101**
Folly Way. M'head —7B **20**
Fontmell Clo. Ashf —9N **73**
Fontmell Pk. Ashf —9N **73**
Fontwell Clo. M'head —6K **19**
Fontwell Dri. Read —7N **61**
Fontwell Rd. Green —1M **101**
Forbes Chase. Col T —2H **119**
Forbe's Ride. Wind —3K **69**
Forbury Ho. Read —5H **63**
Forbury La. Kint —3G **98**
Forbury Pk. Ind. Est. Read —4J **63**
Forbury Rd. Read —4H **63**
(in two parts)
Forbury, The. Read —4H **63**
(in two parts)
Fordbridge Rd. Ashf —9M **73**
Ford Clo. Ashf —9M **73**
Fordham Way. Lwr Ear —2B **88**
Ford La. Far H —7N **109**
Ford La. Iver —7H **25**
Ford Rd. Ashf —8N **73**
Fordwells Dri. Brack —6C **92**
Forehead, The. Mort —6N **107**
Forest Clo. Asc —5F **92**
Forest Clo. Baug —8G **104**
Forest Dean. Read —4J **87**
Forest End. Sand —9D **112**
Forest End Rd. Sand —9D **112**
Foresters Sq. Brack —5B **92**
Foresters Way. Crowt —3J **113**
Forest Grn. Brack —3A **92**
Forest Grn. Rd. M'head —7B **44**
Forest Hill. Tile —2N **61**
Forest Hills. Camb —5M **119**
Forest Rd. Crowt —5G **113**
Forest Rd. Warf & Asc —9B **68**
Forest Rd. Wind —5N **69**
(Cranbourne)
Forest Rd. Wind —8N **45**
(Windsor)
Forest Rd. Wokgm & Binf —1M **89**
Forest Way. Warf P —2C **92**
Forge Clo. Cav —2J **63**
Forge Clo. Kint —9G **77**
(Craven Way)
Forge Clo. Kint —9F **76**
(Station Rd.)
Forge Dri. Farn C —1E **22**
Forge Hill. Hamp N —8K **33**
Forge, The. Hung —5K **75**
Forlease Clo. M'head —8D **20**
Forlease Dri. M'head —8D **20**
Forlease Rd. M'head —7D **20**
Formby Clo. Ear —9D **64**
Formosa Ct. Cook —8N **5**
Forndon Clo. Lwr Ear —1D **88**
Forsters. Aldm —3H **105**
Forsters Farm Ct. Aldm —3H **105**
Forsythia Gdns. Slou —2N **47**
Fort Narrien. Col T —3J **119**
Fortrose Clo. Col T —2H **119**
Fortrose Wlk. Calc —8M **61**
Forty Grn. Dri. Mar —5A **4**
Fosseway. Crowt —5D **112**
Fossewood Dri. Camb —1N **119**
Foster Av. Wind —9A **46**
Fosters Gro. W'sham —4L **115**
Fosters La. Wdly —6D **64**
Fosters Path. Slou —5B **22**
Fotherby Ct. M'head —8D **20**
Fotheringay Gdns. Slou —8C **22**
Foundry Ho. Hung —4L **75**
Foundry La. Hort —9C **48**
Foundry Pl. Read —6C **63**
Fountain Gdns. Wind —9F **46**
Fountains Garth. Brack —5L **91**
Fourth St. Green —5C **102**
Fowler Clo. Ear —9N **63**
Fowlers La. Brack —3M **91**
Foxborough. Swal —4K **109**
Foxborough Clo. Slou —4B **48**
Foxbury. Lamb —3H **27**
Fox Clo. Bfld C —8H **85**
Foxcombe Dri. Tile —5K **61**
Foxcote. Wokgm —3M **111**
Fox Covert. Light —9K **115**
Fox Covert Clo. Asc —7M **93**
Foxdown Clo. Camb —4N **119**
Fox Dri. Yat —2B **118**
Foxes Piece. Mar —5C **4**
Foxes Wlk. Charv —1F **64**
Foxglove Clo. Stai —5L **73**
Foxglove Clo. Wink R —1D **92**
Foxglove Clo. Wokgm —4J **89**
Foxglove Gdns. Read —5E **62**
Foxglove Way. That —6H **81**
Foxhays Rd. Read —3K **87**
Foxheath. Brack —7B **92**
Foxherne. Slou —1L **47**
Foxhill Clo. Play —8N **39**
Fox Hill Ho. Read —7M **63**
Foxhill La. Play —6K **39**
Foxhill Rd. Read —6L **63**
Fox Hunter Way. That —8C **80**
Foxhunt Gro. Calc —8N **61**
Foxley Clo. B'water —4G **119**
Foxley La. Binf —1F **90**
Fox Rd. Brack —6N **91**
Fox Rd. Slou —3M **47**
Framewood Rd. Wex & Ful —1L **23**
Framlingham Dri. Cav —8L **39**
Frampton Clo. Wdly —3D **64**
France Hill Dri. Camb —4N **119**
Frances Av. M'head —5F **20**
Frances Rd. Wind —9E **46**
Frances, The. That —7G **81**
Francis Chichester Clo. Asc —7L **93**
Francis Gdns. Warf —1A **92**
Francis St. Read —6H **63**
Francis Way. Slou —8N **21**
Franklin Av. Slou —6D **22**
Franklin Av. Tadl —9H **105**
Franklin Ct. Read —5F 62
(off Franklin St.)
Franklin St. Read —5F **62**
Franklyn Cres. Wind —9N **45**
Frankswood Av. W Dray —7N **25**
Frank Union Clo. Bour —4N **5**
Frascati Way. M'head —7C **20**
Fraser Av. Cav —7J **39**
Fraser Mead. Col T —3J **119**
Fraser Rd. Brack —3M **91**
Frays Av. W Dray —1L **49**
Frayslea. Uxb —3K **25**
Frays Waye. Uxb —2K **25**
Frederick Pl. Wokgm —5M **89**
Freeborn Way. Brack —3B **92**
Freemans Clo. Hung —6J **75**
Freemans Clo. Stoke P —1H **23**
Freemantle Clo. Bag —6H **115**
Freemantle Rd. Bag —7J **115**
Freesia Clo. Wokgm —4J **89**
French Gdns. B'water —5H **119**
Frenchum Gdns. Slou —8A **22**
Frensham. Brack —8A **92**
Frensham Clo. Yat —3A **118**
Frensham Grn. Read —2M **87**
Frensham Rd. Crowt —4F **112**
Freshfield Clo. Ear —9D **64**
Freshwater Rd. Read —4L **63**
Freshwood Dri. Yat —5B **118**
Friars Keep. Brack —6M **91**
Friars Rd. Newb —2L **101**
Friars Rd. Vir W —6M **95**
Friar St. Read —4G **62**
Friars Wlk. Read —4G **63**
Friary Island. Wray —3L **71**
Friary Rd. Asc —8K **93**
Friary Rd. Wray —4L **71**
Friary, The. Old Win —3L **71**
Friday St. Hen T —4D **16**
Friends Wlk. Stai —9G **72**
Friends Wlk. Uxb —1L **25**
Frieth Clo. Ear —2N **87**
Frilsham Rd. Read —8B **62**
Frimley Bus. Pk. Frim —9N **119**
Frimley By-Pass. Frim —9N **119**
Frimley Clo. Wdly —4C **64**
Frimley High St. Frim —9N **119**
Frimley Rd. Camb & Frim —4L **119**
Fringford Clo. Lwr Ear —2B **88**
Frithe, The. Slou —8L **23**
Frobisher. Brack —9N **91**
Frobisher Cres. Stai —4M **73**
Frobisher Gdns. Stai —4M **73**
Frodsham Way. Owl —8J **113**
Frog Hall Dri. Wokgm —5C **90**
Frog La. Brack —5L **91**
Frogmill. Hur —3A **18**
Frogmore Border. Wind —9G **47**
Frogmore Clo. Slou —1D **46**
Frogmore Ct. B'water —5G **119**
Frogmore Dri. Wind —7G **46**
Frogmore Gro. B'water —5G **119**
Frogmore Pk. Dri. B'water —5G **119**
Frogmore Rd. B'water —4F **118**
Frogmore Way. Read —7B **62**
Fromont Dri. That —8G **80**
Fromow Gdns. W'sham —6N **115**
Front St. E Gar —7B **28**
Froxfield Av. Read —7E **62**
Froxfield Down. Brack —7C **92**
Frymley View. Wind —7N **45**
Fry Rd. Ashf —8L **73**
Fry's La. Yat —2C **118**
Fuchsia Clo. Calc —7K **61**
Fuchsia Pl. Brack —4A **92**
Fullbrook Clo. M'head —6D **20**
Fullbrook Clo. Wokgm —2M **89**
Fullbrook Cres. Tile —1L **61**
Fuller Clo. That —9J **81**
Fuller's La. Graz —7B **86**
Fullers La. Wool H —2N **117**
Fulmead Rd. Read —4C **62**
Fulmer Clo. Ear —1N **87**
Fulmer Comn. Rd. Ful & Iver —1N **23**
Furlong Clo. Bour —4M **5**
Furlong Rd. Bour —4M **5**
Furness. Wind —8M **45**
Furness Pl. Wind —8M **45**
Furness Row. Wind —8M **45**
Furness Sq. Wind —8M **45**
Furness Wlk. Wind —8M **45**
Furness Way. Wind —8M **45**
Furnival Av. Slou —6D **22**
Furnival Clo. Vir W —8M **95**
Furzebank. Asc —6N **93**
Furzeham Rd. W Dray —1M **49**
Furze Hill Cres. Crowt —6G **113**
Furze La. Farnb & Catm —6D **10**
Furzemoors. Brack —7M **91**
Furzen Clo. Slou —4C **22**
Furze Platt Rd. M'head —5L **19**
Furze Rd. M'head —5A **20**
Furze Rd. Tadl —8H **105**
Fuzzens Wlk. Wind —8A **46**
Fydler's Clo. Wink —1L **93**
Fyfield Clo. B'water —4H **119**
Fyfield Rd. That —9G **81**
Fylingdales. That —8F **80**

Gables Av. Ashf —9N **73**
Gables Clo. Dat —5J **47**
Gables Clo. M'head —6E **20**
Gabriels, The. Newb —5H **101**
Gage Clo. M'head —1B **44**
Gailys Rd. Wind —8N **45**
Gainsborough. Brack —8N **91**
Gainsborough. Cook —1C **20**
Gainsborough Av. Kint —9G **76**
Gainsborough Clo. Wdly —6F **64**
Gainsborough Cres. Hen T —6B **16**
Gainsborough Dri. Asc —5G **93**
Gainsborough Dri. M'head —2A **44**
Gainsborough Hill. Hen T —6C **16**
Gainsborough Rd. Hen T —6C **16**
Gainsborough Rd. Read —7B **62**
Gairn Clo. Tile —5A **62**
Galahad Clo. Slou —1C **46**
Gale Dri. Light —9K **115**
Galleons La. Wex —5L **23**
Galley La. Hdly —9G **103**
Galleymead Rd. Coln —7G **48**
Gallop, The. Wind —4E **70**
Gallop, The. Yat —2B **118**
Galloway Cen., The. Newb —9B **80**
Gallys Rd. Wind —8N **45**
Galsworthy Dri. Cav —8K **39**
Galton Rd. Asc —8B **94**
Galvin Rd. Slou —9E **22**
Galway Rd. Yat —5A **118**
Garden Clo. M'head —9L **19**
Garden Clo. La. Newb —5H **101**
Gardeners La. Up Bas —9K **35**
Gardeners Rd. Wink R —1D **92**
Garden M. Slou —9H **23**
Gardens, The. S Sto —6L **15**
Garde Rd. Son —1D **64**
Gardner Rd. M'head —4A **20**
Garfield Pl. Wind —8F **46**
Garfield Rd. Camb —4N **119**
Garford Cres. Newb —2H **101**
Garlands Clo. Bfld C —9G **85**
Garnet Clo. Slou —1C **46**
Garnet Ct. Mar —6A **4**
Garnet Hill. Read —6F **62**
Garnet St. Read —6G **62**
Garrard Rd. Slou —5A **22**
Garrard St. Read —4G **63**
(in two parts)
Garret Rd. Wokgm —2K **111**
Garson La. Wray —4M **71**
Garson's La. Warf —5D **68**

Garston Clo. Read —8A **62**
Garston Cres. Calc —7J **61**
Garston Gro. Wokgm —1K **111**
Garston's Pk. Caravan Site. Tile —6J **61**
Garswood. Brack —8A **92**
Garth Clo. Winn —1H **89**
Garthlands. M'head —4A **20**
Garth Rd. Mort C —5H **107**
Garth Sq. Brack —2M **91**
Gascon's Gro. Slou —5C **22**
Gas Ho. Hill. Lamb —2J **27**
Gaskell M. Newb —2M **101**
Gaskells End. Tok G —5D **38**
Gas La. M'head —2D **44**
Gas Works Rd. Read —5J **63**
Gatcombe Clo. Calc —8K **61**
Gatehampton Rd. Gor —8L **15**
Gatewick Clo. Slou —9G **23**
Gatward Av. M'head —2M **43**
Gaveston Rd. Slou —4B **22**
Gayhurst Clo. Cav —7K **39**
Gays La. M'head —5E **44**
Gaywood Dri. Newb —7A **80**
Gazelle Clo. Winn —9F **64**
Geffers Ride. Asc —4H **93**
Geoffreyson Rd. Cav —8D **38**
George Clo. Mar —3D **4**
George Grn. Dri. G Grn —7N **23**
George Grn. Rd. G Grn —7M **23**
Georgeham Rd. Owl —8H **113**
Georges Dri. F Hth —1N **5**
George St. Cav —3H **63**
George St. Read —4F **62**
George St. Stai —8G **73**
George St. Uxb —1L **25**
Georgian Clo. Stai —8J **73**
Geranium Clo. Crowt —2F **112**
Gerrards Cross Rd. Stoke P —1J **23**
Gibbins La. Warf —9A **68**
Gibbons Clo. Sand —1G **118**
Gibbs Clo. Wokgm —4K **111**
Gibbs Way. Yat —5A **118**
Gibraltar Barracks. B'water —7C **118**
Gibraltar La. Cook —6F **4**
Gibson Ct. Dat —4A **48**
Gibson Pl. Stai —3K **73**
Gidley La. Chvly —3J **55**
Giffard Ho. Cav —3J **63**
Gifford Clo. Cav —8L **39**
Gilbert Rd. Camb —8N **119**
Gilby Wlk. Wbrn G —3N 5
(off Stratford Dri.)
Gilchrist Way. L Grn —9F **18**
Gillette Way. Read —1H **87**
Gilliat Rd. Slou —8G **23**
Gillotts Clo. Hen T —6A **16**
Gillotts Hill. Harp —7B **16**
Gillott's La. Hen T —7A **16**
Gilman Cres. Wind —9N **45**
Gilmore Clo. Slou —1L **47**
Gilroy Clo. Newb —4G **101**
Gingells Farm Rd. Charv —8G **40**
Gipsy La. Brack —4A **92**
Gipsy La. Edd —3L **75**
Gipsy La. Lwr Ear —2C **88**
(in three parts)
Gipsy La. Tile —3M **61**
Gipsy La. Wokgm —6A **90**
Girton Clo. Owl —9J **113**
Glade Rd. Mar —5C **4**
Glade, The. Asc —7M **93**
Glade, The. Newb —2K **101**
Glade, The. Pur T —9K **37**
Gladridge Clo. Ear —8A **64**
Gladstone Clo. Kint —9G **76**
Gladstone La. Cold A —3F **80**
Gladstone Way. Slou —9C **22**
Glaisdale. That —9F **80**
Glaisyer Way. Iver —3E **24**
Glamis Way. Calc —8J **61**
Glanmor Rd. Slou —8K **23**
Glanty, The. Egh —8D **72**
Glasgow Rd. Slou —7C **22**
Glebe Clo. Light —9M **115**
Glebe Clo. Moul —1H **15**
Glebe Clo. Tap —9J **21**
Glebe Cotts. S Sto —3L **15**
Glebe Field. Chadw —5M **29**
Glebe Fields. Newb —6M **79**
Glebeland Rd. Camb —5K **119**
Glebelands. That —8F **80**
Glebelands Rd. Wokgm —4A **90**
Glebe La. Son —1D **64**
Glebe Ride. Gor —8K **15**
Glebe Rd. Egh —9D **72**
Glebe Rd. M'head —9E **20**
Glebe Rd. Old Win —2K **71**
Glebe Rd. Pur T —8J **37**
Glebe Rd. Read —7J **63**
Glebe Rd. Stai —9J **73**
Glebe Rd. Uxb —3K **25**
Glebe, The. Aldw —2B **34**
Glebe, The. B'water —5J **119**
Glebe, The. W Dray —3N **49**
Glebewood. Brack —7N **91**
Glenapp Grange. Mort C —4G **107**
Glen Av. Ashf —8N **73**
Glenavon Gdns. Slou —3L **47**
Glenavon Gdns. Yat —5B **118**
Glenbeigh Ter. Read —6E **62**
Glendale Av. Newb —4G **101**
Glendale Rd. Tadl —9J **105**
Glendevon Rd. Wdly —4E **64**
Gleneagles Clo. Stai —3L **73**
Gleneagles Ct. Read —5K 63
(off Muirfield Clo.)
Gleneagles Ho. Brack —8J **91**
Glenfield Ho. Brack —6N **91**
Glenhurst. W'sham —4K **115**
Glenhurst Clo. B'water —5J **119**
Gleninnes. Col T —9K **113**
Glenmore Clo. That —9G **80**
Glennon Clo. Read —8C **62**
Glenrhondda. Cav —8F **38**
Glenrosa Rd. Tile —4A **62**
Glen, The. Pam H —9N **105**
Glen, The. Slou —3L **47**
Glenthorne Clo. Uxb —4N **25**
Glenwood. Brack —6A **92**
Glenwood Dri. Tile —5K **61**
Glenworth Pl. Slou —9E **22**
Glisson Rd. Uxb —3N **25**
Globe Farm La. B'water —4F **118**
Gloucester Av. Slou —6E **22**
Gloucester Ct. Read —5D **62**
Gloucester Dri. Stai —7D **72**
Gloucester Gdns. Bag —7H **115**
Gloucester Pl. Wind —8F **46**
Gloucester Rd. Bag —7H **115**
Gloucester Rd. M'head —4B **20**
Gloucester Rd. Newb —9J **79**
Gloucester Rd. Read —5D **62**
Gloucestershire Lea. Warf —2C **92**
Glyme Wlk. Calc —9N **61**
Glyncastle. Cav —8F **38**
Goaters Rd. Asc —4F **92**
Goddard Clo. Shin —6L **87**
Goddard Ct. Winn —2G **89**
Goddard Dri. Midg —8B **82**
Goddards La. Camb —6M **119**
Goddington Rd. Bour —2L **5**
Godolphin Rd. Slou —8F **22**
Godstow Clo. Wdly —4D **64**
(in two parts)
Goffs Hill. Cray P —1E **36**
Goldcrest Way. Tile —6J **61**
Goldcup La. Asc —3G **93**
Golden Ball La. M'head —3K **19**
Golden Orb Wood. Binf —3H **91**
Goldfinch La. Bis G —7C 102
(off Linden Rd.)
Golding Clo. That —8J **81**
Goldsmid Rd. Read —5F **62**
Goldsmith Clo. That —6F **80**
Goldsmiths Clo. Finch —1K **111**
Goldsmith Way. Crowt —6F **112**
Goldsworthy Way. Slou —7M **21**
Goldthorpe Gdns. Lwr Ear —3M **87**
Goldwell Dri. Newb —7K **79**
Gooch Clo. Twy —1L **65**
Goodboys La. Graz —8N **85**
Goodchild Rd. Wokgm —5B **90**
Goodings Grn. Wokgm —5D **90**
Goodliffe Gdns. Tile —9K **37**
Goodman Pk. Slou —9L **23**
Goodman Pl. Stai —8G **72**
Goodrich Clo. Cav —8L **39**
Goodways Dri. Brack —4N **91**
Goodwin Clo. Calc —8M **61**
Goodwin Rd. Slou —4B **22**
Goodwood Clo. Bfld C —9G **85**
Goodwood Clo. Camb —1N **119**
Goodwood Way. Green —1N **101**
Goose Corner. Warf —9C **68**
Goose Grn. Farn R —3D **22**
Goose Grn. Lamb —2H **27**
Goose Grn. Way. That —8H **81**
Goose La. Leck —8C **30**
Gordon Av. Camb —5M **119**
Gordon Clo. Stai —9J **73**
Gordon Ct. Camb —4N **119**
Gordon Ct. Newb —9M **79**
Gordon Cres. Camb —5N **119**
Gordon Cres. Comp —1H **33**
Gordon Lodge. Read —5E **62**
Gordon Palmer Ct. Read —4C **62**
Gordon Pl. Read —4C **62**
Gordon Rd. Ashf —7M **73**
Gordon Rd. Camb —5N **119**
Gordon Rd. Crowt —7H **113**
Gordon Rd. M'head —7A **20**
Gordon Rd. Newb —9M **79**
Gordon Rd. Stai —8D **72**
Gordon Rd. That —6D **80**
Gordon Rd. W Dray —8M **25**
Gordon Rd. Wind —8B **46**
Gordon Wlk. Yat —4C **118**
Gore End Rd. Bal H —6N **99**
Gore End Vs. Bal H —6N **99**
Gore Rd. Burn —4L **21**
Gore, The. Burn —4K **21**
Goring La. Bfld C —1G **107**
Goring Rd. Stai —9E **72**
Goring Sq. Stai —8F **72**
Gorrick Sq. Wokgm —8N **89**
Gorse Dri. Wdly —4F **64**
Gorse Hill La. Vir W —6M **95**
Gorse Hill Rd. Vir W —6M **95**
Gorselands. Cav —7G **39**
Gorselands. Newb —5H **101**
Gorselands. Tadl —9K **105**
Gorselands. Yat —5A **118**
Gorse Meade. Slou —9D **22**
Gorse Pl. Wink R —2E **92**
Gorse Ride N. Wokgm —3K **111**
Gorse Ride S. Wokgm —3K **111**
Gorse Rd. Cook —9J **5**
Gorse Wlk. W Dray —7M **25**
Gosbrook Houses. Cav —3J 63
(off Star Rd.)
Gosbrook Rd. Cav —2G **63**
(in two parts)
Gosforth Clo. Lwr Ear —1B **88**
Goslar Way. Wind —8D **46**
Gosling Grn. Slou —2N **47**
Gosling Rd. Slou —2N **47**
Gossage Rd. Uxb —1N **25**
Gossmore Clo. Mar —6D **4**
Gossmore La. Mar —6D **4**
Gossmore Wlk. Mar —6D **4**
Goswell Hill. Wind —7F **46**
Goswell Rd. Wind —7F **46**
Gough's Barn La. Brack —4L **67**
(in two parts)
Gough's La. Brack —2A **92**
Gough's Meadow. Sand —2F **118**
Governor's Rd. Col T —3K **119**
Govett Gro. W'sham —5N **115**
Gower Pk. Col T —2H **119**
Gower St. Read —4E **62**
Grace Bennett Clo. Farn —9L **119**
Grace Ct. Slou —9E **22**
Grace Reynolds Wlk. Camb —3N **119**
Graces La. Chvly —4M **55**
Graffham Clo. Lwr Ear —3A **88**
Grafton Clo. G Grn —7N **23**
Grafton Clo. M'head —4B **20**
Grafton Rd. Tile —5L **61**
Graham Clo. Calc —8M **61**
Graham Clo. M'head —9N **19**
Grahame Av. Pang —8E **36**
Graham Rd. Cook —9J **5**
Graham Rd. W'sham —6M **115**
Grainges Yd. Uxb —1K **25**
Grampian Rd. Sand —8E **112**
Grampian Way. Slou —4B **48**
Gramp's Hill. Let B —2C **8**
Granby Ct. Read —5L **63**
Granby End. Bfld C —8J **85**
Granby Gdns. Read —5L **63**
Grand Av. Camb —3N **119**
Grand Union Office Pk., The. Uxb —7K **25**
Grange Av. Crowt —4F **112**
Grange Av. Read —6M **63**
Grange Clo. Gor —9K **15**
Grange Clo. Stai —9H **73**
Grange Clo. Wray —3N **71**
Grange Ct. Ear —4A **64**
Grange Ct. Egh —9A **72**
Grange Ct. Newb —9M **79**
Grange Ct. Stai —9H **73**
Grange Dri. Wbrn G —4N **5**
Grange La. Cook —7K **5**
Grange Lodge. Wind —6N **45**
Grangely Clo. Calc —8L **61**
Grange Rd. Brack —3N **91**
Grange Rd. Cook —8K **5**
Grange Rd. Egh —9A **72**
(in two parts)
Grange Rd. Farn —9M **119**
Grange Rd. Hen T —5D **16**
Grange, The. Burn —4M 21
(off Green La.)
Grange Way. Iver —7G **24**
Grangewood. Wex —6L **23**
Grant Av. Slou —7G **23**
Grantham Clo. Owl —9J **113**
Grantham Rd. Read —8N **61**
Granthams, The. Lamb —2H **27**
Grant Rd. Crowt —7G **112**
Grant Wlk. Asc —1N **115**
Granville Av. Slou —6F **22**
Granville Rd. Read —7A **62**
Grasmere Av. Slou —8J **23**
Grasmere Av. Tile —2N **61**
Grasmere Clo. Winn —2H **89**
Grasmere Pde. Slou —8K **23**
Grasmere Rd. Light —9L **115**
Grass Hill. Cav —1E **62**
Grassington Pl. That —8G **80**
Grassmead. That —9J **81**
Grassy La. M'head —7B **20**
Gratton Dri. Wind —1A **70**
Gratton Rd. Read —3J **87**
Gratwicke Rd. Tile —4M **61**
Gravel Hill. Cav —7F **38**
Gravel Hill. Hen T —4C **16**
Gravel Hill. Stcks —6C **78**
Gravelly Clo. N End —7M **99**
Gravelpithill La. Wokgm —6E **88**
Gravel Rd. Bin H —4M **39**
Graveney Dri. Cav —1E **62**
Gravett Clo. Hen T —6B **16**
Grayling Clo. Mar —7A **4**
Grayling Ct. Read —3G 63
(off De Montfort Rd.)
Grays All. M'head —7K **19**
Grays Cres. Wdly —5B **64**
Grayshot Dri. B'water —4G **119**
Grays Pk. Rd. Stoke P —3J **23**
Grays Pl. Slou —9H **23**
Gray's Rd. Slou —9H **23**
Grays Rd. Uxb —3M **25**
Grazeley Rd. Three M —7G **86**
Gt. Auclum Pl. Bfld C —9J **85**
Gt. Barn Ct. That —8F **80**
Gt. Benty. W Dray —3M **49**
Greatfield Clo. Farn —9M **119**
Greatfield Rd. Farn —9L **119**
Greatfields Dri. Uxb —6N **25**
Gt. Hill Cres. M'head —9M **19**
Gt. Hollands Rd. Brack —8J **91**
Gt. Hollands Sq. Brack —8K **91**
Greathouse Wlk. Brad —5J **59**
Gt. Knollys St. Read —4F **62**
Gt. Lea Cotts. Three M —6G **86**
Gt. Lea Ter. Three M —6G **86**
Gt. Severals. Kint —9F **76**
Greenacre. Wind —8A **46**
Greenacre Ct. Egh —1L **95**
Greenacre Mt. Tile —4L **61**
Greenacres. Wool H —9C **100**
Greenacres Av. Winn —9F **64**
Greenacres La. Winn —9F **64**
Greenbank Way. Camb —7N **119**
Green Bus. Cen., The. Stai —8D **72**
Green Clo. M'head —5C **20**
Green Clo. Tap —7K **21**
Green Cres. F Hth —1N **5**
Green Croft. Wokgm —3C **90**
Greencroft Gdns. Read —7N **61**
Greendale M. Slou —8J **23**
Green Dean Hill. Tok G —3B **38**
Green Dragon La. F Hth —1M **5**
Green Dri. Slou —3N **47**
(in two parts)
Green Dri. Wokgm —7C **90**
Green End. Yat —2B **118**
Green End Clo. Spen W —9H **87**
Green Farm Rd. Bag —7J **115**
Greenfern Av. Slou —7M **21**
Greenfields. M'head —8D **20**
Greenfields Rd. Read —3H **87**
Greenfield Way. Crowt —3E **112**
Green Finch Clo. Crowt —4D **112**
Greenfinch Clo. Tile —6J **61**
Greenham Clo. Wdly —6F **64**
Greenham Mill. Newb —8M **79**
Greenham Rd. Newb & Green —9L **79**
Green Hams La. Comp & Hamp N —1C **32**
Greenham Wood. Brack —8N **91**
Greenhaven. Yat —4A **118**
Greenhow. Brack —5L **91**
Greenlands. Wool H —9C **100**
Greenlands Rd. Camb —8M **119**
Greenlands Rd. Newb —1M **101**
Greenlands Rd. Stai —8H **73**
Green La. Asc —3A **94**
Green La. Bag —8J **115**
Green La. Bin H —4N **39**
Green La. B'water —5J **119**
Green La. Box —4E **54**
Green La. Burn —4M **21**
Green La. Chvly —5M **55**
Green La. Crowt —3E **114**
Green La. Dat —7K **47**
Green La. Egh —9C **72**
(in two parts)
Green La. Fac —9G **117**
Green La. Fif —7E **44**
Green La. Frogm —5F **118**
Green La. Hen T —6C **16**
Green La. Hurst —9K **65**
Green La. L Grn —9F **18**
Green La. M'head —8D **20**
Green La. Mort —9M **107**
Green La. Newb —9J **79**
Green La. Pang —9D **36**
Green La. P'mre —2K **31**
Green La. Read —1A **86**
Green La. Sand —2G **118**
Green La. Son C —1F **38**
Green La. Tap —8L **43**
Green La. That —8F **80**
Green La. Tut C —9H **59**
Green La. Uft N —9D **84**
Green La. Wind —8C **46**
Green La. Wokgm —9E **66**
Green La. Ct. Burn —4M **21**
Greenleas Av. Emm G —6H **39**
Greenleas Clo. Yat —2A **118**
Green Leys. M'head —4C **20**
Greenock Rd. Slou —7C **22**
Green Pk. Stai —7F **72**
Green Ride. Brack —9C **92**
Green Rd. Read —7M **63**
Greenside. Bour —2L **5**
Greenside. Crowt —5D **112**
Greenside. Slou —6C **22**
Greensward La. Arbor —8B **88**
Green, The. B'water —5G **118**
Green, The. Brack —6M **91**
Green, The. Burn —6L **21**
Green, The. Dat —6K **47**
Green, The. Kint —1G **98**
Green, The. Leck —7D **30**
Green, The. Slou —2F **46**
Green, The. Thea —1D **84**
Green, The. W Dray —2L **49**
Green, The. Woos —4K **89**
Green, The. Wray —3N **71**
Green, The. Yat —3A **118**
Green Verges. Mar —4C **4**
Greenview Ct. Ashf —8N **73**
Greenway. Burn —4L **21**
Greenway. Wool H —9C **100**
Greenways. Egh —9N **71**
Greenways. Lamb —3H **27**
Greenways. Sand —9F **112**
Greenways Dri. Asc —1N **115**
Greenways Dri. M'head —6L **19**
Greenway, The. Slou —9N **21**
Greenway, The. Uxb —3L **25**
Green Wood. Asc —3F **92**
Greenwood Gro. Winn —9J **65**
Greenwood Rd. Crowt —4E **112**
Greenwood Rd. Tile —7N **61**
Gregory Clo. Lwr Ear —3B **88**
Gregory Dri. Old Win —3K **71**
Grenfell. M'head —6E **20**
Grenfell Av. M'head —8C **20**
Grenfell Pl. M'head —8C **20**
Grenfell Rd. M'head —7B **20**
Grenville Clo. Burn —3L **21**
Gresham Rd. Slou —7C **22**
Gresham Rd. Stai —9G **73**
Gresham Rd. Uxb —3N **25**
Gresham Way. Read —2A **62**
Gresham Way Ind. Est. Tile —2A **62**
Greyberry Copse Rd. That —2A **102**
Greyfriars Dri. Asc —7L **93**
Greyfriars Rd. Read —4G **63**
Grey's Ct. Read —5J **63**
Greys Hill. Hen T —5C **16**
Greys Rd. Hen T —6A **16**
Greystoke Ct. Crowt —6E **112**
Greystoke Rd. Cav —9J **39**
Greystoke Rd. Slou —6A **22**
Griffin Clo. M'head —9B **20**
Griffin Clo. Slou —1E **46**
Griffiths Clo. That —9J **81**
Grindle Clo. That —6F **80**
Gringer Hill. M'head —5A **20**
Groombridge Pl. Don —5J **79**
Grosvenor Clo. Iver —4E **24**
Grosvenor Ct. B'water —6H **119**
Grosvenor Ct. Slou —7G **23**
Grosvenor Dri. M'head —6F **20**
Grosvenor Rd. Cav —1H **63**
Grove Clo. Old Win —4K **71**
Grove Clo. Slou —2H **47**
Grove Clo. Wokgm —3C **112**
Grove Cotts. Cav —8G **39**
Grove Ct. Egh —9B **72**
Grove End. Bag —6J **115**
Grove Hill. Cav —9G **39**
Groveland Pl. Read —4B **62**
Groveland Rd. Speen —6H **79**
Grovelands Av. Winn —1J **89**
Grovelands Clo. Winn —9J **65**
Grovelands Rd. Read —5B **62**
Grovelands Rd. Spen W —9J **87**
Grove La. Uxb —5N **25**
Grove La. Wink R —9E **68**
Grove Pde. Slou —1J **47**
Grove Rd. Burn —4N **21**
Grove Rd. Emm G —8G **39**
Grove Rd. Hen T —5D **16**
Grove Rd. M'head —7C **20**
Grove Rd. Newb —6H **79**
Grove Rd. Son C —1F **38**
Grove Rd. Uxb —1L **25**
Grove Rd. Wind —8E **46**
Groves Clo. Bour —4N **5**
Groves Lea. Mort —4G **107**
Groves, The. Chilt F —1G **75**
Groves Way. Cook —9J **5**
Grove, The. Asc —3F **92**
Grove, The. Egh —9B **72**
Grove, The. Read —5J **63**
Grove, The. Slou —1J **47**
Grove, The. That —7G **80**
Grove, The. Twy —8J **41**
Grove Way. Uxb —1L **25**
Grubwood La. Cook —9E **4**
Guards Club Rd. M'head —7F **20**
Guards Rd. Wind —8M **45**
Guildford Rd. Bag —7H **115**
(in two parts)
Guildford Rd. Light —9K **115**
(in two parts)
Gullane Ct. Read —5K 63
(off Muirfield Clo.)
Gull Clo. Wokgm —6K **89**
Gullet Path. M'head —9A **20**
Gun St. Read —5G **63**
Gunthorpe Rd. Mar —4D **4**
Gurnard Clo. W Dray —8L **25**
Gurney Clo. Cav —8D **38**
Gurney Dri. Cav —9D **38**
Gwendale. M'head —5N **19**
Gwent Clo. M'head —1M **43**
Gwyn Clo. Newb —2K **101**
Gwynne Clo. Tile —1L **61**
Gwynne Clo. Wind —7A **46**
Gwyns Piece. Lamb —2H **27**
Gypsey La. Mar —2C **4**
Gypsy La. Mar —3C **4**

Haddenhurst Ct. Binf —1G **90**
Haddon Dri. Wdly —4D **64**
Haddon Rd. M'head —9N **19**
Hadfield Rd. Stai —3L **73**
Hadleigh Rise. Cav —8L **39**
Hadlow Ct. Slou —9E **22**
Hadrian Clo. Stai —5M **73**
Hadrian Wlk. E. Read —8J **63**
Hadrian Wlk. W. Read —8J **63**
Hadrian Way. Stai —4L **73**
Hafod. Cav —7F **38**
Hag Hill La. Tap —7K **21**
Hag Hill Rise. Tap —7K **21**
Hagley Rd. Read —8H **63**
Haig Dri. Slou —1D **46**
Haig Rd. Col T —3K **119**
Hailey La. P'mre —5H **31**
Hailsham Clo. Owl —9H **113**
Halcyon Ter. Tile —4M **61**
Haldane Rd. Cav —8E **38**
Hale End. Brack —6C **92**
Hale St. Stai —8F **72**
Hale Way. Frim —9N **119**
Halewood. Brack —9K **91**
Halfacre Clo. Spen W —8H **87**
Half Mile Rd. Hung —3G **50**
Half Moon St. Bag —7H **115**
Halfpenny Catch La. Beed —3N **31**
Halfpenny La. Asc —9D **94**
Halfpenny La. Chol —2E **14**
Halifax Clo. M'head —6L **19**
Halifax Pl. That —7F **80**
Halifax Rd. M'head —6L **19**
Halifax Way. M'head —6L **19**
Halkingcroft. Slou —1L **47**
Hallbrooke Gdns. Binf —2J **91**
Hall Clo. Leck —8D **30**
Hall Ct. Dat —6K **47**
Halldore Hill. Cook —8J **5**
Halley Dri. Asc —4G **93**
Hall Farm Cres. Yat —4B **118**
Hallgrove Bottom. Bag —5J **115**
Hall La. Yat —4A **118**
Hall Meadow. Burn —3M **21**
Hall Pl. La. Bur G —6F **18**
Halls La. Shin —2L **87**
Halls La. Wal L —6E **42**
Hallsmead Ct. Read —3G 63
(off De Montfort Rd.)
Halls Rd. Tile —6K **61**
Halpin Clo. Calc —8K **61**
Halstead Clo. Wdly —5D **64**
Halstead Ho. Baug —9H **105**
Hamble Av. B'water —4H **119**
Hambleberry Ct. Tile —4K **61**
Hamble Ct. Read —6H **63**
Hambleden Wlk. M'head —3B **20**
Hambledon Clo. Lwr Ear —2D **88**
Hambledon Ct. Brack —6B **92**
Hamble Dri. Tadl —9M **105**
Hamblin Meadow. Edd —4L **75**
Hambridge La. Newb —9B **80**
Hambridge Rd. Newb —9M **79**
Hamilton Av. Hen T —5D **16**
Hamilton Clo. Newb —2L **101**
Hamilton Dri. Asc —9A **94**
Hamilton Gdns. Burn —4L **21**
Hamilton Pk. M'head —8L **19**
Hamilton Rd. Read —5L **63**
Hamilton Rd. Slou —7C **22**
Hamilton Rd. Uxb —5L **25**
Hamilton Rd. Warg —3K **41**
Ham La. Egh —8K **71**
Ham La. Old Win —2L **71**
Hamlet St. Warf —3B **92**
Hamlet, The. Gall C —1B **38**
Hammond Clo. That —9J **81**
Hammond's Heath. Mort —4J **107**
Hammond Way. Light —9L **115**
Hampden Clo. Stoke P —4J **23**
Hampden Rd. Cav —2H **63**
Hampden Rd. M'head —6M **19**
Hampden Rd. Slou —2A **48**
Hampshire Av. Slou —6E **22**
Hampshire Rise. Warf —1C **92**
Hampshire Rd. Camb —9C **114**
Hampshire Wlk. Tile —6J 61
(off Barton Rd.)
Hampshire Way. Wokgm —5J **89**
Hampstead Bottom. Son —5B **40**
Hampstead Ct. Read —4B **62**
Hampstead Hill. Son —5B **40**
Hampstead Norreys Rd. Herm —5E **56**
Hampton Towers. Read —6E **62**
Ham Rd. Shalb —7F **96**
Hanbury Clo. Burn —6K **21**
Hanbury Dri. Calc —8L **61**
Hanbury Way. Camb —6N **119**
Hancocks Mt. Asc —8N **93**
Hancombe Rd. Sand —9E **112**
Handford La. Yat —4B **118**
Hangerfield Clo. Yat —4A **118**
Hanger Rd. Tadl —9H **105**
Hangman's Stone La. Chad —7K **29**

Hankin's La. Ham M —1J 99
Hanley Clo. Wind —7N 45
Hannibal Rd. Stai —4L 73
Hanningtons Way. Bfld C —8K 85
Hanover Clo. Egh —1K 95
Hanover Clo. Slou —2J 47
Hanover Clo. Wind —7B 46
Hanover Clo. Yat —2B 118
Hanover Ct. Cav —7J 39
Hanover Gdns. Brack —9K 91
Hanover Mead. Bray —2F 44
Hanover Mead. Newb —4H 101
Hanover Way. Wind —8B 46
Hanwood Clo. Wdly —4B 64
Hanworth Clo. Brack —8N 91
Hanworth Rd. Brack —1L 113
Harborough Clo. Slou —9N 21
Harbour Clo. Farn —9L 119
Harcourt Clo. Dor R —2H 45
Harcourt Clo. Egh —9D 72
Harcourt Clo. Hen T —5B 16
Harcourt Dri. Ear —1M 87
Harcourt Rd. Brack —8M 91
Harcourt Rd. Camb —4M 119
Harcourt Rd. Dor R —2J 45
Harcourt Rd. Wind —7A 46
Hardell Clo. Egh —9B 72
Harding Rd. Wdly —4B 64
Hardings Clo. Iver —4D 24
Hardings Row. Iver —4D 24
Hardwell Way. Brack —6B 92
Hardwick Clo. M'head —6K 19
Hardwick Rd. Tile —4N 61
Hardwick Rd. Whit T —6D 36
Hardy Av. Yat —5A 118
Hardy Clo. Cav —2J 63
Hardy Clo. Slou —9C 22
Hardy Clo. That —6F 80
Hardy Grn. Crowt —6F 112
Harebell Dri. That —7H 81
Harefield Clo. Winn —1H 89
Harefield Rd. M'head —7L 19
Harefield Rd. Uxb —1K 25
Hare Shoots. M'head —9B 20
Harewood Dri. Cold A —3F 80
Harewood Pl. Slou —2J 47
Hargrave Rd. M'head —6A 20
Hargreaves Wlk. Calc —8N 61
Hargreaves Way. Calc —8N 61 (off Bayford Dri.)
Harkness Rd. Burn —6L 21
Harlech Av. Cav —8L 39
Harlech Rd. B'water —5H 119
Harleyford La. Mar —7A 4
Harley Rd. Cav —2H 63
Harlington Rd. Uxb —4N 25
Harlton Clo. Lwr Ear —3B 88
Harman Ct. Winn —1G 89
Harman's Water Rd. Brack —7A 92
Harmar Clo. Wokgm —5C 90
Harmondsworth La. W Dray —5M 49
Harmondsworth Rd. W Dray —4M 49
Harness Clo. Read —5H 87
Harold Rd. Kint —9G 77
Harpesford Av. Vir W —7K 95
Harpsden Rd. Bin H —2N 39
Harpsden Rd. Hen T —6D 16
Harpsden Way. Hen T —6D 16
Harpton Clo. Yat —2B 118
Harpton Pde. Yat —2B 118
Harrier Clo. Wdly —6F 64
Harrington Clo. Lwr Ear —1B 88
Harrington Clo. Newb —9M 79 (King's Rd.)
Harrington Clo. Newb —6B 80 (Waller Dri.)
Harrington Clo. Wind —1B 70
Harris Arc. Read —4H 63
Harris Clo. Wdly —4G 65
Harrison Clo. Twy —1L 65
Harrison Way. Slou —9N 21
Harrogate Ct. Slou —4B 48
Harrogate Rd. Cav —9E 38
Harrow Bottom Rd. Vir W —8N 95
Harrow Clo. M'head —5B 20
Harrow Ct. Read —6F 62
Harrow La. M'head —5A 20
Harrow Rd. Felt —6N 73
Harrow Rd. Slou —2A 48
Hart Clo. Brack —2M 91
Hart Clo. Farn —9J 119
Hart Dyke Clo. Wokgm —9N 89
Hartford Rise. Camb —3N 119
Hartigan Pl. Wdly —4F 64
Hartin Clo. Uxb —3M 25
Hartland Clo. Slou —9F 22
Hartland Rd. Read —2H 87
Hartley Clo. B'water —4F 118
Hartley Clo. Stoke P —2L 23
Hartley Copse. Old Win —3J 71
Hartley Ct. Rd. Three M —5E 86
Hartleys. Sil —9C 106
Hartley Way. That —7H 81
Hartmead Rd. That —8H 81
Hartsbourne Rd. Ear —9M 63
Harts Clo. Arbor —9D 88
Harts Clo. Lamb —2H 27
Hartshill Rd. Tadl —9H 105
Harts Hill Rd. That & Up Buck —7H 81
Hart's La. Uft N —6C 84
Harts Leap Clo. Sand —9F 112
Harts Leap Rd. Sand —1E 118
Hartslock Ct. Pang —7C 36
Hartslock View. Lwr B —3N 35
Hartslock Way. Tile —2K 61
Hart St. Hen T —4D 16
Hart St. Read —4E 62
Harvard Clo. Wdly —4G 64
Harvard Rd. Owl —9J 113
Harvaston Pde. Tile —5N 61
Harvest Clo. Tile —6J 61
Harvest Clo. Yat —5A 118
Harvest Grn. Newb —1J 101
Harvest Hill. Bour & Wbrn G —5N 5
Harvest Hill Rd. M'head —1B 44
Harvest Ride. Brack —1L 91
Harvest Rd. Egh —9M 71
Harvey Ho. Read —6D 62
Harvey Rd. Slou —2C 48
Harvey Rd. Uxb —3N 25
Harwich Clo. Lwr Ear —2C 88
Harwich Rd. Slou —7C 22
Harwood Dri. Uxb —2N 25
Harwood Gdns. Old Win —4K 71
Harwood Rise. Wool H —8D 100 (in two parts)
Harwood Rd. Mar —6A 4
Haslemere Rd. Wind —7C 46
Hasting Clo. M'head —3F 44
Hastings Clo. Read —8A 62
Hatch Clo. Chap R —4E 82
Hatch End. W'sham —6M 115
Hatchet La. Asc & Wind —1K 93
Hatchet La. Wink —7L 69
Hatchets La. Fril —5L 57
Hatchgate Clo. Cold A —5F 80
Hatchgate Copse. Brack —8J 91
Hatchgate Gdns. Burn —4N 21
Hatch Ga. La. C Grn —7L 17
Hatch La. Chap R —3E 82
Hatch La. W Dray —6L 49
Hatch La. Wind —9C 46
Hatch Ride. Crowt —3E 112
Hatch Rd. Bfld —5L 85
Hatch, The. Wind —6M 45
Hatchway. Read —4J 87
Hatfield Clo. M'head —8N 19
Hatfield Ct. Calc —8J 61
Hatfield Rd. Slou —1J 47
Hatford Rd. Read —8B 62
Hatherley Rd. Read —6L 63
Hatherwood. Yat —4D 118
Hatt Clo. P'mre —6H 31
Hatton Av. Slou —5F 22
Hatton Gro. W Dray —1L 49
Hatton Hill. Ash'd —6D 34
Hatton Hill. W'sham —4L 115
Haughurst Hill. Baug —9E 104
Havelock Cres. M'head —7M 19
Havelock Rd. M'head —7M 19
Havelock Rd. Wokgm —5M 89
Havelock St. Wokgm —5M 89
Haven Ct. Read —5L 63
Haven, The. Kint —9F 76
Haversham Dri. Brack —8M 91
Hawkchurch Rd. Read —3K 87
Hawkedon Way. Lwr Ear —1C 88
Hawker Ct. Langl —2B 48
Hawker Way. Wdly —6F 64
Hawkesbury Dri. Calc —9M 61
Hawkes Clo. Wokgm —4M 89
Hawkes Leap. W'sham —4L 115
Hawkesworth Dri. Bag —9G 115
Hawkins Clo. Brack —4D 92
Hawkins Way. Wokgm —5C 90
Hawk La. Brack —6A 92
Hawkridge Ct. Brack —6B 92
Hawkridge Hill. Fril —6L 57
Hawks Hill. Bour —5N 5
Hawkshill Rd. Slou —4C 22
Hawks Way. Stai —7G 73
Hawkswood Gro. Ful —1A 24
Hawkswood Ho. Brack —3J 91
Hawksworth Rd. Bfld C —8J 85
Haw La. Hamp N & Ash'd —6A 34
Hawley Clo. Calc —8K 61
Hawley Ct. Farn —9J 119
Hawley Grn. B'water —6J 119
Hawley La. Farn —8L 119 (in two parts)
Hawley Rd. B'water —5H 119
Haws La. Stai —3H 73
Hawthorn Clo. Brack —3L 91
Hawthorn Clo. Mar —3C 4
Hawthorn Cotts. Graz —8C 86
Hawthorn Dri. Den —1K 25
Hawthorne Ct. Stai —4L 73 (off Hawthorne Way)
Hawthorne Cres. B'water —5J 119
Hawthorne Cres. Slou —7G 23
Hawthorne Cres. W Dray —1N 49
Hawthorne Rd. Cav —9L 39
Hawthorne Rd. Stai —8D 72
Hawthornes. Tile —1J 61
Hawthorne Way. Gt Shef —9G 28
Hawthorne Way. Stai —4L 73
Hawthorne Way. Wink —5L 69
Hawthorn Gdns. M'head —9B 20
Hawthorn Gdns. Read —1L 87
Hawthorn Hill Rd. M'head —1N 67
Hawthorn La. Brack —4B 68
Hawthorn La. Farn C —1B 22
Hawthorn La. Wind —4A 68
Hawthorn Rd. Newb —7L 79
Hawthorns, The. Charv —1F 64
Hawthorns, The. Coln —7G 48
Hawthorn Way. Son —2D 64
Hawtrey Clo. Slou —1K 47
Hawtrey Rd. Wind —8E 46
Haydon La. E Ils —7B 12
Hayes La. Wokgm —7G 89
Hayes Pl. Mar —6B 4
Hayfield Clo. Tile —4K 61
Hayfield Ct. E'bury —7M 27
Hayley Grn. Warf —9C 68
Haymaker Clo. Uxb —1N 25
Haymill Rd. Slou —5N 21
Haynes Clo. Slou —4A 48
Hay Rd. Read —7F 62
Hayse Hill. Wind —7N 45
Haywards Clo. Hen T —5B 16
Haywards Mead. Eton W —4B 46
Haywards, The. That —7G 81
Haywood. Brack —9N 91
Haywood Ct. Read —5M 63
Haywood Way. Read —7N 61
Hazel Av. W Dray —2N 49
Hazelbank. Finch —4J 111
Hazelby Cotts. N End —6M 99
Hazel Clo. Bfld —6J 85
Hazel Clo. Egh —1K 95
Hazel Clo. Mar —1A 4
Hazel Clo. Wokgm —6L 89
Hazel Cres. Read —1L 87
Hazelcroft Clo. Uxb —1N 25
Hazeldene. Chvly —3M 55
Hazel Dri. Wdly —7B 64
Hazel Grn. Baug —9F 104
Hazel Gro. That —6G 80
Hazelhurst Rd. Burn —3M 21
Hazell Clo. M'head —6C 20
Hazell Hill. Brack —5N 91
Hazell Way. Stoke P —1H 23
Hazelmoor La. Gall C —1C 38
Hazel Rd. Pur T —8K 37
Hazelwood Clo. Tile —3K 61
Hazelwood La. Binf —9K 67
Hazlemere Rd. Slou —9K 23
Heacham Clo. Lwr Ear —3N 87
Headington Clo. M'head —7L 19
Headington Clo. Wokgm —3B 90
Headington Dri. Wokgm —3B 90
Headington Rd. M'head —6L 19
Headley Clo. Wdly —4F 64
Headley Pk. Ind. Est. Wdly —5E 64
Headley Rd. Wdly —5D 64
Headley Rd. E. Wdly —5E 64
Head's La. Ink C —5F 98
Heardman Clo. That —9J 81
Hearmon Clo. Yat —3C 118
Hearne Dri. Holyp —4D 44
Hearn Rd. Wdly —7D 64
Hearn Wlk. Brack —3B 92
Hearsey Gdns. B'water —3F 118 (in two parts)
Heathacre. Coln —7E 48
Heath Clo. Stai —3K 73
Heath Clo. Vir W —6M 95
Heath Clo. Wokgm —7N 89
Heathcote. M'head —3E 44
Heathcote Rd. Camb —4N 119
Heathcote Way. W Dray —9L 25
Heath Ct. Bag —7H 115
Heath Ct. Baug —8G 105
Heath Croft. Cav —9H 39
Heath Dri. Bin H —4N 39
Heath End Rd. Baug —9F 104
Heather Clo. Uxb —6N 25
Heather Clo. Wokgm —3K 111
Heatherdale Rd. Camb —5N 119
Heatherdene Av. Crowt —6C 112
Heatherdene Clo. Read —4J 87
Heatherden Grn. Iver —2D 24
Heather Dri. Asc —9D 94
Heather Dri. Tadl —8H 105
Heather La. W Dray —7M 25
Heatherley Clo. Camb —4M 119
Heatherley Rd. Camb —4M 119
Heathermount. Brack —6B 92
Heathermount Dri. Crowt —4D 112
Heathermount Gdns. Crowt —4D 112
Heatherside Dri. Vir W —8J 95
Heathers, The. Stai —4N 73
Heatherway. Crowt —5E 112
Heathfield. Mort C —4H 107
Heathfield Av. Asc —7A 94
Heathfield Av. Bin H —4A 40
Heathfield Av. Tile —6L 61
Heathfield Clo. Bin H —4A 40
Heathfields. Chvly —4L 55
Heath Hanger La. Hung —1B 76
Heath Hill Rd. N. Crowt —5F 112
Heath Hill Rd. S. Crowt —5F 112
Heathlands. Baug —9G 104
Heathlands. Brack —6L 91
Heathlands Ct. Wokgm —2D 112
Heathlands Ct. Yat —5C 118
Heathlands Dri. M'head —8L 19
Heathlands Rd. Wokgm —8D 90
Heath La. Henw —6F 80
Heathmoors. Brack —7N 91
Heathpark Dri. W'sham —6N 115
Heath Pl. Bag —7H 115
Heath Ride. Wokgm —4N 111
Heath Rise. Vir W —6M 95
Heath Rd. Bag —7H 115
Heath Rd. Pam H —9N 105
Heath Rd. Read —7N 63
Heath Rd. South —1J 83
Heathrow Airport. Houn —8M 49
Heathrow Clo. W Dray —7J 49
Heathrow Copse. Baug —9F 104
Heathrow Summit Cen. W Dray —6L 49
Heathway. Asc —3H 93
Heathway. Iver —3E 24
Heathway. Tile —4K 61
Heathwood Clo. Yat —2B 118
Heavens Lea. Bour —5N 5
Hedge Way. Newb —7N 79
Hedingham M. M'head —7A 20
Hedsor Hill. Bour —5M 5
Hedsor Rd. Bour —5M 5
Heelas Rd. Wokgm —5M 89
Helena Rd. Wind —8F 46
Helen Ct. Read —7A 62
Hellas Rd. Wokgm —5M 89
Hellyer Way. Bour —4M 5
Helmsdale. Brack —7B 92
Helmsdale Clo. Read —4B 62
Helson La. Wind —7D 46
Helston Gdns. Read —2H 87
Helston La. Wind —7D 46
Hemdean Hill. Cav —1G 63
Hemdean Rise. Cav —1G 62
Hemdean Rd. Cav —2G 63
Hempson Av. Slou —2L 47
Hemsdale. M'head —5M 19
Hemwood Rd. Wind —9N 45
Hencroft St. Slou —2H 47
Hendons Way. Holyp —4E 44
Hendon Way. Stai —3L 73
Hengrove Clo. Lwr Ear —1D 88
Hengrove Cres. Ashf —7L 73
Henley Bri. Hen T —4D 16
Henley Clo. Farn —9J 119
Henley Gdns. Yat —4B 118
Henley Rd. Cav —1H 63
Henley Rd. M'head —6H 19
Henley Rd. Mar —7A 4
Henley Rd. Medm —1K 17
Henley Rd. Slou —7A 22
Henley Rd. Warg —8H 17
Henley Wood Rd. Ear —8C 64
Henry Rd. Slou —1F 46
Henrys, The. That —7G 80
Henry St. Read —6H 63
Henshaw Cres. Newb —2H 101
Hensworth Rd. Ashf —9L 73
Henwick Clo. Henw —5E 80
Henwick La. That —6D 80
Henwood Copse. Up Bas —7J 35
Hepplewhite Clo. Baug —9G 105
Hepworth Croft. Col T —3J 119
Herald Way. Wdly —5F 64
Herbert Clo. Brack —7M 91
Hercies Rd. Uxb —1N 25
Herewood Clo. Newb —7K 79
Heritage Clo. Uxb —5K 25
Heritage Ct. Read —5F 62
Hermes Clo. Wokgm —4G 89
Hermitage Clo. Slou —2L 47
Hermitage Dri. Asc —4H 93
Hermitage Dri. Twy —8J 41
Hermitage La. Wind —1C 70
Hermitage Pde. Asc —5L 93
Hermitage Rd. Cold A —9E 56
Hermitage, The. E'bury —5L 27
Hermitage, The. Uxb —1M 25
Hermits Clo. Bfld C —8J 85
Hermit's Hill. Bfld —7K 85
Herndon Clo. Egh —8B 72
Heroes Wlk. Read —4H 87
Heron Clo. Asc —3G 93
Herondale. Brack —9N 91
Heron Dri. Slou —3C 48
Heron Dri. Twy —7K 41
Heronfield. Egh —1K 95
Herongate. Hung —4K 75
Heron Island. Cav —3J 63
Heron Rd. Wokgm —5K 89
Heronsbrook. Asc —4A 94
Herons Ct. Light —9M 115
Heron Shaw. Gor —7L 15
Herons Pl. Mar —5C 4
Heron's Way. Wokgm —4C 90
Heron Way. Read —8E 62
Heron Way. That —8E 80
Herrings La. W'sham —5N 115
Herriot Clo. Yat —5A 118
Herschel Pk. Dri. Slou —1H 47
Herschel St. Slou —1H 47
Hertford Clo. Cav —7K 39
Hertford Clo. Wokgm —6K 89
Hetherington Clo. Slou —4B 22
Hever Clo. M'head —8N 19
Hewett Av. Cav —9D 38
Hewett Clo. Cav —9D 38
Hewgate Ct. Hen T —5D 16
Hewlett Pl. Bag —7J 115
Hexham Clo. Owl —8H 113
Hexham Rd. Read —9J 63
Heywood Av. M'head —4L 43
Heywood Ct. M'head —4L 43
Heywood Ct. Clo. M'head —3L 43
Heywood Gdns. M'head —4L 43
Hibbert Rd. M'head —2D 44
Hibbert's All. Wind —7F 46
Hicks La. B'water —4F 118
Higgs La. Bag —7G 114
High Beech. Brack —6C 92
Highbeeches Clo. Mar —1A 4
Highbridge Clo. Cav —8L 39
High Bri. Wharf. Read —5H 63
Highbury Rd. Tile —5H 61
Highclere. Asc —7N 93
Highclere Clo. Brack —4B 92
Highdown Av. Cav —7G 38
Highdown Hill Rd. Cav —6G 38
Higher Alham. Brack —9B 92
Highfield. Brack —8K 91
Highfield. Lwr Ear —1A 88
Highfield Av. Newb —9L 79
Highfield Clo. Egh —1L 95
Highfield Clo. Wokgm —5A 90
Highfield Ct. Bfld C —8J 85
Highfield Ct. Farn R —2D 22
Highfield Ct. Twy —9K 41
Highfield La. M'head —1L 43
Highfield Pk. Mar —6A 4
Highfield Rd. Bour —4M 5
Highfield Rd. M'head —6M 19
Highfield Rd. Newb —1K 101
Highfield Rd. Tile —9J 37
Highfield Rd. Wind —9B 46
High Fields. Asc —7B 94
Highgate Rd. Wdly —7C 64
Highgrove. Farn —9M 119
Highgrove Pk. M'head —6B 20
Highgrove St. Read —7J 63
Highgrove Ter. Read —6H 63
Highland Av. Wokgm —6H 89
Highmead Clo. Read —1L 87
High Meadow. Cav —1D 62
Highmoor Rd. Cav —1E 62
High Rd. Cook —8J 5
High Rd. Uxb —6K 25
High St. Bray, Bray —1F 44
High St. Eton, Eton —5F 46
High St. Iver, Iver —7F 24
High St. Ascot, Asc —5J 93
High St. Bagshot, Bag —7H 115
High St. Boxford, Box —2M 77
High St. Bracknell, Brack —4M 91
High St. Burnham, Burn —4M 21
High St. Camberley, Camb —3N 119
High St. Chalvey, Chalv —2E 46
High St. Chieveley, Chvly —4M 55
High St. Colnbrook, Coln —6D 48
High St. Compton, Comp —1G 33
High St. Cookham, Cook —8M 5
High St. Cowley, Cow —5K 25
High St. Crowthorne, Crowt —6G 112
High St. Datchet, Dat —7K 47
High St. East Ilsley, E Ils —8B 12
High St. Egham, Egh —9A 72
High St. Goring, Gor —8K 15
High St. Harmondsworth, Harm —5L 49
High St. Hungerford, Hung —6K 75
High St. Kintbury, Kint —9E 76
High St. Lambourn, Lamb —3H 27
High St. Langley, Langl —4A 48
High St. Little Bedwyn, L Bed —2A 96
High St. Little Sandhurst, L Sand —9D 112
High St. Maidenhead, M'head (in two parts) —7C 20
High St. Marlow, Mar —5B 4
High St. Pangbourne, Pang —8D 36
High St. Sandhurst, Sand —9D 112
High St. Slough, Slou —9H 23
High St. Sonning, Son —1C 64
High St. Staines, Stai —8G 72
High St. Stanwell, Stanw —3L 73
High St. Streatley, Streat —8H 15
High St. Sunningdale, S'dale —7C 94
High St. Sunninghill, S'hill —7N 93
High St. Taplow, Tap —5H 21
High St. Thatcham, That —8G 80
High St. Theale, Thea —9F 60
High St. Twyford, Twy —8J 41
High St. Upper Lambourn, Up Lamb —9D 6
High St. Uxbridge, Uxb —1K 25 (in two parts)
High St. Wargrave, Warg —4H 41
High St. W. Slou —1G 47
High St. Whitchurch on Thames, Whit T —6D 36
High St. Windsor, Wind —7F 46
High St. Wraysbury, Wray —3N 71
High St. Yiewsley, Yiew —8L 25
High Town Rd. M'head —8B 20 (in two parts)
High Tree Dri. Ear —6A 64
Highview. Calc —7J 61
Highview Cres. Camb —9C 114
Highway. Crowt —5E 112
Highway Av. M'head —7L 19
Highwayman's Ridge. W'sham —4L 115
Highway Rd. M'head —8M 19
Highwood. Shaw —5M 79
Highwood Clo. Yat —5B 118
Highwoods Clo. Mar —1A 4
Highwoods Dri. Mar —1A 4
Highworth Cotts. Baug —9E 104
Highworth Way. Tile —2J 61
Hilary Clo. Read —4J 87
Hilborn Way. Arbor X —1F 110
Hilbury Rd. Ear —9N 63
Hilcot Rd. Read —4D 62
Hildens Dri. Tile —5K 61
Hildesley Ct. E Ils —8B 12
Hilfield. Yat —4D 118
Hillary Dri. Crowt —4F 112
Hillary Rd. Slou —1N 47
Hillberry. Brack —9N 91
Hill Bottom Clo. Whit H —2F 36
Hillbrow. Read —2L 87
Hill Clo. Newb —3H 101
Hill Copse View. Brack —3B 92
Hill Cres. Woolh —8E 82
Hillcrest. Tadl —9K 105
Hillcrest Av. Cook —1B 20
Hillersdon. Slou —6K 23
Hill Farm La. Binf —7J 67
Hill Farm Rd. Binf —7J 67
Hill Farm Rd. Mar —1B 4
Hill Farm Rd. Tap —3H 21
Hill Gdns. Streat —8H 15
Hillgreen La. P'mre —7G 31
Hill Ho. Cav —9H 39
Hillhouse La. Hdly —9K 103
Hilliards Rd. Uxb —7L 25
Hilliary Dri. Crowt —4F 112
Hilliers Av. Uxb —4N 25
Hillingdon Av. Stai —5M 73
Hillingdon Hill. Uxb —3M 25
Hillingdon Rd. Uxb —2L 25
Hill Lands. Warg —3J 41
Hillmead Ct. Tap —6J 21
Hill Pl. Farn C —1D 22
Hill Rise. Slou —5B 48
Hill Rd. Arbor —1E 110
Hill Rd. Newb —7J 79
Hillside. Bfld C —8K 85
Hillside. Ear —9C 64
Hillside. M'head —9A 20
Hillside. Read —7J 63
Hillside. Sand —2K 119
Hillside. Slou —1G 46
Hillside. Vir W —8L 95
Hillside. Whit T —5E 36
Hillside Dri. Binf —1G 91
Hillside Pk. Asc —9B 94
Hillside Rd. Hung —7K 75
Hillside Rd. Mar —3C 4
Hills La. Cook —8G 5
Hill St. Read —6H 63
Hilltop Clo. Asc —4A 94
Hilltop Rd. Cav —8D 38
Hilltop Rd. Ear —5A 64
Hilltop Rd. Twy —6K 41
Hilltopr Rd. Ear —4A 64
Hilltop View. Yat —4A 118
Hillview Clo. Tile —2J 61
Hillview Rd. Wray —3M 71
Hilmanton. Lwr Ear —3M 87
Hilperton Rd. Slou —1G 46
Hilton Clo. Uxb —3J 25
Hindell Clo. Farn —9L 119
Hindhay La. M'head —3M 19
Hindhead Rd. Ear —9N 63
Hinksey Clo. Slou —2C 48
Hinton Clo. Crowt —3F 112
Hinton Dri. Crowt —3F 112
Hinton Rd. Hurst —4L 65
Hinton Rd. Slou —8A 22
Hinton Rd. Uxb —2K 25
Hirstwood. Tile —3M 61
Hirtes Av. Shin —6L 87
Hitcham La. Tap & Slou —4H 21
Hitcham Rd. Tap & Slou —7J 21
Hitherhooks Hill. Binf —3J 91
Hithermoor Rd. Stai —3G 73

Hobbis Dri. M'head —8L 19
Hobley La. Wool H —9B 100
Hocket, The. Hen T —3C 16
Hockett La. Cook —9D 4
Hocketts Clo. Whit H —2F 36
Hockford La. Brimp C —7B 104
Hockham Rd. Comp —9G 13
Hockley La. Stoke P —1K 23
Hodgedale La. Hur & War R —4A 18
Hodge La. Wink —9K 69
(in two parts)
Hodges Clo. Bag —9G 115
Hodsoll Rd. Read —4F 62
Hoe Benham La. Half —5L 77
Hogarth Av. Read —7N 61
Hogarth Clo. Col T —3J 119
Hogarth Clo. Slou —8A 22
Hogfair La. Burn —4M 21
Hogg Robinson Ho. Read
(off Greyfriars Rd.) —4G 63
Hogmoor La. Hurst —3L 65
Hogoak La. Wind —4D 68
Hogwood Ind. Est. Finch —4F 110
Hogwood La. Finch —4F 110
Holbeck. Brack —8K 91
Holberton Rd. Read —3K 87
Holborne Clo. Newb —5G 101
Holford Clo. Tile —4K 61
Holkam Clo. Tile —3N 61
Holland Pines. Brack —9K 91
Holland Rd. Mar —5D 4
Holland Rd. Tile —5L 61
Hollands, The. That —8H 81
Hollicombe Clo. Read —5M 61
Hollies, The. Newb —5H 101
Hollington Pl. That —8F 80
Hollins Wlk. Read —6C 62
Holloway Clo. W Dray —4M 49
Holloway La. W Dray —5L 49
Hollow Hill La. Iver —8C 24
Hollow La. Shin —5L 87
Hollow La. Vir W —5L 95
Holly Acre. Yat —4B 118
Hollybush Hill. Stoke P —1J 23
Hollybush La. Bfld C —8F 84
Hollybush La. Cook D —9E 4
Hollybush La. Iver —7C 24
Hollybush Ride. W'sham —3J 115
Hollybush Ride. Wokgm —6A 112
Holly Clo. Egh —1K 95
Hollycombe. Egh —8L 71
Holly Cres. Wind —8N 45
Hollycroft Clo. W Dray —5N 49
Hollycroft Gdns. W Dray —5N 49
Hollydale Clo. Read —2L 87
Holly Dri. M'head —6C 20
Holly Dri. Old Win —2G 71
Hollyfields Clo. Camb —4M 119
Holly Gdns. W Dray —1N 49
Hollyhook Clo. Crowt —4E 112
Holly Ho. Brack —8M 91
Holly La. Ash'd —7D 34
Holly La. Sil —2J 81
Holly La. W Wood —6H 99
Hollym Clo. Lwr Ear —1D 88
Holly Rd. Wdly —6F 64
Holly Spring Cotts. Brack —2A 92
Holly Spring La. Brack —3N 91
Hollytree Gdns. Frim —9N 119
Holly Wlk. Wind —8A 70
Holly Way. B'water —5H 119
Holmanleaze. M'head —6D 20
Holmbury Av. Crowt —3E 112
Holme Clo. Crowt —3E 112
Holmedale. Slou —8L 23
Holmedene. Bfld C —8J 85
Holmemoor Dri. Son —2C 64
Holme Pk. Farm La. Son —2B 64
Holmes Clo. Asc —8M 93
Holmes Clo. Wokgm —7M 89
Holmes Cres. Wokgm —7L 89
Holmesdale Clo. Iver —7G 25
Holmes Rd. Read —7N 63
Holmewood Clo. Wokgm —9M 89
Holmlea Rd. Dat —7L 47
Holmlea Rd. Gor —9L 15
Holmlea Wlk. Dat —7L 47
Holmwood Av. Read —7N 61
Holmwood Clo. M'head —9M 19
Holsworthy Clo. Lwr Ear —9D 64
Holt Clo. Farn —9N 119
Holt La. Bright —4B 30
Holt La. Wokgm —4N 89
Holton Heath. Brack —6C 92
Holt Rd. Kint —9G 77
Holt, The. Pur T —9L 37
Holtwood Rd. Ham M —5N 99
Holybrook Cres. Read —8A 62
Holybrook Rd. Read —7F 62
Holyport Rd. M'head —5D 44
Holyport St. Holyp —5D 44
Holyrood Clo. Cav —7K 39
Holywell Clo. Stai —5M 73
Holywell Ct. That —8G 81
Holywell Way. Stai —5M 73
Hombrook Dri. Brack —3J 91
Hombrook Ho. Brack —3J 91
Home Croft. Tile —3J 61
Home Farm Clo. Read —9H 63
Home Farm Way. Stoke P —2L 23
Homefield Way. Hung —6J 75
Homelea Clo. Farn —9M 119
Homemead Clo. Newb —2J 101
Home Meadow. Farn R —3E 22
Home Meadow Dri. F Hth —1M 5
Home Pk. Rd. Yat —3B 118
Homers Rd. Wind —7N 45
Homestead Rd. M'head —1A 44
Homestead Rd. Stai —9J 73
Homestead, The. Bin H —4A 40
Homewood. G Grn —7M 23
Hone Hill. Sand —1F 118
Honestey Bottom. Bright —3B 30
Honeybottom Rd. Tadl —9K 105
Honeycroft Hill. Uxb —1M 25
Honey End La. Read —6A 62
(in two parts)
Honeyfields. Hung —6K 75
Honey Hill. Lamb —2H 27
Honey Hill. Uxb —1N 25
Honey Hill. Wokgm —9D 90
Honeyhill Rd. Brack —3L 91
Honey La. Hur —5C 18
Honeysuckle Clo. Crowt —3E 112
Honeysuckle Clo. Iver —7D 24
Honiton Rd. Read —1J 87
Hook End La. Lwr B —7J 35
Hook Mill La. Light —8N 115
Hope Av. Brack —9B 92
Hope Cotts. Brack —5N 91
Hopeman Clo. Col T —2H 119
Hop Gdns. Hen T —4C 16
Hopwood Clo. Newb —7A 80
Horatio Av. Warf —3B 92
Horewood Rd. Brack —8M 91
Horizon W. Ind. Est. Newb —8A 80
Hormer Clo. Owl —9H 113
Hornbeam Clo. Owl —9H 113
Hornbeam Clo. Pur T —8K 37
Hornbeam Clo. Wokgm —8J 89
Hornbeam Gdns. Slou —2J 47
Hornbeams. Swal —4J 109
Hornbill Clo. Uxb —7L 25
Horncastle Dri. Read —7N 61
Horndean Rd. Brack —8C 92
Horne Rd. That —9G 81
Hornsea Clo. Tile —3M 61
Horn St. Comp —1H 33
Horsebrass Dri. Bag —8H 115
Horse Clo., The. Cav —9J 39
Horsegate Ride. Asc —7E 92
Horsegate Ride. S Asc —8K 93
Horseguards Dri. M'head —7E 20
Horsemoor Clo. Slou —3B 48
Horsepond Rd. Gall C —1A 38
Horseshoe Clo. Camb —9C 114
Horseshoe Cres. Bfld C —8H 85
Horseshoe Cres. Camb —9C 114
Horseshoe Pk. Pang —8E 36
Horseshoe Rd. Pang —8E 36
Horsham Rd. Owl —9H 113
Horsnape Gdns. Binf —1F 90
Horsneile La. Brack —2M 91
Horton Bri. Rd. W Dray —9N 25
Horton Clo. M'head —5F 20
Horton Clo. W Dray —9N 25
Horton Gdns. Hort —9A 48
Horton Grange. M'head —5F 20
Horton Ind. Pk. W Dray —9N 25
Horton Rd. Coln —9F 48
Horton Rd. Dat —7L 47
Horton Rd. Hort —8B 48
Horton Rd. Stai —1G 73
Horton Rd. W Dray —9M 25
Hose Hill. Thea —3H 85
Hosier St. Read —5G 63
Houlton Ct. Bag —8H 115
Houston Way. Crowt —5B 112
Howard Av. Slou —6F 22
Howard Rd. Ashf —8L 73
Howard Rd. Newb —1L 101
Howard Rd. Wokgm —6A 90
Howard St. Read —5F 62
Howarth Rd. M'head —8D 20
Howe La. Binf —4J 67
Howe La. M'head —1L 67
Howorth Ct. Brack —6B 92
Hows Clo. Uxb —2K 25
Hows Rd. Uxb —2K 25
Howth Dri. Wdly —5C 64
Hubberholme. Brack —5L 91
Hubert Rd. Slou —2M 47
Huckleberry Clo. Pur T —9K 37
Hudson Rd. Wdly —7E 64
Hughenden Clo. M'head —8N 19
Hughenden Rd. Slou —7F 22
Hughes Rd. Wokgm —4B 90
Hugh Fraser Dri. Tile —6K 61
Hull Clo. Slou —1E 46
Humber Clo. That —6E 80
Humber Clo. Wokgm —4K 89
Humber Way. Sand —1H 119
Humber Way. Slou —3B 48
Hummer Rd. Egh —8B 72
Humphrey's La. E Gar —7B 28
Humphries Yd. Brack —6N 91
Hungerford Av. Slou —6G 22
Hungerford Clo. Sand —1G 119
Hungerford Dri. M'head —3B 20
Hungerford Dri. Read —7E 62
Hungerford Hill. Gt Shef —4D 52
Hungerford Hill. Lamb —4G 26
Hungerford La. Shur R —2A 66
Hungerford La. South —1G 83
Hungerford Rd. Kint —9D 76
Huntercombe Clo. Tap —7L 21
Huntercombe La. N. Slou & Tap —6M 21
Huntercombe La. S. Tap —9L 21
Huntercombe Spur. Slou —9M 21
Hunter Ct. Burn —6M 21
Hunters Chase. Cav —8E 38
Hunters Hill. Bfld C —8G 85
Hunters Meadow. Gt Shef —1F 52
Hunters Way. Spen W —9H 87
Huntingdon Clo. Lwr Ear —1D 88
Huntingdonshire Clo. Wokgm —5J 89
Huntley Ct. Read —6L 63
Hunt's Cotts. Don —5J 79
Huntsgreen Ct. Brack —4N 91
Hunts La. Camb —6M 119
Hunt's La. Tap —3H 21
Huntsmans Meadow. Asc —3J 93
Huntsmoor Rd. Tadl —9H 105
Huntswood La. Tap —1H 21
Hurley Ct. Brack —6B 92
Hurley High St. Hur —1D 18
Hurley La. Hur —3E 18
Hurricane Way. Wdly —5F 64
Hursley Clo. Tile —5M 61
Hurstfield Dri. Tap —7L 21
Hurst Pk. Rd. Twy —2K 65
Hurst Rd. Farn —9M 119
Hurst Rd. Slou —6N 21
Hurst Rd. Twy —9K 41
Hurstwood. Asc —8K 93
Hurworth Rd. Slou —2L 47
Huscarle Way. Tile —9K 37
Hutsons Clo. Wokgm —3B 90
Hutton Clo. Ear —1N 87
Hutton Clo. Newb —7M 79
Hutton Clo. W'sham —7N 115
Huxley Clo. Uxb —5L 25
Hyacinth Dri. Uxb —1M 25
Hyde End La. Brimp —5N 103
Hyde End La. Three M —7H 87
Hyde End Rd. Spen W & Shin —9H 87
Hyde Grn. Mar —6D 4
Hyde La. Ecc —8D 102
Hydes, The. Tile —9K 37
Hylle Clo. Wind —7A 46
Hyperion Way. Read —9H 63
Hythe Clo. Brack —7B 92
Hythe End Rd. Wray —6A 72
Hythe Field Av. Egh —9E 72
Hythe Pk. Rd. Egh —9D 72
Hythe Rd. Stai —9E 72
Hythe, The. Stai —9F 72

Ian Mikardo Way. Cav —2K 63
Ibstock Clo. Read —5B 62
Ibstone Av. Cav —8L 39
Icknield Pl. Gor —6M 15
Icknield Rd. Gor —6M 15
Iffley Clo. Uxb —1L 25
Ilbury Clo. Shin —6L 87
Ilchester Clo. M'head —9N 19
Ilchester Ct. Newb —9L 79
(off Link Rd.)
Ilchester M. Cav —7L 39
Ilex Clo. Egh —2K 95
Ilex Clo. Pam H —9N 105
Ilex Clo. Son C —1F 38
Ilfracombe Way. Lwr Ear —9D 64
Ilkley Rd. Cav —9E 38
Ilkley Way. That —9F 80
Illingworth. Wind —9A 46
Illingworth Av. Cav —7L 39
Illingworth Gro. Brack —3C 92
Ilsey Rd. Comp —1F 32
Ilsley Clo. Son C —1F 38
Imperial Ct. Hen T —5D 16
Imperial Ct. Wind —9C 46
Imperial Rd. Wind —9C 46
Imperial Way. Read —4G 87
Impstone Rd. Pam H —9A 106
Inch's Yd. Newb —9L 79
Inchwood. Brack —1N 113
India Rd. Slou —1K 47
Ingle Glen. Wokgm —3M 111
Ingleside. Coln —7G 48
Ingleton. Brack —5L 91
Inglewood Ct. Read —6C 62
Inglewood Rd. Kint —9C 76
Inhams Way. Sil —9B 106
Inhurst Way. Tadl —9H 105
Inkerman Rd. Eton W —3B 46
Inkpen Clo. Read —8A 62
Inkpen Rd. Hung —8L 75
Inkpen Rd. Kint —9F 76
Innings La. Warf —3B 92
Innings La. White —6H 43
Institute Rd. Mar —6C 4
Institute Rd. Tap —7J 21
Instow Rd. Ear —1A 88
In-the-Ray. M'head —6E 20
Invergordon Clo. Calc —8M 61
Inverness Way. Col T —2H 119
Inwood Clo. Cook —9F 4
Iona Cres. Slou —7A 22
Ipswich Rd. Slou —7B 22
Irainworth Clo. Lwr Ear —3N 87
Iris Ct. Read —5M 61
Irish Hill Rd. Kint —9G 77
Irvine Dri. Farn —9J 119
Irvine Pl. Vir W —7N 95
Irvine Way. Lwr Ear —3B 88
Isaac Newton Rd. Arbor X —1F 110
Isambard Clo. Uxb —5L 25
Isis Clo. Winn —2C 80
Isis Ct. Read —3H 63
Isis Way. Bour —3M 5
Isis Way. Sand —1H 119
Island Clo. Stai —8F 72
Island Farm Rd. Uft N —8E 84
Island Rd. Read —1F 86
Islandstone La. Hurst —6M 65
Island, The. W Dray —6K 49
Island, The. Wray —7B 72
Islet Pk. M'head —3F 20
Islet Pk. Dri. M'head —3F 20
Islet Rd. M'head —3E 20
Ismay Ct. Slou —7G 23
Ivanhoe Clo. Uxb —6L 25
Iveagh Ct. Brack —7A 92
Iverdale Clo. Iver —8D 24
Iver La. Iver & Uxb —7H 25
Ives Clo. Yat —2A 118
Ives Rd. Slou —2A 48
Ivybank. Tile —3K 61
Ivybridge Clo. Uxb —4M 25
Ivy Clo. Holyp —6D 44
Ivy Cres. Slou —8B 22
Ivydene Rd. Read —3C 62

Jackson Clo. Brack —7M 91
Jackson Clo. Uxb —1M 25
Jackson Ind. Est. Bour —4M 5
Jackson Rd. Uxb —1M 25
Jacksons La. Cav —7C 38
Jack St. Newb —8L 79
Jacob Clo. Brack —4H 91
Jacob Clo. Wind —7A 46
Jacob Rd. Col T —2L 119
Jakes Ho. M'head —6D 20
James Butcher Dri. Thea —9F 60
James Clo. Mar —3D 4
James Ct. Read —7D 62
James Rd. Camb —7M 119
James's La. Bfld —8N 85
James St. Read —5F 62
James St. Wind —7F 46
Jameston. Brack —1N 113
James Watt Rd. Arbor X —3E 110
James Way. Camb —7M 119
Janson Ct. Read —6F 62
Japonica Clo. Wokgm —7J 89
Jaques's La. Bfld C —5H 85
Jasmine Clo. Wokgm —4J 89
Jays Nest Clo. B'water —5H 119
Jedburgh Clo. That —8J 81
Jefferson Clo. Slou —3B 48
Jeffries Ct. Bour —5L 5
Jellicoe Clo. Slou —1D 46
Jenkins Hill. Bag —8G 114
Jenner Wlk. Tile —5J 61
(off Stratford Way)
Jennery La. Burn —4M 21
Jennetts Clo. Tut C —9G 59
Jennys Wlk. Yat —3C 118
Jerome Clo. Mar —3D 4
Jerome Rd. Wdly —6C 64
Jerrymoor Hill. Wokgm —2L 111
Jesmond Dene. Newb —7K 79
Jesse Clo. Yat —4D 118
Jesse Ter. Read —5F 62
Jevington. Brack —1N 113
Jig's La. Warf —3B 92
Jig's La. N. Warf —1B 92
Jig's La. S. Warf —3B 92
Job's La. Cook —7F 4
Jock's La. Brack —3J 91
Johannes Ct. Read —6D 62
John Boys Ho. Newb —4H 101
John Childs Clo. Newb —1L 101
John Nike Way. Brack —4G 91
Johnson's La. Cold A —3F 80
Johnson's Yd. Uxb —1K 25
John Taylor Ct. Slou —9E 22
Jonathan Hill. Newt C —7M 101
Jordan Clo. Cav —8L 39
Jordan Clo. Spen W —9K 87
Jordans Clo. Stai —4K 73
Jordan's La. Bfld C —9G 85
Joseph Ct. Warf —1B 92
Josephine Ct. Read —6D 62
Jouldings La. Far H —6B 110
Journeys End. Stoke P —6G 23
Jubilee Av. Asc —3H 93
Jubilee Av. Wokgm —4M 89
Jubilee Clo. Asc —3H 93
Jubilee Clo. Pam H —9N 105
Jubilee Clo. Stai —4K 73
Jubilee Ct. Brack —5N 91
Jubilee Ct. Stai —8H 73
Jubilee Rd. Finch —5L 111
Jubilee Rd. L Grn —1F 42
Jubilee Rd. Newb —9M 79
Jubilee Rd. Read —6N 63
Jubilee Sq. Read —6H 63
Juliet Gdns. Warf —3C 92
Julius Hill. Warf —3C 92
Julkes La. Arbor —4D 88
Junction Rd. Light —9L 115
Junction Rd. Read —6L 63
Juniper. Brack —1N 113
Juniper Ct. Slou —1J 47
Juniper Dri. M'head —6E 20
Juniper Rd. Mar —2B 4
Junipers, The. Wokgm —7J 89
Juniper Way. Tile —2L 61
Jupiter Way. Wokgm —5K 89
Justice Clo. That —9J 81
Jutland Clo. Wokgm —5K 89
Jutland Pl. Egh —9D 72

Katesgrove La. Read —6G 63
Kathleen Sanders Ct. Thea —8F 60
Kaynes Pk. Asc —3H 93
Kaywood Clo. Slou —2M 47
Keane Clo. Wdly —4D 64
Kearsley Rd. Read —6C 62
Keates Grn. Brack —3M 91
Keats Clo. Wdly —8D 64
Keats La. Eton —5E 46
Keats Rd. Wdly —8D 64
Keats Way. Crowt —3F 112
Keats Way. W Dray —3N 49
Keats Way. Yat —5A 118
Keble Rd. M'head —6A 20
Keble Way. Owl —8J 113
Keel Dri. Slou —1D 46
Keeler Clo. Wind —9A 46
Keensacre. Iver —3E 24
Keepers Combe. Brack —8A 92
Keepers Farm Clo. Wind —8A 46
(in two parts)
Keepers Wlk. Vir W —7M 95
Keephatch Rd. Wokgm —3C 90
Keighley Clo. That —9F 80
Keilder Clo. Uxb —3N 25
Keith Pk. Rd. Uxb —1N 25
Kelburne Clo. Winn —9H 65
Keldholme. Brack —5L 91
Kelmscott Clo. Cav —2E 62
Kelpatrick Rd. Slou —7N 21
Kelsey Av. Wokgm —4K 111
Kelsey Clo. M'head —2A 44
Kelsey Gro. Yat —4C 118
Kelso M. Cav —7L 39
Kelston Rd. L Bed —3A 96
Kelton Clo. Lwr Ear —1D 88
Kelvedon Way. Cav —8E 38
Kelvin Clo. Arbor —3D 110
Kelvin Rd. Newb —7M 79
Kemble Ct. Calc —8L 61
Kemerton Clo. Calc —8L 61
Kemp Ct. Bag —8J 115
Kempton Clo. Green —1N 101
Kenavon Dri. Read —4J 63
Kendal Av. Cav —8L 39
Kendal Clo. Slou —8J 23
Kendal Dri. Slou —8J 23
Kendall Av. Shin —5L 87
Kendrick Clo. Wokgm —6N 89
Kendrick Ct. Read —6H 63
Kendrick Rd. Newb —5H 101
Kendrick Rd. Read —6J 63
Kendrick Rd. Slou —2K 47
Keneally. Wind —8M 45
Kenilworth Av. Brack —3A 92
Kenilworth Av. Read —7D 62
Kenilworth Clo. Slou —2H 47
Kenilworth Gdns. Stai —9K 73
Kenilworth Rd. Ashf —7L 73
Kenneally Clo. Wind —8M 45
Kenneally Pl. Wind —8M 45
(off Kenneally)
Kenneally Row. Wind —8M 45
Kenneally Wlk. Wind —8M 45
Kennedy Clo. Farn C —1E 22
Kennedy Clo. M'head —8N 19
Kennedy Clo. Mar —4C 4
Kennedy Clo. Newb —4H 101
Kennedy Dri. Pang —8E 36
Kennedy Gdns. Ear —9A 64
Kennel Av. Asc —3J 93
Kennel Clo. Asc —1J 93
Kennel Grn. Asc —3H 93
Kennel La. Brack —2M 91
Kennel La. Cook D —8G 4
(in two parts)
Kennel La. W'sham —5M 115
Kennel Ride. Asc —3J 93
Kennel Wood. Asc —3J 93
Kennet Cen., The. Newb —9L 79
Kennet Clo. That —8H 81
Kennet Ct. Wokgm —5L 89
Kennet Pl. Bfld C —8J 85
Kennet Pl. Newb —7M 79
(off London Rd.)
Kennet Rd. Kint —9G 76
Kennet Rd. M'head —6C 20
Kennet Rd. Newb —9K 79
Kennet Side. Newb —8N 79
Kennet Side. Read —5H 63
(in four parts)
Kennet St. Read —5J 63
Kennett Rd. Bour —3M 5
Kennett Rd. Slou —2C 48
Kennet Way. Hung —4K 75
Kennylands Rd. Son C —1F 38
Kensington Clo. Lwr Ear —2A 88
Kensington Rd. Read —5D 62
Kent Av. Slou —6E 22
Kent Clo. Wokgm —6J 89
Kent Folly. Warf —1C 92
Kentford Clo. Lwr Ear —1C 88
Kentigern Dri. Crowt —5H 113
Kenton Clo. Brack —4A 92
Kenton Clo. Mar —5C 4
Kenton Rd. Ear —8B 64
Kenton's La. Up Cul —8H 17
Kentons La. Wind —8A 46
Kent Rd. Read —5D 62
Kent Rd. W'sham —5N 115
Kent Way. M'head —5B 20
Kentwood Clo. Tile —3M 61
Kentwood Hill. Tile —3M 61
Kentwood Ho. Tile —3M 61
Kentwood Ter. Tile —3M 61
Kenwood Clo. M'head —7L 19
Keppel Spur. Old Win —4K 71
Kepple Pl. Bag —7H 115
Kepple St. Wind —8F 46
Kernham Dri. Tile —9K 37
Kerris Way. Ear —2N 87
Kersey Cres. Speen —6H 79
Kesteven Way. Wokgm —5K 89
Keston Clo. Cav —2J 63
Kestrel Av. Stai —7G 73
Kestrel Clo. That —8E 80
Kestrel Path. Slou —5A 22
Kestrel Way. Read —8A 62
Kestrel Way. Wokgm —5K 89
Keswick Clo. Tile —5L 61
Keswick Ct. Slou —8H 23
Keswick Dri. Light —9L 115
Keswick Gdns. Wdly —7D 64
Ketcher Grn. Binf —8G 66
Kettering Clo. Calc —8M 61
Kevins Dri. Yat —2C 118
Kew Cotts. Newb —1K 101
Kew Gdns. Shalb —7G 96
Kew Ter. Tile —3M 61
Keynsham Way. Owl —8H 113
Keys La. M'head —8C 20
Kibble Grn. Brack —8N 91
Kibblewhite Cres. Twy —7J 41
Kidby's Ind. Est. Read —6G 63
Kidderminster Rd. Slou —4C 22
Kidmore End Rd. Emm G —4F 38
Kidmore La. Kid E —2D 38
Kidmore Rd. Cav —7E 38
Kidwells Clo. M'head —7C 20
Kidwells Pk. Dri. M'head —7C 20
Kier Pk. Asc —5M 93
Kiff Grn. Up Wool —5E 82
Kilburn Clo. Calc —8L 61
Kildare Gdns. Cav —1J 63
Killarney Dri. M'head —7B 20
Kilmington Clo. Brack —9B 92
Kilmuir Clo. Col T —2H 119
Kiln Brook Ho. Read —7G 63
Kiln Clo. Herm —5F 56
Kiln Croft Clo. Mar —4E 4
Kiln Dri. Cur —7B 56
Kiln Hill. Far H —3A 110
Kiln La. Asc —7C 94
Kiln La. Bin H —3A 40
Kiln La. Bour & Wbrn G —4N 5
Kiln La. Brack —4L 91
Kiln La. Mort —6K 107
Kiln La. Spen W —9F 86
Kiln La. Tile —4H 61
Kiln La. Wink —1L 93
Kiln Pl. M'head —3L 19
Kiln Ride. Up Bas —8H 35
Kiln Ride. Wokgm —2M 111
Kiln Ride Extension. Wokgm —4M 111
Kiln Rd. Cav —7J 39
Kiln Rd. Newb —6M 79
Kilnsea Dri. Lwr Ear —1C 88
Kiln Ter. Cur —7B 56
Kiln View Rd. Read —1K 87
Kilowna Clo. Charv —9F 40
Kimber Clo. Wind —9C 46
Kimberley. Brack —1N 113
Kimberley Clo. Read —7E 62
Kimberley Clo. Slou —3A 48
Kimber's Almshouses. Newb
(off Kennet Rd.) —8K 79
Kimber's Clo. Newb —8K 79
Kimbers Dri. Burn —4N 21
Kimbers Dri. Speen —6G 79
Kimbers La. M'head —2B 44
Kimmeridge. Brack —8B 92

Kimpton Clo. Lwr Ear —3L 87
Kinburn Dri. Egh —9N 71
King Acre Ct. Stai —7F 72
King Edward Ct. Wind —7F 46
King Edward's Clo. Asc —3H 93
King Edward VII Av. Wind —6G 46
King Edward's Rise. Asc —2H 93
King Edward's Rd. Asc —3H 93
King Edward St. Slou —1F 46
Kingfisher Ct. Slou —5D 22
Kingfisher Ct. Twy —1K 65
Kingfisher Ct. Ind. Est. Newb —8A 80
Kingfisher Dri. Stai —8G 72
Kingfisher Dri. Wdly —6B 64
Kingfisher Dri. Yat —3A 118
Kingfisher Pl. Read —4H 63
Kinghorn La. M'head —3A 20
Kinghorn Pk. M'head —3A 20
King James Way. Hen T —6B 16
King John's Clo. Stai —3L 71
Kingsbridge Cotts. Wokgm —3B 112
Kingsbridge Hill. Swal —4G 109
Kingsbridge Rd. Newb —1J 101
Kingsbridge Rd. Read —1J 87
Kingsbury Cres. Stai —8E 72
Kingsbury Dri. Old Win —4J 71
Kingsclear Pk. Camb —5N 119
Kings Clo. Hen T —4C 16
King's Cres. Camb —1N 119
Kingscroft La. Brack —6C 68
Kingsdown Clo. Ear —1A 88
Kings Dri. M'head —8B 20
Kingsfield. Wind —7N 45
Kingsford Clo. Wdly —7F 64
Kingsgate Pl. Read —5K 63
(off Kingsgate St.)
Kingsgate St. Read —5K 63
Kings Gro. M'head —8B 20
King's Keep. Sand —9F 112
Kingsland Cen. That —8G 81
Kingsland Grange. Newb —2J 101
Kings La. Cook —7F 4
Kings La. Egh —9J 71
Kings La. W'sham —5N 115
Kingsley Av. Camb —5N 119
Kingsley Av. Egh —1K 95
Kingsley Clo. Charv —8F 40
Kingsley Clo. Crowt —7F 112
Kingsley Clo. Read —4H 87
Kingsley Clo. Shaw —6M 79
Kingsley Dri. Mar —1A 4
Kingsley Path. Slou —5N 21
Kings Mead. Newb —5G 100
King's Meadow Rd. Read —4H 63
Kingsmere Rd. Brack —3K 91
Kings Reach Ct. Read —5H 63
(off Crane Wharf)
King's Ride. Asc —7F 92
Kings Ride. Camb —9A 114
King's Rd. Cav —2H 63
King's Rd. Crowt —6F 112
Kings Rd. Egh —8B 72
King's Rd. Hen T —4C 16
Kings Rd. Newb —9L 79
King's Rd. Read —5H 63
(in three parts)
King's Rd. Slou —2G 46
King's Rd. S'hill —7N 93
King's Rd. Uxb —3L 25
King's Rd. W Dray —1N 49
King's Rd. Wind —1F 70
Kings Rd. W. Newb —9L 79
Kingstable St. Eton —6F 46
Kingston Av. W Dray —8N 25
(in two parts)
Kingston Cres. Ashf —9K 73
Kingston Gdns. Read —1J 87
Kingston La. Sul'd —5D 84
Kingston La. Uxb —4M 25
Kingston La. W Dray —1N 49
Kingston Rd. Camb —9D 114
Kingston Rd. Stai & Ashf —8H 73
King St. M'head —7C 20
(in three parts)
King St. Mort C —4H 107
King St. Read —5H 63
King St. La. Winn —3G 88
Kingsvale Ct. W Dray —8L 25
King's Wlk. Col T —3K 119
Kings Wlk. Hen T —3C 16
King's Wlk. Read —5H 63
Kingsway. B'water —4H 119
Kingsway. Cav —7L 39
Kingsway. Iver —7F 24
Kingsway. Stai —5L 73
Kingswick Clo. Asc —6N 93
Kingswick Dri. Asc —6N 93
Kingswood Clo. Egh —8M 71
Kingswood Ct. M'head —9C 20
Kingswood Ct. Read —6D 62
Kingswood Creek. Wray —2M 71
Kingswood Ho. Slou —6E 22
Kingswood Pde. Mar —2B 4
Kingswood Rise. Egh —9M 71
Kinnaird Clo. Slou —7M 21
Kinross Av. Asc —7J 93
Kinross Ct. Asc —7J 93
Kinson Rd. Tile —3A 62
Kintbury Rd. Ink —4E 98
Kintbury Wlk. Read —8C 62
Kinver Wlk. Read —7H 63
Kipling Clo. That —6F 80
Kipling Clo. Yat —5A 118
Kipling Ct. Wind —8D 46
Kirkfell Clo. Tile —2K 61
Kirkham Clo. Cav —7L 39
Kirkham Clo. Owl —8H 113
Kirkstall Ct. Calc —8L 61
Kirkwall Spur. Slou —6G 22
Kirkwood Cres. Bfld C —8G 85
Kirton Clo. Read —5B 62
Kittiwake Clo. Wdly —5G 64
Kitwood Dri. Lwr Ear —2D 88
Klondyke. Mar —5B 4
Knappe Clo. Hen T —6B 16
Knapp Rd. Ashf —8N 73
Knapp, The. Ear —8A 64
Knighton Clo. Cav —1G 62
Knighton Way La. Den —1J 25
Knightsbridge Dri. Hdly —7E 102
Knights Clo. Wind —7N 45
Knights La. Bal H —7A 100
Knights Way. Emm G —8H 39
Knightswood. Brack —1M 113
Knole Wood. Asc —1N 115
Knollmead. Calc —8L 61
Knoll Rd. Camb —3N 119
Knoll, The. Tile —2J 61
Knoll Wlk. Camb —3N 119
Knollys Rd. Pam H —9A 106
Knolton Way. Slou —7K 23
Knossington Clo. Lwr Ear —1B 88
Knott La. Lwr P —7K 83
Knowle Clo. Cav —9D 38
Knowle Grn. Stai —9H 73
Knowle Gro. Vir W —9L 95
Knowle Gro. Clo. Vir W —9L 95
Knowle Hill. Vir W —9K 95
Knowle Pk. Av. Stai —9J 73
Knowle Rd. Wdly —8D 64
Knowles Av. Crowt —5D 112
Knowles Clo. W Dray —9M 25
Knowl Hill Comn. Know H —2C 42
Knowl Hill Ter. Know H —1C 42
Knowsley Clo. M'head —5L 19
Knowsley Rd. Tile —1J 61
Knox Grn. Binf —9G 66
Koya Ct. Wex —7K 23
Krooner Rd. Camb —6M 119
Kyle Clo. Brack —5M 91

Laburnham Rd. M'head —8A 20
Laburnum Av. W Dray —8N 25
Laburnum Clo. Mar —3C 4
Laburnum Gdns. Read —2L 87
Laburnum Gro. Newb —7L 79
Laburnum Gro. Slou —5C 48
Laburnum Pl. Egh —1K 95
Laburnum Rd. Winn —2H 89
Laburnums, The. B'water —4F 118
Laburnum Way. Stai —5N 73
Lackman's Hill. Brack —1M 91
Ladbroke Clo. Wdly —6E 64
Ladbrooke Rd. Slou —2E 46
Ladwell Clo. Newb —5H 101
Ladybank. Brack —1M 113
Ladyday Pl. Slou —9E 22
Lady Jane Ct. Cav —1H 63
Lady Margaret Rd. Asc —9B 94
Ladymask Clo. Calc —8N 61
Laffords, The. South —1J 83
Laggan Rd. M'head —4C 20
Laggan Sq. M'head —5C 20
Laird Ct. Bag —9H 115
Lake Av. Slou —8F 22
Lake End. Crowt —6E 112
Lake End Ct. Tap —7K 21
Lake End Rd. Tap —8L 21
Lake Rd. Vir W —6K 95
Lakeside. Brack —2N 91
Lakeside. Ear —9A 64
Lakeside. M'head —4E 20
Lakeside Dri. Stoke P —2G 23
Lakeside Est. Coln —6G 49
Lakeside Gdns. Farn —9H 119
Lakeside Rd. Coln —6G 49
Lakeside, The. B'water —5H 119
Lake View Caravan Site. Wink —5H 69
Lalande Clo. Wokgm —5K 89
Laleham Rd. Stai —9G 72
Lamb Clo. That —6F 80
Lambert Av. Slou —2N 47
Lambert Ct. Read —5N 61
Lambert Cres. B'water —5G 119
Lambfields. Thea —9E 60
Lambly Hill. Vir W —5N 95
Lamborne Clo. Sand —9E 112
Lambourn. Newb —6M 79
Lambourn Ct. Caravan Pk. Lamb —3H 27
Lambourne Clo. Tile —4L 61
Lambourne Ct. Uxb —2J 25
Lambourne Dri. Bag —8G 115
Lambourne Dri. M'head —2N 43
Lambourne Gdns. Ear —8C 64
Lambourne Gro. Brack —4B 92
Lambourn Pl. Lamb —2H 27
Lambourn Rd. Woods —5G 79
Lambridge La. Hen T —3A 16
Lambridge Wood Rd. Hen T —2A 16
Lamb's La. Spen W —4G 109
Lambswoodhill. Graz —1D 108
Lamerton Rd. Read —2J 87
Lammas Ct. Stai —6E 72
Lammas Ct. Wind —8E 46
Lammas Dri. Stai —8E 72
Lammas Mead. Binf —2J 91
Lammas Rd. Slou —6N 21
Lamorna Cres. Tile —3K 61
Lamp Acres. Shaw —6M 79
Lamplighters Wlk. Calc —8N 61
Lamsden Way. Bfld C —8J 85
Lanark Clo. Wdly —6F 64
Lancashire Hill. Warf —1C 92
Lancaster Av. Slou —5E 22
Lancaster Clo. Egh —9M 71
Lancaster Clo. Hung —7J 75
Lancaster Clo. Read —7J 63
Lancaster Clo. That —7F 80
Lancaster Gdns. Ear —9A 64
Lancaster Ho. Brack —7M 91
Lancaster Rd. M'head —6M 19
Lancaster Rd. Uxb —1L 25
Lancaster Sq. Hung —7K 75
Lancaster Way. Farn —9N 119
Lancastria M. M'head —7A 20
Lancelot Clo. Slou —1C 46
Lanchester Dri. Crowt —3G 113
Lancing Clo. Read —5D 62
Lancresse Clo. Uxb —1L 25
Landen Ct. Wokgm —7N 89
Landrake Cres. Read —2J 87
Landseer Clo. Col T —3J 119
Lane End Clo. Shin —5L 87
Laneswood. Mort —5F 106
Lane, The. Sil —9C 106
Lane, The. Vir W —5N 95
Langborough Rd. Wokgm —6A 90
Langdale Clo. M'head —8D 20
Langdale Dri. Asc —4H 93
Langdale Gdns. Ear —1M 87
Langford Clo. Cav —8J 39
Langham Pl. Egh —9A 72
Langhams Way. Warg —3K 41
Langley Broom. Slou —4A 48
Langley Bus. Cen. Langl —1B 48
Langley Bus. Pk. Langl —1A 48
Langley Comn. Rd. Arbor X & B'ham —1D 110
Langley Farm Cotts. Beed —7B 32
Langley Hill. Tile —6K 61
Langley Hill Clo. Tile —6K 61
Langley La. Arbor —5C 88
Langley Pk. Rd. Iver —8C 24
Langley Pk. Rd. Slou & Iver —1B 48
Langley Quay. Langl —1B 48
Langley Rd. Slou —1L 47
Langley Rd. Stai —9G 73
Langley Wlk. Mar —5A 4
Langton Clo. M'head —5A 20
Langton Clo. Slou —9N 21
Langworthy End. M'head —5E 44
Langworthy La. M'head —5D 44
Laniver Clo. Ear —2A 88
Lansdowne Av. Slou —9G 22
Lansdowne Ct. Slou —9G 23
Lansdowne Rd. Tile —5K 61
Lantern Wlk. M'head —7E 20
Lapwing Clo. Tile —6K 61
Larch Av. Asc —7A 94
Larch Av. Wokgm —4M 89
Larch Clo. Bfld —7J 85
Larch Clo. Camb —9B 114
Larch Clo. Slou —6D 22
Larch Clo. Speen —6H 79
Larch Dri. Wdly —7D 64
Larches, The. Warf P —2D 92
Larchfield Rd. M'head —9A 20
Larchside Clo. Spen W —9H 87
Larch Way. Frogm —4F 118
Larchwood. Brack —7C 92
Larchwood Dri. Egh —1K 95
Lardon Cotts. Streat —8J 15
Larges Bri. Dri. Brack —5N 91
Larges La. Brack —4N 91
Larissa Clo. Tile —3M 61
Lark Av. Stai —7G 72
Larkings La. Stoke P —2K 23
Larksfield. Egh —2L 95
Larks Meade. Ear —2N 87
Larkspur Clo. Wokgm —4J 89
Larkspur Gdns. That —7J 81
Larkswood Clo. Sand —9E 112
Larkswood Clo. Tile —1L 61
Larkswood Dri. Crowt —5F 112
La Roche Clo. Slou —2L 47
Lascelles Rd. Slou —2K 47
Lashbrook Mead. Lwr S —1G 40
Lashbrook Rd. Lwr S —1G 40
Lassell Ct. M'head —7E 20
Lassell Gdns. M'head —7E 20
Latimer. Brack —1M 113
Latimer Dri. Calc —8K 61
Latimer Rd. Wokgm —6N 89
Laud's Clo. Hen T —5B 16
Laud Way. Wokgm —5C 90
Launceston Av. Cav —7L 39
Launcestone Clo. Lwr Ear —1A 88
Laundry La. Col T —3J 119
Lauradale. Brack —6L 91
Laurel Av. Egh —9K 71
Laurel Av. Slou —1N 47
Laurel Clo. Camb —5N 119
Laurel Clo. Coln —6F 48
Laurel Clo. Wokgm —6L 89
Laurel Dri. Tile —4J 61
Laurel La. W Dray —3M 49
Laurels End. Iver —3E 24
Lauser Rd. Stai —4K 73
Lavender Rise. W Dray —1N 49
Lavender Rd. Uxb —6N 25
Lavenham Dri. Wdly —4E 64
Laverheath Clo. Lwr Ear —1D 88
Lawford Cres. Yat —3B 118
Lawkland. Farn R —4E 22
Lawn Av. W Dray —1K 49
Lawn Clo. Dat —6L 47
Lawn Rd. Uxb —1K 25
Lawnsend La. Charv —2G 65
Lawns, The. Asc —5G 92
Lawns, The. Coln —7F 48
Lawns, The. Read —9K 63
Lawrence Clo. Wokgm —5B 90
Lawrence Ct. Wind —8E 46
Lawrence Cres. W'sham —6N 115
Lawrence Gro. Binf —3H 91
Lawrence Mead. Kint —9F 76
Lawrence Rd. Tile —4A 62
Lawrences La. That —6G 80
Lawrence Way. Camb —5K 119
Lawrence Way. Slou —6N 21
Lawson Way. Asc —8D 94
Laxton Grn. M'head —2N 43
Layburn Cres. Slou —5C 48
Layland's Grn. Kint —1G 98
Layton Rise. Tile —1K 61
Lea Clo. Mar —1B 4
Lea Clo. Read —9A 62
Leacroft. Asc —7C 94
Lea Croft. Crowt —4F 112
Leacroft. Stai —9H 73
Leacroft Clo. Stai —8J 73
Leacroft Clo. W Dray —7M 25
Leacroft Rd. Iver —7F 24
Leafield Copse. Brack —6C 92
Leaholme Gdns. Slou —6M 21
Lea Rd. Camb —7M 119
Lea Rd. Son C —1F 38
Leas Dri. Iver —7F 24
Lea, The. Wokgm —2L 111
Leaver Rd. Hen T —5B 16
Leaves Grn. Brack —8A 92
Ledbury Clo. Read —4C 62
Ledbury Dri. Calc —8L 61
Ledger La. M'head —8G 45
Ledgers Rd. Slou —1F 46
Ledran Clo. Lwr Ear —2B 88
Leeds Rd. Slou —8G 22
Lee La. M'head —3J 19
Lees Clo. M'head —9M 19
Lees Gdns. M'head —9M 19
Leeson Gdns. Eton W —3A 46
Lees Wlk. Mar —5A 4
Leicester. Brack —9B 92
Leicester Clo. Hen T —3C 16
Leigh Field. Mort C —4G 107
Leigh Pk. Dat —6L 47
Leigh Rd. Slou —8D 22
Leigh Sq. Wind —8N 45
Leighton Ct. Ear —9L 63
Leighton Gdns. M'head —5E 20
Leiston Clo. Lwr Ear —2C 88
Leiston Spur. Slou —7G 22
Leith Clo. Crowt —3E 112
Lemart Clo. Tile —4M 61
Lemington Gro. Brack —8M 91
Lendore Rd. Frim —9N 119
Leney Clo. Wokgm —3B 90
Lenham Clo. Winn —2K 89
Lennox Clo. Calc —8J 61
Lennox Rd. Read —7N 63
Lent Grn. Burn —5L 21
Lent Grn. La. Burn —5L 21
Lent Rise Rd. Tap & Burn —7L 21
Leonard Clo. Frim —9N 119
Leonard Ct. Thea —9F 60
Leopold Wlk. Read —5K 63
Leppington. Brack —9M 91
Lerwick Dri. Slou —6G 22
Lesford Rd. Read —8E 62
Lesley Ct. Read —6D 62
Leslie Dunne Ho. Wind —8A 46
Leslie Southern Ct. Newb —7M 79
Lesters Rd. Cook —9H 5
Letcombe Sq. Brack —6B 92
Letcombe St. Read —5H 63
Letcomb Sq. Brack —6B 92
Leverton Cotts. Hung —3J 75
Leverton La. Chilt F —2G 75
Lewendon Rd. Speen —6J 79
Lewins Farm Ct. Cipp —8B 22
Lewins Way. Slou —8B 22
Lewisham Way. Owl —9H 113
Lewis Ho. Brack —8M 91
Lewis Wlk. Newb —4G 101
Lexington Av. M'head —9A 20
Lexington Gro. Read —5J 87
Leyburn Clo. Wdly —4F 64
Leycester Clo. W'sham —4L 115
Leyland Gdns. Shin —5L 87
Leylands La. Stai —1G 73
(in two parts)
Ley Rd. Farn —9L 119
Leys Gdns. Newb —7K 79
Ley Side. Crowt —5E 112
Lichfield Clo. Lwr Ear —2B 88
Lichfields. Brack —4B 92
Liddall Way. W Dray —9N 25
Liddell. Wind —9M 45
Liddell Clo. Finch —7K 111
Liddell Pl. Wind —9M 45
Liddell Sq. Wind —8M 45
Liddell Way. Asc —7J 93
Liddell Way. Wind —9M 45
Lidstone Clo. Lwr Ear —2C 88
Liebenrood Rd. Read —6C 62
Lightlands La. Cook —1C 20
Lightwater By-Pass. Light —8K 115
Lightwater Meadow. Light —9L 115
Lightwater Rd. Light —9M 115
Lightwood. Brack —8A 92
Liguel Clo. Hung —7K 75
Lilac Clo. Pur T —8K 37
Lilac Ct. Slou —4B 22
Lilac Pl. W Dray —8N 25
Lilacs, The. Wokgm —7J 89
Lilac Wlk. Calc —7K 61
Lilley Ct. Crowt —6F 112
Lillibrooke Cres. M'head —2L 43
Lily Hill Dri. Brack —4B 92
Lily Hill Rd. Brack —4B 92
Lima Ct. Read —6F 62
Lime Av. Asc —8E 92
Lime Av. W Dray —8N 25
Lime Av. Wind —7B 70
(Windsor Great Park)
Lime Av. Wind —7H 47
(Windsor)
Lime Clo. Newb —7A 80
Lime Clo. Wokgm —6L 89
Limecroft. Yat —4A 118
Limerick Clo. Brack —3L 91
Limes Clo. Ashf —9N 73
Limes Rd. Egh —9A 72
Limetree Rd. Gor —8K 15
Lime View. Newb —7L 79
(off Victoria Rd.)
Lime Wlk. Brack —6N 91
Lime Wlk. M'head —6L 19
Limmer Clo. Wokgm —7H 89
Limmerhill Rd. Wokgm —6K 89
Linchfield Rd. Dat —7L 47
Lincoln Clo. Winn —9F 64
Lincoln Ct. Newb —9K 79
Lincoln Gdns. Twy —8J 41
Lincoln Hatch La. Burn —5M 21
Lincoln Rd. M'head —6M 19
Lincoln Rd. Read —8J 63
Lincolnshire Gdns. Warf —2B 92
Lincoln Way. Slou —8N 21
Lindale Clo. Vir W —6H 95
Lindberg Way. Wdly —3G 64
Lind Clo. Ear —1A 88
Linden. Brack —7C 92
Linden Av. M'head —5A 20
Linden Clo. M'head —5E 44
Linden Clo. Newb —7K 79
Linden Clo. Wokgm —6L 89
Linden Ct. Egh —1K 95
Linden Dri. Farn R —2E 22
Linden Hill La. Kiln G —2A 42
Lindenhill Rd. Brack —3K 91
Linden Ho. Langl —4C 48
Linden Pl. Stai —8H 73
Linden Rd. Bis G —7C 102
Linden Rd. Read —1L 87
Linden Rd. Wdly —8C 64
Lindores Rd. Holyp —5E 44
Lindsay Clo. Stai —2L 73
Lindsey Clo. Wokgm —6K 89
Linear Way. Calc —8K 61
Lines Rd. Hurst —6K 65
Lingfield Caravan Pk. Wind —5G 45
Lingfield Rd. Green —2N 101
Lingholm Clo. M'head —8N 19
Lingholm Clo. Tile —7N 61
Lingwood. Brack —8N 91
Link Ho. Newb —9L 79
Link Rd. Dat —7L 47
Link Rd. Newb —9L 79
Links Dri. Tile —4A 62
Links Rd. Ashf —9M 73
Links, The. Asc —4H 93
Linkswood Rd. Burn —3M 21
Link, The. Slou —7K 23
Link, The. Yat —3A 118
Link Way. Arbor X —9D 88
Linkway. Camb —5N 119
Linkway. Crowt —5D 112
Link Way. That —7E 80
Linnet Clo. Tile —6J 61
Linnet La. Bis G —7C 102
(off Linden Rd.)
Linnet Wlk. Wokgm —5K 89
Linstead Rd. Farn —9J 119
Lintott Ct. Stanw —3L 73
Lip La. Elc —3J 77
(in three parts)
Lipscomb Clo. Herm —6E 56
Lipscombe Clo. Newb —9J 79
Liscombe. Brack —9M 91
Liscombe Ho. Brack —9M 91
Lisle Clo. Newb —6K 79
Lismore Clo. Wdly —8D 64
Lismore Pk. Slou —7H 23
Lissett Rd. M'head —8D 20
Lister Clo. Pur T —8K 37
Liston Ct. Mar —5B 4
Liston Rd. Mar —5B 4
Litcham Spur. Slou —7F 22
Litchfield Ho. Tadl —9K 105
Littington Clo. Lwr Ear —3B 88
Lit. Benty. W Dray —4L 49
Lit. Bowden La. Pang —9A 36
Littlebrook Av. Slou —6A 22
Lit. Buntings. Wind —9B 46
Little Clo. F Hth —1M 5
Lit. Copse. Yat —2B 118
Littlecote Dri. Read —6E 62
Littlecote Rd. Frox —6B 74
Lit. Croft. Yat —5B 118
Littlecroft Rd. Egh —9A 72
Lit. Croft Rd. Gor —9L 15
Littledale Clo. Brack —5B 92
Littledown Rd. Slou —9H 23
Littlefield Grn. White —7K 43
Lit. Fryth. Wokgm —4A 112
Lit. Glebe. Son —1D 64
Lit. Heath Rd. Tile —5H 61
Lit. Hill Rd. Hurst —8J 65
Littlejohn's La. Read —4C 62
(in two parts)
Little La. Up Buck —5M 81
Lit. London Rd. Sil —9C 106
Lit. Marlow Rd. Mar —5C 4
Lit. Moor. Sand —9G 112
Lit. Oaks Dri. Tile —4K 61
Lit. Paddock. Camb —9D 114
Littleport Spur. Slou —7G 22
Lit. Ringdale. Brack —6B 92
Littlestead Clo. Cav —7L 39
Little St. Read —4E 62
Lit. Sutton La. Slou —4D 48
Lit. Vigo. Yat —5A 118
Lit. Woodlands. Wind —9B 46
Liverpool Rd. Read —4L 63
Liverpool Rd. Slou —7D 22
Livery Clo. Read —5H 63
Livingstone Gdns. Wdly —7D 64
Livingstone Rd. Newb —9M 79
Llangar Gro. Crowt —5E 112
Llanvair Clo. Asc —8K 93
Llanvair Dri. Asc —8J 93
Loader's La. Arbor —4D 88
Lochinvar Clo. Slou —1D 46
Lochinver. Brack —9M 91
Lock Av. M'head —4F 20
Lock Bri. Rd. Bour —4L 5
Locke Gdns. Slou —1L 47
Lockets Clo. Wind —7N 45
Lock La. M'head —1N 43
Lock Mead. M'head —4F 20
Lock Path. Dor —5N 45
Lock Pl. Read —4K 63
Lockram Rd. Bfld C —1J 107
Lock Rd. Mar —5C 4
Locks Ride. Asc —2E 92
Lockstile Mead. Gor —7L 15
Lockstile Way. Gor —8L 15
Lockton Chase. Asc —5G 93
Lockwood Clo. Farn —9J 119
Loddon Bri. Rd. Wdly —7E 64
Loddon Dri. M'head —6A 20
Loddon Dri. Warg —5F 40
Loddon Hall Rd. Twy —7K 41
Loddon Rd. Bour —3L 5
Loddon Spur. Slou —8G 22
Loddon Vale Cen. Wdly —5F 64
Lodge Clo. Egh —9M 71
Lodge Clo. Mar —6C 4
Lodge Clo. Slou —1E 46
Lodge Clo. Uxb —5K 25
Lodge Gro. Yat —3D 118
Lodge Rd. Hurst —5K 65
Lodge Way. Ashf —6M 73
Lodge Way. Wind —9A 46
Logan Clo. Tile —5N 61
Lomond Av. Cav —8L 39
London Ct. Read —5H 63
London La. Fac —9H 117
London Rd. Asc & S'hill —5L 93
London Rd. Bag —9E 114
London Rd. B'water —7A 118
London Rd. Brack & Asc —4A 92
London Rd. Camb —4K 119
London Rd. Egh —4K 95
London Rd. Newb & That —7L 79
London Rd. Read —6J 63
London Rd. Slou —2L 47
London Rd. Stai & Ashf —8H 73
London Rd. S'dale —9B 94
London Rd. That —8H 81

London Rd. Vir W —7G **94**
London Rd. W'sham —4K **115**
London Rd. Wokgm & Brack —5B **90**
London St. Read —5H **63**
London View. Twy —1K **65**
Loneacre. W'sham —6N **115**
Longacre. Newb —2H **101**
Longbarn La. Read —9H **63**
Longbridge Rd. That —9J **81**
Longbridge Way. Cow —3J **25**
Long Clo. Farn C —1D **22**
Long Clo. Kint —9G **76**
Longcroft Rd. That —9H **81**
Longdon Rd. Winn —2G **89**
Longdown Lodge. Sand —1F **118**
Longdown Rd. Sand —9E **112**
Long Dri. Burn —4M **21**
Longfield Clo. Farn —9L **119**
Longfield Rd. Twy —7J **41**
Longford Av. Stai —5M **73**
Longford Cir. W Dray —7J **49**
Longford Way. Stai —5M **73**
Long Furlong Dri. Slou —5A **22**
Long Gro. Baug —8F **104**
Long Gro. Up Buck —6L **81**
Long Hedge. Lamb —4K **27**
Long Hill Rd. Asc —4D **92**
Longhurst Clo. Cav —1J **63**
Long La. Bright —2C **30**
Long La. M'head —9A **44**
Long La. Shaw —5N **79**
Long La. Stai —6N **73**
Long La. Tile —3H **61**
Longleat Dri. Tile —1J **61**
Longleat Gdns. M'head —8A **20**
Longmead. Wind —7A **46**
Longmead. Wool H —9D **100**
Longmead La. Burn —1N **21**
Long Mickle. Sand —9E **112**
Longmoor La. Mort C —3G **107**
Longmoors. Brack —3J **91**
Longmore Rd. Read —5K **87**
Long Readings La. Slou —4D **22**
Longridge Clo. Read —5B **62**
Long Row. Chad —6M **29**
Longshot Ind. Est. Brack —4J **91**
Longshot La. Brack —5J **91**
(in two parts)
Longstone Rd. Iver —3D **24**
Long's Way. Wokgm —4C **90**
Long Toll. Whit H —1H **37**
Long Wlk. Hung —1D **96**
Long Wlk., The. Wind —2F **70**
Longwater La. Eve —9K **111**
Longwater La. Finch —8K **111**
Longwater Rd. Brack —8N **91**
Longwater Rd. Eve —9K **111**
Longworth Av. Tile —5J **61**
Longworth Dri. M'head —5F **20**
Lonsdale Clo. M'head —5D **20**
Lonsdale Way. M'head —4F **44**
Loosen Dri. M'head —2L **43**
Lord Harris Ct. Sind —2F **88**
Lord Knyvett Clo. Stai —3L **73**
Lord Mayor's Dri. Farn C —1B **22**
Lordswood. Sil —9B **106**
Loring Rd. Wind —7B **46**
Lorne Clo. Slou —2D **46**
Lorne Ct. Chalv —2E **46**
Lorne Pl. Read —5E **62**
Lorne St. Read —5E **62**
Lory Ridge. Bag —6H **115**
Losfield Rd. Wind —7A **46**
Lossie Dri. Iver —8C **24**
Loughborough. Brack —8B **92**
Loundeys Clo. That —7E **80**
Lovatt Clo. Tile —5J **61**
Lovedean Ct. Brack —8B **92**
Love Grn. La. Iver —6E **24**
Love Hill La. Slou —8B **24**
Lovejoy La. Wind —8N **45**
Lovelace Clo. Hur —1D **18**
Lovelace Rd. Brack —6J **91**
Love La. Don —5K **79**
Love La. Iver —7E **24**
Lovel La. Wink —8L **69**
Lovell Clo. Hen T —6B **16**
Lovells Clo. Light —9L **115**
Lovel Rd. Wink —8J **69**
Loverock Rd. Read —3C **62**
Love's Clo. Bfld C —8H **85**
Loves Wood. Mort C —5G **107**
Lovett Gdns. M'head —3E **20**
Lovett Rd. Stai —8D **72**
Lovibonds Av. W Dray —7N **25**
Lowbrook Dri. M'head —2L **43**
Lowbury. Brack —6B **92**
Lowdell Clo. W Dray —7M **25**
Lwr. Armour Rd. Tile —3L **61**
Lwr. Boyndon Rd. M'head —8B **20**
Lwr. Britwell Rd. Slou —5N **21**
Lwr. Broadmoor Rd. Crowt —6G **112**
Lwr. Brook St. Read —6G **63**
Lwr. Charles St. Camb —3N **119**
Lwr. Church Rd. Sand —9C **112**
Lwr. Cippenham La. Slou —9A **22**
Lwr. Common. Eve —9D **110**
Lwr. Cookham Rd. M'head —2E **20**
Lwr. Earley Way. Lwr Ear —3A **88**
Lwr. Earley Way N. Winn —1E **88**
Lwr. Earley Way W. Read & Lwr Ear —4L **87**
Lwr. Elmstone Dri. Tile —3K **61**
Lwr. Farm Ct. That —1C **102**
Lwr. Field Rd. Read —6G **62**
Lwr. Henley Rd. Cav —2J **63**
Lwr. Lees Rd. Slou —4C **22**
Lwr. Mead. Iver —4E **24**
Lwr. Meadow Rd. Read —1K **87**
Lwr. Mill Field. Bag —8G **115**
Lwr. Moor. Yat —4B **118**
Lwr. Mount. Read —7J **63**
Lwr. Nursery. Asc —7C **94**
Lwr. Pound La. Mar —8A **4**
Lwr. Ridge. Bour —3M **5**
Lower Rd. Cook —8J **5**
Lwr. Sandhurst Rd. Finch & Sand —8L **111**
Lwr. Village Rd. Asc —7L **93**
Lower Way. That —8B **80**
Lwr. Wokingham Rd. Wokgm & Crowt —4B **112**
Lowes Clo. S'lake —1G **40**
Lowestoft Clo. Lwr Ear —1C **88**
Lowestoft Dri. Slou —7N **21**
Lowfield Grn. Cav —9L **39**
Lowfield Rd. Cav —8J **39**
Lowlands Dri. Stai —2L **73**
Lowlands Rd. B'water —5G **119**
Low La. Calc —8N **61**
Lowry Clo. Col T —3H **119**
Lowther Clo. Wokgm —3L **89**
Lowther Rd. Wokgm —2K **89**
Loxwood. Ear —1B **88**
Lucas Clo. Yat —4B **118**
Lucas Dri. Yat —4B **118**
Lucey Clo. Tile —1J **61**
Luckley Path. Wokgm —5A **90**
Luckley Rd. Wokgm —8N **89**
Luckley Wood. Wokgm —8N **89**
Luckmore Rd. Ear —9N **63**
Luddington Av. Vir W —4N **95**
Ludlow. Brack —9M **91**
Ludlow Clo. Newb —7B **80**
Ludlow Rd. M'head —8B **20**
Luff Clo. Wind —9A **46**
Luker Av. Hen T —3B **16**
Lulworth Clo. Farn —9L **119**
Lulworth Rd. Read —3J **87**
Lunds Farm Rd. Wdly —4F **64**
Lundy La. Read —5C **62**
Lupin Clo. Bag —9F **114**
Lupin Clo. W Dray —4L **49**
Lupin Ride. Crowt —3F **112**
Luscombe Clo. Cav —2K **63**
Lutman La. M'head —4C **20**
Lutman's Haven. Know H —8B **18**
Lutterworth Clo. Brack —2N **91**
Lutton Clo. Lwr Ear —3M **87**
Lych Ga. Clo. Sand —1D **118**
Lycroft Clo. Gor —7L **15**
Lydbury. Brack —5C **92**
Lydford Av. Slou —6F **22**
Lydford Rd. Read —7L **63**
Lydney. Brack —9M **91**
Lydsell Clo. Slou —4C **22**
Lye Copse Av. Farn —9M **119**
Lyefield Ct. Emm G —7H **39**
Lyell. Wind —9M **45**
Lyell Pl. E. Wind —9M **45**
Lyell Pl. W. Wind —9M 45
(off Lyell)
Lyell Wlk. E. Wind —9M **45**
Lyell Wlk. W. Wind —9M **45**
Lyme Gro. Tile —3L **61**
Lymington Av. Yat —4A **118**
Lymington Ga. Cav —8E **38**
Lynch Clo. Uxb —1K **25**
Lynch Hill La. Slou —5A **22**
Lynch La. Lamb —2H **27**
Lynch, The. Shalb —8F **96**
Lynch, The. Uxb —1K **25**
Lynden M. Read —7H **63**
Lyndhurst Av. B'water —3G **118**
Lyndhurst Av. Cook —9J **5**
Lyndhurst Clo. Brack —5D **92**
Lyndhurst Rd. Asc —6K **93**
Lyndhurst Rd. Gor —8L **15**
Lyndhurst Rd. Tile —3N **61**
Lyndwood Dri. Old Win —3J **71**
Lyne Clo. Vir W —8N **95**
Lyneham Gdns. M'head —5M **19**
Lyneham Rd. Crowt —5F **112**
Lyne Rd. Vir W —8M **95**
Lynmouth Ct. Read —3H **63**
Lynmouth Rd. Read —3G **63**
Lynton Clo. Wdly —7B **64**
Lynton Ct. Newb —7L **79**
Lynton Grn. M'head —7B **20**
Lynwood Av. Egh —1N **95**
Lynwood Av. Slou —2M **47**
Lynwood Chase. Brack —2N **91**
Lynwood Cres. Asc —8A **94**
Lyon Clo. That —9J **81**
Lyon Rd. Crowt —4G **112**
Lyon Sq. Tile —4A **62**
Lyon Way. Frim —8N **119**
Lysander Clo. Wdly —4F **64**
Lysander Mead. M'head —6F **20**
Lytchett Minster Clo. Brack —6C **92**
Lytham. Brack —8J **91**
Lytham Clo. Read —8C **62**
Lytham Ct. S'hill —7M **93**
Lytham End. Tile —1J **61**
Lytham Rd. Wdly —5D **64**

Macadam Av. Crowt —3G **113**
Macbeth Ct. Warf —3B **92**
McCarthy Way. Wokgm —2L **111**
McCrae's Wlk. Warg —3J **41**
Macdonald Rd. Light —9K **115**
Mace Clo. Ear —2N **87**
Mackay Clo. Calc —9M **61**
McKay Trading Est. Coln —8F **48**
Mackenzie Mall. Slou —1H **47**
McKernan Ct. Sand —1D **118**
Macklin Clo. Hung —6K **75**
McNair Clo. Lwr Ear —2N **87**
Macphail Clo. Wokgm —3C **90**
Macrae Rd. Yat —3A **118**
Maddle Rd. Up Lamb —6C **6**
Madeira Wlk. Wind —7F **46**
Madingley. Brack —1M **113**
Madox Brown End. Col T —2J **119**
Mafeking Rd. Wray —6C **72**
Magdalene Rd. Owl —8K **113**
Magill Clo. Spen W —9H **87**
Magna Carta La. Wray —5M **71**
Magna Rd. Egh —1K **95**
Magnolia Clo. Owl —9H **113**
Magnolia Ct. Wdly —5F **64**
Magnolia Gdns. Slou —2L **47**
Magnolia St. W Dray —4L **49**
Magnolia Way. Wokgm —6L **89**
Magpie Clo. That —8E **80**
Magpie Way. Slou —5A **22**
Magpie Way. Tile —6J **61**
Maiden Erlegh Dri. Ear —8A **64**
Maidenfield. Winn —1J **89**
Maidenhead Bus. Campus, The. White —3J **43**
Maidenhead Ct. Pk. M'head —2E **20**
Maidenhead Rd. Binf —6M **67**
Maidenhead Rd. Cook —1B **20**
Maidenhead Rd. M'head —2B **20**
Maidenhead Rd. Wind —6M **45**
Maidenhead Rd. Wokgm —9B **66**
Maiden La. Cen. Lwr Ear —2C **88**
Maiden Pl. Lwr Ear —1B **88**
Maiden's Grn. Wink —6E **68**
Main Dri. Brack —2C **92**
Main Dri. Iver —3F **48**
Mainprize Rd. Brack —3B **92**
Main Rd. Wind —6M **45**
Main St. Green —5D **102**
Main St. Yat —2B **118**
Maisie Webster Clo. Stai —4K **73**
Maitland Rd. Read —5E **62**
Maize La. Warf —1A **92**
Majendie Clo. Speen —6H **79**
Majors Farm Rd. Dat —6M **47**
Makepiece Rd. Brack —2M **91**
Maker Clo. Read —7B **62**
Makins Rd. Hen T —6A **16**
Malders La. M'head —3L **19**
Maldon Clo. Read —6D **62**
Malet Clo. Egh —9E **72**
Malham Fell. Brack —6L **91**
Malham Rd. That —8F **80**
Mallard Clo. Ear —9N **63**
Mallard Clo. Twy —1K **65**
Mallard Dri. Slou —8B **22**
Mallard Row. Read —6G **63**
Mallards. Spen W —1G **109**
Mallards, The. Gt Shef —1F **52**
Mallards Way. Light —9K **115**
Mallard Way. Yat —3A **118**
Mallory Av. Cav —7K **39**
Mallowdale Rd. Brack —9B **92**
Mallow Pk. M'head —5N **19**
Malone Rd. Wdly —6C **64**
Malpas Rd. Slou —8K **23**
Maltby Way. Lwr Ear —3M **87**
Malt Clo. Wick —7J **53**
Malt Hill. Egh —9N **71**
Malt Hill. Warf —8B **68**
Malt Ho. Clo. Old Win —4K **71**
Malthouse Clo. That —9J **81**
Malthouse La. Read —4F **62**
Maltings Pl. Read —5G **63**
Maltings, The. Stai —8F **72**
Maltings, The. That —9J **81**
Maltings, The. W Ils —5M **11**
Malton Av. Slou —7D **22**
Malt Shovel La. Lamb —1F **26**
Malvern Clo. Wdly —6E **64**
Malvern Ct. Coln —5B **48**
Malvern Ct. Newb —1K **101**
Malvern Ct. Read —6K **63**
Malvern Rd. M'head —5A **20**
Malvern Way. Twy —6J **41**
Manchester Rd. Read —4L **63**
Mandarin Ct. Newb —9N **79**
Mandela Ct. Read —5K **63**
Mander Ct. Cav —1H **63**
Mandeville Clo. Tile —7N **61**
Mandeville Ct. Egh —9B **72**
Manea Clo. Lwr Ear —3B **88**
Manfield Clo. Slou —4C **22**
Manners Rd. Wdly —4C **64**
Mannock Way. Wdly —4G **64**
Manor Clo. Brack —2L **91**
Manor Cotts. Fac —8H **117**
Manor Cres. Comp —1G **33**
Manorcrofts Rd. Egh —9B **72**
Manor Farm Clo. Wind —9B **46**
Manor Farm Ct. Egh —9B **72**
Manor Farm La. Egh —9B **72**
Manor Farm La. Tid —2D **60**
Manor Farm Rd. Read —1H **87**
Manor Gro. Fif —7G **45**
Manor Ho. Ct. Read —7N **63**
Manor Ho. Dri. Asc —2K **93**
Manor Ho. La. Dat —6K **47**
Manor La. Brimp —3N **103**
Manor La. Chvly —3M **55**
Manor La. Herm —3E **56**
Manor La. Leck —8C **30**
Manor La. M'head —1B **44**
Manor La. Newb —6B **80**
Manor Leaze. Egh —9C **72**
Manor Pk. Clo. Tile —6K **61**
Manor Pk. Dri. Finch —4J **111**
Manor Pk. Dri. Yat —4B **118**
Manor Pl. Speen —6H **79**
Manor Pl. Stai —9J **73**
Manor Rd. Ashf —9N **73**
Manor Rd. Gor —8K **15**
Manor Rd. Hen T —6C **16**
Manor Rd. M'head —1B **44**
Manor Rd. Shur R —3E **66**
Manor Rd. Want —1H **9**
Manor Rd. Whit T —6D **36**
Manor Rd. Wind —8A **46**
Manor Rd. Wokgm —9M **89**
Manor Way. Bag —8H **115**
Manor Way. Holyp —5D **44**
Manor Waye. Uxb —2L **25**
Manor Wood Ga. Lwr S —1F **40**
Mansel Clo. Slou —6K **23**
Mansell Clo. Wind —7A **46**
Mansell Ct. Read —1L **87**
Mansell Dri. Newb —5G **101**
Mansfield Clo. Asc —3G **93**
Mansfield Cres. Brack —8M **91**
Mansfield Hall. Read —6J **63**
Mansfield Pl. Asc —4G **93**
Mansfield Rd. Read —6F **62**
Mansfield Rd. Wokgm —6L **89**
Man's Hill. Bfld C —8K **85**
Mansion Ho. St. Newb —8L **79**
Mansion La. Iver —9D **24**
Manston Dri. Brack —8N **91**
Manstone La. Hamp N —9N **33**
Maple Av. W Dray —8M **25**
Maple Bank. Rusc —7K **41**
Maple Clo. B'water —4G **118**
Maple Clo. M'head —9N **19**
Maple Clo. Sand —9D **112**
Maple Clo. Son C —1G **38**
Maple Clo. Winn —9J 65
(off Meadow View)
Maple Ct. Brack —6C **92**
Maple Ct. Egh —1K **95**
Maple Ct. Gor —8K **15**
Maple Cres. Newb —6L **79**
Maple Cres. Slou —8K **23**
Mapledene. Cav —1E **62**
Maple Dri. Crowt —3G **112**
Maple Dri. Light —9J **115**
Mapledurham Dri. Pur T —8K **37**
Mapledurham View. Tile —2L **61**
Mapledurham Wlk. M'head —3B **20**
Maple Gdns. Read —1L **87**
Maple Gdns. Stai —6M **73**
Maple Gdns. Yat —4B **118**
Maple Pl. W Dray —9M **25**
Maple Rise. Mar —4C **4**
Maplin Pk. Slou —1C **48**
Marathon Clo. Wdly —4G **64**
Marbeck Clo. Wind —7N **45**
Marchwood Av. Cav —5J **39**
Marconi Rd. Newb —7M **79**
Marcus Clo. Tile —5B **62**
Marefield. Lwr Ear —1B **88**
Marefield Rd. Mar —5B **4**
Mare La. Binf —3J **67**
(in two parts)
Marescroft Rd. Slou —5A **22**
Marfleet Clo. Lwr Ear —1D **88**
Margaret Clo. Read —4J **87**
Margaret Sq. Uxb —2K **25**
Maria Ct. Read —6D **62**
Marigold Clo. Crowt —3D **112**
Marina Way. Finch —4F **110**
Marina Way. Iver —8H **25**
Marina Way. Slou —8N **21**
Mariners La. South —8J **59**
Marish Ct. Langl —2B **48**
Marish Wharf. Mid —1N **47**
Markby Way. Lwr Ear —1C **88**
Market La. Hen T —4C **16**
Market La. Slou & Iver —2D **48**
Market Pl. Brack —4M **91**
Market Pl. Hen T —4C **16**
Market Pl. Lamb —3H **27**
Market Pl. Newb —8L **79**
Market Pl. Read —5H **63**
Market Pl. Wokgm —5A **90**
Market Sq. Stai —8F **72**
Market Sq. Uxb —1K **25**
Market St. Brack —4M **91**
Market St. M'head —7C **20**
Market St. Newb —9L **79**
Market St. Wind —7F **46**
Market Way. Read —5H **63**
Marks Rd. Wokgm —3M **89**
Marlborough Av. Read —7K **63**
Marlborough Clo. M'head —8L **19**
Marlborough Cotts. Tile —3J **61**
Marlborough Ct. Read —6F **62**
Marlborough Ct. Wokgm —4B **90**
Marlborough Ho. Read —8K **63**
Marlborough Rd. Ashf —9L **73**
Marlborough Rd. M'head —8L **19**
Marlborough Rd. Slou —3M **47**
Marlborough Way. Calc —8J **61**
Marlin Ct. Mar —6B **4**
Marling Clo. Tile —2K **61**
Marlow Bottom. Mar —1A **4**
Marlow Bri. La. Mar —7C **4**
Marlow Ct. Read —6K **63**
Marlowes, The. Newb —2K **101**
Marlow Rd. Bish —9B **4**
Marlow Rd. Hen T —3D **16**
Marlow Rd. L Mar & Bour —3E **4**
Marlow Rd. M'head —7B **20**
Marlow Rd. M'head —1H **19**
(Pinkeys Green)
Marlow Rd. Mar —1A **4**
Marlston Rd. Herm —6E **56**
Marmion Rd. Hen T —6D **16**
Marquis Pl. Read —5L **63**
Marsack St. Cav —2J **63**
Mars Clo. Wokgm —5K **89**
Marshall Clo. Farn —9K **119**
Marshall Clo. Pur T —9L **37**
Marshall Rd. Col T —2H **119**
Marshalls Ct. Speen —6H **79**
Marsham Ho. Brack —2M **91**
Marshaw Ct. Read —9J **63**
Marsh Ct. Read —5D **62**
Marshfield. Dat —7M **47**
Marshland Sq. Emm G —8H **39**
Marsh La. Cav —1N **63**
Marsh La. Cur —7N **55**
Marsh La. Hung —6H **75**
Marsh La. Newb —8L **79**
Marsh La. Tap & Wind —9H **21**
Marsh Rd. That —7H **81**
Marshwood Rd. Light —9N **115**
Marston Dri. Farn —9M **119**
Marston Way. Asc —4H **93**
Marten Pl. Tile —1K **61**
Martin Clo. Wind —7M **45**
Martin Clo. Wdly —6D **64**
Martindale. Iver —5E **24**
Martineaux La. Hurst —5K **65**
Martin Rd. M'head —6C **20**
Martin Rd. Slou —2G **46**
Martins Clo. B'water —5H **119**
Martin's Dri. Wokgm —3N **89**
Martin's La. Brack —5B **92**
Martins Plain. Stoke P —4H **23**
Martins, The. Thea —9J **81**
Marunden Grn. Slou —4B **22**
Mary Drew Almshouses. Egh —1M **95**
Maryland Clo. Wokgm —2K **111**
Mary Lyne Almshouses. Read
(off New La. Hill) —7N 61
Mary Mead. Warf —1A **92**
Mary Morgan Ct. Slou —6F **22**
Maryside. Slou —1N **47**
Mascoll Path. Slou —4B **22**
Masefield Rd. That —7F **80**
Masefield Way. Stai —5N **73**
Mason Clo. Yat —4C **118**
Mason Ct. Wool H —9D **100**
Mason Pl. Sand —1D **118**
Masons Ct. Cipp —8A **22**
Masons Rd. Slou —8A **22**
Mason St. Read —4E **62**
Master Clo. Wdly —4G **64**
Mathews Chase. Brack —2K **91**
Mathisen Way. Coln —7F **48**
Matlock Rd. Cav —9E **38**
Matson Dri. Rem —4E **16**
Matthews Clo. That —7E **80**
Matthews Ct. Asc —6N **93**
Matthewsgreen Rd. Wokgm —3M **89**
Matthews La. Stai —8G **73**
Matthews Rd. Camb —1N **119**
Mattland Rd. Read —5E **62**
Maultway Clo. Camb —9E **114**
Maultway Cres. Camb —9E **114**
Maultway N. Camb —9D **114**
Maultway, The. Camb —9E **114**
Mawbray Clo. Lwr Ear —1B **88**
Maxine Clo. Sand —9F **112**
Maxwell Clo. Wdly —4D **64**
Maxwell Rd. W Dray —3N **49**
Maybrick Clo. Sand —9D **112**
Maybury Clo. Frim —9N **119**
Maybury Clo. Slou —7N **21**
May Clo. Owl —1H **119**
Mayfair. Tile —5L **61**
Mayfair Dri. Newb —1J **101**
Mayfield Av. Calc —8J **61**
Mayfield Caravan Pk. W Dray —2K **49**
Mayfield Cotts. Comp —1F **32**
Mayfield Dri. Cav —1K **63**
Mayfield Rd. Camb —8M **119**
May Fields. Sind —2F **88**
Maygoods Clo. Uxb —6L **25**
Maygoods Grn. Uxb —6L **25**
Maygoods La. Uxb —6L **25**
Maygoods View. Cow —6K **25**
Maying, The. Read —5H **87**
Maynard Clo. That —6F **80**
Maynard Ct. Stai —8H **73**
Mayow Clo. That —9J **81**
May Pk. Calc —8M **61**
Maypole Rd. Tap —6K **21**
Mays Croft. Brack —6L **91**
May's Hill. B Hill —3E **108**
Mays La. Ear —7A **64**
(in two parts)
May's La. Pad C —3B **106**
May's La. Stcks —8N **77**
May's Rd. Wokgm —5C **90**
May Tree Clo. Mar —1A **4**
Meachen Ct. Wokgm —5A **90**
Mead Av. Slou —1C **48**
Mead Clo. Egh —9C **72**
Mead Clo. Mar —4D **4**
Mead Clo. Slou —1C **48**
Mead Clo. Tile —6J **61**
Meade Ct. Bag —7J **115**
Meadfield Av. Slou —1B **48**
Meadfield Rd. Slou —2B **48**
Mead La. Up Bas —8K **35**
Meadow Bank. Bour —4M **5**
Meadowbank Rd. Light —9M **115**
Meadow Brook Clo. Coln —7G **48**
Meadow Clo. B'water —5H **119**
Meadow Clo. Gor —8L **15**
Meadow Clo. Mar —6D **4**
Meadow Clo. Old Win —2K **71**
Meadow Clo. That —8F **80**
Meadow Ct. Stai —7F **72**
Meadowcroft Rd. Read —3J **87**
Meadow Gdns. Stai —9E **72**
Meadow La. Eton —5D **46**
Meadow La. Pang —8E **36**
Meadow La. Stai —8G **73**
Meadow Rd. Ear —9C **64**
Meadow Rd. Hen T —5D **16**
Meadow Rd. Newb —2K **101**
Meadow Rd. Read —3F **62**
Meadow Rd. Slou —2N **47**
Meadow Rd. Vir W —7G **94**
Meadow Rd. Wokgm —5M **89**
Meadowside. Stai —9H **73**
Meadowside Rd. Pang —8E **36**
Meadows, The. Camb —4J **119**
Meadowsweet Dri. That —7H **81**
Meadow View. Mar —1C **4**
Meadowview. Stai —2H **73**
Meadow View. Winn —9J **65**
Meadow View La. Holyp —5B **44**
Meadow Wlk. Bour —2L **5**
Meadow Wlk. Wokgm —5M **89**
Meadow Way. B'water —4G **119**
Meadow Way. Brack —2L **91**
Meadow Way. Dor R —1J **45**
Meadow Way. Fif —7G **45**
Meadow Way. Old Win —3K **71**
Meadow Way. Thea —9E **60**
Meadow Way. Wokgm —6M **89**
Mead Rd. Uxb —1L **25**
Meads, The. Uxb —5M **25**
Mead, The. Gt Shef —1G **52**
Mead Wlk. Slou —1C **48**
Meadway. Ashf —8N **73**
Mead Way. Slou —6N **21**
Meadway Precinct. Tile —6A **62**
Meadway, The. Tile —5M **61**
Mearings, The. Bfld —6N **85**
Measham Way. Lwr Ear —2B **88**
Meavy Gdns. Read —1H **87**
Medallion Pl. M'head —7E **20**
Mede Clo. Wray —5M **71**
Mede Ct. Stai —7F **72**
Mediar Ct. Slou —9L **23**
Medina Clo. Wokgm —4K **89**
Medlar Dri. B'water —6K **119**
Medman Clo. Uxb —3K **25**
Medway Clo. That —6E **80**
Medway Clo. Wokgm —4K **89**
Melbourne Av. Slou —7E **22**
Melbourne Av. Winn —2H **89**
Meldreth Way. Lwr Ear —2B **88**
Meldrum Clo. Newb —4G **100**
Melford Grn. Cav —7L **39**
Melksham Clo. Lwr Ear —3L **87**
Melksham Clo. Owl —9H **113**

Melling Clo. Ear —9D 64
Mellor Wlk. Read —7H 63
Melody Clo. Winn —9H 65
Melrose. Brack —1M 113
Melrose Av. Read —7N 63
Melrose Gdns. Arbor X —9D 88
Membury Wlk. Brack —6B 92
Memorial Av. S'lake X —3E 40
Mendip Clo. Charv —9G 41
Mendip Clo. Slou —4B 48
Mendip Dri. Tile —6H 61
Mendip Rd. Brack —7B 92
Mendip Rd. Farn —9J 119
Menpes Rd. Tile —9K 37
Mentone Cotts. Wal L —8C 42
Meon Clo. Tadl —9J 105
Mercer Wlk. Uxb —1K 25
Merchants Pl. Read —4G 63
Mercian Way. Slou —9N 21
Mercia Rd. M'head —1M 43
Mercury Av. Wokgm —5K 89
Mere Clo. Mar —5D 4
Mereoak La. Graz —8E 86
Mere Rd. Slou —2H 47
Mereside Pl. Vir W —9J 95 (Knowle Hill)
Mereside Pl. Vir W —7M 95 (Virginia Water)
Meridian Ct. S'dale —1L 115
Merlewood. Brack —7A 92
Merlin Clo. Slou —5C 48
Merlin Clove. Wink R —1E 92
Merrivale Gdns. Read —2J 87
Merrivale M. W Dray —9L 25
Merron Clo. Yat —4A 118
Merryfields. Uxb —3M 25 (in two parts)
Merryhill Chase. Winn —9H 65
Merryhill Grn. La. Winn —9J 65
Merryhill Rd. Brack —2L 91
Merryman Dri. Crowt —4D 112
Merryweather Clo. Finch —1L 111
Mersey Way. That —6E 80
Merton Clo. M'head —2N 43
Merton Clo. Owl —8K 113
Merton Rd. Slou —2J 47
Merton Rd. N. Read —2H 87
Merton Rd. S. Read —2H 87
Merwin Way. Wind —8N 45
Meteor Clo. Wdly —5F 64
Metro Cen., The. Wokgm —1M 89
Mews, The. Read —6L 63
Mews, The. Slou —2G 47
Mey Clo. Calc —7K 61
Meyrick Dri. Newb —5G 100
Micawber Av. Uxb —5N 25
Michael Clo. M'head —9N 19
Michaelmas Clo. Yat —5B 118
Michael's Path. M'head —5H 19
Micheldever Way. Brack —8C 92
Michelet Clo. Light —9L 115
Micklands Rd. Cav —9K 39
Mickle Hill. Sand —9E 112
Micro Cen., The. Read —9H 63
Midas Ind. Est. Cow —3J 25
Midcroft. Slou —5D 22
Middle Clo. Newb —3H 101
Middlefields. Rusc —7K 41
Middlefields Ct. Rusc —7K 41
Middle Gordon Rd. Camb —4N 119
Middle Grn. Slou —9N 23
Middlegreen Rd. Slou —1M 47
Middle Hill. Egh —8L 71
Middleton Ct. Newb —6B 80
Middle Wlk. Burn —4L 21
Midsummer Meadow. Cav —7F 38
Mid Winter Clo. Tile —4M 61
Milbanke Ct. Brack —4K 91
Milbanke Way. Brack —4K 91
Milburn Dri. W Dray —7M 25
Mildenhall Clo. Lwr Ear —1C 88
Mildenhall Rd. Slou —7G 22
Mile Elm. Mar —4E 4
Milestone Av. Charv —9F 40
Milestone Cres. Charv —9F 40
Milestone Way. Cav —7K 39
Miles Way. Wdly —5F 64
Milford Ct. Slou —1J 47
Milford Rd. Read —3F 62
Milkhouse Rd. Stcks —8A 78
Milkingbarn La. Shin —8N 87
Mill Av. Uxb —3K 25
Mill Bank. Kint —8F 76
Millbank Cres. Wdly —6E 64
Millboard Rd. Bour —4M 5
Mill Bri. Rd. Yat —1A 118
Millbrook Way. Coln —8F 48
Mill Clo. W Dray —2L 49
Mill Clo. Wokgm —4L 89
Mill Ct. Slou —9H 23
Milldown Av. Gor —7L 15
Milldown Rd. Gor —7L 15
Millenium Ct. Read —1H 87
Millers Clo. Gor —7K 15
Millers Clo. Stai —9J 73
Millers Ct. Egh —9E 72
Miller's Field. Gt Shef —1F 52
Millers Gro. Calc —8M 61
Miller's La. Old Win —3H 71
Millers Rd. Tadl —9K 105
Milley La. Hare H —5M 41
Milley Rd. Wal L —6B 42
Mill Field. Bag —7G 115
Millfield. Lamb —3H 27
Mill Grn. Brack —2J 91
Mill Grn. Cav —3J 63 (in two parts)
Millgreen La. Hdly —8J 103
Mill Ho. La. Stai —9E 72
Millins Clo. Owl —9J 113
Mill La. Asc —4B 94
Mill La. Brack —6K 91
Mill La. Calc —9M 61
Mill La. Cook —8M 5
Mill La. Ear —9D 64 (in two parts)
Mill La. Hen T —6E 16
Mill La. Hort —9C 48
Mill La. Hur —1D 18
Mill La. Lamb —3J 27
Mill La. Lwr P —8L 83
Mill La. Newb —8L 79
Mill La. Read —5H 63 (in two parts)
Mill La. S'lake —3E 40
Mill La. Sind —2E 88
Mill La. Tap —7F 20
Mill La. Tok G —4C 38
Mill La. Wind —6C 46
Mill La. Yat —1B 118
Mill Mead. Stai —8G 72
Mill Mead. Wokgm —4M 89
Millmere. Yat —2B 118
Mill Pl. Dat —8M 47
Mill Pond Rd. W'sham —4L 115
Mill Reef Clo. That —8C 80
Mill Ride. Asc —3G 92
Mill Rd. Bfld —2M 85
Mill Rd. Cav —3J 63
Mill Rd. Gor —6L 15
Mill Rd. Lwr S —3G 40
Mill Rd. Mar —6C 4
Mill Rd. W Dray —2K 49
Mill Side. Bour —4N 5
Mills Spur. Old Win —4K 71
Millstream La. Slou —9A 22
Mill St. Coln —6E 48
Mill St. Slou —9H 23
Millworth La. Shin —7L 87
Milman Clo. Brack —4D 92
Milman Rd. Read —7H 63
Milner Rd. Burn —6K 21
Milsom Clo. Shin —6L 87
Milton Clo. Brack —8M 91
Milton Clo. Hen T —5C 16
Milton Clo. Hort —9B 48
Milton Ct. Wokgm —4N 89
Milton Dri. Wokgm —4N 89
Milton Gdns. Stai —5N 73
Milton Gdns. Wokgm —5N 89
Milton Rd. Ear —5N 63
Milton Rd. Egh —9A 72
Milton Rd. Slou —5F 22
Milton Rd. Wokgm —3N 89
Milton Way. Rusc —8L 41
Milton Way. W Dray —3N 49
Milverton Clo. M'head —2M 43
Milward Gdns. Binf —4G 91
Mina Av. Slou —1M 47
Minchin Grn. Binf —9G 67
Minden Clo. Wokgm —5K 89
Minerva Clo. Stai —2H 73
Minerva Ho. Read —4H 63 (off Valpy St.)
Ministry Rd. Green —5D 102
Minley La. Yat —7B 118
Minley Mnr. B'water —9C 118
Minley Rd. B'water & Fleet —9A 118
Minley Rd. Farn —9D 118 (in two parts)
Minniecroft Rd. Burn —4L 21
Minstead Clo. Brack —5C 92
Minstead Dri. Yat —4A 118
Minster Ct. Camb —5K 119
Minster St. Read —5H 63
Minster Way. Slou —1A 48
Mint Clo. Ear —2M 87
Minton Clo. Tile —4N 61
Minton Rise. Tap —7L 21
Mirador Cres. Slou —8K 23
Mire La. Wal L —8B 42
Misbourne Ct. Langl —3B 48
Misbourne Rd. Uxb —2N 25
Missenden Gdns. Burn —7L 21
Mistletoe Rd. Yat —5B 118
Mitcham Clo. Read —7H 63
Mitcham Rd. Camb —9D 114
Mitchell Clo. Slou —2C 46
Mitchell Way. Wdly —5G 64
Mitford Clo. Read —3K 87
Moat Dri. Slou —6L 23
Modbury Gdns. Read —1J 87
Moffat Clo. Wdly —6F 64
Moffatts Clo. Sand —1E 118
Moffy Hill. M'head —4B 20
Mohawk Way. Wdly —4G 64
Mole Rd. Sind —7E 88
Moles Clo. Wokgm —6B 90
Mollison Clo. Wdly —4G 65
Molly Millars Bri. Wokgm —7N 89
Molly Millars Clo. Wokgm —7N 89
Molly Millar's La. Wokgm —6M 89
Molyneux Rd. W'sham —6N 115
Monarch Ho. Read —3G 62
Monck Ct. Read —6D 62
Money La. W Dray —2L 49
Moneyrow Grn. Holyp —7C 44
Monkey Island La. Bray —2G 45
Monkley Ct. Cav —3J 63
Monks All. Binf —9F 66
Monks Clo. Asc —8L 93
Monks Dri. Asc —8L 93
Monksfield Way. Slou —5C 22
Monks Hollow. Mar —2C 4
Monks Hood Clo. Wokgm —4C 90
Monk's La. Newb —3J 101
Monks Rd. Vir W —6M 95
Monks Rd. Wind —8N 45
Monks Wlk. Asc —8L 93
Monks Way. Read —7D 62
Monks Way. W Dray —5M 49
Monkswood Clo. Newb —3H 101
Monmouth Ct. Read —4F 62 (North St.)
Monmouth Ct. Read —3G 62 (off Northfield Rd.)
Mons Clo. Wokgm —5K 89
Monsell Gdns. Stai —9F 72
Mons Wlk. Egh —9D 72
Montacute Dri. That —9J 81
Montague Clo. Camb —4M 119
Montague Clo. Light —9K 115
Montague Pas. Uxb —1L 25
Montague Rd. Slou —8H 23
Montague Rd. Uxb —1L 25
Montague St. Cav —2J 63
Montague St. Read —5K 63
Montague Ter. Newb —2L 101
Montagu Rd. Dat —7K 47
Monteagle La. Yat —4A 118
Montem La. Slou —9F 22
Montgomery Clo. Sand —1F 118
Montgomery Dri. Spen W —9H 87
Montgomery of Alamein Ct. Brack —3A 92
Montgomery Pl. Slou —7L 23
Montgomery Rd. Newb —2J 101
Montpelier Ct. Wind —8E 46
Montpelier Dri. Cav —8K 39
Montrose Av. Dat —6L 47
Montrose Av. Slou —7D 22
Montrose Dri. M'head —8L 19
Montrose Ter. W Dray —8L 25
Montrose Wlk. Calc —8N 61
Montrose Way. Dat —7M 47
Monycrower Dri. M'head —7B 20
Moorbridge Rd. M'head —7D 20
Moor Clo. Owl —9J 113
Moor Clo. Wokgm —3K 111
Moor Copse Clo. Ear —9A 64
Moorcroft La. Uxb —6N 25
Moordale Av. Brack —3J 91
Moore Clo. Slou —1D 46
Moore Gro. Cres. Egh —1N 95
Moor End. M'head —4F 44
Moores Grn. Wokgm —3C 90
Moores La. Eton W —3B 46
Moore's Pl. Hung —6J 75
Moorfield Rd. Uxb —7L 25
Moorfield Ter. M'head —6D 20
Moorland Rd. W Dray —5K 49
Moorlands Dri. M'head —6K 19
Moorlands Pl. Camb —4L 119
Moorlands Rd. Camb —5M 119
Moor La. Brack —5G 91
Moor La. M'head —5C 20
Moor La. Newb —8H 79
Moor La. Stai —5E 72
Moor La. W Dray —5K 49
Moormead Cres. Stai —8G 73
Moor Pk. Ho. Brack —8J 91
Moor Pl. W'sham —5L 115
Moor Rd. Farn —9L 119
Moor Rd. Stai —3H 73
Moors Ct. Winn —9F 64 (off Ditchfield La.)
Moorside Clo. Farn —8L 119
Moorside Clo. M'head —5C 20
Moors, The. Pang —8E 36
Moors, The. That —8F 80
Moorstown Ct. Slou —1G 47
Moor, The. Mar —3G 5
Moray Av. Col T —1H 119 (in two parts)
Moray Dri. Slou —7J 23
Mordaunt Dri. Wel C —7F 112
Morden Clo. Brack —6C 92
Moreau Wlk. G Grn —7N 23
Morecambe Av. Cav —8E 38
Moreland Av. Coln —6D 48
Moreland Clo. Coln —6D 48
Moreleigh Clo. Read —3J 87
Morella Clo. Vir W —6M 95
Moretaine Rd. Ashf —7L 73
Moreton Way. Slou —9N 21
Morgan Rd. Read —7J 63
Moriston Clo. Read —4B 62
Morlais. Cav —8G 38
Morland Clo. W Ils —4L 11
Morlands Av. Read —7A 62
Morley Clo. Slou —1A 48
Morley Pl. Hung —6K 75
Mornington Av. Wokgm —2L 111
Mornington Clo. Baug —9F 104
Morpeth Clo. Read —8J 63
Morrice Clo. Slou —3A 48
Morriss Ct. Read —5K 63 (off Orts Rd.)
Mortimer Clo. Read —4J 87
Mortimer La. Mort —2L 107
Mortimer La. Strat S —9L 107
Mortimer Rd. Slou —2M 47
Morton Ct. Read —7K 63
Morton Pl. Thea —8F 60
Moss Clo. Cav —1J 63
Mossy Vale. M'head —5A 20
Mostyn Ho. Brack —2M 91 (off Merryhill Rd.)
Moulsham Copse La. Yat —2A 118
Moulsham Grn. Yat —2A 118
Moulsham La. Yat —2A 118
Mountain Ash. Mar —1B 4
Mountbatten Clo. Newb —6M 79
Mountbatten Clo. Slou —2J 47
Mountbatten Rise. Sand —9D 112
Mountbatten Sq. Wind —7E 46
Mount Clo. Newb —1L 101
Mount Clo., The. Vir W —8M 95
Mountfield. Gor —7L 15
Mount Hill. Wink —6M 69
Mount La. Brack —5N 91
Mount La. Chad —5L 29
Mt. Lee. Egh —9A 72
Mt. Pleasant. Been —5H 83
Mt. Pleasant. Brack —5N 91 (in two parts)
Mt. Pleasant. L Sand —9E 112
Mt. Pleasant. Read —6H 63
Mt. Pleasant. Tadl —9J 105
Mt. Pleasant. Wokgm —5M 89
Mt. Pleasant Clo. Light —9K 115
Mt. Pleasant Dri. Tadl —9J 105
Mt. Pleasant Gro. Read —6H 63
Mount Rd. That —7G 81
Mountsfield Clo. Stai —3H 73
Mounts Hill. Wind —6M 69
Mount St. Read —7H 63 (in two parts)
Mount, The. Cav —1F 62
Mount, The. Read —7K 63
Mount, The. Vir W —8M 95
Mt. View. Hen T —4C 16
Mowbray Cres. Egh —9B 72
Mowbray Dri. Tile —4A 62
Mower Clo. Wokgm —4D 90
Moyleen Rise. Mar —6A 4
Muddy La. Slou —6G 23
Mud La. Eve —9E 110
Mud La. P'mre —7G 31
Muirfield Clo. Read —5K 63
Muirfield Ho. Brack —8J 91
Mulberry Av. Stai —5M 73
Mulberry Av. Wind —9H 47
Mulberry Bus. Pk. Wokgm —7M 89
Mulberry Clo. Crowt —6G 113
Mulberry Clo. Owl —1H 119
Mulberry Clo. Wdly —6D 64
Mulberry Ct. Brack —7B 92
Mulberry Ct. Wokgm —5A 90
Mulberry Cres. W Dray —1N 49
Mulberry Dri. Slou —4N 47
Mulberry Ho. Brack —2M 91
Mulberry Pde. W Dray —2N 49
Mulberry Wlk. M'head —6N 19
Mulberry Way. Thea —9F 60
Mulfords Hill. Tadl —9K 105
Mullens Rd. Egh —9D 72
Mullens Ter. Chaz H —5D 38
Mumbery Hill. Warg —4K 41
Muncaster Clo. Ashf —8N 73
Munces Rd. Mar —1B 4
Munday Ct. Binf —2J 91
Mundaydean La. Mar —3A 4
Mundesley Spur. Slou —7G 22
Mundesley St. Read —6H 63 (off Southampton St.)
Munkle Marsh. That —8K 81
Munnings Dri. Col T —3H 119
Munro Av. Wdly —8E 64
Murdoch Clo. Stai —9H 73
Murdoch Rd. Wokgm —6A 90
Murray Ct. Asc —7M 93
Murray Rd. Wokgm —5M 89
Murrellhill La. Binf —2G 90
Murrells La. Camb —6M 119
Murrin Rd. M'head —6N 19
Mushroom Castle. Brack —1E 92
Mustard La. Son —3D 64
Mustard Mill Rd. Stai —8F 72
Muswell Clo. Thea —9F 60
Mutton Hill. Brack —3G 91
Mutton Oaks. Binf —3H 91
Myddleton Rd. Uxb —2K 25
Mylne Sq. Wokgm —5B 90
Myrke, The. Dat —3H 47
Myrtle Clo. Bfld C —8J 85
Myrtle Clo. Coln —7F 48
Myrtle Clo. Tile —1K 61
Myrtle Clo. Uxb —6N 25
Myrtle Clo. W Dray —2N 49
Myrtle Cres. Slou —8H 23
Myrtle Dri. B'water —4J 119
Myton Wlk. Thea —9F 60

Nabbs Hill Clo. Tile —7K 61
Nalderhill Rd. Stcks —3N 77
Napier Clo. Crowt —5G 113
Napier Clo. W Dray —2N 49
Napier Ct. Trading Est. Read —4H 63
Napier Rd. Crowt —6G 112
Napier Rd. Houn —7L 49
Napier Rd. M'head —8M 19
Napier Rd. Read —4H 63
Napper Clo. Asc —4F 92
Narromine Dri. Calc —8N 61
Naseby. Brack —1M 113
Nash Clo. Ear —9N 63
Nashdom La. Burn —1K 21
Nash Gdns. Asc —4H 93
Nash Gro. La. Wokgm —9K 89
Nashgrove Ride. Wokgm —9H 89
Nash Pk. Binf —1F 90
Nash Rd. Slou —3A 48
Nash's Yd. Uxb —1L 25
Navahoe Rd. Finch —4F 110
Neath Gdns. Tile —5N 61
Needham Clo. Wind —7A 46
Nell Gwynne Clo. Asc —6N 93
Nelson Clo. Brack —3B 92
Nelson Clo. Slou —3M 47
Nelson Rd. Ashf —9M 73
Nelson Rd. Cav —2J 63
Nelson Rd. H'row A —7N 49
Nelson Rd. Wind —9B 46
Nelson's La. Hurst —7N 65
Nelson Way. Camb —5K 119
Neptune Clo. Wokgm —5K 89
Netherton. Brack —6L 91
Netley Clo. Cav —7L 39
Nettlecombe. Brack —8A 92
Nevelle Clo. Binf —3H 91
Nevil Ct. That —9G 80
Neville Clo. Stoke P —1H 23
Neville Clo. Wal L —7D 42
Neville Ct. Burn —4M 21
Neville Dri. That —8H 81
Neville Duke Rd. Farn —9K 119
Nevis Rd. Tile —1L 61
Newalls Rise. Warg —3K 41
Newark St. Read —6H 63
New Bath Rd. Charv —8G 40
Newberry Cres. Wind —8N 45
Newbery Clo. Tile —3L 61
Newbery Way. Slou —1F 46
Newbold Rd. Speen —6H 79
Newbolt Clo. That —6F 80
New Bright St. Read —6G 63
Newbury Bus. Pk. Newb —7N 79
Newbury Dri. M'head —8E 20
Newbury Hill. Hamp N —8J 33
Newbury La. Comp —1G 32
Newbury Racecourse. Green —1A 102
Newbury Rd. Gt Shef —1F 52
Newbury Rd. Herm —6D 56
Newbury Rd. Houn —7N 49
Newbury Rd. Lamb —3J 27
Newbury St. Kint —9G 76
Newbury St. Lamb —3H 27
Newcastle Rd. Read —8J 63
Newchurch Rd. Slou —6B 22
Newchurch Rd. Tadl —9J 105
Newcombe Rise. W Dray —7M 25
New Cotts. Fac —9G 116
New Ct. Mar —5C 4
Newcourt. Uxb —6K 25
Newcroft Clo. Uxb —6N 25
New Cut. Slou —5K 21
Newell's La. Cav —7B 38
Newfield Gdns. Mar —4D 4
Newfield Rd. Mar —5D 4
Newfield Way. Mar —5D 4
New Forest Ride. Brack —9B 92
New Garden Dri. W Dray —1M 49
Newhaven Spur. Slou —5D 22
New Hayward Farm Cotts. Hung —1K 75
New Hill. Pur T —8K 37
Newhurst Gdns. Warf —9A 68
Newlands Av. Cav —1H 63
Newlands Clo. Yat —4B 118
Newlands Cotts. Wokgm —4E 88
Newlands Dri. Coln —9F 48
Newlands Dri. M'head —7L 19
Newlands Rd. Camb —8M 119
New La. Hill. Tile —5M 61
Newlyn Gdns. Read —2H 87
Newmarket Clo. Lwr Ear —1C 88
New Meadow. Asc —3G 93
New Mile Rd. Asc —4L 93
New Mill La. Eve —8D 110
New Mill Rd. Eve —8D 110
Newnham Clo. Slou —9J 23
New Pde. Ashf —8N 73
New Peachey La. Uxb —7L 25
Newport Clo. Newb —7M 79
Newport Rd. Houn —7N 49
Newport Rd. Newb —7M 79
Newport Rd. Read —3G 62
Newport Rd. Slou —5A 22
New Rd. Asc —2H 93
New Rd. Bag & W'sham —7J 115
New Rd. B'water —5J 119
New Rd. Bour —4M 5
New Rd. Brack —4A 92
New Rd. Bfld C —9M 85
New Rd. Chvly —1K 55
New Rd. Cook —8J 5
New Rd. Crowt —5G 112
New Rd. Dat —7M 47
New Rd. Green —1N 101
New Rd. Hur —3D 18
New Rd. Langl —2B 48
New Rd. M'head —5E 44
New Rd. Mar —1B 4
New Rd. Read —7K 63
New Rd. Rusc —7L 41
New Rd. Sand —1E 118
New Rd. S'lake —3E 40
New Rd. Stai —9D 72
New Rd. Twy —6J 41
New Rd. Hill. Midg —7D 82
New Sq. Slou —1H 47
New St. Hen T —4D 16
New St. Stai —8H 73
New St. Strat S —9A 108
Newton Av. Cav —8K 39
Newton Clo. Slou —1A 48
Newton Ct. Old Win —3J 71
Newton La. Old Win —3K 71
Newton Rd. Houn —7M 49
Newton's La. Bagn —4G 79
Newton's M. Hung —5K 75
Newtown. Tadl —9J 105
Newtown Gdns. Hen T —6D 16
Newtown Rd. Den —1J 25
Newtown Rd. Hen T —6E 16
Newtown Rd. Mar —4D 4
Newtown Rd. Newb —1L 101
Newtown Rd. Sand —1F 118
New Villas. Bal H —7N 99
New Way. South —1J 83
New Windsor St. Uxb —2K 25
New Wokingham Rd. Crowt —3E 112
Niagara Rd. Hen T —6D 16
Nicholas Ct. Read —5F 62 (off Prospect St.)
Nicholas Rd. Hen T —6A 16
Nicholls. Wind —9M 45
Nicholls Wlk. Wind —9M 45
Nicholson M. Egh —9B 72 (off Nicholson Wlk.)
Nicholsons La. M'head —7C 20
Nicholsons Wlk. M'head —7C 20
Nicholson Wlk. Egh —9B 72
Nideggen Clo. That —8G 81
Nightingale Cres. Brack —7N 91
Nightingale Gdns. Sand —1F 118
Nightingale La. M'head —3A 20
Nightingale La. Mort —3J 107
Nightingale Pk. Farn C —1B 22
Nightingale Rd. Wdly —7B 64
Nightingales, The. Newb —2M 101
Nightingales, The. Stai —5N 73
Nimrod Clo. Wdly —5G 64
Nimrod Way. Read —7H 63
Nine Elms Av. Uxb —6L 25
Nine Elms Clo. Uxb —6L 25
Nine Mile Ride. Asc —9H 93
Nine Mile Ride. Crowt & Brack —1K 113
Nine Mile Ride. Finch —4G 111
Nine Mile Ride. Wokgm —4M 111
Niven Ct. S'hill —6N 93
Nixley Clo. Slou —1J 47
Noakes Hill. Ash'd —6D 34
Nobles Way. Egh —1N 95
Nodmore. Chadw —6N 29
Nonsuch Clo. Wokgm —4N 89
Norcot Rd. Tile —4M 61
Norden Clo. M'head —1N 43
Norden Rd. M'head —9N 19
Norelands Dri. Burn —3M 21
Nores Rd. Read —4K 87
Norfolk Av. Slou —6E 22
Norfolk Chase. Warf —2C 92
Norfolk Clo. Wokgm —5K 89
Norfolk Pk. Cotts. M'head —6C 20
Norfolk Rd. M'head —6B 20
Norfolk Rd. Read —5C 62
Norfolk Rd. Uxb —1L 25
Norlands. That —6F 80
Norman Av. Hen T —5D 16
Normandy Wlk. Egh —9D 72
Normanhurst. Ashf —9N 73
Norman Rd. Cav —9J 39
Normans Clo. Uxb —5N 25
Normanstead Rd. Tile —4K 61

Normans, The. Slou —7K 23
Normay Rise. Newb —5G 101
Normoor Rd. Bfld C —1G 106
Norreys Av. Wokgm —5B 90
Norreys Dri. M'head —1N 43
Norris Field. Chadw —5N 29
Norris Grn. Land E —3F 64
Norris La. Chadw —5N 29
Norris Rd. Read —6N 63
Norris Rd. Stai —8G 72
Nortbourne Clo. Lwr Ear —1A 88
Northam Clo. Lwr Ear —9D 64
Northampton Av. Slou —7E 22
Northampton Clo. Brack —5B 92
Northborough Rd. Slou —5C 22
Northbrook Copse. Brack —8C 92
Northbrook Rd. Cav —8K 39
Northbrook St. Newb —7L 79
N. Burnham Clo. Burn —3L 21
Northbury Av. Rusc —7K 41
Northbury La. Rusc —7K 41
North Clo. Farn —9L 119
North Clo. Wind —7B 46
Northcott. Brack —1L 113
Northcourt Av. Read —8K 63
Northcroft. Slou —5D 22
Northcroft Clo. Egh —9K 71
Northcroft Gdns. Egh —9K 71
Northcroft La. Newb —8K 79
Northcroft Rd. Egh —9K 71
Northcroft Ter. Newb —8K 79
Northcroft Vs. Egh —9K 71
N. Dean. M'head —5C 20
North Dri. Stoke P —4G 22
North Dri. Sul'd —4E 84
North Dri. Vir W —7G 94
N. End La. Asc —9D 94
Northern Av. Don —5L 79
Northern Heights. Bour —2M 5
Northern Perimeter Rd. W. Houn —7M 49
Northern Rd. Slou —5F 22
Northern Woods. F Hth —1N 5
N. Farm Rd. Farn —9K 119
Northfield. Light —9L 115
Northfield Av. Lwr S —1F 40
Northfield Clo. Hen T —3C 16
(off Badgemore La.)
Northfield Cotts. Read —3G 62
Northfield End. Hen T —3C 16
Northfield Rd. Eton W —3B 46
Northfield Rd. Lwr S —1G 40
Northfield Rd. M'head —5C 20
Northfield Rd. Read —3G 62
Northfield Rd. That —7E 80
Northfields. Chvly —8L 31
Northfields. Lamb —2H 27
Northfields Ter. Lamb —2H 27
N. Fryerne. Yat —1B 118
North Grn. Brack —3A 92
North Grn. M'head —5C 20
North Grn. Slou —8G 23
Northington Clo. Brack —8C 92
N. Lodge Dri. Asc —4F 92
North Mall. Stai —8G 72
Northmead Rd. Slou —6B 22
Northolt Rd. Houn —7L 49
N. Park Rd. Iver —2E 48
North Rd. Asc —3E 92
North Rd. M'head —7B 20
North Rd. Moul —2F 14
North Rd. W Dray —2N 49
N. Standen Rd. Hung —8E 74
N. Star La. M'head —8N 19
North St. Cav —2H 63
North St. Egh —9A 72
North St. Read —4F 62
North St. Wink —8J 69
North Ter. Wind —6G 46
N. Town Clo. M'head —5C 20
N. Town Mead. M'head —5C 20
N. Town Moor. M'head —4C 20
N. Town Rd. M'head —5C 20
Northumberland Av. Read —8J 63
Northumberland Clo. Stai —3M 73
Northumberland Clo. Warf —2C 92
Northumbria Rd. M'head —1M 43
North View. Binf —5G 91
Northview. Hung —6K 75
North Wlk. Thea —8F 60
Northway. Newb —9M 79
Northway. That —6F 80
North Way. Uxb —1M 25
North Way. Wokgm —4J 89
Northwood Dri. Newb —7N 79
Northwood Rd. Houn —7L 49
Norton Clo. Newb —4G 100
Norton Pk. Asc —7M 93
Norton Rd. Read —5L 63
Norton Rd. Rise —7J 109
Norton Rd. Uxb —4L 25
Norton Rd. Wokgm —6A 90
Norton Rd. Wdly —7E 64
Norway Dri. Slou —6K 23
Norwich Dri. Wdly —4B 64
Norwood La. Iver —5E 24
Norwood Rd. Read —5K 63
Notley End. Egh —2L 95
Notton Way. Lwr Ear —3M 87
Nuffield Dri. Owl —9K 113
Nuffield Rd. Arbor X —3E 110
Nugee Ct. Crowt —5F 112
Nugent Ct. Mar —4D 4
Nuneaton. Brack —8B 92
Nunhide La. Sul —3G 60
Nun's Acre. Gor —7K 15
Nuns Wlk. Vir W —7M 95
Nuptown La. Nup —5C 68
Nursery Gdns. Pur T —8J 37
Nursery La. Asc —3H 93
Nursery La. Slou —9L 23
Nursery La. Uxb —5L 25
Nursery Rd. Tap —7L 21
Nursery Wlk. Mar —6A 4
Nursery Way. Wray —3M 71
Nursery Waye. Uxb —2L 25
Nutbean La. Swal —4M 109
Nuthatch Clo. Stai —5N 73
Nuthatch Dri. Ear —8A 64
Nuthurst. Brack —7B 92
Nut La. Wal L —7C 42
Nutley. Brack —1L 113
Nutley Clo. Yat —4B 118
Nutmeg Clo. Ear —2M 87
Nutter's La. Arbor X —2N 109
Nuttingtons. Leck —7D 30
Nut Wlk., The. Hung —1D 76

Oak Av. Owl —9H 113
Oak Av. W Dray —2N 49
Oakdale. Brack —8A 92
Oakdale Clo. Tile —4K 61
Oakdale Way. Wdly —4F 64
Oakdene. Asc —8B 94
Oakdene. Bfld C —9H 85
Oakdown Clo. Whit H —2F 36
Oak Dri. Bfld C —9G 85
Oak Dri. Wdly —6F 64
Oaken Copse Cres. Farn —9M 119
Oak End Way. Iver —3D 24
Oak End Way. Pad —7L 83
Oakengates. Brack —1L 113
Oaken Gro. M'head —6M 19
Oaken Gro. Newb —2H 101
Oak Farm Clo. B'water —4G 118
Oakfield Av. Slou —9D 22
Oakfield Rd. B'water —5J 119
Oakfield Rd. Bour —4L 5
Oakfield Rd. Pam H —9N 105
Oakfields. Camb —4M 119
Oak Grn. Read —3K 87
Oak Gro. Cres. Col T —3J 119
Oakham Clo. Tile —2L 61
Oak Hill. Frox —8C 74
Oakhurst. M'head —2E 20
Oaklands. Read —6L 63
(in two parts)
Oaklands. Yat —3B 118
Oaklands Bus. Pk. Wokgm —8L 89
Oaklands Clo. Asc —2J 93
Oaklands Dri. Asc —2J 93
Oaklands Dri. Wokgm —7L 89
Oaklands La. Crowt —3E 112
Oaklands Pk. Wokgm —7M 89
Oak La. Egh —7L 71
Oak La. Wind —7C 46
Oaklea Dri. Eve —8D 110
Oak Leaf Ct. Asc —3G 92
Oakley Ct. Water —5K 45
Oakley Cres. Slou —8G 22
Oakley Grn. Rd. Oak G —8H 45
Oakley M. Wind —8A 46
Oakley Rd. Camb —5M 119
Oakley Rd. Cav —9F 38
Oakley Rd. Newb —7A 80
Oak Lodge. Crowt —5G 112
Oakmede Pl. Binf —1G 90
Oakside Way. Shin —3L 87
Oaks Rd. S'lake —1F 40
Oaks Rd. Stai —3L 73
Oaks, The. Brack —4A 92
Oaks, The. Stai —8G 73
Oaks, The. Yat —4B 118
Oak Stubbs La. Dor R —1J 45
Oak Tree Av. Mar —4B 4
Oak Tree Clo. Tadl —9K 105
Oak Tree Clo. Vir W —8M 95
Oak Tree Copse. Tile —1M 61
Oak Tree Dri. Egh —9L 71
Oak Tree M. Brack —5A 92
Oak Tree Rd. Mar —3B 4
Oak Tree Rd. That —9H 81
Oak Tree Rd. Tile —2L 61
Oak Tree Wlk. Pur T —8L 37
Oaktree Way. Sand —9E 112
Oak View. Tile —4K 61
Oak Way. Wdly —8C 64
Oakwood Rd. Brack —4B 92
Oakwood Rd. Vir W —7L 95
Oakwood Rd. W'sham —6N 115
Oarborough. Brack —6B 92
Oareborough. Brack —6B 92
Oareborough La. Chvly & Herm —1B 56
Oast Ho. Clo. Wray —4N 71
Oatlands Dri. Slou —7F 22
Oatlands Rd. Shin —6M 87
Oban Ct. Chalv —1F 46
Oban Gdns. Wdly —8D 64
Obelisk Way. Camb —3N 119
Observatory Shopping Cen., The. Slou —1J 47
Ocean Ho. Brack —4M 91
Ockwells Rd. M'head —2M 43
Octavia. Brack —1L 113
Oddfellow Rd. Newb —9K 79
Odd La. Mort —9H 107
Odell Clo. Lwr Ear —3A 88
Odencroft Rd. Slou —4C 22
Odiham Av. Cav —8L 39
Odiham Rd. Rise & Hook —7J 109
Odney La. Cook —8M 5
Ogmore Clo. Tile —5M 61
Okingham Clo. Owl —8H 113
Oldacres. M'head —7E 20
Old Acres La. Charv —8G 41
Old Barn Clo. Cav —7G 39
Old Bath Rd. Calc —8K 61
Old Bath Rd. Charv —9F 40
(In two parts)
Old Bath Rd. Newb —7J 79
Old Bath Rd. Son —3B 64
(in two parts)
Old Beechwood Gdns. Slou —1G 47
Old Bracknell Clo. Brack —5M 91
Old Bracknell La. E. Brack —5M 91
Old Bracknell La. W. Brack —5L 91
Oldbury. Brack —5K 91
Old Court Clo. M'head —2M 43
Old Crown Cen. Slou —1H 47
Old Dean Rd. Camb —2N 119
Olde Farm Dri. B'water —3F 118
Old Elm Dri. Tile —5L 61
Oldershaw M. M'head —6M 19
Old Farm Cres. Tile —2K 61
Old Farm Dri. Brack —2N 91
Old Farm Rd. W Dray —1L 49
Old Ferry Dri. Wray —3M 71
Oldfield Clo. Ear —5A 64
Oldfield Rd. M'head —8E 20
Old Files Ct. Burn —4L 21
Old Forest Rd. Wokgm —3K 89
Old Forge Clo. M'head —2D 44
Old Forge, The. Baug —9G 104
Old Green La. Camb —2N 119
Old Hayward La. Hung —2J 75
Old House Ct. Wex —6M 23
Oldhouse La. W'sham & Light —7L 115
Old Kennel's Ct. Read —7A 62
Old Lands Hill. Brack —3A 92
Old La. Ham M —1K 99
Old La., The. Read —7F 62
Old Marsh La. Tap —1J 45
Old Mill La. Bray —1F 44
Old Mill La. Uxb —7J 25
Old Mills Pde. Sand —2E 118
Old Newtown Rd. Newb —1K 101
Old Orchard, The. Calc —8M 61
Old Pharmacy Ct. Crowt —6F 112
Old Pond Clo. Camb —8N 119
Old Sawmill La. Crowt —4G 112
Old Sawmills, The. Ink —4D 98
Old School Ct. Wray —4N 71
Old School La. Yat —3A 118
Old School Yd. Lamb —3H 27
Old Slade La. Iver —2F 48
Oldstead. Brack —7A 92
Old St. Beed —8N 31
(in four parts)
Old St. Catm —7G 10
Old St. Chvly —2B 56
Old St. Farnb & Catm —4F 10
Old St. Herm —4C 56
Old St. La. P'mre —3K 31
Oldway La. Slou —1N 45
(in three parts)
Old Well Ct. Son —9C 40
Old Welmore. Yat —4C 118
Old Whitley Wood La. Read —5J 87
Old Windsor Lock. Old Win —2L 71
Old Wokingham Rd. Wokgm —9F 90
Old Woosehill La. Wokgm —4L 89
Oleander Clo. Crowt —3D 112
Oliver Dri. Calc —7J 61
Oliver Rd. Asc —6K 93
Oliver's Paddock. Mar —2B 4
Olivia Ct. Wokgm —5N 89
Ollerton. Brack —1L 113
Omer's Rise. Bfld C —8G 85
Onslow Dri. Asc —2K 93
Onslow Gdns. Cav —1J 63
Onslow Rd. Asc —9D 94
Opal Way. Wokgm —4K 89
Opendale Rd. Burn —6L 21
Opladen Way. Brack —7N 91
Oracle Cen. Brack —4N 91
Orbit Clo. Finch —4L 111
Orchard Av. Slou —6N 21
Orchard Av. Wind —7C 46
Orchard Chase. Hurst —5L 65
Orchard Clo. B'water —8K 119
Orchard Clo. Egh —8C 72
Orchard Clo. Hen T —6D 16
Orchard Clo. Herm —4F 56
Orchard Clo. M'head —2D 44
Orchard Clo. Midg —9E 82
Orchard Clo. Newb —6N 79
Orchard Clo. S'lake —3E 40
Orchard Clo. Spen W —9H 87
Orchard Clo. Tile —9J 37
Orchard Clo. Wokgm —5B 90
Orchard Coombe. Whit H —2E 36
Orchard Ct. Brack —4N 91
Orchard Ct. Read —4J 87
Orchard Ct. That —8H 81
Orchard Ct. W Dray —6K 49
Orchard Dri. Uxb —5L 25
Orchard Dri. Wbrn G —3N 5
Orchardene. Newb —7M 79
Orchard Est. Twy —8K 41
Orchard Field. Gall C —1C 38
Orchard Ga. Sand —1F 118
Orchard Gro. Cav —9L 39
Orchard Gro. M'head —7N 19
Orchard Hill. W'sham —7N 115
Orchard Ho. Bour —3L 5
Orchard Pk. Clo. Hung —6K 75
Orchard Pl. Cow —1L 25
Orchard Pl. Wokgm —5A 90
Orchard Rd. Hurst —5L 65
Orchard Rd. Mort —5J 107
Orchard Rd. Old Win —3K 71
Orchard St. Read —6H 63
Orchard, The. F Hth —1M 5
Orchard, The. Mar —4C 4
Orchard, The. Tadl —9M 105
Orchard, The. Thea —8F 60
Orchard, The. Vir W —7N 95
Orchard View. Uxb —5L 25
Orchardville. Burn —5L 21
Orchard Way. Ashf —6N 73
Orchard Way. Camb —7M 119
Orchard Way. Uxb —3L 25
Orchid Ct. Egh —8C 72
Oregon Av. Tile —1L 61
Oregon Wlk. Wokgm —3J 111
Oriel Hill. Camb —5N 119
Oriental Rd. Asc —6N 93
Orion. Brack —1L 113
Orkney Clo. Calc —8M 61
Ormathwaites Corner. Warf —2B 92
Ormonde Rd. Wokgm —6M 89
Ormsby St. Read —5E 62
Orrin Clo. Tile —5B 62
Orts Rd. Newb —9M 79
Orts Rd. Read —5J 63
(in two parts)
Orville Clo. Wdly —5F 64
Orwell Clo. Cav —9F 38
Orwell Clo. Wind —9F 46
Osborne Av. Stai —5N 73
Osborne Ct. Wind —8E 46
Osborne La. Warf —9N 67
Osborne M. Wind —8E 46
Osborne Rd. Egh —9A 72
Osborne Rd. Read —4B 62
Osborne Rd. Uxb —1K 25
Osborne Rd. Wind —8E 46
Osborne Rd. Wokgm —5A 90
Osborne St. Slou —1H 47
Osman's Clo. Brack —2E 92
Osnaburgh Hill. Camb —4M 119
Osney Rd. M'head —4B 20
Osprey Clo. W Dray —1M 49
Osprey Ct. Read —5J 63
Osterley Clo. Wokgm —6D 90
Osterley Dri. Cav —7L 39
Ostler Ga. M'head —5N 19
Oswald Clo. Warf —1A 92
Othello Gro. Warf —3B 92
Otter Clo. Crowt —3E 112
Otterfield Rd. W Dray —8M 25
Ouseley Rd. Old Win —4L 71
Ouseley Rd. Wray —4L 71
Overbridge Sq. Newb —8B 80
Overbury Av. Wokgm —2L 89
Overdown Rd. Tile —2K 61
Overlanders End. Tile —1M 61
Overlord Clo. Camb —1N 119
Owen Rd. Shaw —5M 79
Owen Rd. W'sham —5N 115
Owl Clo. Wokgm —6K 89
Owlsmoor Rd. Owl —1H 119
Owston. Lwr Ear —1B 88
Ox Drove. Burc —9L 101
Oxenhope. Brack —6L 91
Oxford Av. Burn —3L 21
Oxford Av. Slou —6B 22
Oxford Rd. Mar —5A 4
Oxford Rd. Newb —6K 79
Oxford Rd. Owl —8J 113
Oxford Rd. Tile & Read —8K 37
Oxford Rd. Uxb —1K 25
Oxford Rd. Wokgm —5N 89
Oxford Rd. E. Wind —7F 46
Oxford Rd. N. Chvly —4N 55
Oxford Sq. Newb —7K 79
Oxford St. Cav —2G 63
Oxford St. Hung —4L 75
Oxford St. Lamb —3H 27
Oxford St. Newb —7K 79

Pacific Ho. Read —3G 87
Pack and Prime La. Hen T —5A 16
Packet Boat La. Uxb —7J 25
Packway, The. M'head —1H 21
Padcroft Rd. W Dray —9L 25
Paddick Clo. Son —1D 64
Paddock Clo. M'head —3L 43
Paddock Heights. Twy —9K 41
Paddock Rd. Cav —3K 63
Paddock Rd. Newb —1K 101
Paddock, The. Brack —5N 91
Paddock, The. Crowt —4E 112
Paddock, The. Dat —7K 47
Paddock, The. M'head —4N 19
Paddock, The. Newb —9N 79
Paddock, The. Wink —5L 69
Padley Ct. Read —5J 63
(off Dell, The)
Padstow Clo. Slou —2N 47
Padstow Gdns. Read —2H 87
Page's Croft. Wokgm —6D 90
Pages La. Uxb —1K 25
Pages Orchard. Son C —1E 38
Paget Clo. Mar —3D 4
Paget Dri. M'head —1L 43
Paget Rd. Slou —3A 48
Pagoda, The. M'head —5E 20
Paice Grn. Wokgm —4B 90
Paices Hill. Aldm —7H 105
Paley St. M'head —7M 43
Palmera Av. Calc —8K 61
Palmer Clo. Wokgm —2E 112
Palmer Ct. Wokgm —5A 90
Palmer Pk. Av. Read —6M 63
Palmer School Rd. Wokgm —5A 90
Palmers Clo. M'head —2L 43
Palmer's Hill. Ash'd —8E 34
Palmer's La. Bfld C —9H 85
Palmer's La. Graz —8A 86
Palmer's Moor La. Iver —5H 25
Palmerston Av. Slou —2K 47
Palmerstone Rd. Ear —5N 63
Pamber Heath Rd. Pam H —9M 105
Pamela Row. Holyp —5D 44
Pangbourne Hill. Pang —8C 36
Pangbourne Rd. Thea & Tid —1D 84
Pangbourne Rd. Up Bas —9L 35
Pangbourne St. Read —4B 62
Pankhurst Dri. Brack —7A 92
Pantile Row. Slou —3B 48
Pantiles Wlk. Uxb —1K 25
Paprika Clo. Ear —2M 87
Parade, The. Bour —4L 5
Parade, The. Frim —9N 119
Parade, The. Read —8D 62
Parade, The. Tadl —9K 105
Parade, The. Vir W —8M 95
Parade, The. Wind —7N 45
Parade, The. Wdly —8D 64
Parade, The. Yat —4C 118
Paradise La. Chap R —3E 82
Paradise M. Hen T —4C 16
Paradise Rd. Hen T —5C 16
Paradise Way. Chap R —4E 82
Park Av. Camb —5N 119
Park Av. Stai —9M 73
Park Av. That —7G 80
Park Av. Wokgm —6N 89
(in two parts)
Park Av. Wray —2M 71
Park Clo. Wind —8F 46
Park Corner. Wind —9A 46
Parkcorner La. Wokgm —5E 88
Park Cres. Asc —8B 94
Park Cres. Read —6D 62
Park Dri. Asc —8B 94
Park End. Newb —7L 79
Parkers La. Wink R —7E 68
Park Farm Ind. Est. Camb —8N 119
Parkgate. Burn —5M 21
Park Gro. Read —6B 62
Parkhill Clo. B'water —5H 119
Parkhill Dri. Tile —2L 61
Parkhill Rd. B'water —5H 119
Parkhouse La. Read —6D 62
Parkland Av. Slou —3M 47
Parkland Dri. Brack —3B 92
Parkland Gro. Ashf —7N 73
Park La. Binf —2J 91
Park La. Camb —4N 119
Park La. Can E —1N 37
Park La. Charv —9F 40
Park La. Finch —4F 110
Park La. Ham M —9N 77
Park La. Hdly —8L 103
Park La. Newb —7L 79
Park La. Slou —2K 47
Park La. Strat S —8L 107
Park La. That —6G 80
Park La. Tile —6K 61
Park La. Wink —5L 69
Park Ride. Wind —4N 69
Park Rd. Brack —4A 92
Park Rd. Camb —6M 119
Park Rd. Egh —8B 72
Park Rd. Farn R —3E 22
Park Rd. Hen T —5D 16
Park Rd. Sand —2G 118
Park Rd. Stai —3J 73
Park Rd. Uxb —1M 25
Park Rd. Wokgm —5N 89
Park Rd. E. Uxb —3L 25
Parkside. Hen T —4B 16
Parkside. M'head —5A 20
Parkside Rd. Asc —7C 94
Parkside Rd. Read —6D 62
Parkside Rd. That —6G 80
Park Sq. Wink —5L 69
Parkstone Dri. Camb —5N 119
Park St. Bag —7H 115
Park St. Camb —3N 119
Park St. Coln —7E 48
Park St. Hung —6K 75
Park St. M'head —7C 20
Park St. Newb —7L 79
Park St. Slou —2H 47
Park St. Wind —7F 46
Park Ter. Newb —7L 79
Park, The. Lamb —2G 27
Park View. Bag —7G 115
Park View. B Hill —5D 108
Parkview. F Hth —1M 5
Parkview Chase. Slou —7A 22
Park View Dri. N. Charv —8F 40
Park View Dri. S. Charv —8F 40
Park View Rd. Uxb —7N 25
Park Wlk. Pur T —8L 37
(in two parts)
Park Wall La. Up Bas —6K 35
Parkway. Camb —6N 119
Parkway. Crowt —5E 112
Park Way. Hung —7K 75
Parkway. Mar —5E 4
Park Way. Newb —7L 79
Parkway Dri. Son —1D 64
Parkway, The. Iver —2D 24
Parlaunt Rd. Slou —3B 48
Parliament La. Burn —1J 21
Parnham Av. Light —9N 115
Parry Grn. Langl —3A 48
Parsley Clo. Ear —2M 87
Parsonage Gdns. Mar —6C 4
Parsonage La. Farn C —1E 22
Parsonage La. Hung —5J 75
Parsonage La. Lamb —3H 27
Parsonage La. Wind —7C 46
Parsonage Pl. Lamb —2G 27
Parsonage Rd. Egh —9M 71
Parsons Clo. Arbor —2F 110
Parsons Clo. Newb —9J 79
Parsons Field. Sand —1F 118
Parson's Ride. Brack —9C 92
Parthia Clo. Read —6H 63
Part La. Rise —7J 109
Partridge Av. Yat —3A 118
Partridge Dri. Tile —6J 61
Partridge Mead. M'head —4C 20
Pasture Clo. Lwr Ear —3A 88
Patch Clo. Uxb —2N 25
Patches Field. Mar —2C 4
Paterson Rd. Ashf —9L 73
Pathway, The. Binf —9G 67
Patricia Clo. Slou —8A 22
Patrick Gdns. Warf —2B 92
Patrick Rd. Cav —2H 63
Patrington Clo. Uxb —4K 25
Patriot Pl. Read —5J 63
Patten Ash Dri. Wokgm —4C 90
Patten Av. Yat —4A 118
Pattinson Rd. Read —5K 87
Pavenham Clo. Lwr Ear —3A 88
Pavilions, The. Uxb —1K 25
Pavy Clo. That —9J 81
Paxton Av. Slou —2E 46
Payley Dri. Wokgm —3C 90
Paynesdown Rd. That —8E 80
Peace La. Cook —9K 5
Peace Rd. Slou & Iver —4A 24
Peachey Clo. Uxb —7L 25
Peachey La. Uxb —6L 25
Peach St. Wokgm —5A 90
Peach Tree Av. W Dray —7N 25
Peachy Dri. That —9J 81
Peacock Cotts. Brack —6G 91
Peacock Ga. Slou —8F 22
Peacock La. Wokgm & Brack —7F 90
Peacock Rd. Mar —4E 4
Peacock Wlk. Wokgm —6K 89
Pearce Clo. M'head —5C 20
Pearce Rd. M'head —5C 20
Pearces Orchard. Hen T —3C 16
Pear Gdns. Chalv —9D 22
Pearman's Glade. Read —3L 87
Pearman's La. Lwr Ear —4M 87
(in two parts)
Pearson Rd. Son —1C 64
Pearson Way. Wdly —7D 64
Pear Tree Av. W Dray —7N 25
Pear Tree La. Newb —6N 79
Peascod Pl. Wind —7F 46
Peascod St. Wind —7E 46
Pease Hill. Bckby —1B 82
Peasemore Hill. P'mre —4F 30
Pebble Hill. Kint —3F 98
Pebble La. Wint & Snel —7H 55
Peddlars Gro. Yat —3C 118

Peel Cen., The. Brack —4L 91
Peel Clo. Cav —2K 63
Peel Clo. Wind —9D 46
Peel Clo. Wdly —4G 64
Peel Ct. Slou —6E 22
Peel Way. Uxb —6M 25
Pegasus Clo. That —7D 80
Pegasus Ct. Lamb —3H 27
Pegasus Ct. Tile —5K 61
Pegasus Rd. Farn —9K 119
Peggotty Pl. Owl —8J 113
Peg's Grn. Clo. Read —6B 62
Pelham Ct. Read —6D 62
Pelican La. Newb —7K 79
Pelican Rd. Pam H —8N 105
Pelling Hill. Old Win —4K 71
Pell St. Read —6H 63
Pemberton Gdns. Calc —8L 61
Pemberton Rd. Slou —5A 22
Pembroke. Brack —9K 91
Pembroke B'way. Camb —4N 119
Pembroke Clo. Asc —7N 93
Pembroke Clo. Bfld C —8K 85
Pembroke Ho. Cav —3J 63
Pembroke M. Asc —7N 93
Pembroke Pde. Yat —3C 118
Pembroke Pl. Cav —1J 63
Pembroke Rd. Newb —8K 79
Pendals Clo. Hamp N —8J 33
Pendennis Av. Cav —7L 39
Pendine Pl. Brack —7M 91
Pendlebury. Brack —9L 91
Pendragon Ct. Read —7D 62
Pendred Rd. Read —5K 87
Pendry's La. Binf —3L 67
Penling Clo. Cook —9J 5
Penn Clo. Cav —7G 38
Penn Clo. Uxb —5L 25
Pennfields. Rusc —7K 41
Pennine Clo. Tile —6J 61
Pennine Rd. Slou —6C 22
Pennine Way. Charv —9G 40
Pennine Way. Farn —9J 119
Penn Meadow. Stoke P —2H 23
Penn Rd. Dat —7M 47
Penn Rd. Slou —5F 22
Penn Rd. Speen —6H 79
Pennylets Grn. Stoke P —1H 23
Penny Piece. Gor —7L 15
Pennyroyal Ct. Read —6G 62
Penny's La. C Grn —8J 17
Penrith Clo. Uxb —1L 25
Penroath Av. Read —6C 62
Penrose Av. Wdly —6D 64
Penrose Clo. Newb —6K 79
Penrose Ct. Egh —1L 95
Pensford Clo. Crowt —3F 112
Penshurst Rd. M'head —9A 20
Pentangle, The. Newb —7L 79
Pentland Clo. Read —7N 61
Pentland Rd. Slou —6C 22
Pentridge Ho. Read —3J 87
Penwood Ct. M'head —7M 19
Penwood Gdns. Brack —8H 91
Penwood Heights. Burc —9E 100
Penwood La. Mar —6A 4
Penyston Rd. M'head —7N 19
Penzance Spur. Slou —5D 22
Peplow Clo. W Dray —9L 25
Peppard La. Hen T —7C 16
Peppard Rd. Cav —1H 63
Peppard Rd. Son C —1G 38
Pepper La. Ear —8L 63
Pepys Clo. Slou —5C 48
Perch Clo. Mar —7A 4
Percy Av. Ashf —9N 73
Percy Pl. Dat —7K 47
Peregrine Clo. Brack —7M 91
Peregrine Clo. Wokgm —6L 89
Periam Clo. Hen T —6B 16
Perimeter Rd. Wind —7F 46
Perimeter Rd. Wdly —4F 64
Perkins Ct. Ashf —9N 73
Perkins Way. Wokgm —6M 89
Perrin Clo. Ashf —9N 73
Perring Av. Farn —9J 119
Perrycroft. Wind —9A 46
Perryfields. Burn —5M 21
Perryhill Dri. Sand —9D 112
Perryman Way. Slou —4B 22
Perry Oaks. Brack —4B 92
Perry Oaks Dri. W Dray & Houn —8J 49
Perry Way. Brack —4B 92
Perseverance Hill. Hen T —9A 16
Perth Av. Slou —7D 22
Perth Clo. Wdly —3F 64
Perth Trading Est. Slou —6D 22
Peterhead M. Langl —4B 48
Peterhouse Clo. Owl —8K 113
Petersfield Av. Slou —9J 23
Petersfield Av. Stai —9K 73
Petersfield Rd. Stai —9K 73
Peters La. Holyp —5E 44
Petrel Clo. Wokgm —6K 89
Petworth Av. Read —9N 61
Petworth Ct. Read —6E 62
Pevensey Av. Cav —8L 39
Pevensey Rd. Slou —6C 22
Pewsey Vale. Brack —7C 92
Pheasant Clo. Winn —1H 89
Pheasant La. Bis G —7C 102
Pheasants Croft. M'head —1L 43
Pheasants Rise. Mar —1A 4
Philip Dri. F Hth —1N 5
Phillimore Rd. Cav —5J 39
Phillips Clo. Wdly —3G 65
Philpots Clo. W Dray —8L 25
Phipps Clo. M'head —3L 43
Phipps Rd. Slou —6N 21
(in three parts)
Phoebe Ct. Read —6G 63
Phoenix Bus. Pk. Brack —4G 91
Phoenix Clo. Wokgm —5K 89
Phoenix Wlk. Newb —4G 101
(off Glendale Av.)
Phyllis Ct. Dri. Hen T —3D 16
Pickering. Brack —6L 91
Picket Post Clo. Brack —5C 92
Picketts La. Pang —9N 35
Pickins Piece. Hort —8B 48
Pickwell Clo. Lwr Ear —2B 88
Picton Way. Cav —9H 39
Pield Heath Av. Uxb —5N 25
Pield Heath Rd. Uxb —5M 25
Pierce Field. Calc —8K 61
Pierce's Hill. Tile —3K 61
Pierson Rd. Wind —7N 45
Pigeonhouse La. Wink —7G 69
Pigeon's Farm Rd. Green —3A 102
Piggott's Rd. Cav —3J 63
Pightle, The. Graz —8N 85
Pigott Rd. Wokgm —3B 90
Pike Clo. Uxb —2N 25
Pikeshaw Way. Tile —2K 61
Pike St. Newb —7M 79
Pills La. Ham —7J 97
Pimento Dri. Ear —2M 87
Pimpernell Pl. That —7J 81
Pincents Kiln Trading Est. Tile —8H 61
Pincents La. Tile —8G 61
Pinchcut. Bfld C —8H 85
Pinchington La. Green —3L 101
Pindar Pl. Newb —6B 80
Pine Av. Camb —5N 119
Pine Clo. M'head —7M 19
Pine Clo. Sand —2J 119
Pinecote Dri. Asc —9B 94
Pine Ct. Brack —6B 92
Pinecroft. Mar —4B 4
Pine Croft Rd. Wokgm —9M 89
Pine Dri. B'water —6J 119
Pine Dri. Mort C —4G 107
Pine Dri. Wokgm —3M 111
Pinefields Clo. Crowt —5F 112
Pine Gro. Twy —8J 41
Pine Gro. W'sham —6N 115
Pinehill Rise. Sand —1G 118
Pinehill Rd. Crowt —6F 112
Pinehurst. S'hill —7N 93
Pine Mt. Rd. Camb —5N 119
Pine Ridge. Newb —6N 79
Pine Ridge Rd. Bfld C —8H 85
Pine Tree Ct. Emm G —8G 39
Pine Trees Bus. Pk. Stai —9F 72
Pine Way. Egh —1K 95
Pinewood Av. Crowt —4G 112
Pinewood Av. Uxb —7N 25
Pinewood Caravan Pk. Wokgm —2G 112
Pinewood Clo. Baug —9F 104
Pinewood Clo. Iver —1D 24
Pinewood Clo. Sand —1D 118
Pinewood Dri. Stai —9H 73
Pinewood Gdns. Bag —7F 114
Pinewood Grn. Iver —1D 24
Pinewood M. Stai —3L 73
Pinewood Pk. Farn —9G 119
Pinewood Rd. Iver —1C 24
Pinewood Rd. Vir W —6J 95
Pinfold La. Ash'd —8D 34
Pingewood Rd. Ping —3N 85
Pinglestone Clo. W Dray —6M 49
Pink La. Burn —3L 21
Pinkneys Dri. M'head —7J 19
Pinkneys Rd. M'head —5L 19
Pink's La. Baug —8G 105
Pinn Clo. Uxb —7L 25
Pipers Clo. Burn —4M 21
Pipers Ct. That —9K 81
Piper's End. Vir W —5M 95
Pipers La. That —1J 103
Pipers Way. That —9J 81
Pipers Way Ind. Est. That —9J 81
Pipit Clo. That —8E 80
Pippins Clo. W Dray —2L 49
Pipson La. Yat —4B 118
Pipsons Clo. Yat —3B 118
Pitch Pl. Binf —9H 67
Pitcroft Av. Read —6N 63
Pitfield La. Mort —6K 107
Pitford Rd. Wdly —4F 64
Pitts Clo. Binf —1H 91
Pitts La. Ear —5A 64
Pitts Rd. Slou —9E 22
Plackett Way. Slou —9N 21
Plain Ride. Wind —5M 69
Plantation Clo. Cur —7C 56
Plantation Rd. Tadl —8H 105
Plantation Row. Camb —4M 119
Plateau, The. Warf P —2D 92
Players Grn. Wdly —7D 64
Playhatch Rd. Play —8N 39
Play Platt. Thea —8E 60
Play Platt Houses. Thea —8E 60
Pleasant Hill. Tadl —9K 105
Ploughlands. Brack —3K 91
Plough La. S'lake —3C 40
Plough La. Stoke P —2K 23
Plough La. Wokgm —4D 90
Plough Lees La. Slou —8G 23
Plough Rd. Yat —2C 118
Plover Clo. Stai —7G 72
Plover Clo. Wokgm —6L 89
Plowden Way. S'lake X —4D 40
Plummery, The. Read —5J 63
(off Blakes Cotts.)
Plumpton Rd. Green —1N 101
Plumtrees. Ear —1A 88
Plymouth Av. Wdly —7B 64
Plymouth Rd. Slou —6A 22
Plympton Clo. Ear —9D 64
Pococks La. Eton —4G 46
Poffley Pl. That —8K 81
Pointers Clo. Chvly —2M 55
Points, The. M'head —2M 43
Polden Clo. Farn —9J 119
Polehampton Clo. Twy —9J 41
Polehampton Ct. Twy —9J 41
Pollard Clo. Old Win —2K 71
Pollard Cotts. Bal H —7N 99
Pollardrow Av. Brack —3K 91
(in two parts)
Pollards Way. Calc —8K 61
Polsted Rd. Tile —3L 61
Polyanthus Way. Crowt —2F 112
Polygon Bus. Cen. Coln —8G 48
Pond Clo. Newb —3H 101
Pond Croft. Yat —3C 118
Pond Head La. Ear —8C 64
Pond La. Herm —5F 56
Pond La. Map —6N 37
Pond Moor Rd. Brack —7M 91
Pond Rd. Egh —9D 72
Poole Clo. Tile —5N 61
Pooley Av. Egh —9C 72
Pooley Grn. Clo. Egh —9D 72
Pooley Grn. Rd. Egh —9C 72
Pool La. Slou —8G 22
Pool La. Wal L —8E 42
Poolmans Rd. Wind —9N 45
Popes Clo. Coln —6C 48
Popes La. Cook —7G 5
Popeswood Rd. Binf —2H 91
Popham Clo. Brack —7C 92
Poplar Av. Tile —7N 61
Poplar Av. W Dray —8N 25
Poplar Av. W'sham —4K 115
Poplar Clo. Baug —9F 104
Poplar Clo. Coln —7F 48
Poplar Gdns. Read —2L 87
Poplar Ho. Langl —4A 48
Poplar La. Hurst —3L 65
Poplar La. Winn —9J 65
Poplar Pl. Newb —6L 79
Poplars Gro. M'head —4E 20
Poplars, The. Asc —7K 93
Poppy Dri. That —7J 81
Poppy Pl. Wokgm —5N 89
Poppy Way. Calc —7K 61
Porchester. Asc —6K 93
Porchester Rd. Newb —1L 101
Porchfield Clo. Ear —2N 87
Porlock Clo. That —9G 80
Porlock Pl. Calc —8J 61
Portal Clo. Uxb —1M 25
(in two parts)
Porter Clo. Lwr Ear —3B 88
Porter End. Green —2M 101
Porters Way. W Dray —2N 49
Portesbery Rd. Camb —3N 119
Portia Gro. Warf —3B 92
Portland Bus. Cen. Dat —7K 47
(off Manor Ho. La.)
Portland Clo. Slou —5N 21
Portland Gdns. Tile —5K 61
Portland Rd. Ashf —7M 73
Portlands. Mar —6B 4
Portlock Rd. M'head —7N 19
Portman Clo. Brack —3L 91
Portman Gdns. Uxb —1N 25
Portman Rd. Read —3B 62
Portmeirion Gdns. Tile —3N 61
Portnall Dri. Vir W —8G 94
Portnall Rise. Vir W —7H 95
Portnall Rd. Vir W —7H 95
Portrush Clo. Wdly —6C 64
Portsmouth Ct. Slou —8G 23
Portsmouth Rd. Frim & Camb —8N 119
Portswood. Tadl —9M 105
Portway. Baug —9F 104
Portway. Rise —8J 109
Portway Clo. Read —6E 62
Post Horn Pl. Calc —8N 61
Posting Ho. M. Newb —7J 79
Post Meadow. Iver —4E 24
Post Office La. G Grn —7M 23
Post Office Rd. Ink —6D 98
Potley Hill Rd. Yat —3D 118
Potters Cross. Iver —4F 24
Pottery La. Ink —5C 98
Pottery Rd. Tile —3N 61
Poulcott. Wray —3N 71
Pound Cres. Mar —6A 4
Poundfield La. Cook —8K 5
Poundfield Way. Twy —1L 65
Pound La. Hurst —7M 65
Pound La. Mar —7A 4
Pound La. Newb —7H 79
Pound La. Son —2D 64
Pound La. That —8D 80
Pound La. W'sham —6M 115
Pound Piece. Hung —5J 75
Pound St. Newb —9K 79
Pound, The. Burn —5N 21
Pound, The. Cook —8K 5
Powis Clo. M'head —1M 43
Powney Rd. M'head —7N 19
Poyle Clo. Coln —8F 48
Poyle Gdns. Brack —3A 92
Poyle Ind. Est. Coln —9G 48
Poyle La. Burn —2L 21
Poyle Rd. Coln —9F 48
Poyle Technical Cen. Coln —8F 48
Poyle Trading Est. Coln —9F 48
Poynings, The. Iver —3G 48
Precincts, The. Burn —5L 21
Precinct, The. Cav —8J 39
Precinct, The. Egh —9B 72
Prentice Clo. Farn —9M 119
Prescott. Brack —9K 91
Prescott Rd. Coln —8F 48
Press Rd. Uxb —1L 25
Preston Rd. Read —7H 63
Preston Rd. Slou —8L 23
Prestwood. Slou —7K 23
Prides Crossing. Asc —2K 93
Priest Av. Wokgm —6D 90
Priest Hill. Cav —1G 62
Priest Hill. Egh & Old Win —7L 71
Priestwood Av. Brack —3K 91
Priestwood Ct. Brack —3L 91
Priestwood Ct. Rd. Brack —3L 91
Priestwood Sq. Brack —3L 91
Priestwood Ter. Brack —3L 91
Primrose Clo. Pur T —8K 37
Primrose La. M'head —7D 44
Primrose La. Winn —9H 65
Primrose Wlk. Brack —7N 91
Primrose Wlk. Yat —3A 118
Primrose Way. Sand —9F 112
Prince Albert Dri. Asc —6G 93
Prince Albert's Wlk. Wind —7J 47
Prince Andrew Clo. M'head —6E 20
Prince Andrew Rd. M'head —5E 20
Prince Andrew Way. Asc —4G 93
Prince Charles Cres. Farn —9M 119
Prince Consort Cotts. Wind —8F 46
Prince Consort Dri. Asc —6G 92
Prince Consort's Dri. Wind —3B 70
Prince Dri. Sand —9E 112
Prince of Wales Av. Read —5D 62
Prince of Wales Wlk. Camb —3N 119
Princes Clo. Eton W —4B 46
Prince's La. P'mre —7H 31
Princes Rd. Ashf —9N 73
Princes Rd. Bour —4N 5
Princes Rd. Egh —9A 72
Princess Av. Wind —9D 46
Princess Marina Dri. Arbor X (in two parts) —1F 110
Princess Sq. Brack —4M 91
Princess St. M'head —8C 20
Prince's St. Read —5J 63
Princes St. Slou —1K 47
Princess Way. Camb —3N 119
Princes Way. Bag —9H 115
Prince William Dri. Tile —3K 61
Priors Clo. Farn —9L 119
Priors Clo. M'head —3E 44
Priors Ct. Slou —2J 47
Priors Ct. Rd. Herm —4N 55
Prior's La. B'water —4E 118
Priors Rd. Tadl —8J 105
Priors Rd. Wind —9N 45
Priors Way. M'head —3E 44
Priors Wood. Crowt —6B 112
Priory Av. Cav —2G 62
Priory Av. Hung —7K 75
Priory Clo. Asc —9C 94
Priory Clo. Hung —7K 75
Priory Ct. Camb —4K 119
Priory Ct. Winn —9H 65
Priory Grn. Stai —9J 73
Priory La. Warf —2N 91
(in two parts)
Priory M. Stai —9J 73
Priory Pl. Hung —6K 75
(off Tarrant's Hill)
Priory Rd. Chav D —3E 92
Priory Rd. Hung —7K 75
Priory Rd. Newb —1L 101
Priory Rd. Slou —6M 21
Priory Rd. S'dale —9C 94
Priory, The. Winn —9H 65
Priory Wlk. Brack —6C 92
Priory Way. Dat —6K 47
Priory Way. W Dray —5M 49
Proctors Rd. Wokgm —5D 90
Progress Bus. Cen. Burn —7N 21
Promenade Rd. Cav —2G 62
Prospect Ct. Read —6B 62
Prospect La. Egh —9J 71
Prospect Pl. Hur —3D 18
Prospect Pl. Newb —1L 101
Prospect Pl. Stai —9G 73
Prospect Rd. Hung —6K 75
Prospect Rd. Mar —5A 4
Prospect St. Cav —2G 63
Prospect St. Read —5F 62
Providence Pl. M'head —7C 20
Providence Rd. W Dray —9M 25
Prune Hill. Egh —2M 95
Pudding Hill. War R —8B 18
Pudding La. Arbor —8C 88
Pudding La. Bright —4C 30
Puffers Way. Newb —9J 79
Pumpkin Hill. Farn C —1A 22
Pump La. Asc —3A 94
Pump La. Graz —8C 86
Pump La. N. Mar —1D 4
Pump La. S. Mar —2E 4
Pundles La. White —7G 43
Purbeck Ho. Read —3J 87
Purbrook Ct. Brack —8B 92
Purcell Rd. Crowt —3F 112
Purfield Dri. Warg —3K 41
Purley La. Pur T —8K 37
Purley Village. Pur T —8K 37
Purley Way. Pang —8F 36
Purslane. Wokgm —6B 90
Purssell Clo. M'head —2L 43
Purton Ct. Farn C —1E 22
Purton La. Farn R —1E 22
Putman Pl. Hen T —5D 16
Pyegrove Chase. Brack —9B 92
Pyke's Hill. Ash'd C —9F 34

Quadrant Ct. Brack —5B 92
Qualitas. Brack —1K 113
Quantock Av. Cav —8K 39
Quantock Clo. Charv —9G 40
Quantock Clo. Slou —4B 48
Quantocks, The. That —9G 80
Quarrington Clo. That —9H 81
Quarrydale Dri. Mar —5D 4
Quarry La. Yat —4C 118
Quarry Wood. Cook —7E 4
Quarry Wood Rd. Mar & Cook D —7C 4
Quartz Clo. Wokgm —4J 89
Quaves Rd. Slou —2K 47
Quebec Gdns. B'water —5H 119
Quebec Rd. Hen T —6D 16
Queen Adelaide's Ride. Wind —3N 69
Queen Anne's Ga. Cav —2J 63
Queen Anne's Ride. Asc & Wind —1C 94
Queen Anne's Rd. Wind —1E 70
Queen Ann's Ct. Wind —7E 46
Queen Clo. Hen T —5D 16
Queen Elizabeth Rd. Camb —9A 114
Queen Elizabeth's Wlk. Wind —8G 47
Queen Mary Av. Camb —4L 119
Queens Acre. Wind —1F 70
Queensborough Dri. Cav —8E 38
Queensbury Pl. B'water —6G 119
Queen's Clo. Asc —2H 93
Queen's Clo. Old Win —2J 71
Queen's Cotts. Read —5H 63
Queens Ct. Newb —1L 101
Queens Ct. Slou —8H 23
Queen's Dri. Slou —3A 24
Queen's Dri., The. Ear —8L 63
Queens Hill Rise. Asc —5M 93
Queens La. Ashf —8N 73
Queens Lawns. Read —6K 63
Queensmead. Dat —7K 47
Queensmere. Slou —1H 47
Queensmere Rd. Slou —1J 47
Queens Pine. Brack —8B 92
Queens Pl. Asc —5K 93
Queen's Rd. Asc —7N 93
Queens Rd. Camb —5M 119
Queen's Rd. Cav —3H 63
Queen's Rd. Dat —6K 47
Queen's Rd. Egh —9A 72
Queens Rd. Eton W —4B 46
Queen's Rd. Mar —5B 4
Queen's Rd. Newb —9M 79
Queen's Rd. Read —5H 63
(in two parts)
Queen's Rd. Slou —8H 23
Queen's Rd. Uxb —4K 25
Queens Rd. W Dray —1N 49
Queen's Rd. Wind —8E 46
Queen St. Cav —1G 62
Queen St. Hen T —5D 16
Queen St. M'head —8C 20
(in three parts)
Queen's Wlk. Ashf —8L 73
Queens Wlk. Read —5G 62
Queensway. Brack —3K 91
Queensway. Cav —7K 39
Queens Way. Kint —9G 77
Queensway. M'head —5B 20
Queen Victoria St. Read —4H 63
Queen Victoria's Wlk. Col T —3K 119
Queen Victoria Wlk. Wind —7G 47
Quelmans Head Ride. Wind —6N 69
Quelm La. Brack —1M 91
Quentin Rd. Wdly —6C 64
Quentin Way. Vir W —6K 95
Quinbrookes. Wex —7L 23
Quince Clo. S'hill —6M 93
Quincy Rd. Egh —9B 72
Quintilis. Brack —1K 113
(in two parts)
Quoitings Dri. Mar —5A 4
Quoiting Sq. Mar —5B 4

Rabbs Mill Ho. Uxb —3K 25
Racecourse Rd. Newb —1M 101
Raceview Bus. Cen. Newb —9M 79
Rachael's Lake View. Warf —2B 92
Rackstraw Rd. Camb —9G 113
Radbourne Rd. Calc —8L 61
Radcliffe Way. Brack —3J 91
Radcot Av. Langl —2C 48
Radcot Clo. M'head —3B 20
Radcot Clo. Wdly —3D 64
Radical Ride. Wokgm —3L 111
Radley Bottom. Newt —3B 76
Radnor Clo. Hen T —4D 16
Radnor Gro. Uxb —3N 25
Radnor Rd. Brack —5C 92
Radnor Rd. Ear —9B 64
Radnor Way. Slou —3N 47
Radstock La. Ear —9N 63
Radstock Rd. Read —5L 63
Raeburn Way. Col T —3H 119
Ragdale. Bfld C —8H 85
Raggett's La. Far H —4N 109
Raggleswood Clo. Ear —9B 64
Raghill. Aldm —4M 105
Raglan Ct. Read —1K 87
Raglan Gdns. Cav —9J 39
Raglan Ho. Slou —9H 23
Ragley M. Cav —7K 39
Ragstone Rd. Slou —2F 46
Railside Cotts. Midg —9H 83
Railton Clo. Read —4K 87
Railway Cotts. Bag —6H 115
Railway Cotts. Gor —8L 15
Railway Cotts. Graz —8C 86
Railway Rd. Newb —9M 79
Railway Ter. Hamp N —7J 33
Railway Ter. Slou —9H 23
Railway Ter. Stai —9E 72
Rainbow Ind. Est. W Dray —8L 25
Rainsborough Chase. M'head —2M 43
Raleigh Clo. Slou —9C 22
Raleigh Ct. Stai —8H 73
Ralph's Ride. Brack —5B 92
(in two parts)
Rambler Clo. Tap —7L 21
Rambler La. Slou —2L 47
Ramsay Rd. W'sham —5N 115
Ramsbury Clo. Brack —8J 91
Ramsbury Dri. Ear —8N 63
Ramsey Ct. Slou —5N 21
Ramslade Cotts. Brack —5N 91
Ramslade Rd. Brack —6A 92
Ranald Ct. Asc —1K 93
Rances La. Wokgm —6C 90
Randall Clo. Slou —4A 48
Randall Mead. Binf —1F 90
Randell Clo. B'water —8J 119
Randell Ho. Hawl —8J 119
Randolph Rd. Read —3G 62
Randolph Rd. Slou —2N 47
Ranelagh Cres. Asc —3F 92
Ranelagh Dri. Brack —5N 91
Range Ride. Sand —2K 119
Range Rd. Wokgm —3N 111
Range View. Col T —1J 119
Rangewood Av. Read —9N 61
Rapley Grn. Brack —8N 91
Ratby Clo. Lwr Ear —1B 88
Ratcliffe Clo. Uxb —4L 25
Ratcliffe Rd. Farn —9K 119
Raven Clo. Yat —3A 118
Ravenglass Clo. Lwr Ear —9B 64
Ravensbourne Av. Stai —5M 73
Ravensbourne Dri. Wdly —4D 64
Ravenscroft Rd. Hen T —4C 16
Ravensdale Ho. Stai —9J 73
Ravensdale Rd. Asc —7K 93
Ravensfield. Egh —1L 95
Ravensfield. Slou —1M 47
Ravenshoe Clo. Bour —4L 5
Ravenswood Av. Crowt —5C 112
Ravensworth Rd. Mort —4F 106
Ravensworth Rd. Slou —4C 22
Rawling Ct. Read —4J 87

Rawlinson Rd. Camb —3L 119
Ray Dri. M'head —7E 20
Ray Lea Clo. M'head —6E 20
Ray Lea Rd. M'head —5E 20
Rayleigh Clo. Wdly —7D 64
Ray Mead Ct. M'head —5F 20
Ray Mead Rd. M'head —7F 20
Ray Mill Rd. E. M'head —5D 20
Ray Mill Rd. W. M'head —6C 20
Raymond Clo. Coln —7F 48
Raymond Rd. M'head —7A 20
Raymond Rd. Slou —2B 48
Rayners Clo. Coln —6D 48
Ray Pk. Av. M'head —5E 20
Ray Pk. La. M'head —7E 20
Ray Pk. Rd. M'head —6E 20
Ray's Av. Wind —6B 46
Ray St. M'head —7E 20
Reade's La. Gall C —1C 38
Reading Link Retail Pk. Read —7G 62
Reading Retail Pk. Read —3B 62
Reading Rd. Arbor —7A 88
Reading Rd. Bfld —6L 85
Reading Rd. Bfld C —1G 107
Reading Rd. Chol —1J 15
Reading Rd. Finch —5D 110
Reading Rd. Gor —8L 15
Reading Rd. Hen T —5D 16
Reading Rd. Pang —8E 36
Reading Rd. Streat —3J 15
Reading Rd. Winn & Wokgm —1H 89
Reading Rd. Wdly —4B 64
Reading Rd. Yat —2A 118
Reckitt Ho. Read —1L 87
Recreation La. Spen W —9H 87
Recreation Rd. Bour —4M 5
Recreation Rd. Bfld C —9H 85
Recreation Rd. Tile —4M 61
Recreation Rd. Warg —3K 41
Rectory Clo. Brack —6N 91
Rectory Clo. Farn R —4E 22
Rectory Clo. Newb —9K 79
Rectory Clo. Sand —1D 118
Rectory Clo. Wind —7C 46
Rectory Clo. Wokgm —5A 90
Rectory La. Brack —7M 91
Rectory La. W'sham —6M 115
Rectory Rd. Cav —2G 63
Rectory Rd. Pad C —2A 106
Rectory Rd. Streat —7D 14
Rectory Rd. Tap —5G 21
Rectory Rd. Wokgm —5A 90
Rectory Row. Brack —6M 91
Redberry Clo. Cav —8K 39
Red Cottage Dri. Calc —8K 61
Red Cottage M. Slou —2L 47
Red Ct. Slou —9G 22
Red Cross Rd. Gor —8L 15
Reddington Dri. Slou —3N 47
Redditch. Brack —9A 92
Redfern Clo. Uxb —2K 25
Redfield Ct. Newb —7A 80
Redford Rd. Wind —7N 45
Redford Way. Uxb —1L 25
Redgauntlet. Finch —4J 111
Redhatch Dri. Ear —1M 87
Red Hill. Bin H —1M 39
Redhouse Clo. Lwr Ear —3A 88
Red Ho. Dri. Son C —1G 38
Redlake Hill. Aldm —4L 105
Redlands Rd. Read —6J 63
Red La. Aldm —4L 105
Redlane Ct. Read —7K 63
Redlane Rd. P'mre —1K 31
Redriff Clo. M'head —8A 20
Red Rose. Binf —9G 67
Redruth Gdns. Read —2H 87
Redshots Clo. Mar —3C 4
Red Shute Hill. Herm —8D 56
Redvers Rd. Brack —7M 91
Redwood. Burn —3L 21
Redwood Av. Wdly —7F 64
Redwood Dri. Asc —8D 94
Redwood Gdns. Slou —8F 22
Redwood Way. Tile —1L 61
Reed Clo. Iver —7F 24
Reeds Av. Ear —9M 63
Reed's Hill. Brack —7M 91
Reeve Rd. Holyp —5E 44
Reeves Way. Wokgm —7M 89
Reform Rd. M'head —7E 20
Regency Heights. Cav —9E 38
Regent Clo. Hung —6J 75
Regent Clo. Lwr Ear —2B 88
Regent Ct. Bag —8J 115
Regent Ct. M'head —7C 20
Regent Ct. Read —4G 62
Regent Ct. Slou —7G 22
Regents Ga. Read —6H 63
Regents Pl. Sand —1G 118
Regent St. Read —5L 63
Regents Wlk. Asc —9M 93
Regis Clo. Read —4K 87
Regnum Dri. Shaw —6M 79
Reid Av. M'head —9A 20
Rembrandt Clo. Wokgm —5J 89
Rembrandt Way. Read —7E 62
Remembrance Rd. Newb —9J 79
Remenham Chu. La. Rem —2F 16
Remenham La. Rem —4E 16
Renault Rd. Wdly —6F 64
Rennie Clo. Ashf —7L 73
Repton Clo. M'head —2N 43
Repton Rd. Ear —9B 64
Restwold Clo. Read —8C 62
Retford Clo. Wdly —3E 64
Retreat, The. Egh —9M 71
Retreat, The. M'head —6G 45
Revesby Clo. M'head —2A 44
Reynards Clo. Tadl —9K 105
Reynards Clo. Winn —1H 89
Reynolds Ct. That —8G 80
Reynolds Grn. Col T —3H 119
Rhigos. Cav —7F 38
Rhodes Clo. Ear —9D 64
Rhodes Clo. Egh —9D 72
Rhodes Ct. Egh —9D 72
(off Pooley Grn. Clo.)
Rhododendron Clo. Asc —2H 93
Rhododendron Ride. Egh —1H 95
Rhododendron Wlk. Asc —2H 93
Ribbleton Clo. Ear —9D 64
Ribstone Rd. M'head —2M 43
Ricardo Rd. Old Win —3K 71
Richard Nevill Ct. Cav —2J 63
(off Nelson Rd.)
Richards Clo. Uxb —2N 25
Richborough Clo. Ear —1A 88
Richfield Av. Read —3E 62
Richings Way. Iver —2F 48
Richmond Cres. Slou —9J 23
Richmond Cres. Stai —9G 73
Richmond Ho. Col T —2J 119
Richmond Rise. Wokgm —4K 89
Richmond Rd. Cav —9E 38
Richmond Rd. Col T —1J 119
Richmond Rd. Read —4D 62
Richmond Rd. Stai —9G 73
Richmondwood. Asc —9D 94
Rickard Clo. W Dray —2L 49
Rickman Clo. Arbor X —1D 110
Rickman Clo. Brack —8N 91
Rickman Clo. Wdly —7C 64
Rickman's La. Stoke P —1G 23
Riddings La. Hdly —8M 103
Rider's La. Graz —7A 86
Rideway Clo. Camb —5M 119
Ridgebank. Slou —8B 22
Ridge Hall Clo. Cav —1E 62
Ridgemead Rd. Egh —7J 71
Ridgemount Clo. Tile —2J 61
Ridge Mt. Rd. Asc —9C 94
Ridge, The. Cold A —2F 80
Ridge, The. Pang —5A 36
Ridge Way. Iver —8G 24
Ridge Way. Warg —3J 41
Ridgeway Clo. Herm —5E 56
Ridgeway Clo. Light —9K 115
Ridgeway Clo. Mar —3C 4
Ridgeway, The. Brack —5N 91
Ridgeway, The. Cav —1H 63
Ridgeway, The. Light —9L 115
Ridgeway, The. Mar —3C 4
Ridgeway, The. Wdly —7E 64
Ridgeway Trading Est. Iver —8G 24
Riding Ct. Rd. Dat —6L 47
Ridings, The. Emm G —5J 39
Ridings, The. Iver —3G 49
Ridings, The. M'head —8L 19
Riding Way. Wokgm —5J 89
Ridlington Clo. Lwr Ear —1D 88
Riley Rd. Mar —5B 4
Riley Rd. Tile —4N 61
Ringmead. Brack —7J 91
Ring, The. Brack —4N 91
Ringwood. Brack —9K 91
Ringwood Clo. Asc —6L 93
Ringwood Rd. B'water —3G 118
Ringwood Rd. Tile —3A 62
Ripley Av. Egh —1N 95
Ripley Clo. Slou —3N 47
Ripley Rd. Tile —3A 62
Ripplesmere. Brack —6A 92
Ripplesmore Clo. Sand —1F 118
Risborough Rd. M'head —6B 20
Riseley Rd. M'head —7A 20
Rise Rd. Asc —7A 94
Rise, The. Cav —9H 39
Rise, The. Cold A —4F 80
Rise, The. Crowt —5D 112
Rise, The. S'dale —8A 94
Rise, The. Uxb —3N 25
Rissington Clo. Tile —1M 61
Rivacres. Whit H —2F 36
Rivar Rd. Shalb —8E 96
Riverbank. Stai —9G 73
Riverbank, The. Wind —6D 46
Riverdene Dri. Winn —9E 64
Riverfield Rd. Stai —9G 73
River Gdns. Bray —1G 45
River Gdns. Pur T —8L 37
Rivermead. That —1J 103
Rivermead Ct. Mar —7C 4
Rivermead Rd. Camb —7M 119
Rivermead Rd. Wdly —7E 64
River Pk. Newb —8M 79
River Pk. Av. Stai —8E 72
Riverpark Dri. Mar —6D 4
River Rd. Cav —1D 62
River Rd. Read —6G 63
River Rd. Tap —8F 20
River Rd. Wind —6M 45
River Rd. Yat —1A 118
Riversdale. Bour —6M 5
Riversdale Ct. Read —4L 63
Riverside. Bour —4M 5
Riverside. Brad —6L 59
Riverside. Egh —7B 72
Riverside. Stai —9G 72
Riverside. Wray —4L 71
Riverside Av. Light —9M 115
Riverside Caravan Pk. Read —2A 62
Riverside Ct. Cav —2G 63
Riverside Dri. Stai —9F 72
(Chertsey La.)
Riverside Pk. Camb —6L 119
Riverside Pk. Coln —8F 48
Riverside Pl. Stai —3L 73
Riverside Rd. Stanw —2L 73
Riverside Way. Camb —6L 119
Riverside Way. Cow —2J 25
River St. Wind —6F 46
River Ter. Hen T —4D 16
Riverview Rd. Pang —7D 36
Riverway. Gt Shef —1F 52
Riverwoods Dri. Mar —6E 4
River Yd. Twy —8H 41
Rixman Clo. M'head —9A 20
Rixon Clo. G Grn —7N 23
Roasthill La. Eton W —5N 45
Roberts Clo. Stai —3K 73
Roberts Clo. W Dray —9M 25
Robertsfield. That —8C 80
Roberts Gro. Wokgm —7L 89
Robertson Clo. Green —2M 101
Roberts Rd. Camb —3L 119
Roberts Way. Egh —2L 95
Robin Clo. Bfld C —8J 85
Robindale Av. Ear —9C 64
Robin Hood Clo. Farn —9L 119
Robin Hood Clo. Slou —9B 22
Robin Hood La. Winn —1H 89
Robin Hood Way. Winn —9H 65
Robin La. Bis G —7C 102
Robin La. Sand —1F 118
Robin's Bow. Camb —5M 119
Robins Clo. Newb —3K 101
Robins Clo. Uxb —6K 25
Robins Gro. Cres. Yat —3A 118
Robins Hill. Ink —4D 98
Robin Way. Stai —7G 72
Robin Way. Tile —6J 61
Robin Willis Way. Old Win —3J 71
Robinwood Gro. Uxb —5N 25
Rochester Av. Wdly —3D 64
Rochester Rd. Stai —9E 72
Rochfords Gdns. Slou —9L 23
Rochford Way. Tap —8K 21
Rockall Ct. Slou —2C 48
Rockbourne Gdns. Tile —3A 62
Rockfel Rd. Lamb —3G 27
Rockfield Way. Col T —1H 119
Rockingham Clo. Uxb —2K 25
Rockingham Pde. Uxb —1K 25
Rockingham Rd. Newb —9K 79
Rockingham Rd. Uxb —2J 25
Rodney Ct. Read —6G 62
Rodney Way. Coln —7F 48
Rodway Rd. Tile —2M 61
Roebuck Est. Binf —2G 91
Roebuck Grn. Slou —9A 22
Roebuts Clo. Newb —2K 101
Roger's La. E Gar —7A 28
Roger's La. Stoke P —1H 23
Rokeby Clo. Brack —3A 92
Rokeby Clo. Newb —3L 101
Rokeby Dri. Tok G —5C 38
Rokesby Rd. Slou —4B 22
Rollington Clo. Lwr Ear —1D 88
Rolls La. Holyp —5B 44
Romana Ct. Stai —8H 73
Roman Fields. Sil —9C 106
Roman Lea. Cook —8K 5
Roman Ride. Crowt —5B 112
Romans Ga. Pam H —9A 106
Roman Way. Bour —3L 5
(in two parts)
Roman Way. Ear —9C 64
Roman Way. That —7D 80
Romany Clo. Tile —3A 62
Romany La. Tile —4N 61
(in two parts)
Romeo Hill. Warf —3C 92
Romney Ho. Brack —6B 92
Romney Lock Rd. Wind —6F 46
Romsey Clo. B'water —3G 119
Romsey Clo. Ear —9D 64
Romsey Clo. Slou —2A 48
Romsey Rd. Tile —3A 62
Rona Ct. Read —4B 62
Ronaldsay Spur. Slou —6G 22
Rood Hill. E'ton —7N 53
Rook Clo. Wokgm —6K 89
Rookery Ct. Finch —4F 110
Rookery Ct. Mar —5B 4
Rookery Rd. Stai —9J 73
Rooksfield. Bis G —8D 102
Rooksnest La. Kint —5F 98
Rookswood. Brack —2M 91
Rookwood Av. Owl —8J 113
Rope Wlk. That —8F 80
Rosary Gdns. Yat —3B 118
Roseary Clo. W Dray —3L 49
Rosebank Clo. Cook —8J 5
Rosebay. Wokgm —3C 90
Rosebery Rd. Tok G —6D 38
Rose Clo. Wdly —5G 64
Rose Ct. Wokgm —5A 90
Rosecroft Way. Shin —6L 87
Rosedale. Binf —9G 67
Rosedale Cres. Ear —4N 63
Rosedale Gdns. Brack —7L 91
Rosedale Gdns. That —9F 80
Rosedene La. Col T —3H 119
Rosefield Rd. Stai —8H 73
Rose Gdns. Stai —4L 73
Rose Gdns. Wokgm —5A 90
Rose Hill. Binf —9G 67
Rose Hill. Burn —2K 21
Rosehill Ct. Slou —2J 47
Rosehill Houses. Cav —6J 39
Rosehill Pk. Cav —6H 39
Rose Ind. Est. Bour —4M 5
Rose Kiln La. Read —6G 62
Rose La. C Grn —7M 17
Roseleigh Clo. M'head —7L 19
Rosemary Av. Ear —2M 87
Rosemary Clo. Uxb —6N 25
Rosemary Gdns. B'water —4G 119
Rosemary La. B'water —3G 118
Rosemary Ter. Newb —9J 79
Rosemead Av. Tile —1J 61
Rosen Ct. That —8H 81
Rose Rd. M'head —9A 20
Rosery, The. Bour —4L 5
Roses La. Wind —8N 45
Rose St. Wokgm —5A 90
Rose Ter. Newb —1K 101
Rose Wlk. Read —5G 63
Rose Wlk. Slou —6D 22
Rosewood. Wdly —7C 64
Rosier Clo. That —9J 81
Rosken Gdns. Farn R —3D 22
Roslyn Rd. Wdly —6C 64
Rossendale Rd. Cav —1K 63
Rossett Clo. Brack —6M 91
Rossington Pl. Read —3J 87
Rossiter Clo. Slou —3N 47
Ross Rd. M'head —9A 20
Ross Rd. Read —3G 62
Rostrevor Gdns. Iver —3E 24
Rother Clo. Sand —1G 119
Rotherfield Av. Wokgm —4L 89
Rotherfield Clo. Thea —8G 60
Rotherfield Rd. Hen T —7C 16
Rotherfield Way. Cav —9G 39
Rothwell Gdns. Wdly —3E 64
Rothwell Ho. Crowt —6G 113
Rothwell Wlk. Cav —2K 63
Rotten Row Hill. Tut C —9H 59
Roughgrove Copse. Binf —1F 90
Roundabout La. Winn —3J 89
Round Clo. Yat —4D 118
Round End. Newb —5H 101
Roundfield. Up Buck —5L 81
(in two parts)
Roundhead Rd. Thea —9E 60
Roundway. Egh —9D 72
Routh La. Tile —6M 61
Rowallan Clo. Cav —7K 39
Rowan. Brack —7C 92
Rowan Av. Egh —9D 72
Rowan Clo. Camb —9C 114
Rowan Clo. Son C —1F 38
Rowan Clo. Wokgm —6L 89
Rowan Dri. Crowt —3G 112
Rowan Dri. Newb —6L 79
Rowan Dri. Wdly —4D 64
Rowan Gdns. Iver —3D 24
Rowan Rd. W Dray —3L 49
Rowans Clo. Farn —8J 119
Rowan Way. Bfld —7J 85
Rowan Way. Slou —6D 22
Rowanwood. Finch —4F 110
Rowcroft Rd. Arbor X —3E 110
Rowe Ct. Read —4B 62
Rowland Clo. Wind —9N 45
Rowland Way. Ear —1M 87
Row La. D'den —5L 39
Rowles Paddock. W Ils —4L 11
Rowley Clo. Brack —5B 92
Rowley La. Wex —2L 23
Rowley Rd. Read —8H 63
Rowlheys Pl. W Dray —2M 49
Roxborough Way. M'head —1K 43
Roxwell Clo. Slou —9A 22
Royal Av. Calc —8J 61
Royal Clo. Uxb —7N 25
Royal Ct. Read —5J 63
Royal La. Uxb & W Dray —6N 25
Royal Mans. Hen T —5D 16
Royal M. Wind —7F 46
Royal Sta. Ct. Twy —9J 41
Royal Victoria Gdns. S Asc —6K 93
Roy Clo. Herm —6C 56
Roycroft La. Wokgm —2K 111
Royston Clo. Tile —5N 61
Royston Gdns. Wokgm —4M 111
Royston Way. Slou —6M 21
Ruby Clo. Slou —2C 46
Ruby Clo. Wokgm —4J 89
Ruddlesway. Wind —7N 45
(in three parts)
Rudland Clo. That —9G 80
Rudsworth Clo. Coln —6E 48
Rugby Clo. Owl —9J 113
Ruggles-Brise Rd. Ashf —9L 73
Runnemede Rd. Egh —8B 72
Runnymede Ct. Egh —8B 72
Rupert Clo. Hen T —3D 16
Rupert Rd. Newb —2K 101
Ruperts La. Hen T —3D 16
Rupert Sq. Read —5K 63
Rupert St. Read —5K 63
Rupert Wlk. Read —5K 63
Ruscombe Gdns. Dat —5J 47
Ruscombe La. Rusc —8K 41
Ruscombe Pk. Ind. Est. Rusc —8K 41
Ruscombe Rd. Twy —8K 41
Rushall Clo. Lwr Ear —4L 87
Rusham Ct. Egh —9B 72
Rusham Pk. Av. Egh —9A 72
Rusham Rd. Egh —9A 72
Rushbrook Rd. Wdly —5B 64
Rushden Dri. Read —2L 87
Rushes M. Uxb —2K 25
Rushes, The. M'head —8E 20
Rushey Way. Lwr Ear —3M 87
Rushington Av. M'head —8C 20
Rushmoor Gdns. Calc —8J 61
Ruskin Ct. Crowt —6C 112
Ruskin Way. Wokgm —5J 89
Russell Ct. B'water —4H 119
Russell Ct. M'head —7C 20
Russell Dri. Stai —3L 73
Russell Gdns. W Dray —4N 49
Russell Rd. Newb —9J 79
Russell Rd. Tok G —6D 38
Russell St. Read —5F 62
Russell St. Wind —7F 46
Russell Way. Winn —2G 89
Russet Clo. Stai —3G 73
Russet Glade. Bfld C —9J 85
Russet Glade. Cav —6J 39
Russet Rd. M'head —2N 43
Russley Grn. Wokgm —1M 111
Rustington Clo. Ear —2A 88
Ruston Way. Asc —4H 93
Rutherford Clo. Wind —7B 46
Rutherford Wlk. Tile —5H 61
Rutland Av. Slou —6E 22
Rutland Pl. M'head —8N 19
Rutland Rd. M'head —8A 20
Rutland Rd. Read —5D 62
Rutters Clo. W Dray —1N 49
Ryan Mt. Sand —1E 118
Ryans Mt. Mar —5A 4
Rycroft. Wind —9B 46
Rycroft Clo. Warg —2K 41
Rydal Av. Tile —2N 61
Rydal Dri. That —8D 80
Rydal Pl. Light —9L 115
Ryde Gdns. Yat —3A 118
Rydings. Wind —9B 46
Rye Clo. Brack —2A 92
Rye Clo. M'head —1L 43
Rye Ct. Slou —2J 47
Ryecroft Clo. Wdly —3C 64
Ryecroft Gdns. B'water —5J 119
Rye Gro. Light —9N 115
Ryehurst La. Binf —8J 67
Ryeish La. Spen W —8J 87
Ryeland Clo. W Dray —7M 25
Ryemead La. Wink —7F 68
Ryhill Way. Lwr Ear —3L 87
Rylstone Clo. M'head —2N 43
Rylstone Rd. Read —4D 62
Ryvers Rd. Slou —2A 48

Sabah Ct. Ashf —8N 73
Sackville St. Read —4G 62
Saddleback Rd. Camb —9B 114
Saddlewood. Camb —5N 119
Sadlers Ct. Winn —3J 89
Sadlers End. Sind —4G 89
Sadlers La. Winn —3J 89
Sadlers M. M'head —7E 20
Sadlers Rd. Ink —5M 97
Saffron Clo. Dat —7K 47
Saffron Clo. Ear —8B 64
Saffron Clo. Newb —8K 79
Saffron Rd. Brack —6M 91
Sage Clo. Ear —2N 87
Sagecroft Rd. That —6F 80
Sage Rd. Tile —1K 61
Sage Wlk. Warf —2A 92
Sailing Club La. Bour —4L 5
St Adrians Clo. M'head —1M 43
St Agnes Ter. Lamb —3H 27
St Alban's Clo. Wind —7F 46
St Alban's St. Wind —7F 46
St Andrews. Brack —8J 91
St Andrew's Av. Wind —8B 46
St Andrew's Clo. Crowt —4D 112
St Andrew's Clo. Old Win —3J 71
St Andrews Clo. Wray —3N 71
St Andrew's Ct. Read —5K 63
St Andrew's Cres. Wind —8B 46
St Andrew's Hall. Read —6J 63
St Andrew's Rd. Cav —9F 38
St Andrews Rd. Hen T —6B 16
St Andrew's Rd. Uxb —2M 25
St Andrew's Way. Slou —8N 21
St Anne's Av. Stai —4L 73
St Annes Clo. Hen T —5C 16
St Annes Glade. Bag —7G 114
St Anne's Rd. Cav —2G 62
St Anthonys Clo. Brack —3L 91
St Barnabas Rd. Cav —7G 39
St Barnabas Rd. Read —2M 87
St Bartholomews Rd. Read —5M 63
St Bernards Rd. Slou —2L 47
St Birinus Rd. Calc —7K 61
St Catherine's Clo. Sind —2F 88
St Catherines Ct. Stai —8H 73
St Cecelia Ct. Read —1J 87
St Chads Rd. M'head —1M 43
St Christopher Rd. Uxb —7L 25
St Christophers Gdns. Asc —3G 92
St Clement Clo. Uxb —7L 25
St Clements Clo. Lwr Ear —2B 88
St Cloud Way. Tap —7C 20
St Columbus Clo. M'head —1M 43
St Cuthberts Clo. Egh —9M 71
St David Clo. Uxb —6L 25
St David's Clo. Cav —8F 38
St David's Clo. Farn —9K 119
St David's Clo. Iver —2E 24
St Davids Clo. M'head —1L 43
St David's Rd. Newb —9K 79
St Donats Pl. Newb —9L 79
St Edwards Rd. Read —6N 63
St Elizabeth Clo. Read —4H 87
St Elmo Clo. Slou —5F 22
St Elmo Cres. Slou —5F 22
St George's Av. Newb —9J 79
St Georges Clo. Wind —7A 46
St Georges Ct. Owl —8J 113
St George's Cres. Slou —8N 21
St George's Hall. Read —7K 63
St George's Ind. Est. Camb —6M 119
St George's La. Asc —5L 93
St George's Rd. Read —4B 62
St George's Ter. Read —4B 62
St Giles Clo. Read —6H 63
St Giles Ct. Read —6H 63
(off Southampton St.)
St Helen Clo. Uxb —6L 25
St Helens Cres. Sand —1F 118
St Helier Clo. Wokgm —8N 89
St Hilda's Av. Ashf —9M 73
St Ives Clo. Thea —1E 84
St Ives Rd. M'head —7D 20
St James Clo. Pang —7D 36
St James Clo. Twy —8K 41
St James' Courtyard. Mar —5B 4
(off Claremont Gdns.)
St James Pl. Slou —7M 21
St James Rd. Wokgm —2K 111
St James Wlk. Iver —1F 48
St Johns Clo. Uxb —2J 25
St Johns Clo. Wdly —4E 64
St John's Ct. Egh —9B 72
St John's Dri. Wind —8C 46
St Johns Gdns. Newb —1K 101
(off Old Newbury Rd.)
St Johns Ga. Read —4H 63
(off Valpy St.)
St John's Hill. Read —5J 63
St John's Rd. Asc —2J 93
St John's Rd. Cav —2J 63
St John's Rd. Mort C —5H 107
St John's Rd. Newb —1L 101
St John's Rd. Read —5J 63
St John's Rd. Sand —2F 118
St Johns Rd. Slou —8J 23
St John's Rd. That —8F 80
St John's Rd. Uxb —2J 25
St John's Rd. Wind —8C 46
St John's St. Read —5J 63
St Joseph's Ct. Newb —7M 79
(off Charlton Pl.)
St Jude's Clo. Egh —9L 71
St Jude's Rd. Egh —8L 71
St Katherine's Rd. Hen T —7C 16
St Laurence Clo. Uxb —6K 25
St Laurence Way. Slou —2J 47
St Lawrence Sq. Hung —6J 75
St Leger Ct. Newb —7J 79
St Leonard's Av. Wind —8E 46
St Leonard's Hill. Wind —1N 69
St Leonard's Rd. Wind —3M 69
(Windsor Safari Park)
St Leonard's Rd. Wind —9C 46
(Windsor)
St Leonards Wlk. Iver —2G 48
St Luke Clo. Uxb —7L 25
St Lukes Ct. Cav —9H 39
St Luke's Rd. M'head —7C 20
St Luke's Rd. Old Win —3J 71
St Luke's Rd. Uxb —1M 25
St Lukes Way. Cav —9H 39
St Margarets Av. Uxb —5N 25
St Margarets Clo. Iver —3E 24

St Margarets Ga. Iver —3E 24
St Margarets Rd. M'head —7L 19
St Mark's Clo. Eng —7C 60
St Marks Clo. That —8F 80
St Mark's Cres. M'head —7M 19
St Marks Pl. Wind —8E 46
St Mark's Rd. Binf —2G 91
St Mark's Rd. Hen T —6C 16
St Mark's Rd. M'head —7N 19
St Marks Rd. Wind —8E 46
St Martin Clo. Uxb —7L 25
St Martin's Cen. Cav —2G 63
St Martins Clo. Lwr Ear —2B 88
St Martin's Clo. W Dray —2L 49
St Martin's Ct. Ashf —9K 73
St Martin's Rd. W Dray —2L 49
St Mary's Av. Pur T —8K 37
St Mary's Av. Stai —4L 73
St Mary's Butts. Read —5G 63
St Mary's Clo. Hen T —6A 16
St Mary's Clo. M'head —7C 20
St Mary's Clo. Sand —1G 119
St Mary's Clo. Stai —4L 73
St Mary's Cres. Stai —4L 73
St Mary's Gdns. Bag —7H 115
St Mary's Hill. Asc —8M 93
St Mary's La. Wink —7G 68
St Mary's Rd. Asc —9L 93
St Mary's Rd. Camb —3N 119
St Mary's Rd. Langl —9N 23
St Mary's Rd. Mort C —5H 107
St Mary's Rd. Newb —7L 79
St Mary's Rd. Sind —3G 88
St Mary's Way. Bfld C —8J 85
St Matthew Clo. Uxb —7L 25
St Michaels Clo. Lamb —3G 27
St Michael's Ct. Rusc —7K 41
St Michaels Ct. Slou —5N 21
St Michael's Rd. Camb —4M 119
St Michael's Rd. Newb —9K 79
St Michael's Rd. Sand —1D 118
St Michael's Rd. Tile —4L 61
St Nazaire Clo. Egh —9E 72
St Neot's Rd. Eve —9E 110
St Nicholas Clo. Uxb —7L 25
St Nicholas's Rd. Newb —9K 79
St Patrick's Av. Charv —8F 40
St Patricks Clo. E Ils —7B 12
St Patricks Clo. M'head —1M 43
St Patrick's Hall. Read —8K 63
St Paul Clo. Uxb —6L 25
St Pauls Av. Slou —8H 23
St Paul's Ct. Read —6G 62
St Paul's Ga. Wokgm —4M 89
St Paul's Rd. Stai —9E 72
St Peter's Av. Cav —9E 38
St Peter's Clo. Burn —5L 21
St Peter's Clo. Old Win —2J 71
St Peter's Clo. Stai —9G 73
St Peter's Gdns. Yat —3B 118
St Peter's Hill. Cav —1F 62
St Peter's Rd. M'head —4A 20
St Peter's Rd. Read —6N 63
St Peters Rd. Uxb —6L 25
St Peter St. Mar —6C 4
St Ronan's Rd. Read —4B 62
St Saviour's Rd. Read —7F 62
St Saviours Ter. Read —6F 62
St Sebastian's Clo. Wokgm —3C 112
St Stephen's Clo. Cav —2G 63
St Stephens Ct. Read —5K 63 (off Rupert St.)
St Stephen's Rd. W Dray —9L 25
St Swithins Clo. Wick —8J 53
St Swithin's Ct. Twy —9J 41
St Thomas Wlk. Coln —6E 48
Salamanca. Crowt —5C 112
Salcombe Dri. Ear —8A 64
Salcombe Rd. Ashf —8M 73
Salcombe Rd. Newb —1J 101
Salcombe Rd. Read —9K 63
Saleby Clo. Lwr Ear —1D 88
Sale Garden Cotts. Wokgm —6A 90
Salford Clo. Read —4J 87
Salisbury Av. Slou —5E 22
Salisbury Clo. Wokgm —9M 89
Salisbury Rd. B'water —5G 119
Salisbury Rd. Hung —8J 75
Salisbury Rd. Read —4E 62
Salisbury Rd. Uxb —3J 25
Salmon Clo. Spen W —9H 87
Salmond Rd. Read —5J 87
Salters Clo. M'head —7D 20
Saltersgate Clo. Lwr Ear —1C 88
Salters Rd. M'head —7E 20
Salt Hill Av. Slou —9E 22
Salt Hill Dri. Slou —9E 22
Salt Hill Mans. Slou —9E 22
Salt Hill Way. Slou —9E 22
Salwey Clo. Brack —8M 91
Samian Pl. Binf —2J 91
Sampage Clo. Read —5J 87
Sampson Pk. Binf —3H 91
Sampson's Grn. Slou —4B 22
Sanctuary Clo. Tile —4M 61
Sandcroft Rd. Cav —7E 38
Sanden Clo. Hung —6J 75
Sandford Down. Brack —7C 92
Sandford Dri. Wdly —3E 64
Sandford La. Wdly & Hurst —5G 65
Sandford Rd. Tadl —9J 105
Sandgate Av. Tile —2N 61
Sand Hill Ct. Farn —9M 119
Sandhills Ct. Vir W —7N 95
Sandhills La. Vir W —7N 95
Sandhills Way. Calc —8M 61
Sandhurst-Crowthorne By-Pass. Col T —4J 119
Sandhurst-Crowthorne By-Pass. Crowt —3J 113
Sandhurst La. B'water —3F 118
Sandhurst Rd. Crowt —7F 112
Sandhurst Rd. Wokgm —2N 111
Sandhurst Rd. Yat —2D 118
Sandisplatt Rd. M'head —8L 19
Sandleford Clo. Read —5J 87
Sandleford Rise. Newb —3L 101
Sandlers End. Slou —5D 22
Sandown Av. Calc —8J 61
Sandown Clo. B'water —4H 119
Sandown Rd. Slou —6B 22
Sandown Way. Green —1N 101
Sandpit Hill. Newb —6G 101
Sandpit La. D'den —5M 39
Sandpit La. Far H —6N 109
Sandringham Ct. Slou —7N 21
Sandringham Dri. Ashf —8L 73
Sandringham Rd. H'row A —2M 73
Sandringham Rd. M'head —4B 20
Sandringham Way. Calc —8J 61
Sands Drove. Hung —5A 98
Sands Farm Dri. Burn —5M 21
Sandstone Clo. Winn —2H 89
Sandygate Clo. Mar —4B 4
Sandygate Rd. Mar —4B 4
Sandy La. Brack —3N 91
Sandy La. Chvly —2B 56
Sandy La. Cur —8C 56
Sandy La. Farn —9J 119
Sandy La. N Asc —3F 92
Sandy La. Sand —9D 112
Sandy La. Shalb —9D 96
Sandy La. S'dale —7C 94
Sandy La. Vir W —6N 95
Sandy La. Wokgm —7H 89
Sandy Mead. M'head —4F 44
Sandy Ride. S'hill —6A 94
Sapphire Clo. Wokgm —4K 89
Sargeants Clo. Uxb —4L 25
Sarsby Dri. Stai —6B 72
Sarum. Brack —1K 113
Sarum Complex. Uxb —4J 25
Sarum Cres. Wokgm —4B 90
Sarum Rd. Tadl —9J 105
Sarum Way. Hung —7K 75
Saturn Clo. Wokgm —5K 89
Saturn Croft. Wink R —1D 92
Saunders Ct. Pur T —8J 37
Saunders Rd. Uxb —1N 25
Savernake Clo. Tile —5N 61
Savernake Way. Brack —8B 92
Savill Way. Mar —5D 4
Savory Wlk. Binf —1F 90
Savoy Gro. B'water —6H 119
Sawpit Rd. Hurst —5K 65
Sawtry Clo. Lwr Ear —1D 88
Sawyers Clo. M'head —3L 43
Sawyers Clo. Wind —6A 46
Sawyers Cres. M'head —3L 43
Saxby Clo. Bfld C —8J 85
Saxon Clo. Slou —1A 48
Saxon Clo. Uxb —6N 25
Saxon Gdns. Tap —5G 21
Saxon Ho. Cotts. Lamb —1F 26
Saxon Way. Old Win —3K 71
Saxon Way. W Dray —5K 49
Saxony Way. Yat —5A 118
Sayers Clo. Green —2M 101
Scafell Clo. Tile —2J 61
Scafell Rd. Slou —5B 22
Scampton Rd. Houn —3N 73
Scania Wlk. Wink R —1E 92
Scarborough Way. Slou —2D 46
Scarletts La. Kiln G —5N 41
Scholars Clo. Cav —1F 62
Scholars Clo. Gt Shef —1F 52
School Allotment Ride. Wind —4L 69
School Cotts. Asc —3G 93
Schoolfields. S'lake X —3D 40
School Grn. Shin —7L 87
School Hill. Crowt —6H 113
School Hill. Sand —9E 112
School Hill. Warg —4J 41
School La. Bag —8G 115
School La. Box —8B 54
School La. Bfld C —8G 85
School La. Cav —2G 63
School La. Cook —8L 5
School La. Cook D —8F 4
School La. Egh —9B 72
School La. Emm G —8H 39
School La. L Bed —1D 96
School La. L Mar —2G 5
School La. M'head —5B 20
School La. Stoke P —1K 23
School La. Warg —3J 41
School La. W'sham —5N 115
School La. Yat —3A 118
School Rd. Arbor X & B'ham —9D 88
School Rd. Asc —7N 93
School Rd. B'ham —5B 90
School Rd. Bfld —5K 85
School Rd. Chvly —3J 55
School Rd. Comp —1H 33
School Rd. Hurst —5L 65
School Rd. Pad —1A 106
School Rd. Rise —6L 109
School Rd. Tile —4L 61
School Rd. W Dray —5L 49
School Rd. W'sham —4K 115
School Ter. Read —4L 63
School Wlk. Slou —8K 23
Schroder Ct. Egh —9K 71
Scotland Hill. Sand —9E 112
Scotlands Dri. Farn C —1D 22
Scots Clo. Stanw —5L 73
Scots Dri. Wokgm —3K 89
Scottalls La. Hamp N —8J 33
Scott Clo. Emm G —8G 39
Scott Clo. W Dray —3N 49
Scott Clo. Wdly —5F 64
Scott's Ct. Farn —9M 119
Scott Ter. Brack —3B 92
Scours La. Tile —3B 62
Scratchface La. Brad —4E 58
Scrivens Mead. That —8J 81
Scutley La. Light —8N 115
Seacourt Rd. Slou —3C 48
Seaford Gdns. Wdly —6D 64
Seaford Rd. Houn —2L 73
Seaford Rd. Wokgm —5B 90
Sealand Rd. Houn —3N 73
Searles Farm La. Read —2B 86
Seaton Dri. Ashf —6M 73
Seaton Gdns. Read —1J 87
Seaton Rd. Camb —4M 119
Second Cres. Slou —6E 22
Second St. Green —5C 102
Sedgefield Rd. Green —2N 101
Seebys Oak. Col T —3J 119
Sefton Clo. Stoke P —2H 23
Sefton Paddock. Stoke P —1J 23
Sefton Way. Uxb —7K 25
Segsbury Gro. Brack —6B 92
Selborne Clo. B'water —3G 119
Selborne Ct. Read —5J 63
Selborne Gdns. Read —3A 62
Selcourt Clo. Wdly —4C 64
Sellafield Way. Lwr Ear —1B 88
Selsdon Av. Wdly —4E 64
Selsey Way. Lwr Ear —3A 88
Selva Ct. Read —6J 63
Selwood Clo. Stai —3K 73
Selwood Gdns. Stai —3K 73
Selwyn Dri. Yat —3A 118
Selwyn Pl. Cipp —8B 22
Send Rd. Cav —2J 63
September Ct. Uxb —3L 25
Sermed Ct. Slou —9L 23
Setley Way. Brack —5C 92
Seton Dri. Calc —8N 61
Settringham Clo. Lwr Ear —1D 88
Sett, The. Yat —4A 118
Seven Hills Rd. Iver —1E 24
Sevenoaks Dri. Spen W —8G 87
Sevenoaks Rd. Ear —9A 64
Seventh St. Green —5C 102
Severalls, The. Ham —7J 97
Severn Clo. Sand —1G 119
Severn Clo. That —6E 80
Severn Cres. Slou —4C 48
Severn Way. Tile —6N 61
Sewell Av. Wokgm —3M 89
Sewell Clo. Cold A —2E 80
Seymour Av. Shin —6L 87
Seymour Clo. M'head —2M 43
Seymour Ct. Crowt —6C 112
Seymour Ct. Rd. Mar —2A 4
Seymour Pk. Rd. Mar —4B 4
Seymour Plain. Mar —2A 4
Seymour Rd. Slou —1F 46
Shackleton Rd. Slou —8H 23
Shackleton Way. Wdly —5F 64
Shaftesbury Clo. Brack —7A 92
Shaftesbury Ct. Slou —1G 47
Shaftesbury Ct. Wokgm —4B 90
Shaftesbury Mt. B'water —6H 119
Shaftesbury Rd. Read —4B 62
Shaggy Calf La. Slou —8J 23
Shakespeare Clo. Cav —8K 39
Shakespeare Rd. That —7F 80
Shakespeare Way. Warf —3B 92
Shalbourne Clo. Hung —6H 75
Sharney Av. Slou —2C 48
Sharnwood Dri. Calc —7N 61
Sharpethorpe Clo. Lwr Ear —2A 88
Shaw Ct. Old Win —2J 71
Shaw Farm Rd. Newb —4M 79
Shawfield Ct. W Dray —2M 49
Shaw Hill. Newb —6M 79
Shaw Pk. Crowt —7F 112
Shaw Rd. Newb —7M 79
Shaw Rd. Read —7F 62
Shaw, The. Cook —1B 20
Sheehy Way. Slou —8K 23
Sheepcote La. M'head —9N 43
Sheepcote Rd. Eton W —4C 46
Sheepcote Rd. Wind —8A 46
Sheepcot La. Bfld C —9N 85
Sheepdrove Rd. Lamb —2J 27
Sheephouse Rd. M'head —5E 20
Sheephouse Way. Chad —8M 29
Sheep Leaze La. Catm —2E 30
Sheepridge La. Mar —1J 5
Sheep Wlk. Cav —9H 39
Sheepwash. Newt —8K 101
Sheepways La. Tok G —5B 38
Sheerlands Rd. Arbor —3E 110
Sheet St. Wind —8F 46
Sheet St. Rd. Wind —8N 69
Sheffield Rd. Slou —7E 22
Shefford Cres. Wokgm —3B 90
Shefford Lodge. Newb —9L 79
Sheldon Gdns. Read —2J 87
Shelgate Wlk. Wdly —5B 64
Shelley Av. Brack —4B 92
Shelley Clo. Slou —4B 48
Shelley Clo. Wdly —8D 64
Shelley Ct. Camb —4N 119
Shelley Rd. Mar —4D 4
Shelley Rd. That —7F 80
Shelley Wlk. Yat —4A 118
Shelton Ct. Slou —2L 47
Shenstone Clo. Wokgm —2M 111
Shenstone Dri. Burn —5N 21
Shenstone Pk. S'hill —6A 94
Shenstone Rd. Read —8H 63
Shepherd's Av. Ear —4A 64
Shepherds Chase. Bag —8H 115
Shepherds Clo. Hur —3D 18
Shepherds Clo. Uxb —5K 25
Shepherds Hill. Brack —3N 91
Shepherds Hill. Comp —2H 33
Shepherds Hill. Ear —4A 64
Shepherd's Ho. La. Read —4N 63
Shepherd's La. Brack —2L 91
Shepherds La. Cav —7D 38
Shepherds La. Hur —3B 18
Shepherds Mt. Comp —2H 33
Shepherds Rise. Comp —1H 33
Shepherds Wlk. Farn —9N 119
Shepherds Wlk. Wdly —4B 64
Shepherds Way. Crowt —6C 112
Shepherdton La. Graz —9C 86
Shepley Dri. Asc —8E 94
Shepley Dri. Read —8C 62
Shepley End. Asc —7E 94
Sheraton Clo. B'water —5J 119
Sheraton Dri. Tile —3J 61
Sherborne Clo. Coln —7F 48
Sherbourne Dri. Asc —7F 94
Sherbourne Dri. M'head —2N 43
Sherbourne Dri. Wind —1B 70
Sherbourne Dri. Wdly —4E 64
Sherfield Clo. Read —8K 63
Sherfield Dri. Read —8K 63
Sherfield Hall. Read —8K 63
Shergold Way. Cook —9K 5
Sheridan Av. Cav —8F 38
Sheridan Ct. Cipp —8A 22
Sheridan Ct. Newb —8N 79
Sheridan Cres. Baug —9G 104
Sheridan Rd. Frim —9N 119
Sheridan Way. Wokgm —6K 89
Sheringham Ct. Read —7J 63
Sherman Pl. Read —6H 63
Sherman Rd. Read —6H 63
Sherman Rd. Slou —6G 23
Sherrardmead. Shaw —6M 79
Sherring Clo. Brack —2N 91
Sherwin Cres. Farn —9M 119
Sherwood Clo. Brack —4D 92
Sherwood Clo. Slou —2N 47
Sherwood Ct. Coln —4A 48
Sherwood Dri. M'head —8L 19
Sherwood Gdns. Hen T —6B 16
Sherwood Pl. Pur T —9J 37
Sherwood Rise. Pur T —9J 37
Sherwood Rd. Winn —1H 89
Sherwood St. Read —4C 62
Shifford Cres. M'head —4B 20
Shinfield Ct. Three M —6J 87
Shinfield Rise. Read —2L 87
Shinfield Rd. Read —8K 63
Shiplake Ho. Brack —6C 92
Shiplake Row. S'lake —4B 40
Shipley Clo. Wdly —3F 64
Shipton Clo. Tile —2K 61
Shire Clo. Bag —8H 115
Shireshead Clo. Read —6D 62
Shires, The. Wokgm —7K 89
Shires Way. Yat —2B 118
Shirley Av. Read —4J 87
Shirley Av. Wind —7B 46
Shirley Rd. M'head —9N 19
Shoesmiths Ct. Read —4G 63 (off Merchants Pl.)
Shootersbrook La. Uft N —9B 84
Shooter's Hill. Pang —6C 36
Shop La. Leck —8D 30
Shop La. Newb —5K 79
Shoppenhangers Rd. M'head —2M 43
Shop Rd. Wind —6M 45
Shoreham Rise. Slou —5N 21
Shoreham Rd. E. H'row A —2M 73
Shoreham Rd. W. H'row A —2M 73
Shortfern. Slou —7L 23
Shortheath La. Sul'd —8E 84
Shortlands Hill. Chol —2E 14
Short La. Stai —4N 73
Short Rd. Houn —3M 73
Short St. Cav —2H 63
Short St. Pang —8E 36
Short St. Read —6H 63
Short, The. Pur T —8L 37
Shortwood Av. Stai —7J 73
Shrewsbury Ter. Newb —1K 101
Shrivenham Clo. Col T —1H 119
Shropshire Gdns. Warf —2C 92
Shrubbs Hill La. S'dale —8E 94
Shrubland Dri. Read —8A 62
Shute End. Wokgm —5N 89
Shyshack La. Baug —9G 105
Sibley Pk. Rd. Ear —1N 87
Sibson. Lwr Ear —1B 88
Sidbury Clo. Asc —7C 94
Sidestrand Rd. Newb —2J 101
Sidings, The. Stai —8J 73
Sidmouth Grange Clo. Ear —5A 64
Sidmouth Grange Rd. Ear —5A 64
Sidmouth St. Read —5J 63 (in two parts)
Sidney Harrison Ho. Lwr S —2G 40
Sidney Rd. Stai —8H 73
Sidney Rd. Wind —9M 45
Silbury Clo. Calc —8H 61
Silchester Rd. Pam H —9K 105
Silchester Rd. Read —8C 62
Silco Dri. M'head —8B 20
Silton Clo. Ear —9D 64
Silver Birches. Wokgm —8H 89
Silver Clo. M'head —9L 19
Silverdale Ct. Stai —8J 73
Silverdale Rd. Ear —9A 64
Silverdale Rd. Tadl —9K 105
Silverdale Rd. Warg —4K 41
Silver Fox Cres. Wdly —6C 64
Silver Glades. Yat —5A 118
Silver Hill. Col T —1J 119
Silver La. Pad C —1A 106
Silver St. Read —6H 63
Silver St. Flats. Read —6H 63 (off Silver St.)
Silverthorne Dri. Cav —7D 38
Silvertrees Dri. M'head —9M 19
Silwood. Brack —1J 113
Silwood Clo. Asc —4N 93
Silwood Rd. Asc —6B 94
Simkin's Clo. Wink R —1E 92
Simmonds Clo. Brack —3J 91
Simmonds St. Read —5G 63
Simmons Clo. Slou —3B 48
Simmons Field. That —7J 81
Simmons Pl. Stai —9F 72
Simmons Rd. Hen T —3C 16
Simms Farm La. Mort —6G 107
Simons Clo. Tile —9K 37
Simon's La. Wokgm —5H 89 (in two parts)
Simons Wlk. Egh —2L 95
Simpson Clo. M'head —6E 20
Sindlesham Rd. Arbor —8D 88
Sine Clo. Farn —9M 119
Singers Clo. Hen T —6D 16
Singers La. Hen T —6D 16
Singret Pl. Cow —5K 25
Sinhurst Rd. Camb —5M 119
Sinkins Ho. Chalv —9E 22
Sipson Clo. W Dray —5N 49
Sipson La. W Dray —5N 49
Sipson Rd. W Dray —2N 49
Sir Henry Peeks Dri. Farn C —1D 22
Sirius Clo. Wokgm —5K 89
Six Acre La. Hung —4F 96
Sixth St. Green —5C 102
Skeffling Clo. Lwr Ear —1D 88
Skerries Ct. Langl —3B 48
Skerrit Way. Pur T —9L 37
Skilman Dri. That —8J 81
Skilton Rd. Tile —1K 61
Skimerdale Way. Ear —9D 64
Skimped Hill La. Brack —4L 91
Skinners Grn. La. Newb —2F 100
Skydmore Path. Slou —4B 22
Skye Clo. Calc —8M 61
Skye Lodge. Slou —9G 22
Skylings. Newb —7N 79
Skyport Dri. Harm —6L 49
Skyway Trading Est. Coln —9G 48
Slaidburn Grn. Brack —9B 92
Slanting Hill. Herm —9E 56
Sloane Clo. Gor —8L 15
Slopes, The. Cav —2K 63
Slough By-Pass. Slou —3F 46
Slough Ind. Est. Slou —7C 22
Slough Rd. Dat —4J 47
Slough Rd. Eton C & Slou —5F 46
Slough Rd. Iver —4D 24
Slough Trading Est. Slou —6B 22
Smallmead Rd. Read —2D 86 (in two parts)
Smewins Rd. White —7H 43
Smitham Bri. Rd. Hung —6J 75
Smithfield Rd. M'head —2K 43
Smith's Hill. Let B —1D 8
Smith's La. Wind —8A 46
Smith Sq. Brack —4A 92
Smiths Wlk. Wokgm —5L 89
Smithy's Grn. W'sham —6N 115
Snape Spur. Slou —7G 22
Snipe La. Bis G —8C 102 (off Willow Rd.)
Snowball Hill. M'head —5M 43
Snowberry Clo. Wokgm —6L 89
Snowden Dri. Tile —6H 61
Snowdon Clo. That —9G 80
Snowdon Clo. Wind —1N 69
Snowdon Rd. Farn —9J 119
Snowdrop Copse. That —7J 81
Snowdrop Gro. Winn —9H 65
Snows Paddock. W'sham —3L 115
Snows Ride. W'sham —5L 115
Sodom La. Ash'd C —9G 35
Soham Clo. Lwr Ear —3B 88
Soho Cres. Wbrn G —3N 5
Soke Rd. Sil —6N 105
Soldiers Rise. Wokgm —3B 112
Solent Ct. Read —6H 63
Solent Rd. Houn —3N 73
Somerford Clo. M'head —6E 20
Somersby Cres. M'head —2B 44
Somerset Clo. Hung —6J 75
Somerset Clo. Wokgm —5J 89
Somerset Wlk. Tile —6J 61 (off Barton Rd.)
Somerset Way. Iver —1G 49
Somerstown Ct. Read —5F 62
Somerton Gdns. Ear —1N 87
Somerton Gro. That —9F 80
Somerville Clo. Wokgm —7J 89
Somerville Cres. Yat —3C 118
Somerville Rd. Eton —4E 46
Sonninge Clo. Col T —1H 119
Sonning La. Son —2C 64
Sonning Meadows. Son —3B 64
Sopwith Clo. Wdly —5F 64
Sorrel Clo. Bfld C —8J 85
Sorrel Clo. Newb —6A 80
Sorrel Clo. Wokgm —3C 90
Sospel Ct. Farn R —3E 22
Southampton Clo. B'water —3G 119
Southampton Rd. H'row A —3M 73
Southampton St. Read —6H 63
South Av. Hen T —6D 16
Southbourne Dri. Bour —4L 5
Southbury La. Rusc —8L 41
South Clo. Slou —8N 21
South Clo. W Dray —2N 49
South Clo. Wokgm —5A 90 (Peach St.)
South Clo. Wokgm —7B 90 (South Dri.)
S. Common Rd. Uxb —1M 25
Southcote Farm La. Read —7D 62
Southcote La. Read —8A 62
Southcote Lodge. Read —8A 62
Southcote Rd. Read —6D 62
South Croft. Egh —9K 71
Southcroft. Slou —5D 22
Southdown Rd. Ben H —8C 80
Southdown Rd. Emm G —8H 39
Southdown Rd. Tadl —9J 105
South Dri. Read —1L 87
South Dri. Son —3B 64
South Dri. Sul'd —4E 84
South Dri. Vir W —9J 95
South Dri. Wokgm —6A 90
Southend. Cold A —5F 80
South End Rd. South —2H 83
Southern Cotts. Stai —2H 73
Southern Ct. Read —5H 63
Southerndene Clo. Tile —2L 61
Southern Hill. Read —7K 63
Southern Perimeter Rd. H'row A —2J 73
Southern Rd. Camb —3N 119
S. Farm La. Bag —8K 115
Southfield Clo. Dor —2M 45
Southfield Gdns. Burn —6L 21
Southfields. Box —9A 54
Southfields. Chvly —4M 55
Southgate Ho. M'head —7C 20
Southglade. Read —3K 87
South Grn. Slou —8G 23
South Groves. Chilt F —1G 74
S. Hill Rd. Brack —8L 91
S. Lake Cres. Wdly —7D 64
Southlands Clo. Wokgm —6B 90
Southlands Rd. Wokgm —7B 90
Southlea Rd. Dat & Old Win —7K 47
S. Lynn Cres. Brack —7M 91
South Mall. Stai —8G 72
S. Meadow. Crowt —7H 113 (in three parts)
S. Meadow La. Eton —5E 46
S. Path. Wind —7E 46
South Pl. Mar —6C 4

South Rd. Crowt —7J **113**
South Rd. Egh —1L **95**
South Rd. M'head —8B **20**
South Rd. W Dray —2N **49**
South Rd. Wokgm —9H **91**
South St. Cav —2H **63**
South St. Read —5H **63**
South St. Stai —9G **72**
South View. Brack —5H **91**
South View. Hung —6K **75**
S. View Av. Cav —2H **63**
Southview Clo. Twy —7K **41**
S. View Gdns. Newb —7M **79**
S. View Pk. Cav —2J **63**
Southview Rd. Mar —3C **4**
Southwark Clo. Yat —3A **118**
Southway. Camb —5M **119**
Southwell Pk. Rd. Camb —4M **119**
Southwick. Bag —9H **115**
Southwick Ct. Brack —8B **92**
Southwold. Brack —1J **113**
Southwold Clo. Lwr Ear —2C **88**
Southwold Spur. Slou —1D **48**
Southwood. Wokgm —7B **90**
Southwood Gdns. Bfld C —8H **85**
Southwood Gdns. Cook —1B **20**
Southwood Rd. Cook —1B **20**
Sovereign Ct. Asc —9D **94**
Sovereign Way. Calc —7K **61**
Sowbury Pk. Chvly —4L **55**
Spackman Clo. That —9G **81**
Spackmans Way. Slou —2E **46**
Span Hill. Son —6A **40**
Sparrowbill. Bright —3C **30**
Sparrow Clo. Wokgm —6K **89**
Sparvell Way. Camb —3N **119**
Speedwell Way. That —7J **81**
Speenhamland Ct. Newb —7L **79**
Speen Hill Clo. Newb —7J **79**
Speen La. Newb —6G **79**
Speen Lodge Ct. Speen —7J **79**
Speen Pl. Speen —7J **79**
Spencer Clo. Pam H —9N **105**
Spencer Clo. Uxb —4K **25**
Spencer Clo. Wokgm —5J **89**
Spencer Gdns. Egh —9M **71**
Spencer Rd. Brack —3K **91**
Spencer Rd. Newb —4H **101**
Spencer Rd. Read —4H **87**
Spencer Rd. Slou —2A **48**
Spencers Clo. M'head —6A **20**
Spencers La. Cook —9J **5**
Spencers Rd. M'head —6A **20**
Spens. M'head —6C **20**
Spenwood Clo. Spen W —9H **87**
Sperling Rd. M'head —5C **20**
Spey Rd. Tile —5A **62**
Spinfield La. Mar —6A **4**
Spinfield La. W. Mar —6A **4**
Spinfield Mt. Mar —6A **4**
Spinfield Pk. Mar —6A **4**
Spinis. Brack —1K **113**
Spinner Grn. Brack —7M **91**
Spinners Wlk. Mar —6A **4**
Spinners Wlk. Wind —7E **46**
Spinney. Slou —9D **22**
Spinney Clo. Emm G —6H **39**
Spinney Clo. W Dray —8M **25**
Spinney La. Wink —5L **69**
Spinney, The. Asc —7A **94**
Spinney, The. Calc —8M **61**
Spinney, The. Wokgm —2L **111**
Spinney, The. Yat —2B **118**
Spinningwheel La. Binf —4G **67**
Spital St. Mar —5B **4**
Spitfire Way. Wdly —5F **64**
Splash, The. Binf —1M **91**
Spode Clo. Tile —4M **61**
Spout La. Stai —1H **73**
Spout La. N. Stai —1J **73**
Spray La. Bright —4A **30**
Spray Rd. Ham —7J **97**
Spray Rd. Hung —7N **97**
Spriggs Clo. That —9G **81**
Springate Field. Slou —1N **47**
Spring Av. Egh —1N **95**
Spring Clo. M'head —4C **20**
Spring Clo. Up Bas —8M **35**
Springcross Av. B'water —6H **119**
Springdale. Ear —1A **88**
Springdale. Wokgm —2K **111**
Springfield. Light —9N **115**
Springfield Clo. Wind —8D **46**
Springfield Ct. Twy —8K **41**
Springfield End. Gor —6L **15**
Springfield La. Newb —2M **101**
Springfield Pk. M'head —4E **44**
Springfield Pk. Twy —8K **41**
Springfield Rd. Ashf —9N **73**
Springfield Rd. Binf —4G **91**
Springfield Rd. Pam H —9N **105**
Springfield Rd. Slou —6C **48**
Springfield Rd. Wind —8D **46**
Spring Gdns. Asc —6L **93**
Spring Gdns. Bour —3L **5**
Spring Gdns. Mar —4C **4**
Spring Gdns. N Asc —2H **93**
Spring Gdns. Spen W —9H **87**
Spring Gro. Read —6H **63**
Spring Hill. M'head —2B **44**
Springhill Ct. Brack —6M **91**
Springhill Rd. Gor —6L **15**
Spring La. Cold A —3F **80**
Spring La. Cook D —9F **4**
Spring La. Farn R —1D **22**
Spring La. Mort —3H **107**
Spring La. Rise —7G **108**
Spring La. Slou —9B **22**
Spring La. Son —7A **40**
Springmead Ct. Owl —9J **113**
Spring Meadow. Brack —3A **92**
Spring Meadows. Gt Shef —9G **29**
Spring Rise. Egh —1N **95**
Spring Ter. Bin H —5N **39**
Spring Ter. Read —7H **63**
Spring Wlk. Warg —3J **41**
Spring Wood La. Bfld C —9H **85**
Spring Woods. Sand —9G **112**
Spring Woods. Vir W —6K **95**
Spruce Ct. Slou —2H **47**
Spruce Rd. Wdly —6F **64**
Spurcroft Rd. That —8G **81**
Spur, The. Slou —6N **21**
Spur, The. Warg —2K **41**
Square, The. Bag —7H **115**
Square, The. Bis G —7D **102**
Square, The. Brack —6B **92**
Square, The. Camb —3N **119**
Square, The. Ear —3N **87**
Square, The. Light —9M **115**
Square, The. Spen W —9H **87**
Square, The. W Dray —7J **49**
Squirrel Clo. Sand —1F **118**
Squirrel Dri. Wink —5L **69**
Squirrel La. Wink —5L **69**
Squirrel Rise. Mar —1B **4**
Squirrels Clo. Uxb —1N **25**
Squirrels Drey. Crowt —5D **112**
Squirrels Way. Ear —1A **88**
Stable Clo. Bfld C —8H **85**
Stable Ct. Newb —5M **79**
Stable Croft. Bag —8G **115**
Stables Ct. Mar —6A **4**
Stable View. Yat —2B **118**
Staddlestone Clo. Tile —2K **61**
Stadium Way. Tile —3B **62**
Stadium Way Ind. Est. Read —3B **62**
Staff College. Camb —3N **119**
Staff College Rd. Camb —3L **119**
Stafferton Way. M'head —8C **20**
Stafford Av. Slou —5E **22**
Stafford Clo. Tap —7L **21**
Stafford Clo. Wdly —4E **64**
Staffordshire Clo. Read —4N **61**
Staffordshire Croft. Warf —1C **92**
Stag Hill. Chilt F —2G **74**
Stainash Cres. Stai —9J **73**
Stainash Pde. Stai —9J 73
(off Kingston Rd.)
Stainby Clo. W Dray —2M **49**
Staines Bri. Stai —9F **72**
Staines By-Pass. Stai —6D **72**
Staines Central Trading Est. Stai —8F **72**
Staines Rd. Wray —4N **71**
Stamford Rd. M'head —8N **19**
Stanbrook Clo. South —1J **83**
Stanfield. Tadl —9K **105**
Stanham Rd. Tile —4N **61**
Stanhope Heath. Stai —3K **73**
Stanhope Rd. Camb —5K **119**
Stanhope Rd. Read —9K **63**
Stanhope Rd. Slou —7N **21**
Stanhope Way. Stai —3K **73**
Stanlake La. Rusc —9L **41**
Stanley Clo. Mar —4D **4**
Stanley Clo. Uxb —2L **25**
Stanley Cotts. Slou —9H **23**
Stanley Grn. Langl —3A **48**
Stanley Gro. Read —4E **62**
Stanley Rd. Ashf —9M **73**
Stanley Rd. Newb —9M **79**
Stanley Rd. Wokgm —5C **90**
Stanley St. Read —4F **62**
Stanley Wlk. Brack —4N **91**
Stanmore Clo. Asc —6K **93**
Stanmore Gdns. Mort C —5G **107**
Stanmore Rd. Beed —3M **31**
Stanmore Rd. E Ils —7B **12**
Stanshawe Rd. Read —4G **62**
Stanstead Rd. Houn —3N **73**
Stanton Clo. Ear —8B **64**
Stanton Way. Slou —3N **47**
Stanway Cotts. Read —6M **63**
Stanwell Clo. Stai —3L **73**
Stanwell Gdns. Stai —3L **73**
Stanwell Moor Rd. Stai & W Dray —7H **73**
Stanwell New Rd. Stai —7H **73**
Stanwell Rd. Ashf —8M **73**
Stanwell Rd. Hort —9B **48**
Stapleford Rd. Read —8C **62**
Staplehurst. Brack —9J **91**
Stapleton Clo. Mar —3D **4**
Stapleton Clo. Newb —4G **101**
Star La. Know H —8A **18**
Star La. Read —5H **63**
Starling Clo. Wokgm —6L **89**
Starlings Dri. Tile —7J **61**
Starmead Dri. Wokgm —6B **90**
Star Post Rd. Camb —9B **114**
Star Rd. Cav —2J **63**
Starting Gates. Newb —1N **101**
Startins La. Cook —7G **4**
Starwood Ct. Slou —2L **47**
Statham Ct. Brack —3J **91**
Station App. Ashf —8N **73**
Station App. B'water —5J **119**
Station App. Frim —9N **119**
Station App. M'head —8C **20**
Station App. Mar —5C **4**
Station App. Read —4G **63**
Station App. Vir W —6M **95**
Station App. W Dray —9M **25**
Station App. Wind —7F **46**
Station Cres. Ashf —7L **73**
Station Hill. Asc —5K **93**
Station Hill. Cook —8K **5**
Station Hill. Hamp N —7J **33**
Station Hill. Read —4G **63**
Station Ind. Est. Wokgm —5N **89**
Station Pde. Ashf —8N **73**
Station Pde. Cook —8K **5**
Station Pde. S'dale —9C **94**
Station Pde. Vir W —6M **95**
Station Path. Stai —8G **73**
Station Rise. Mar —5C **4**
Station Rd. Ashf —8N **73**
Station Rd. Bag —6H **115**
Station Rd. Bour —4L **5**
Station Rd. Brack —4M **91**
Station Rd. Cipp —7A **22**
Station Rd. Cook —8K **5**
Station Rd. Ear —8B **64**
Station Rd. E Gar —7B **28**
Station Rd. E Wood —8D **100**
Station Rd. Egh —9B **72**
Station Rd. Frim —8N **119**
Station Rd. Gor —8K **15**
Station Rd. Gt Shef —1F **52**
Station Rd. Hen T —5D **16**
Station Rd. Hung —6K **75**
Station Rd. Kint —9G **76**
Station Rd. Lamb —3H **27**
Station Rd. Langl —2B **48**
Station Rd. Lwr S —1F **40**
Station Rd. Mar —6C **4**
Station Rd. Midg —9E **82**
Station Rd. Mort —5M **107**
Station Rd. Newb —9L **79**
Station Rd. Pang —7D **36**
Station Rd. Read —4G **63**
Station Rd. Speen —6H **79**
Station Rd. S'dale —8C **94**
Station Rd. Tap —7J **21**
Station Rd. That —8G **81**
Station Rd. Thea —9F **60**
Station Rd. Twy —9J **41**
Station Rd. Uxb —5K **25**
Station Rd. Warg —4H **41**
Station Rd. W Dray —1M **49**
Station Rd. Wokgm —5N **89**
Station Rd. Wray —3A **72**
Station Rd. N. Egh —9B **72**
Staunton Rd. Slou —6F **22**
Staverton Clo. Brack —2M **91**
Staverton Clo. Wokgm —5D **90**
Staverton Rd. Read —9J **63**
Stayne End. Vir W —6J **95**
Steeple Wlk. Lwr Ear —3M **87**
Steerforth Copse. Owl —8J **113**
Stephanie Chase Ct. Wokgm —4B **90**
Stephen Clo. Twy —1L **65**
Stephens Clo. Mort C —4G **106**
Stephens Firs. Mort —4F **106**
Stephenson Ct. Slou —1H **47**
Stephenson Dri. Wind —6D **46**
Stephenson Rd. Arbor —3F **110**
Stephen's Rd. Mort C —4G **107**
Stephens Rd. Tadl —9L **105**
Sterling Cen. Brack —4A **92**
Sterling Way. Read —3A **62**
Stevens Hill. Yat —4C **118**
Stevenson Dri. Binf —9G **66**
Stewart Av. Slou —6H **23**
Stewart Clo. M'head —7G **44**
Stile Rd. Slou —2M **47**
Stilwell Clo. Yat —3C **118**
Stirling Clo. Cav —7K **39**
Stirling Clo. Uxb —4K **25**
Stirling Clo. Wind —8N **45**
Stirling Gro. M'head —6L **19**
Stirling Rd. Houn —3N **73**
Stirling Rd. Slou —6C **22**
Stirling Way. That —7F **80**
Stockbridge Way. Yat —5B **118**
Stockbury Clo. Ear —2A **88**
Stockdales Rd. Eton W —3B **46**
Stockley Rd. Uxb & W Dray —7N **25**
Stockton Rd. Read —2H **87**
Stockwells. Tap —5G **20**
Stoke Cotts. Slou —9H **23**
Stoke Ct. Read —2H **87**
Stoke Ct. Dri. Stoke P —2G **23**
Stokeford Clo. Brack —7C **92**
Stoke Gdns. Slou —9G **23**
Stoke Grn. Stoke P —5J **23**
Stoke Ho. Tadl —9K **105**
Stoke Pk. Av. Farn R —4E **22**
Stoke Poges La. Slou —9G **22**
Stoke Rd. Slou —9H **23**
Stokesay. Slou —8H **23**
Stokes View. Pang —8D **36**
Stompits Rd. Holyp —5E **44**
Stomp Rd. Burn —6L **21**
Stonea Clo. Lwr Ear —3B **88**
Stonebridge Field. Eton —4D **46**
Stone Clo. W Dray —9N **25**
Stonecroft Av. Iver —7F **24**
Stonefield Pk. M'head —7N **19**
Stoneham Clo. Tile —6A **62**
Stonehaven Dri. Wdly —6F **64**
Stonehill Rd. Light —9K **115**
Stone Ho. La. Cook —6G **5**
Stone St. Read —3B **62**
Stoney Clo. Yat —5B **118**
Stoney Drove. Link —9A **116**
Stoneyfield. Been —5J **83**
Stoneylands Ct. Egh —9A **72**
Stoneylands Rd. Egh —9A **72**
Stoney La. Farn C —2C **22**
Stoney La. Newb & That —6A **80**
Stoney La. That —8H **81**
Stoney Meade. Slou —9D **22**
Stoney Rd. Brack —3L **91**
Stoney Ware. Mar —7C **4**
Stoney Ware Clo. Mar —7B **4**
Stony La. Wood M —8J **27**
Stour Clo. Slou —2D **46**
Stour Clo. Tile —4A **62**
Stovell Rd. Wind —6D **46**
Stowe Clo. Lwr Ear —1C **88**
Stowe Rd. Slou —8A **22**
Stowmarket Clo. Lwr Ear —1C **88**
Straight La. Hung —1L **51**
Straight Mile, The. Shur R & Wokgm —3B **66**
Straight Rd. Old Win —2J **71**
Strande Pk. Cook —1C **20**
Strande View Wlk. Cook —1C **20**
Strand La. Cook —1C **20**
Strand Way. Lwr Ear —2A **88**
Stranraer Rd. Houn —3M **73**
Stratfield. Brack —1J **113**
Stratfield Ct. M'head —6E **20**
Stratfield Rd. Slou —1J **47**
Stratford Av. Uxb —3N **25**
Stratford Clo. Slou —5N **21**
Stratford Dri. Wbrn G —3N **5**
Stratford Gdns. M'head —1N **43**
Stratford Way. Tile —6H **61**
Strathdean Pl. Read —4F **62**
Strathmore Ct. Camb —3N **119**
Strathmore Dri. Charv —9F **40**
Strathy Clo. Read —4B **62**
Stratton Gdns. Read —2J **87**
Strawberry Hill. Newb —7K **79**
Strawberry Hill. Warf —1B **92**
Streatley Hill. Streat —8G **15**
Street, The. Aldm —3J **105**
Street, The. Eng —7C **60**
Street, The. Mort —4H **107**
Street, The. Shur R —2E **66**
Street, The. S Sto —2K **15**
Street, The. Swal —4J **109**
Street, The. Tid —2E **60**
Street, The. Wal L —7D **42**
Stretton Clo. South —2J **83**
Strode's Cres. Stai —9K **73**
Strode St. Egh —8B **72**
Stroma Ct. Cipp —8N **21**
Strongrove Hill. Hung —5H **75**
Strood La. Asc —1M **93**
Stroud Clo. Wind —9N **45**
Stroud Farm Rd. Holyp —5E **44**
Strouds, The. Been —5H **83**
Stuart Clo. Emm G —8H **39**
Stuart Clo. Wind —8B **46**
Stuart Rd. Newb —4H **101**
Stuart Way. Vir W —6J **95**
Stuart Way. Wind —8A **46**
Stubbles. Ash'd —8E **34**
Stubbles La. Cook —9F **4**
Stubbs Folly. Col T —2H **119**
Stubbs Hill. Binf —8J **67**
Studland Clo. Read —4J **87**
Studland Ind. Est. Bal H —6A **100**
Sturbridge Clo. Lwr Ear —2B **88**
Sturges Rd. Wokgm —6A **90**
Sturt Grn. M'head —5B **44**
Suck's La. Ash'd C —2E **58**
Suffolk Clo. Bag —8H **115**
Suffolk Clo. Slou —7A **22**
Suffolk Clo. Wokgm —5J **89**
Suffolk Rd. M'head —1A **44**
Suffolk Rd. Read —5D **62**
Sulham Hill. Sul —3F **60**
Sulham La. Sul —1F **60**
Sulhamstead Hill. Sul'd —5D **84**
Sulhamstead Rd. Sul'd —7E **84**
Sulhamstead Rd. Uft N —7H **85**
Sulham Wlk. Read —8B **62**
Sullivan Rd. Camb —4L **119**
Sumburgh Way. Slou —6G **22**
Summerfield Clo. Wokgm —2L **89**
Summerfield Rise. Gor —7M **15**
Summerhouse La. W Dray —5L **49**
Summerlea. Slou —9D **22**
Summerleaze Rd. M'head —5D **20**
Summers Rd. Burn —4M **21**
Summit Clo. Wokgm —3L **111**
Sunbury Rd. Eton —5F **46**
Sun Clo. Eton —5F **46**
Sunderland Clo. Wdly —4G **65**
Sunderland Ct. Stanw —3M **73**
Sunderland Pl. That —7F **80**
Sunderland Rd. Houn —3M **73**
Sunderland Rd. M'head —6M **19**
Sundew Clo. Light —9N **115**
Sundew Clo. Wokgm —3C **90**
Sundon Cres. Vir W —7K **95**
Sun Gdns. Bfld C —9H **85**
Sun Hill Cotts. Midg —9H **83**
Sun La. M'head —7B **20**
Sun La. Rise —8H **109**
Sunning Av. Asc —9A **94**
Sunninghill Clo. Asc —6N **93**
Sunninghill Ct. Asc —6N **93**
Sunninghill Rd. Asc —3B **94**
Sunninghill Rd. S'hill —7N **93**
Sunninghill Rd. W'sham —3K **115**
Sunninghill Rd. Wind & Asc —9N **69**
Sunnybank. Mar —3A **4**
Sun Pas. Wind —7F **46**
Sunray Av. W Dray —1L **49**
Sun Ray Est. Sand —1E **118**
Sun St. Read —5K **63**
Surbiton Rd. Camb —9D **114**
Surley Row. Cav —7G **39**
(in three parts)
Surly Hall Wlk. Wind —7B **46**
Surrey Av. Camb —5L **119**
Surrey Av. Slou —6E **22**
Surrey Ct. Warf —2C **92**
Surrey Rd. Read —8H **63**
Surridge Ct. Bag —8H **115**
Sussex Clo. Slou —1K **47**
Sussex Gdns. Wdly —5D **64**
Sussex Keep. Slou —1K **47**
Sussex La. Spen W —9J **87**
Sussex Pl. Slou —1J **47**
Sutcliffe Av. Ear —8C **64**
Sutherland Chase. Asc —4G **93**
Sutherland Gro. Calc —8M **61**
Sutherlands. Newb —3J **101**
Sutherlands Av. Read —7J **63**
Sutton Av. Slou —1L **47**
Sutton Clo. Cook —8M **5**
Sutton Clo. M'head —8N **19**
Sutton La. Coln —5C **48**
Sutton Pl. Slou —5C **48**
Sutton Rd. Camb —9D **114**
Sutton Rd. Cook —8M **5**
Sutton Rd. Speen —6H **79**
Suttons Bus. Pk. Read —4M **63**
Suttons Pk. Av. Read —4L **63**
Sutton Wlk. Read —7J **63**
Swabey Rd. Slou —3B **48**
Swains Clo. W Dray —1M **49**
Swainstone Rd. Read —7H **63**
Swaledale. Brack —7L **91**
Swallow Clo. Stai —8G **72**
Swallow Clo. Tile —6K **61**
Swallow Clo. Yat —3A **118**
Swallowdale. Iver —4E **24**
Swallowfield. Egh —1K **95**
Swallowfield Dri. Read —5H **87**
Swallowfield Gdns. Thea —8F **60**
Swallowfield Rd. Arbor —9B **88**
Swallowfield Rd. Far H & Arbor —3N **109**
Swallowfield St. Swal —3J **109**
Swallow St. Iver —4E **24**
Swallow Way. Wokgm —6K **89**
Swanbrook Ct. M'head —7D **20**
Swancote Grn. Brack —7M **91**
Swan Ct. Newb —8K **79**
Swangate. Hung —4K **75**
Swanholm Gdns. Calc —8N **61**
Swan La. Sand —2F **118**
Swanmore Clo. Lwr Ear —2D **88**
Swann Ct. Chalv —2G **46**
Swan Pl. Read —5G **63**
Swan Rd. Iver —7G **25**
Swan Rd. W Dray —1L **49**
Swans Ct. Twy —1K **65**
Swansdown Wlk. That —8E **80**
Swansea Cotts. Tile —3M **61**
Swansea Rd. Read —3G **62**
Swansea Ter. Tile —3M **61**
Swanston Field. Whit T —6E **36**
Swan Ter. Wind —6D **46**
Sweeps La. Egh —9A **72**
Sweetbriar. Crowt —3E **112**
Sweet Briar Dri. Calc —8K **61**
Sweetcroft La. Uxb —1N **25**
Sweetwell Rd. Brack —4J **91**
Sweetzer's Piece. Mort —4F **106**
Swepstone Clo. Lwr Ear —1B **88**
Swift Clo. Wokgm —6K **89**
Swift La. Bag —7J **115**
Swinbrook Clo. Tile —1L **61**
Swing Brook Clo. Tile —1L **61**
Swinley Rd. Asc —5F **92**
Swinley Rd. Bag —4G **114**
Swiss Cotts. Clo. Tile —4K **61**
Swiss Farm Caravan Site. Hen T —2C **16**
Switchback Clo. M'head —4A **20**
Switchback Rd. N. M'head —2B **20**
Switchback Rd. S. M'head —4A **20**
Sycamore Clo. Bfld —6J **85**
Sycamore Clo. M'head —1N **43**
Sycamore Clo. Sand —1F **118**
Sycamore Clo. W Dray —8N **25**
Sycamore Clo. Wdly —7B **64**
Sycamore Cotts. Camb —6M 119
(off Frimley Rd.)
Sycamore Ct. Pang —7D **36**
Sycamore Dri. Mar —2B **4**
Sycamore Dri. Twy —8J **41**
Sycamore Rise. Brack —5A **92**
Sycamore Rise. Newb —6N **79**
Sycamore Rd. Read —1L **87**
Sycamores, The. B'water —4F **118**
Sycamore Wlk. Egh —1K **95**
Sycamore Wlk. G Grn —7N **23**
Sydings, The. Speen —6H **79**
Sydney Clo. Crowt —3G **112**
Sydney Clo. That —8H **81**
Sydney Gro. Slou —7E **22**
Sykecluan. Iver —1F **48**
Sykeings. Iver —2F **48**
Sykes Dri. Stai —9J **73**
Sykes Rd. Slou —7D **22**
Sylvana Clo. Uxb —2N **25**
Sylvan Ridge. Sand —9E **112**
Sylvanus. Brack —9K **91**
Sylvan Wlk. Read —8C **62**
Sylverns Ct. Warf —2A **92**
Sylvester Clo. Speen —6J **79**
Sylvester Rd. M'head —4B **20**
Symondson M. Binf —8G **66**
Sympson Rd. Tadl —9M **105**

Tachbrook Rd. Uxb —3K **25**
Tachbrook Rd. W Dray —9M **25**
Tadcroft Wlk. Calc —9M **61**
Tadham Pl. That —9F **80**
Tadley Comn. Rd. Tadl —9L **105**
Taff Way. Tile —5A **62**
Tagg La. D'den —5M **39**
Tag La. Hare H —4M **41**
Talbot Av. Slou —1A **48**
Talbot Clo. Cav —2K **63**
Talbot Clo. Newb —6J **79**
Talbot Ct. Read —5G **62**
Talbot Pl. Bag —7H **115**
Talbot Pl. Dat —7L **47**
Talbot Rd. Ashf —9M **73**
Talbots Dri. M'head —8M **19**
Talbot Way. Tile —1K **61**
Talfourd Av. Read —7N **63**
Talisman Clo. Crowt —5B **112**
Tallis La. Read —8D **62**
Tall Trees. Coln —7E **48**
Tamar Gdns. Read —9J **63**
Tamarind Way. Ear —2M **87**
Tamarisk Av. Read —2L **87**
Tamarisk Ct. That —7J **81**
Tamarisk Rise. Wokgm —4A **90**
Tamarisk Way. Slou —1D **46**
Tamar Way. Slou —4C **48**
Tamar Way. Wokgm —5K **89**
Tamworth. Brack —9A **92**
Tamworth Clo. Lwr Ear —2B **88**
Tanfield. Read —9J **63**
Tangier Ct. Eton —5F **46**
Tangier La. Eton —5F **46**
Tanglewood. Wokgm —3M **111**
Tangley Dri. Wokgm —7N **89**
Tanhouse La. Wokgm —6M **89**
Tank Rd. Camb —4K **119**
Tanners Clo. Bfld C —9G **85**
Tanners La. Chalk —5F **38**
Tanners Yd. Bag —7H **115**
Tape La. Hurst —4L **65**
Tapling Trading Est. W Dray —8L **25**
Taplow Comn. Rd. Burn —1J **21**
Taplow Rd. Tap —7K **21**
Tarbat Clo. Owl —1H **119**
Tarbay La. Oak G —9L **45**
Target Hill. Warf —2A **92**
Targett Ct. Winn —1G **89**
Tarlton Ct. Tile —6N **61**
Tarmac Way. W Dray —6J **49**
Tarnbrook Way. Brack —9B **92**
Tarn La. Newb —2K **101**
Tarragon Clo. Ear —2M **87**
Tarragon Way. Bfld C —8J **85**
Tarrant's Hill. Hung —6K **75**
Tatchbrook Clo. M'head —6D **20**
Tattersall Clo. Wokgm —6C **90**
Tavistock Clo. M'head —6L **19**
Tavistock Rd. Read —9H **63**
Tavistock Rd. W Dray —9L **25**
Tawfield. Brack —9J **91**
Tawny Croft. Owl —1J **119**
Taylor Ct. Read —5E **62**
Taylor's Bushes Ride. Wind —6M **69**
Taylor's Clo. Mar —5D **4**
Taylors Ct. M'head —6M **19**
Taylor's La. Rise —6H **109**
Taynton Wlk. Read —7H **63**
Tay Rd. Tile —4A **62**

Tazewell Ct. Read —6F 62
Tealgate. Hung —4K 75
Tebbit Clo. Brack —4A 92
Technology Cen. Thea —1F 84
Tedder Clo. Uxb —1N 25
Teesdale Rd. Slou —6B 22
Tekels Av. Camb —4N 119
Telford Av. Crowt —3G 112
Telford Cres. Wdly —3E 64
Telford Dri. Slou —1C 46
Telston Clo. Bour —2L 5
Templar Clo. Sand —1E 118
Temple La. Bish —1G 18
Temple M. Wdly —5E 64
Temple Mill Island. Mar —1F 18
Temple Pk. Hur —3D 18
Temple Pk. Uxb —4N 25
Temple Pl. Read —6G 63
Temple Rd. Wind —8E 46
Templeton Gdns. Read —2J 87
Temple Way. Brack —2J 91
Tenaplas Dri. Up Bas —8H 35
Tenby Av. Cav —8K 39
Tenby Dri. Asc —7N 93
Tennyson Rd. Ashf —9M 73
Tennyson Rd. That —7F 80
Tennyson Rd. Wdly —8D 64
Tennyson Way. Slou —5A 22
Tern Clo. Tile —5A 62
Terrace Rd. N. Binf —9G 66
Terrace Rd. S. Binf —1G 90
Terrace, The. Asc —7N 93
Terrace, The. Bray —2F 44
Terrace, The. Crowt —5J 113
Terrace, The. Sand —4L 119
Terrace, The. Wokgm —5N 89
Terrington Hill. Mar —5A 4
Terry Pl. Cow —6K 25
Terry's La. Cook —6J 5
Tessa Rd. Read —3F 62
Test Clo. Tile —4A 62
Test Way. Link —7B 116
Testwood Rd. Wind —7N 45
Tetbury Ct. Read —5E 62
Teviot Rd. Tile —5M 61
Textile Est. Yat —2B 118
Thames Av. Pang —7E 36
Thames Av. Read —3G 63
Thames Av. Wind —6F 46
Thames Bank S. Whit T —6E 36
Thamesbourne M. Bour —4L 5
(off Station Rd.)
Thames Clo. Bour —3L 5
Thames Cres. M'head —4E 20
Thames Dri. Charv —7E 40
Thamesfield Gdns. Mar —6C 4
Thames Ind. Est. Mar —5D 4
Thames Mead. Wind —7A 46
Thames Reach. Pur T —9L 37
Thames Rd. Gor —8K 15
Thames Rd. Slou —3B 48
Thames Rd. That —6E 80
Thames Rd. Wind —6M 45
Thames Side. Hen T —4D 16
(in two parts)
Thames Side. Read —3G 63
(in two parts)
Thames Side. Wind —6F 46
Thames Side Promenade. Read —2F 62
Thames St. Son —9C 40
Thames St. Stai —9G 72
Thames St. Wind —7F 46
Thames Ter. Son —9C 40
Thames Valley Bus. Pk. Cav —3N 63
Thames Valley Pk. Dri. Cav —4M 63
Thanington Way. Lwr Ear —1A 88
Thanksgiving La. Bin H —3M 39
Thatcher Clo. W Dray —1M 49
Thatchers Dri. M'head —9L 19
Theal Clo. Col T —1H 119
Theale Commercial Est. Thea —9G 60
Theale Rd. Bfld —4J 85
Theobald Dri. Tile —9L 37
Thetford M. Cav —7K 39
Thetford Rd. Ashf —8M 73
Thibet Rd. Sand —1G 118
Thicket Gro. M'head —7K 19
Thicket Rd. Tile —4M 61
Thicket, The. W Dray —7M 25
Third Cres. Slou —6E 22
Third St. Green —5C 102
Thirkleby Clo. Slou —9E 22
Thirlmere Av. Slou —6M 21
Thirlmere Av. Tile —2N 61
Thirtover. Cold A —2E 80
Thistledown. Tile —3K 61
Thistleton Way. Lwr Ear —1D 88
Thomas Dri. Warf —2B 92
Thomas La. Wokgm —2K 111
Thomas Rd. Wbrn G —3N 5
Thompkins La. Farn R —1B 22
Thompson Clo. Herm —6C 56
Thompson Clo. Slou —3A 48
Thompson Dri. That —9H 81
Thompson Rd. Uxb —2M 25
Thomson Wlk. Calc —8M 61
Thorburn Chase. Col T —3J 119
Thornbank Clo. Stai —2H 73
Thornbers Way. Charv —8G 40
Thornbridge Rd. Iver —2D 24
Thornbridge Rd. Read —3H 87
Thornbury Clo. Crowt —5F 112
Thornbury Grn. Twy —8J 41
Thorncroft. Egh —2L 95
Thorndike. Slou —6C 22
Thorndown La. W'sham —7N 115
Thorn Dri. G Grn —7N 23
Thorne Clo. Crowt —3E 112
Thorney Clo. Lwr Ear —1D 88
Thorney La. N. Iver —7G 25
Thorney La. S. Iver —1G 49
Thorney Mill Rd. Iver & W Dray —2H 49
Thornfield. Hdly —7G 103
Thornfield Grn. B'water —6K 119
Thornford Rd. Crook C —6E 102
Thornford Rd. Hdly —8G 103
Thornhill. Brack —6B 92
Thorn La. Read —5H 63
Thorn St. Read —5G 62
Thornton Av. W Dray —2N 49
Thornton Clo. W Dray —2N 49
Thornton M. Read —4D 62
Thornton Rd. Read —4C 62
Thorn Wlk. Read —4F 62
(off Weldale St.)
Thorp Clo. Binf —9G 67
Thorpe Clo. Wokgm —8M 89
Thorpe Lea Rd. Egh —9D 72
Thorpe Rd. Stai —9E 72
Thrale M. Read —4B 62
Three Acre Rd. Newb —2K 101
Three Firs Way. Bfld C —1G 106
Three Gables La. Streat —7J 15
Threepost La. Lamb —2H 27
(off Big La.)
Threshfield. Brack —7L 91
Thrift La. M'head —3N 43
(in two parts)
Thrush Clo. Bfld C —8J 85
Thurlby Way. M'head —2A 44
Thurlestone Gdns. Read —1J 87
Thurnscoe Clo. Lwr Ear —3M 87
Thurso Clo. Tile —4A 62
Thurston Rd. Slou —7G 22
Thyme Clo. Ear —2M 87
Tichborne Clo. B'water —4H 119
Tickenor Dri. Wokgm —3L 111
Tickhill Clo. Lwr Ear —4M 87
Tickleback Row. Warf —6M 67
Ticklecorner La. Mort —8K 107
Tidmarsh La. Tid —2A 60
Tidmarsh Rd. Pang —1E 60
Tidmarsh St. Read —3B 62
Tidwells Lea. Warf —3B 92
Tierney Ct. Mar —6C 4
Tiffany Clo. Wokgm —5J 89
Tiger Clo. Wdly —5G 64
Tigerseye Clo. Wokgm —4J 89
Tilbury Clo. Cav —1J 63
Tilebarn Clo. Hen T —5B 16
Tilebarn La. Hen T —5B 16
Tile Barn Row. Wool H —9C 100
Tilecotes Clo. Mar —5B 4
Tilehurst La. Binf —9G 67
Tilehurst Rd. Read —6B 62
Tilling Clo. Tile —2J 61
Tillington Way. That —5F 80
Tillys La. Stai —8G 72
Tilney Way. Lwr Ear —3M 87
Tilstone Av. Eton W —4A 46
Tilstone Clo. Eton W —4A 46
Timbers Wlk. M'head —9M 19
Timline Grn. Brack —4C 92
Timsway. Stai —9G 72
Tindal Clo. Yat —3B 118
Tinkers La. S'dale —8D 94
Tinkers La. Wind —8N 45
Tinsey Clo. Egh —9B 72
Tinsley Clo. Lwr Ear —3M 87
Tintagel Rd. Wokgm —2N 111
Tintern Clo. Slou —2E 46
Tintern Cres. Read —7F 62
Tippett Rise. Read —7H 63
Tippings La. Wdly —3F 64
Tippits Mead. Brack —3H 91
Tippitts Mead. Brack —3J 91
Tiree Ho. Slou —5D 22
Titcombe Way. Kint —9F 76
Tite Hill. Egh —9M 71
Tithe Barn Dri. M'head —4G 45
(in two parts)
Tithebarn Gro. Calc —8N 61
Tithe Clo. M'head —4F 44
Tithe Ct. Slou —3B 48
Tithe La. Wray —3B 72
Tithe Meadows. Vir W —8L 95
Titness Pk. S'hill —5C 94
Tiverton Clo. Wdly —3D 64
Tiwell Clo. Lwr Ear —1D 88
Toad La. B'water —5J 119
Tockington Ct. Yat —3B 118
Tockley Rd. Burn —4L 21
Tofrek Ter. Read —5C 62
Tokersgreen La. Kid E —6D 38
Tokers Grn. Rd. Tok G —4D 38
Toll Gdns. Brack —5C 92
Tollgate. M'head —8L 19
Tolpuddle Way. Yat —4D 118
Tomlin Rd. Slou —5A 22
Tomlinson Dri. Wokgm —3M 111
Topaz Clo. Slou —9D 22
Topaz Clo. Wokgm —4K 89
Top Common. Warf —2A 92
Tope Cres. Arbor —3E 110
Tope Rd. Arbor —2E 110
Topping La. Uxb —4L 25
Torcross Gro. Calc —8J 61
Torin Ct. Egh —9L 71
Torquay Spur. Slou —4D 22
Torridge Rd. Slou —5C 48
Torrington Rd. Read —1J 87
Toseland Way. Lwr Ear —9D 64
Totnes Rd. Read —1J 87
Tottenham Wlk. Owl —9H 113
Totterdown. Bfld C —9G 85
Touchen End Rd. M'head —7A 44
Toutley Clo. Wokgm —2K 89
Toutley Rd. Wokgm —1L 89
Tower Clo. Cav —5J 39
Towerhill. Chad —5M 29
Tower Ho. Chalv —2G 46
Tower Ho. Iver —7F 24
Tower Ride. Wind —7A 70
Towers Dri. Crowt —6F 112
Town Farm Way. Stanw —4L 73
Town La. Stai —3L 73
(in two parts)
Town La. Wbrn G —3N 5
Town Mills. Newb —8K 79
Town Pl. Read —5K 63
Townsend Clo. Brack —7B 92
Townsend Rd. Aldw —1A 34
Townsend Rd. Ashf —9M 73
Townsend Rd. Streat —7J 15
Town Sq. Brack —4N 91
Tozer Wlk. Wind —9N 45
Trafalgar Clo. Wokgm —5K 89
Trafalgar Ct. Read —6D 62
Trafalgar Ho. Read —3F 62
Trafalgar Way. Camb —5K 119
Trafford Rd. Frim —9N 119
Trafford Rd. Read —3E 62
Travic Rd. Slou —4B 22
Travis Ct. Farn R —4D 22
Travis La. Sand —2G 118
Treacher Ct. Twy —8K 41
Tredegar Rd. Cav —8F 38
Tree Clo. Tile —4L 61
Treeside Clo. W Dray —3L 49
Treesmill Dri. M'head —2M 43
Trees Rd. Bour —4M 5
Trefoil Clo. Wokgm —4C 90
Trefoil Drove. That —7J 81
Treforgan. Cav —8F 38
Trelawney Av. Slou —2M 47
Trelawney Dri. Tile —3J 61
Trelleck Rd. Read —7F 62
Trenchard Rd. Holyp —5E 44
Trenches La. Slou —8B 24
Trent Clo. Wokgm —4K 89
Trent Cres. That —6E 80
Trenthams Clo. Pur T —8J 37
Trent Rd. Slou —5C 48
Trevelyan. Brack —9J 91
Trewarden Av. Iver —3E 24
Treyarnon Ct. Read —6L 63
Triangle, The. Tile —4L 61
Triangle, The. Up Bas —8K 35
Trident Ind. Est. Coln —9F 48
Trindledown. Brack —1L 91
Tring Rd. Tile —1K 61
Trinity. Owl —8J 113
Trinity Av. Mar —4B 4
Trinity Clo. Hen T —5C 16
Trinity Clo. Stai —3K 73
Trinity Ct. Wokgm —4L 89
Trinity Cres. Asc —7C 94
Trinity Pl. Read —5F 62
Trinity Pl. Wind —8E 46
Trinity Rd. Mar —5B 4
Triptree Clo. Lwr Ear —3M 87
Troon Ct. Brack —8J 91
Troon Ct. Read —5K 63
Troon Ct. S'hill —7M 93
Trotsworth Av. Vir W —6N 95
Trotsworth Ct. Vir W —6M 95
Trotwood Clo. Owl —8J 113
Troutbeck Clo. Slou —8H 23
Troutbeck Clo. Twy —7J 41
Trout Clo. Mar —7A 4
Trout La. Uxb —4J 25
Trout Rd. W Dray —9L 25
Trout Wlk. Newb —7N 79
Trowe's La. B Hill —5C 108
Trowe's La. Swal —4J 109
Trumbull Rd. Brack —2L 91
Trumper Way. Uxb —1K 25
Trumpsgreen Av. Vir W —8M 95
Trumpsgreen Clo. Vir W —7N 95
Trumpsgreen Rd. Vir W —9L 95
Trumps Mill La. Vir W —8N 95
Truro Clo. M'head —7L 19
Truss Hill Rd. Asc —7M 93
Trust Corner. Hen T —6D 16
Trusthorpe Clo. Lwr Ear —1D 88
Tubbs Farm Clo. Lamb —3H 27
Tubwell Rd. Stoke P —2K 23
Tudor Clo. Ashf —8M 73
Tudor Clo. Wokgm —6D 90
Tudor Ct. M'head —4F 20
Tudor Ct. Stanw —3M 73
Tudor Ct. Tadl —9K 105
Tudor Dri. Yat —5B 118
Tudor Gdns. Slou —7M 21
Tudor Ho. Brack —7M 91
Tudor La. Old Win —4L 71
Tudor Rd. Newb —1L 101
Tudor Rd. Read —4G 62
Tudor Way. Uxb —1N 25
Tudor Way. Wind —7A 46
Tuns Hill Cotts. Read —7N 63
Tuns La. Hen T —4D 16
Tuns La. Slou —2E 46
Tupsley Rd. Read —7F 62
Turks Clo. Uxb —4N 25
Turk's La. Mort C —5G 107
Turmeric Clo. Ear —2M 87
Turnberry. Brack —8J 91
Turnberry Ct. Read —5K 63
(off Muirfield Clo.)
Turnbridge Clo. Lwr Ear —3A 88
Turner Pl. Col T —3H 119
Turner Rd. Slou —1L 47
Turners Clo. Stai —9J 73
Turners Dri. That —8H 81
Turnery, The. That —8F 80
Turnfields. That —8G 81
Turnoak Pk. Wind —1A 70
Turnpike Ind. Est. Newb —6B 80
Turnpike La. Uxb —4M 25
Turnpike Rd. Brack —4H 91
Turnpike Rd. Newb —7A 80
Turnstone Clo. Winn —9G 64
Turnvill Clo. Light —9K 115
Turpins Grn. M'head —9L 19
Turpins Rise. W'sham —4L 115
Turton Way. Slou —2F 46
Tuscam Way. Camb —5K 119
Tuscan Clo. Tile —3M 61
Tuscany Way. Yat —5A 118
Tuxford M. Read —5B 62
Tweed Ct. Tile —5B 62
Tweed Rd. Slou —5C 48
Twinches La. Slou —9D 22
Twin Oaks. Emm G —7H 39
Two Tree Hill. Hen T —6A 16
Twyford Rd. Binf —3N 89
Twyford Rd. Twy —6J 41
Twyford Rd. Wokgm —3N 89
Twynham Rd. Camb —4N 119
Twynham Rd. M'head —7M 19
Tyberton Pl. Read —7F 62
Tydehams. Newb —3J 101
Tyle Pl. Old Win —2J 71
Tyler Clo. Cav —8E 38
Tyle Rd. Tile —4L 61
Tyler's La. Bckby —2L 81
Tylers Pl. Tile —4N 61
Tylorstown. Cav —8F 38
Tyne Way. That —6E 80
Tyrell Gdns. Wind —9B 46
Tyrrel Ct. Read —5J 63
Tytherton. Brack —4N 91

Uffington Clo. Tile —4K 61
Uffington Dri. Brack —6B 92
Uffoot Clo. Lwr Ear —3M 87
Ufton Ct. Yd. Bour —3M 5
Ullswater. Brack —9J 91
Ullswater Clo. Slou —6M 21
Ullswater Clo. That —8D 80
Ullswater Dri. Tile —1L 61
Ulster Clo. Cav —8K 39
Ulswater Clo. Light —9L 115
Ulswater Rd. Light —9L 115
Umberville Way. Slou —4B 22
Uncles La. Wal L —1D 66
Underhill. Moul —3H 15
Underhill Clo. M'head —8B 20
Underwood. Brack —8J 91
Underwood Ct. Binf —1G 91
Underwood Rd. Read —8N 61
Union Clo. Owl —8J 113
Union Rd. Brad —9L 59
Union St. Read —4G 63
Unity Clo. Emm G —8H 39
Unity Ct. Emm G —8H 39
Uong La. Cook D —1N 19
Upavon Dri. Read —7E 62
Upavon Gdns. Brack —7C 92
Upcroft. Wind —9D 46
Updown Hill. W'sham —6N 115
Upland Rd. Camb —2N 119
Uplands. Hung —6J 75
Uplands. Mar —1B 4
Uplands Clo. Sand —1F 118
Uplands Rd. Cav —8E 38
Up. Bray Rd. Bray —3F 44
Up. Broadmoor Rd. Crowt —5G 113
Up. Charles St. Camb —3N 119
Up. College Ride. Camb —9C 114
Up. Crown St. Read —6H 63
Up. Culham Rd. C Grn —4H 17
Up. Eddington. Edd —4L 75
Upper End. Chadw —5M 29
Up. Gordon Rd. Camb —4N 119
Up. Lambourn Rd. Lamb —1G 26
Up. Lees Rd. Slou —4D 22
Up. Meadow Rd. Read —1K 87
Up. Nursery. S'dale —7C 94
Up. Park Rd. Camb —4N 119
Up. Raymond Almshouses. Newb
(off Newtown Rd.) —9K 79
Up. Red Cross Rd. Gor —8L 15
Up. Redlands Rd. Read —7K 63
Up. Star Post Ride. Crowt —3M 113
Up. Verran Rd. Camb —6N 119
Up. Village Rd. Asc —7M 93
Up. Warren Av. Cav —1C 62
Up. Woodcote Rd. Cav —8D 38
Uppingham Dri. Wdly —3E 64
Uppingham Gdns. Cav —7K 39
Upshire Gdns. Brack —6C 92
Upton Clo. Hen T —5D 16
Upton Clo. Slou —2H 47
Upton Ct. Rd. Slou —2J 47
Upton Lea Pde. Slou —8K 23
Upton Pk. Slou —2G 47
Upton Rd. Slou —2J 47
Upton Rd. Tile —5B 62
Urquhart Rd. That —1G 103
Usk Rd. Tile —6N 61
Uxbridge Ind. Est. Uxb —3J 25
Uxbridge Rd. Slou —1J 47
Uxbridge Rd. Uxb & Hay —4N 25

Vachel Rd. Read —4G 62
Vale Cres. Tile —3M 61
Vale Gro. Slou —2G 47
Valentia Clo. Read —4D 62
Valentia Rd. Read —4D 62
Valentine Clo. Read —2M 87
Valentine Cres. Cav —9J 39
Valerie Ct. Read —6E 62
Vale Rd. Camb —5L 119
Vale Rd. Wind —6B 46
Vale View Dri. B Hill —5D 108
Valley Clo. Cav —9G 38
Valley Clo. Gor —8L 15
Valley Cres. Wokgm —3M 89
Valley Rd. Bfld C —8H 85
Valley Rd. Hen T —6A 16
Valley Rd. Newb —1J 101
Valley Rd. Uxb —3M 25
Valley Way. Pam H —9N 105
Valon Rd. Arbor —1D 110
Valpy St. Read —4H 63
Valroy Clo. Camb —3N 119
Vanbrugh Ct. Read —5K 63
Vandyke. Brack —8J 91
Vanlore Way. Calc —7K 61
Vanners La. Enb —5B 100
Vansittart Est. Wind —6E 46
Vansittart Rd. Bish —8C 4
Vansittart Rd. Wind —7D 46
Vantage Rd. Slou —9D 22
Vanwall Bus. Pk. M'head —9N 19
Vanwall Rd. M'head —1N 43
Vastern Ct. Read —3G 63
Vastern Rd. Read —3G 63
Vaughan Gdns. Eton W —3B 46
Vaughan Way. Slou —5A 22
Vauxhall Dri. Wdly —6E 64
Vegal Cres. Egh —9L 71
Venetia Clo. Cav —6J 39
Venning Rd. Arbor —2E 110
Ventnor Rd. Tile —4L 61
Venus Clo. Wokgm —5L 89
Verbena Clo. W Dray —4L 49
Verbena Clo. Winn —9F 64
Verey Clo. Twy —1L 65
Vermont Rd. Slou —5B 22
Vermont Woods. Wokgm —3K 111
Verney Clo. Mar —5B 4
Verney M. Read —5C 62
Verney Rd. Slou —3B 48
Vernon Cres. Read —4H 87
Vernon Dri. Asc —4G 93
Verona Clo. Uxb —6K 25
Verran Rd. Camb —6N 119
Vicarage Av. Egh —9C 72
Vicarage Clo. Cook —8M 5
Vicarage Ct. Egh —9C 72
Vicarage Cres. Egh —9C 72
Vicarage Dri. M'head —1F 44
Vicarage Gdns. Asc —7K 93
Vicarage La. Cold A —3F 80
Vicarage La. Crowt & Bag —5D 114
Vicarage La. Wray —5N 71
Vicarage La. Yat —2A 118
Vicarage Meadow. Been —5H 83
Vicarage Pl. Slou —2J 47
Vicarage Rd. Bag —7F 114
Vicarage Rd. B'water —5J 119
Vicarage Rd. Egh —9B 72
Vicarage Rd. Hen T —5D 16
Vicarage Rd. M'head —6C 20
Vicarage Rd. Read —7J 63
Vicarage Rd. Stai —7F 72
Vicarage Rd. Yat —2A 118
Vicarage Wlk. Bray —1F 44
Vicarage Way. Coln —6D 48
Vicarage Wood. Tile —2J 61
Vickers Clo. Shin —7M 87
Vickers Clo. Wdly —6G 64
Victor Clo. M'head —6M 19
Victoria Av. Camb —4L 119
Victoria Ct. Bag —9H 115
Victoria Ct. Hen T —5D 16
Victoria Ct. Mar —5C 4
(off Victoria Rd.)
Victoria Cres. Iver —8G 25
Victoria Dri. B'water —5G 119
Victoria Gdns. Newb —7L 79
Victoria M. Read —3D 62
Victoria Rd. Asc —7K 93
Victoria Rd. Cav —1G 62
Victoria Rd. Eton W —3A 46
Victoria Rd. Mar —5C 4
Victoria Rd. Mort —4G 106
Victoria Rd. Owl —9J 113
Victoria Rd. Slou —9K 23
Victoria Rd. Stai —7F 72
Victoria Rd. Tile —4L 61
Victoria Rd. Uxb —1K 25
Victoria Rd. Warg —3K 41
Victoria Sq. Read —5K 63
Victoria St. Egh —1L 95
Victoria St. Read —5K 63
Victoria St. Slou —1H 47
Victoria St. Wind —7F 46
Victoria Way. Read —5K 63
Victor Pl. Woolh —9E 82
Victor Rd. That —8H 81
Victor Rd. Wind —9E 46
Victor Way. Wdly —5F 64
Vigo La. Yat —4A 118
Viking. Brack —7J 91
Village Clo. Read —5H 87
Village Rd. Dor —2L 45
Village, The. Finch —7K 111
Village Way. Ashf —8N 73
Village Way. Yat —2B 118
Villa M. Read —5L 63
Villiers Mead. Wokgm —5M 89
Villiers Rd. Slou —6F 22
Villier St. Uxb —4L 25
Villiers Wlk. Newb —4G 101
Villiers Way. Newb —4G 100
Vincent Clo. Wdly —6E 64
Vincent Dri. Uxb —2N 25
Vincent Rise. Brack —5B 92
Vincent Rd. That —7H 81
Vine Clo. Stai —2H 73
Vine Clo. W Dray —3N 49
Vine Ct. Newb —1M 101
Vine Cres. Read —8A 62
Vine Gro. Uxb —1N 25
Vine La. Hil —2N 25
Vineries Clo. W Dray —5N 49
Vinery, The. Warg —3J 41
Vines, The. Wokgm —8H 89
Vine St. Uxb —2L 25
Vineyard Dri. Bour —2L 5
Viola Av. Stai —5M 73
Viola Croft. Warf —3C 92
Violet Av. Uxb —6N 25
Virginia Av. Vir W —7L 95
Virginia Beeches. Vir W —5L 95
Virginia Dri. Vir W —7L 95
Virginia Way. Read —8B 62
Viscount Ind. Est. Coln —9F 48
Viscount Rd. Stai —5M 73
Viscount Way. Wdly —5E 64
Vivien Clo. Cook —9K 5
Voller Dri. Tile —6K 61
Volunteer Rd. Thea —1E 84
Vo-Tec Cen. Newb —9C 80
Vulcan Clo. Sand —2E 118
Vulcan Clo. Wdly —3G 64
Vulcan Way. Sand —2F 118

Waborne Rd. Bour —3M 5
Wade Dri. Slou —9C 22
Wadham. Owl —9K 113
Wagbullock Rise. Brack —8N 91
Waggoners Hollow. Bag —8H 115
Wagner Clo. M'head —2K 43
Wagtail Clo. Twy —9K 41
Waingels Rd. Land E —3F 64
Wakefield Cres. Stoke P —1H 23
Wakeford Clo. Pam H —9N 105
Wakeford Ct. Pam H —8N 105
Wakelins End. Cook —8J 5
Wakeman Rd. Bour —4L 5
Wakemans. Up Bas —9M 35
Walbury. Brack —6B 92
Waldeck Rd. M'head —7D 20
Waldeck St. Read —7H 63
Walden Av. Arbor —8B 88
Waldens Clo. Bour —4L 5
Waldorf Heights. B'water —6H 119
Waldron Hill. Brack —3C 92
Waleys Pl. Cav —2J 63
Walford Rd. Uxb —3K 25
Walgrove Gdns. White —6H 43
Walker Rd. M'head —1D 44
Walker's La. Lamb —2H 27
Walkers Pl. Read —5C 62
Walk, The. Eton W —4C 46
Wallace Clo. Mar —3D 4
Wallace Clo. Wdly —7C 64
Wall Clo. Uxb —3M 25
Wallcroft Clo. Binf —2K 91

Walled Gdns. Warg —3J 41
Waller Dri. Newb —6B 80
Wallingford Clo. Brack —6B 92
Wallingford Rd. Comp —9H 13
Wallingford Rd. Gor & N Sto —8L 15
Wallingford Rd. Streat & Moul —8J 15
Wallingford Rd. Uxb —3J 25
Wallington Rd. Camb —9D 114
Wallingtons Rd. Kint —2D 98
Wallis Ct. Slou —1J 47
Wall La. Sil —8E 106
Wallner Way. Wokgm —6C 90
Walmer Clo. Crowt —5G 112
Walmer Clo. Tile —6A 62
Walmer Rd. Wdly —3E 64
Walnut Av. W Dray —2N 49
Walnut Clo. Wokgm —6L 89
Walnut Clo. Yat —5B 118
Walnut Lodge. Chalv —2F 46
Walnut Tree Clo. Rusc —7K 41
Walnut Tree Ct. Bour —5M 5
Walnut Tree Ct. Gor —8L 15
Walnut Way. Bour —5M 5
Walnut Way. Tile —4L 61
Walpole Bus. Cen. Slou —7N 21
Walpole Rd. Old Win —4K 71
Walpole Rd. Slou —7N 21
Walrus Clo. Wdly —5G 65
Walsh Av. Warf —2B 92
Walter Rd. Wokgm —3K 89
Walters Clo. Cold A —3F 80
Waltham Clo. M'head —3K 43
Waltham Clo. Owl —9H 113
Waltham Ct. Gor —6L 15
Waltham Pl. M'head —6K 43
Waltham Rd. Rusc —8L 41
Waltham Rd. Twy —9J 41
Waltham Rd. White —5J 43
Walton Av. Hen T —6D 16
Walton Clo. Wdly —5B 64
Walton Dri. Asc —3J 93
Walton La. Slou —3B 22
Walton Way. Newb —7N 79
Wandhope Way. Tile —2K 61
Wansdyke, The. Hung —6N 97
Wanstraw Gro. Brack —9B 92
Wantage Clo. Brack —7B 92
Wantage Hall. Read —7K 63
Wantage Rd. Chol & Streat —2F 14
Wantage Rd. Col T —1H 119
Wantage Rd. Don —3J 79
Wantage Rd. Edd —4L 75
Wantage Rd. Gt Shef —1F 52
Wantage Rd. Lamb —2J 27
Wantage Rd. Read —5C 62
Wantage Rd. Up Lamb —8J 7
Wapshott Rd. Stai —9F 72
Waram Clo. Edd —4L 75
Warbler Clo. Tile —6J 61
Warborough Av. Tile —5J 61
Warbreck Dri. Tile —1J 61
Warbrook La. Eve —9F 110
Ward Clo. Iver —8G 24
Ward Clo. Wokgm —3B 90
Ward Gdns. Slou —8A 22
Wardle Av. Tile —3L 61
Wardle Clo. Bag —7H 115
Ward Royal Est. Wind —7E 46
Wards Stone Clo. Brack —9B 92
Wards Stone Pk. Brack —9B 92
Wareham Rd. Brack —6C 92
Warehouse Rd. Green —5C 102
Warfield Rd. Brack —9N 67
Warfield St. Brack —9N 67
Wargrave Hill. Warg —3J 41
Wargrave Rd. Hen T & Lwr S —5E 16
Wargrave Rd. Twy —6J 41
Wargrove Dri. Col T —1H 119
Waring Clo. Lwr Ear —3B 88
Waring Ho. That —7G 80
Warley Rise. Tile —9J 37
War Memorial Pl. Hen T —7D 16
Warner Clo. Slou —9A 22
Warners Hill. Cook —8G 5
Warnford Rd. Tile —5N 61
Warnham La. Comp —3D 32
Warnsham Clo. Lwr Ear —2A 88
Warren Clo. Bfld C —8H 85
Warren Clo. Finch —4L 111
Warren Clo. Sand —1E 118
Warren Clo. Slou —2N 47
Warren Ct. Cav —2F 62
Warren Down. Brack —3J 91
Warren Field. Iver —3D 24
Warren Ho. Rd. Wokgm —1B 90
Warren La. Finch —4J 111
Warren Pde. Slou —9L 23
Warren Rd. Son & Wdly —3C 64
Warren Row. Asc —4G 92
Warren Row Rd. Know H —7M 17
Warren, The. Brack —6D 92
Warren, The. Cav —1D 62
Warrington Av. Slou —7E 22
Warrington Spur. Old Win —4K 71
Warwick. Brack —8B 92
Warwick Av. Slou —5E 22
Warwick Av. Stai —9K 73
Warwick Clo. M'head —2M 43
Warwick Dri. Green —1M 101
Warwick Pl. Uxb —1K 25
Warwick Rd. Ashf —9M 73
Warwick Rd. Read —8J 63
Warwick Rd. W Dray —9M 25
Wasdale Clo. Owl —8H 113
Washington Dri. Slou —8N 21
Washington Dri. Wind —9A 46
Washington Rd. Cav —2H 63
Wash Water. Wool H —7D 100
Wasing La. Aldm —4E 104
Watchetts Dri. Camb —7N 119
Watchetts Lake Clo. Camb —6N 119
Watchetts Rd. Camb —5M 119
Watchmoor Pk. Camb —6L 119
Watchmoor Rd. Camb —5L 119
Waterbeach Rd. Slou —7F 22
Waterfall Clo. Vir W —5J 95
Waterford Way. Wokgm —5A 90
Waterham Rd. Brack —8M 91
Waterhouse Mead. Col T —2H 119
Water La. Farn —9L 119
Water La. Green —3N 101
Waterloo Clo. Wokgm —6C 90
Waterloo Cres. Wokgm —6C 90
Waterloo Pl. Crowt —6F 112
Waterloo Rise. Read —8H 63
Waterloo Rd. Crowt —6E 112
Waterloo Rd. Read —7H 63
Waterloo Rd. Uxb —2K 25
Waterloo Rd. Wokgm —6C 90
Waterman Pl. Read —3G 62
Watermans Bus. Pk. Stai —8E 72
Watermans Rd. Hen T —6D 16
Waterman's Way. Warg —4H 41
Watermill Ct. Woolh —9F 82
Water Rd. Read —5B 62
Waters Dri. Stai —7G 72
Watersfield Clo. Lwr Ear —3N 87
Water Side. Uxb —6K 25
Waterside Ct. Newb —8N 79
Waterside Dri. Langl —1A 48
Waterside Dri. Pur T —8L 37
Waterside Dri. Thea —9G 60
Waterside Gdns. Read —5G 63
Waterside Pk. Ind. Est. Brack —4J 91
Watersplash La. Asc —3N 93
Watersplash La. Warf —1M 91
Water St. Hamp N —7J 33
Watery La. N End —5L 99
Watkins Clo. Wokgm —3K 111
Watlington St. Read —5J 63
(in two parts)
Watmore La. Winn —9J 65
Watson Clo. Wokgm —1K 111
Wavell Clo. Read —2M 87
Wavell Gdns. Slou —4B 22
Wavell Rd. M'head —8M 19
Waverley. Brack —7J 91
Waverley Ct. Read —6D 62
(off Southcote Rd.)
Waverley Dri. Vir W —5J 95
Waverley Rd. Bag —7H 115
Waverley Rd. Read —4B 62
Waverley Rd. Slou —6E 22
Waverleys, The. That —7G 80
Waverley Way. Wokgm —1L 111
Waybrook Cres. Read —6M 63
Wayland Clo. Brack —6C 92
Waylen St. Read —5F 62
Wayman Rd. Farn —9J 119
Wayside M. M'head —6C 20
Wealden Way. Tile —3M 61
Weald Rise. Tile —2N 61
Weald Rd. Uxb —3N 25
Weavers La. Ink —5B 98
Weavers Wlk. Newb —8K 79
Webb Clo. Bag —9H 115
Webb Clo. Binf —2J 91
Webb Clo. Slou —3M 47
Webb Ct. Wokgm —3C 90
Webbs Acre. That —9J 81
Webbs La. Been —4K 83
Webster Clo. M'head —9L 19
Wedderburn Clo. Winn —1J 89
Wedgewood Way. Tile —3N 61
Weekes Dri. Slou —9D 22
Weighbridge Row. Read —3F 62
Weir Clo. Calc —8N 61
Weirside Ct. Read —5K 63
Welbeck. Brack —7J 91
Welbeck Rd. M'head —9A 20
Welby Clo. M'head —1L 43
Welby Cres. Winn —2G 88
Weldale St. Read —4F 62
Welden. Slou —7L 23
Welford Rd. Wdly —4F 64
Welland Clo. Slou —5C 48
Welland Clo. Tile —3K 61
Wellbank. M'head —5H 21
Wellburn Clo. Sand —2F 118
Well Clo. Camb —5M 119
Wellcroft Rd. Slou —9D 22
Weller Dri. Camb —6N 119
Weller Dri. Finch —4F 110
Weller's La. Brack —6N 67
Wellesley Av. Iver —2G 48
Wellesley Clo. Bag —7F 114
Wellesley Dri. Crowt —5C 112
Wellesley Rd. Slou —9J 23
Welley Av. Wray —1N 71
Welley Rd. Wray & Hort —3N 71
Wellfield Clo. Tile —5K 61
Wellhill Rd. S Faw —9H 9
Wellhouse La. Herm —7G 56
Wellhouse Rd. M'head —4B 20
Wellington Av. Read —8K 63
Wellington Av. Vir W —7K 95
Wellington Bus. Pk. Crowt —6C 112
Wellington Clo. Newb —6N 79
Wellington Clo. Sand —1G 119
Wellington Ct. Spen W —8G 86
Wellington Ct. Stanw —4M 73
Wellington Cres. Baug —9F 104
Wellington Dri. Brack —7A 92
Wellingtonia Av. Crowt —6N 111
Wellingtonia Roundabout. Crowt —6C 112
Wellingtonias. Warf P —2D 92
Wellington Ind. Est. Spen W —9G 87
Wellington Rd. Ashf —9M 73
Wellington Rd. Crowt —6G 112
Wellington Rd. M'head —7A 20
Wellington Rd. Sand —1F 118
Wellington Rd. Uxb —2K 25
Wellington Rd. Wokgm —5N 89
Wellington St. Slou —9G 23
Wellington Ter. Sand —1G 119
Well La. Herm —5H 57
Well Meadow. Newb —6M 79
Wells Clo. Wind —7C 46
Wells Hall. Read —7K 63
Wells La. Asc —6L 93
Welsh La. Rise —8F 108
Welshman's Rd. Pad C —5A 106
Welwick Clo. Lwr Ear —1D 88
Wendan Rd. Newb —1K 101
Wendover Pl. Stai —9E 72
Wendover Rd. Bour —3L 5
Wendover Rd. Burn —6L 21
Wendover Rd. Stai —9D 72
Wendover Way. Tile —5L 61
Wenlock Edge. Charv —9G 40
Wenlock Way. That —9G 80
Wensley Clo. Twy —8J 41
Wensley Rd. Read —8D 62
Wentworth Av. Asc —4F 92
Wentworth Av. Read —3K 87
Wentworth Av. Slou —4C 22
Wentworth Clo. Crowt —4D 112
Wentworth Clo. Yat —4B 118
Wentworth Ct. Newb —1M 101
Wentworth Cres. M'head —8N 19
Wentworth Dri. Vir W —6H 95
Wentworth Way. Asc —4F 92
Wescott Rd. Wokgm —5B 90
Wescott Way. Uxb —3K 25
Wesley Dri. Egh —9B 72
Wesley Ga. Read —5J 63
Wessex Clo. Hung —6J 75
Wessex Ct. Stanw —3M 73
Wessex Gdns. Twy —1K 65
Wessex Hall. Read —7M 63
Wessex Rd. Bour —5M 5
Wessex Rd. H'row A —1K 73
Wessex Rd. Ind. Est. Bour —5M 5
Wessex Way. M'head —1M 43
Westacott Way. M'head —9H 19
Westborough Ct. M'head —8N 19
Westborough Rd. M'head —8N 19
Westbourne Rd. Col T —2J 119
Westbourne Ter. Read —5C 62
Westbrook. M'head —4H 45
Westbrook Clo. Hung —6J 75
Westbrook Gdns. Brack —3A 92
Westbrook Rd. Read —3C 62
Westbrook Rd. Stai —9G 72
Westbury Clo. Crowt —4F 112
Westbury La. Pur T —7H 37
West Clo. Ashf —8M 73
Westcombe Clo. Brack —9B 92
Westcote Rd. Read —6D 62
Westcott Rd. Wokgm —5B 90
Westcotts Grn. Warf —1A 92
West Cres. Wind —7B 46
Westcroft. Slou —5D 22
West Dean. M'head —6C 20
Westdene Cres. Cav —9E 38
W. Drayton Pk. Av. W Dray —2M 49
West Dri. Asc & Vir W —7F 94
(in two parts)
West Dri. Calc —7M 61
West Dri. Son —3C 64
W. End Ct. Hedg —2H 23
W. End La. Stoke P —2G 23
W. End La. Warf —1M 91
W. End Rd. Mort C —5D 106
W. End Rd. Warf —9M 67
Westerdale. That —8F 80
Westerham Wlk. Read —7H 63
(off Charndon Clo.)
Western Av. Hen T —6D 16
Western Av. Newb —7J 79
Western Av. Wdly —4C 64
Western Cen., The. Brack —4K 91
Western Elms Av. Read —5E 62
Western End. Newb —9J 79
Western Oaks. Tile —2M 61
Western Perimeter Rd. W Dray & H'row A —8J 49
Western Rd. Brack —3J 91
Western Rd. Hen T —6D 16
Western Rd. Read —6E 62
Westfield Clo. Tadl —9M 105
Westfield Cres. S'lake —2G 40
Westfield Cres. That —7E 80
Westfield La. Wex —7M 23
Westfield Rd. Camb —7M 119
Westfield Rd. Cav —2H 63
Westfield Rd. Chol —2E 14
Westfield Rd. M'head —7M 19
Westfield Rd. Slou —5D 22
Westfield Rd. That —6D 80
Westfield Rd. Winn —1G 89
Westfields. Comp —1G 33
Westfields. W Wood —7F 98
Westfield Way. Newb —9J 79
W. Fryerne. Yat —1B 118
Westgate Ct. Newb —9J 79
Westgate Cres. Slou —8B 22
Westgate Rd. Newb —9J 79
West Grn. Yat —2A 118
West Grn. Ct. Read —7F 62
Westhatch La. Brack —8M 67
West Hill. Read —6H 63
Westhorpe Rd. Mar —4D 4
Westland. That —7E 80
Westland Clo. Stai —3M 73
Westlands Av. Read —2L 87
Westlands Av. Slou —7M 21
Westlands Clo. Slou —7M 21
Westlands Rd. Newb —2M 101
Westleigh Dri. Son C —1F 38
Westlyn Rd. Pam H —9N 105
Westmead. Wind —9D 46
Westmead Dri. Newb —2K 101
West Meadow. Farnb —6C 10
West Mills. Newb —8K 79
Westminster Way. Lwr Ear —2B 88
Westmorland Clo. Wokgm —5J 89
Westmorland Dri. Warf —2C 92
Westmorland Rd. M'head —7A 20
Westonbirt Dri. Cav —1E 62
Weston Gro. Bag —8J 115
Weston Rd. Slou —6B 22
Weston St. Beed —5A 32
West Point. Slou —9N 21
West Ramp. Houn —7N 49
West Ridge. Bour —3M 5
Westridge Av. Pur T —8K 37
West Rd. Farn —9M 119
West Rd. M'head —7B 20
West Rd. W Dray —2N 49
West Rd. Wokgm —9G 90
West Sq. Iver —7G 24
West St. Hen T —4C 16
West St. M'head —7C 20
West St. Mar —6A 4
West St. Newb —8K 79
West St. Read —5G 63
West St. Tadl —9M 105
Westview. P'mre —6G 31
Westview Dri. Twy —7K 41
Westward Rd. Wokgm —4L 89
Westwates Clo. Brack —3A 92
Westway. Gor —6L 15
Westwood. Newb —1N 101
Westwood Glen. Tile —4K 61
Westwood Grn. Cook —9K 5
Westwood Rd. Green —2M 101
Westwood Rd. Mar —6A 4
Westwood Rd. Tile —3L 61
Westwood Rd. W'sham —2N 115
Westwood Row. Tile —2K 61
Wetherby Clo. Cav —7J 39
Wethered Dri. Burn —6L 21
Wethered Rd. Mar —5B 4
Wexham Ct. Wex —7L 23
Wexham Pk. La. Wex —5L 23
Wexham Rd. Slou & Wex —1J 47
Wexham St. Wex —5K 23
Wexham Woods. Wex —6L 23
Weybridge Mead. Yat —2C 118
Wey Clo. Camb —4M 119
Weycrofts. Brack —2K 91
Whaley Rd. Wokgm —3B 90
Wharfdale Rd. Winn —9F 64
Wharfe La. Hen T —4D 16
Wharf La. Bour —4L 5
Wharf Rd. Newb —8L 79
Wharf Rd. Wray —4L 71
Wharfside. Pad —8L 83
Wharf St. Newb —8L 79
Wharf, The. Newb —8L 79
Wharf, The. Pang —7D 36
Whatley Grn. Brack —8M 91
Whatmore Clo. Stai —3H 73
Wheatbutts, The. Eton W —3B 46
Wheatfield Clo. M'head —1L 43
Wheatfields Rd. Shin —6L 87
Wheatland Rd. Slou —2K 47
Wheatlands Clo. Calc —8M 61
Wheatlands La. Enb —4F 100
Wheatley. Brack —7J 91
Wheatley Clo. Read —2L 87
Wheatsheaf La. Newb —7M 79
Wheble Dri. Wdly —4C 64
Wheeler Clo. Bfld C —8J 85
Wheelers Grn. Way. That —9H 81
Wheelton Clo. Ear —9D 64
Wheelwrights Pl. Coln —6D 48
Whins Clo. Camb —5M 119
Whins Dri. Camb —5M 119
Whistler Gro. Col T —3H 119
Whistley Clo. Brack —5B 92
Whitamore Row. Hen T —6D 16
(off Trust Corner)
Whitby Ct. Cav —8K 39
Whitby Dri. Read —7J 63
Whitby Grn. Cav —7K 39
Whitby Rd. Slou —8E 22
Whitchurch Clo. M'head —3B 20
Whitchurch Rd. Pang —7E 36
White Acres Dri. M'head —4F 44
Whitebeam Clo. Wokgm —8J 89
Whitebrook Pk. M'head —2F 20
White City. Crowt —5H 113
(in two parts)
White Clo. Herm —6C 56
White Clo. Slou —9F 22
Whitedown Rd. Tadl —9H 105
Whiteford Rd. Slou —6G 23
Whitegates La. Ear —5N 63
Whitehall Clo. Uxb —2K 25
Whitehall Dri. Arbor —2D 110
Whitehall Farm La. Vir W —4N 95
Whitehall La. Egh —2N 95
Whitehall La. Wray —3B 72
Whitehall Rd. Uxb —2L 25
Whitehart Clo. Thea —8F 60
White Hart Ind. Est. B'water —5J 119
Whitehart Rd. M'head —7C 20
White Hart Rd. Slou —2F 46
Whitehaven. Slou —8H 23
White Hill. Ash'd —7F 34
White Hill. Bin H —9A 16
White Hill. Hen T —4E 16
White Hill. W'sham —4L 115
Whitehill Clo. Camb —2N 119
Whitehill Clo. Mar —1A 4
Whitehill Pl. Vir W —7N 95
Whitehills Grn. Gor —8L 15
Whitehorn Av. W Dray —8M 25
White Horse La. Finch —4H 111
White Horse Rd. Wind —9N 45
White Ho. Gdns. Yat —2A 118
Whitehouse Way. Iver —4E 24
Whiteknights Hall. Read —7L 63
Whiteknights Rd. Read —7M 63
Whitelands Dri. Asc —3G 92
Whitelands Rd. That —7G 80
Whiteley. Wind —6A 46
White Lion Way. Yat —2B 118
White Lodge Clo. Tile —1J 61
Whitemoor La. Lwr B —5L 35
Whitemoor La. Up Bas —8F 34
White Paddock. M'head —3L 43
Whitepit La. F Hth —1N 5
White Rd. Col T —3K 119
White Rock. M'head —5E 20
White's Hill. Sul'd —6E 84
White Shute. Lamb —5H 27
White's La. Been —3K 83
Whites La. Dat —5K 47
Whitestone Clo. Lwr Ear —9D 64
Whitethorn Av. W Dray —9N 25
Whitethorn Pl. W Dray —8N 25
White Waltham Airfield. White —4J 43
Whitewell Clo. Arbor X —9D 88
Whitley Clo. Stai —3M 73
Whitley Pk. Farm Ho. Read —8J 63
Whitley Pk. La. Read —8K 63
Whitley Rd. Yat —5B 118
Whitley St. Read —7H 63
Whitley Wood La. Read —4H 87
(in two parts)
Whitley Wood Rd. Read —5H 87
Whitmoor Rd. Bag —7J 115
Whitmore Clo. Owl —1H 119
Whitmore La. S'dale —7C 94
Whitstone Gdns. Read —2J 87
Whittaker Rd. Slou —5N 21
Whittenham Clo. Slou —9J 23
Whittle Clo. Finch —3K 111
Whittle Clo. Sand —9E 112
Whittle Parkway. Slou —7N 21
Whitton Clo. Lwr Ear —2C 88
Whitton Rd. Brack —5C 92
Whitworth Rd. Arbor X —3F 110
Whurley Way. M'head —4B 20
Whynstones Rd. Asc —8K 93
Whyteladyes La. Cook —8H 5
Wickets, The. M'head —7N 19
Wickett, The. Chalv —2G 47
Wickford Way. Lwr Ear —3M 87
Wickham Clo. Bag —4H 115
Wickham Clo. Tadl —9K 105
Wickham Rd. Lwr Ear —2D 88
Wickham Vale. Brack —8J 91
Wick Hill La. Wokgm —4L 111
Wick La. Chad —6N 29
Wick La. Egh —1H 95
Wick Rd. Egh —3J 95
Wick's Grn. Binf —8F 66
Wicks La. Shur R —2C 66
Widbrook Rd. M'head —3E 20
Widecombe Pl. Read —2H 87
Widecroft Rd. Iver —7F 24
Wield Clo. Lwr Ear —2D 88
Wient, The. Coln —6D 48
Wiggett Gro. Binf —1G 90
Wigmoreash Drove. Ham —1A 116
Wigmore La. Read —3B 62
(in two parts)
Wigmore La. Thea —1D 84
Wigmore Rd. Tadl —9H 105
Wilberforce Way. Brack —7A 92
Wild Briar. Wokgm —3L 111
Wild Clo. Lwr Ear —3B 88
Wildcroft Dri. Wokgm —9M 89
Wilder Av. Pang —8F 36
Wilderness Ct. Ear —9N 63
Wilderness Rd. Ear —1M 87
Wilders Clo. Brack —2L 91
Wildgreen N. Slou —3B 48
Wildgreen S. Slou —3B 48
Wildridings Rd. Brack —6L 91
Wildridings Sq. Brack —6L 91
Wildwood Dri. Baug —9F 104
Wildwood Gdns. Yat —5A 118
Wilford Rd. Slou —3N 47
Wilfred Way. That —8K 81
Willant Clo. M'head —3K 43
William Clo. That —9G 81
William Ellis Clo. Old Win —2J 71
William Hitchcock Ho. Farn —9M 119
William Sim Wood. Wink R —1E 92
William St. Read —4F 62
William St. Slou —1H 47
William St. Wind —7F 46
Willington Clo. Camb —3M 119
Willoners. Slou —5C 22
Willoughby Rd. Brack —5K 91
Willoughby Rd. Slou —2B 48
Willow Av. W Dray —8N 25
Willowbrook. Eton —3F 46
Willowbrook Rd. Stai —6M 73
Willow Clo. Bfld —6J 85
Willow Clo. Coln —6D 48
Willow Clo. F Hth —1N 5
Willow Clo. Newb —1K 101
Willow Ct. Newb —7M 79
(off Wheatsheaf La.)
Willow Cres. Farn —9M 119
Willowdale. Finch —2L 111
Willow Dri. Brack —3N 91
Willow Dri. M'head —3E 44
Willow Dri. Twy —7J 41
Willowford. Yat —3B 118
Willow Gdns. Read —2L 87
Willow Gdns. Tile —2J 61
Willowherb Clo. Wokgm —4C 90
Willow La. B'water —5H 119
Willow La. Warg —1H 41
Willowmead Clo. Mar —4D 4
Willowmead Clo. Newb —5G 101
Willowmead Gdns. Mar —4D 4
Willowmead Rd. Mar —4D 4
Willowmead Sq. Mar —4D 4
Willow Pde. Slou —2B 48
Willow Pk. Stoke P —1J 23
Willow Pl. Eton —5E 46
Willow Rd. Bis G —8C 102
Willow Rd. Coln —8F 48
Willows End. Sand —1F 118
Willowside. Wdly —3E 64
Willows Lodge. Wind —6N 45
Willows Riverside Pk. Wind
(off Maidenhead Rd.) —6M 45
Willows Rd. Bour —4M 5
Willows, The. Brack —6C 92
Willows, The. Cav —2G 63
Willows, The. Light —9N 115
Willows, The. Wind —6N 45
Willow St. Read —6G 63
Willow Tree Glade. Calc —8K 61
Willow Wlk. Egh —9L 71
Willow Way. Sand —9D 112
Willson Rd. Egh —9K 71
Wilmar Clo. Uxb —1L 25
Wilmington Clo. Wdly —4E 64
Wilmot Clo. Binf —1G 90
Wilmot Rd. Burn —4L 21
Wilmott Clo. Winn —1G 89
Wilsford Clo. Lwr Ear —4L 87
Wilson Av. Hen T —6D 16
Wilson Clo. Comp —1H 33
Wilson Clo. W Dray —5L 49
Wilson Ct. Winn —2G 89
Wilson Rd. Read —5C 62
Wilson Valkenburg Ct. Newb
(off Old Bath Rd.) —7J 79
Wilton Clo. W Dray —5L 49
Wilton Cres. Wind —1N 69
Wilton Ho. Read —6D 62
Wilton Rd. Camb —6M 119

Wilton Rd. Read —4C **62**
Wiltshire Av. Crowt —4F **112**
Wiltshire Av. Slou —5E **22**
Wiltshire Clo. Hung —6J **75**
Wiltshire Dri. Wokgm —4B **90**
Wiltshire Gro. Warf —1C **92**
Wiltshire Rd. Mar —3D **4**
Wiltshire Rd. Wokgm —3A **90**
Wiltshire Wlk. Tile —6J **61**
Wilwood Rd. Brack —3J **91**
Wilwyne Clo. Cav —9J **39**
Wimbledon Clo. Camb —9C **114**
Wimbledon Rd. Camb —9C **114**
Wimblington Dri. Lwr Ear —3B **88**
Wimborne Gdns. Tile —3A **62**
Wimbushes. Finch —4J **111**
Wimpole Rd. W Dray —9L **25**
Wincanton Rd. Read —4J **87**
Winchbottom La. Mar —1F **4**
Winch Clo. Binf —9G **66**
Winchcombe Rd. Newb —9L **79**
Winchcombe Rd. Twy —1K **65**
Winchester Clo. Coln —7F **48**
Winchester Dri. M'head —2M **43**
Winchester Rd. Read —8H **63**
Winchester Way. B'water —3G **119**
Winchgrove Rd. Brack —2L **91**
Wincroft Rd. Cav —8E **38**
Windermere Clo. Stai —5M **73**
Windermere Clo. Winn —9H **65**
Windermere Rd. Light —9L **115**
Windermere Rd. Read —9K **63**
Windermere Way. Slou —6M **21**
Windermere Way. That —8D **80**
Windermere Way. W Dray —9M **25**
Windingwood La. Shef W & Wick —8F **52**
Windlebrook Grn. Brack —3L **91**
Windle Clo. W'sham —6N **115**
Windlesham Ct. W'sham —3M **115**
Windlesham Ct. Dri. W'sham —4M **115**
Windlesham Rd. Brack —3K **91**
Windmill Av. Wokgm —3K **89**
Windmill Clo. Wind —8D **46**
Windmill Clo. Wokgm —3K **89**
Windmill Corner. Mort C —4H **107**
Windmill Field. W'sham —6M **115**
Windmill La. Midg —6C **82**
Windmill La. Mort —4H **107**
Windmill Rd. Brack —3K **91**
Windmill Rd. Cook —9J **5**
Windmill Rd. Mort C —4H **107**
Windmill Rd. Slou —9F **22**
Windrush Av. Slou —2C **48**
Windrush Ct. Read —5B **62**
Windrush Heights. Sand —1E **118**
Windrush Ho. Bour —3L **5**
Windrush Way. M'head —6C **20**
Windrush Way. Read —5B **62**
Windsor Castle. Wind —7G **46**
Windsor Clo. Burn —5M **21**
Windsor Ct. Brack —6N **91**
Windsor Ct. Read —5E **62**
Windsor Dri. Ashf —8L **73**
Windsor & Eton Relief Rd. Wind —7D **46**
Windsor Forest Ct. Asc —3G **92**
Windsor Hall. Read —7L **63**
Windsor La. Burn —5M **21**
Windsor Ride. Brack & Asc —8C **92**
Windsor Ride. Camb & Crowt —1L **119**
Windsor Ride. Wokgm —3L **111**
Windsor Rd. Asc & Wind —5H **93**
Windsor Rd. Dat —6J **47**
Windsor Rd. M'head & Wind —2E **44**
Windsor Rd. Newb —2N **101**
Windsor Rd. Old Win & Egh —5L **71**
Windsor Rd. Slou —2G **47**
Windsor Rd. Wind —6L **45**
Windsor Rd. Wray —3N **71**
Windsor Sq. Read —6H **63**
Windsor St. Uxb —1L **25**
Windsor Way. Calc —8J **61**
Wingate Rd. Wdly —6D **64**
Wing Clo. Mar —6A **4**
Wingrove Rd. Read —6C **62**
Winkfield Clo. Wokgm —8N **89**
Winkfield La. Wink —5F **68**
Winkfield Rd. Asc —1K **93**
Winkfield Rd. Wind —5M **69**
Winkfield Row. Brack —8D **68**
Winkfield St. Wink —6E **68**
Winnersh Ga. Winn —1J **89**
Winnersh Gro. Winn —2H **89**
Winnersh Triangle Ind. Est. Winn —9G **65**
Winnock Rd. W Dray —9L **25**
Winscombe. Brack —7J **91**
Winser Dri. Read —8D **62**
Winston Clo. Spen W —9K **87**
Winston Way. Pur T —8J **37**
Winston Way. That —7C **80**
Winterberry Way. Cav —7E **38**
Winterbourne Ct. Brack —4A **92**
Winterbourne Rd. Box —8B **54**
Winter Hill. Cook —6G **4**
Winter Hill Rd. M'head —4L **19**
Winterly La. Kint —2D **98**
Winterton Dri. Speen —6H **79**
Winton Cres. Yat —4B **118**
Winton Rd. Read —3K **87**
Wintoun Path. Slou —5A **22**
Wintringham Way. Pur T —8L **37**
Winvale. Slou —2G **47**
Winwood. Slou —7L **23**
Wise La. W Dray —2L **49**
Wise's Firs. Sul'd —8E **84**
Wishmoor Clo. Camb —9B **114**
Wishmoor Rd. Camb —9B **114**
Wispington Clo. Lwr Ear —1C **88**
Wistaria La. Yat —4A **118**
Wisteria Clo. Wokgm —6L **89**
Wiston Ter. Read —4H **63**
Witcham Clo. Lwr Ear —3C **88**
Withey Clo. Wind —7A **46**
Witheygate Av. Stai —9J **73**
Withybed La. Kint —9D **76**
Withybed Way. That —6H **81**
Withy Clo. Light —9M **115**
Withy Clo. Tile —7K **61**
Withycroft. G Grn —7N **23**
Withy's, The. Fril —3A **58**
Wittenham Av. Tile —4J **61**
Wittenham Rd. Brack —3C **92**
Woburn Clo. Cav —9E **38**
Wokefield Row. Mort —2L **107**
Wokingham La. Arbor X —2A **110**
Wokingham Rd. Brack —3J **91**
Wokingham Rd. Crowt & Sand —6C **112**
Wokingham Rd. Hurst —4L **65**
Wokingham Rd. Read —5L **63**
Wolf La. Wind —9N **45**
Wolseley St. Read —6G **62**
Wolsey Ho. Gor —8L **15**
Wolsey Rd. Ashf —8M **73**
Wolsey Rd. Cav —3G **63**
Wolsingham Way. That —9G **80**
Wolverton Rd. Baug —9F **104**
Wondesford Dale. Binf —8G **66**
Woodberry Clo. Cav —9G **38**
Woodbine Clo. Lwr Ear —2B **88**
Woodbine Clo. Sand —2G **118**
Woodbine La. Burc —9K **101**
Woodbourne Clo. Yat —3B **118**
Woodbridge Rd. B'water —4F **118**
Woodbridge Rd. Tile —6J **61**
Woodbury. Lamb —4J **27**
Woodby Dri. Asc —9B **94**
Wood Clo. Wind —1E **70**
Woodcock La. B Hill —3E **108**
Woodcock La. Spen W —9F **86**
Woodcote. M'head —8A **20**
Woodcote Rd. Cav —9E **38**
Woodcote Rd. Gor H —2L **15**
Woodcote Way. Cav —7D **38**
Wood End. Crowt —6D **112**
Woodend Clo. Asc —3H **93**
Woodend Dri. Asc —7L **93**
Woodend Ride. Asc & Wind —2L **93**
Woodenhill. Brack —9J **91**
Woodfield Dri. M'head —8L **19**
Woodfield Way. Thea —9F **60**
Woodford Clo. Cav —9E **38**
Woodford Grn. Brack —6C **92**
Woodford Way. Slou —4C **22**
Wood Grn. Read —3K **87**
Woodgreen Clo. Read —5E **62**
Woodhall La. Asc —2N **115**
Woodhaw. Egh —8C **72**
Woodhouse La. Ash H & RG7 —9N **103**
Woodhouse St. Binf —3J **91**
Woodhurst La. Wokgm —2L **89**
Woodhurst N. M'head —5F **20**
Woodhurst Rd. M'head —5E **20**
Woodhurst S. M'head —5F **20**
Woodies Clo. Brack —2G **91**
Woodland Av. Slou —8F **22**
Woodland Av. Wind —1B **70**
Woodland Av. Wokgm —4J **89** (in two parts)
Woodland Clo. Mar —3C **4**
Woodland Cres. Brack —2N **91**
Woodland Dri. Tile —5L **61**
Woodlands. Yat —6B **118**
Woodlands Av. Bfld C —8H **85**
Woodlands Av. Ear & Wdly —6A **64**
Woodlands Bus. Pk. M'head —3L **43**
Woodlands Clo. Asc —8J **93**
Woodlands Clo. B'water —8J **119**
Woodlands Ct. Owl —9K **113**
Woodlands Gro. Cav —9L **39**
Woodlands La. W'sham —6N **115**
Woodlands Pk. Av. M'head —3L **43**
Woodlands Pk. Rd. M'head —3L **43**
Woodlands Ride. Asc —8J **93**
Woodlands Rd. Baug —9F **104**
Woodlands Rd. Camb —4M **119**
Woodlands Rd. Harp —8C **16**
Woodlands Rd. Vir W —6L **95**
Woodlands Rd. E. Vir W —6L **95**
Woodlands Rd. W. Vir W —6L **95**
Woodlands, The. Wokgm —7J **89**
Woodlands Wlk. B'water —8J **119**
Woodlands Way Cottage. Hen T —5E **16**
Woodland Way. Mar —3C **4**
Wood La. B'ham —9E **88**
Wood La. B Hill —7D **108**
Wood La. Binf —1H **91**
Wood La. Iver —4D **24**
Wood La. Kid E —1B **38**
Wood La. Slou —2B **46**
Wood La. Son C —1F **38**
Wood La. Clo. Iver —4C **24**
Woodlee Clo. Vir W —4L **95**
Woodley Rd. Wdly —4E **64**
Woodman Clo. Read —5J **87**
Woodmancott Clo. Brack —8C **92**
Woodman's La. Bfld C —8G **84**
Woodmere. Brack —6B **92**
Woodmere Clo. Ear —1A **88**
Wood Moor. Finch —8L **111**
Woodmoor End. Cook —8M **5**
Woodpecker Clo. Twy —1K **65**
Woodpecker Wlk. Wokgm —6K **89**
Wood Ridge. Newb —3J **101**
Woodridge Clo. Brack —5N **91**
Wood Rd. Camb —8M **119**
Woodrow Ct. Cav —2F **62**
Woodrow Dri. Wokgm —5C **90**
Woodsend Clo. Lwr Ear —3L **87**
Woodshore Clo. Vir W —8K **95**
Woodside. B'water —7G **118**
Woodside. Farn —9M **119**
Woodside. F Hth —1N **5**
Woodside. Newb —3H **101**
Woodside. Sand —2K **119**
Woodside Av. F Hth —1N **5**
Woodside Bus. Pk. Read —4H **87**
Woodside Clo. Up Buck —5M **81**
Woodside Clo. Wokgm —2K **111**
Woodside La. Wink —9M **69**
Woodside Rd. Wink —9L **69**
Woodside Way. Read —4K **87**
Woodside Way. Vir W —5K **95**
Woods Rd. Cav —9L **39**
Woodstock Av. Slou —3M **47**
Woodstock Clo. M'head —5C **20**
Woodstock St. Read —5K **63**
Woodthorpe Rd. Ashf —9L **73**
Woodview Rd. Pang —8E **36**
Woodville Clo. B'water —4F **118**
Woodward Clo. Winn —2H **89**
Wood Way. Camb —4M **119**
Woodwaye. Wdly —5C **64**
Woodway Rd. Blew —1K **13**
Woodyer Clo. Wdly —7D **64**
Woolacombe Dri. Read —1L **87**
Woolford Clo. Brack —2F **92**
Woolhampton Hill. Woolh —9E **82**
Woolhampton Way. Brack —7A **92**
Woolvers Rd. W Ils —8M **11**
Woosehill. Wokgm —5K **89**
Woosehill Cen. Wokgm —5L **89**
Woosehill Ct. Wokgm —4L **89**
Woosehill La. Wokgm —6L **89**
Wootten Rd. Hen T —6B **16**
Wootton Clo. Tile —4K **61**
Wootton Way. M'head —8N **19**
Worcester Clo. Farn —9M **119**
Worcester Clo. M'head —2N **43**
Worcester Clo. Read —7A **62**
Worcester Gdns. Slou —1F **46**
Worcester Rd. Uxb —6K **25**
Wordsworth. Brack —7J **91**
Wordsworth Av. Yat —5A **118**
Wordsworth Ct. Cav —6J **39**
Wordsworth Rd. Slou —5N **21**
Wordsworth Rd. That —7F **80**
Wordsworth Way. W Dray —3M **49**
Worford Dri. That —8J **81**
Workhouse Grn. Up Buck —4N **81**
Worlds End Hill. Brack —8C **92**
Worple Av. Stai —9J **73**
Worple Rd. Stai —9J **73**
Worple, The. Wray —3A **72**
Worrall Way. Lwr Ear —3M **87**
Worsley Pl. Thea —9F **60**
Worster Rd. Cook —9J **5**
Worton Dri. Read —3G **87**
Worton Grange Ind. Est. Read —3G **87**
Wraysbury Rd. Stai —6C **72**
Wren Clo. Bfld C —8J **85**
Wren Clo. Wokgm —6K **89**
Wren Clo. Yat —3A **118**
Wren Ct. Langl —2B **48**
Wren Dri. W Dray —2L **49**
Wrenfield Dri. Cav —8F **38**
Wrensfield. Mar —5A **4**
Wrenswood Clo. Read —5H **87**
Wren Way. Farn —9K **119**
Wright. Wind —9M **45**
Wright Clo. Wdly —5F **64**
Wright's La. Ham —1B **116**
Wright Sq. Wind —9N **45**
Wright Way. Wind —9M **45**
Wroxham. Brack —7K **91**
Wroxham Rd. Wdly —4C **64**
Wulwyn Ct. Crowt —5D **112**
Wulwyn Side. Crowt —5D **112**
Wyatt Rd. Stai —9H **73**
Wyatt Rd. Wind —9N **45**
Wychcotes. Cav —2F **62**
Wychelm Rd. Light —9M **115**
Wychelm Rd. Shin —6L **87**
Wychwood Av. Brack —6C **92**
Wychwood Clo. Ear —1M **87**
Wychwood Clo. Son C —1F **38**
Wychwood Cres. Ear —9M **63**
Wychwood Pl. Camb —9E **114**
Wycombe Rd. Mar —4C **4**
Wye Clo. Tile —6N **61**
Wykeham Clo. W Dray —4N **49**
Wykeham Rd. Read —6N **63**
Wylam. Brack —7K **91**
Wylands Rd. Slou —3B **48**
Wyld Ct. Hill. Hamp N —8K **33**
Wymers Clo. Burn —3L **21**
Wymer's Wood Rd. Burn —2K **21**
Wyncote Clo. Read —2M **87**
Wyndale Clo. Hen T —5D **16**
Wyndham Clo. Yat —2B **118**
Wyndham Cres. Burn —3L **21**
Wyndham Cres. Wdly —3C **64**
Wyndham Rd. Newb —6A **80**
Wynford Clo. Read —8C **62**
Wynnstay Gdns. Mar —2C **4**
Wynsham Way. W'sham —5L **115**
Wyre Ct. Tile —1K **61**
Wyresdale. Brack —9B **92**
Wythemede. Binf —1F **90**
Wyvern Clo. Brack —6M **91**
Wyvern Way. Uxb —1J **25**

Yale Clo. Owl —8K **113**
Yardley. Brack —7K **91**
Yard Mead. Egh —7B **72**
Yarmouth Rd. Slou —7E **22**
Yarnold Clo. Wokgm —4D **90**
Yarnton Clo. Cav —7J **39**
Yateley Cen. Yat —3A **118**
Yateley Rd. Sand —1D **118**
Yates Copse. Newb —6B **80**
Yattendon La. Ash'd C —2E **58**
Yattendon La. Yatt —1L **57**
Yattendon Rd. Herm —5E **56**
Yaverland Dri. Bag —8G **114**
Yelverton Rd. Read —9J **63**
Ye Meads. Tap —9H **21**
Yeomans La. Newt —9L **101**
Yeoveney Clo. Stai —6E **72**
Yeovil Rd. Owl —9H **113**
Yeovil Rd. Slou —7A **22**
Yew Av. W Dray —8M **25**
Yew Clo. Wokgm —6L **89**
Yew Ga. Newb —5K **79**
Yewhurst Clo. Twy —7H **41**
Yew La. Read —8F **62**
Yew Tree Clo. M'head —6B **20**
Yew Tree Ct. Gor —8L **15**
Yew Tree Rise. Calc —7K **61**
Yew Tree Rd. Slou —2J **47**
Yew Tree Rd. Uxb —2N **25**
Yield Hall La. Read —4H **63**
Yield Hall Pl. Read —5H **63**
Yiewsley Ct. W Dray —9M **25**
Yoreham Clo. Lwr Ear —2D **88**
York Av. Slou —7F **22**
York Av. Wind —8D **46**
York Clo. Newb —9M **79**
York Ho. Brack —3K **91**
York Ho. Calc —8J **61**
York La. Camb —4L **119**
York La. Ter. Camb —4M 119 (off York La.)
York Rd. Binf —9H **67**
York Rd. Camb —2N **119**
York Rd. Hen T —4C **16**
York Rd. Hung —7K **75**
York Rd. M'head —8C **20**
York Rd. Mar —5B **4**
York Rd. Newb —9M **79**
York Rd. Read —3G **62**
York Rd. Uxb —1L **25**
York Rd. Wind —8D **46**
Yorkshire Pl. Warf —2C **92**
Yorktown Rd. Sand & Col T —1E **118**
York Way. Sand —1F **118**
Young's Ind. Est. Aldm —6H **105**

Zealand Av. W Dray —6L **49**
Zinnia Clo. Wokgm —4J **89**
Zinzan Pl. Up Buck —4L **81**
Zinzan St. Read —5F **62**

AREAS COVERED BY THIS ATLAS
with their map square reference

Names in this index shown in CAPITAL LETTERS, followed by its Postcode district, are Postal addresses.

Abbotsbrook. —3K 5
ALDERMASTON. (RG7)
—3J 105
ALDWORTH. (RG8) —2A 34
Amen Corner. —5G 91
Anvilles. —2L 97
ARBORFIELD CROSS. (RG2)
—9D 88
Arborfield Garrison. —2E 110
ARBORFIELD. (RG2) —7B 88
Ascot Heath. —4J 93
ASCOT. (SL5) —6K 93
Ashampstead Green. —6C 34
ASHAMPSTEAD. (RG8) —7C 34
ASHFORD HILL. (RG19)
—9A 104
Ashford Park. —7K 73
ASHFORD. (TW15) —8N 73
ASHMANSWORTH. (RG20)
—9N 117
ASHMORE GREEN. (RG18)
—3E 80
ASTON. (RG9) —1H 17
AVINGTON. (RG17) —6D 76

BAGNOR. (RG20) —4G 79
BAGSHOT. (GU19) —7H 115
BALL HILL. (RG20) —7A 100
Barkham Hill. —8J 89
BARKHAM. (RG40 & RG41)
—7H 89
Baughurst Common. —9F 104
BEECH HILL. (RG7) —5D 108
Beedon Hill. —6A 32
BEEDON. (RG20) —6A 32
Beenham Hill. —5K 83
BEENHAM. (RG7) —5J 83
Beenham's Heath. —1F 66
Beenham Stocks. —4K 83
Beggar's Bush. —6B 94
Bill Hill. —1A 90
BILLINGBEAR. (RG40) —7F 66
BINFIELD HEATH. (RG9)
—3N 39
BINFIELD. (RG12 & RG42)
—9G 67
Birch Green. —8H 73
Birch Hill. —9M 91
BISHAM. (SL7) —8B 4
Bishops Gate. —7J 71
BISHOP'S GREEN. (RG20)
—7D 102
Blacknest. —5D 94
BLACKWATER. (GU17)
—5J 119
Borrough's Grove. —1D 4
Bothamstead. —9E 32
BOURNE END. (SL8) —4L 5
Boveney. —5N 45
BOXFORD. (RG20) —9B 54
Boyn Hill. —8A 20
BRACKNELL. (RG12 & RG42)
—4N 91
BRADFIELD. (RG7) —6L 59
BRANDS HILL. (SL3) —5C 48
BRAY. (SL6) —1F 44
Bray Wick. —1D 44
Braywoodside. —1N 67
Brightwalton Green. —3B 30
BRIGHTWALTON. (RG20)
—2B 30
BRIMPTON COMMON. (RG7)
—7D 104
BRIMPTON. (RG7) —4B 104
BRITWELL. (SL2) —4C 22
Broad Laying. —9D 100
Brock Hill. —8D 68
Brookside. —1J 93
Broomhall. —8C 94
Bucklebury Alley. —1F 80
BUCKLEBURY. (RG7) —1A 82
Bullbrook. —4B 92
BURCHETT'S GREEN. (SL6)
—7F 18
BURGHFIELD COMMON. (RG7)
—9H 85
Burghfield Hill. —8J 85
BURGHFIELD. (RG30) —6L 85
Burleigh. —3H 93
BURNHAM. (SL1) —5M 21
Bury's Bank. —3B 102

CALCOT. (RG31) —8M 61
Calcot Row. —8K 61
CALIFORNIA. (RG40) —4J 111
CAMBERLEY.(GU15, GU16 &
GU17) —3N 119
Cantley. —3N 89

Caversham Heights. —1E 62
Caversham Park. —8J 39
CAVERSHAM. (RG4) —1G 63
CHADDLEWORTH. (RG20)
—5N 29
CHALKHOUSE GREEN. (RG4)
—4G 38
CHALVEY. (SL1) —1F 46
Chapel Green. —7A 90
CHAPEL ROW. (RG7) —3E 82
CHARVIL. (RG10) —8F 40
CHAVEY DOWN. (SL5) —3F 92
CHAZEY HEATH. (RG4) —6C 38
CHEAPSIDE. (SL5) —3A 94
CHIEVELEY. (RG20) —3M 55
CHILTON FOLIAT. (RG17)
—1J 74
Church Lammas. —7E 72
CIPPENHAM. (SL1) —8A 22
City. —1K 101
Clapton. —2F 76
Clay Hill. —1G 82
Cleeve. —7L 15
Clewer Green. —8B 46
Clewer Hill. —9A 46
Clewer New Town. —8D 46
Clewer St Andrew. —6C 46
Clewer St Stephen. —6D 46
Clewer Village. —6C 46
Clewer Within. —8E 46
COCKPOLE GREEN. (RG10)
—7L 17
COLD ASH. (RG18) —4F 80
Cold Harbour. —1D 36
Coley. —6G 62
Coley Park. —7E 62
Colham Green. —6N 25
COLLEGE TOWN. (GU15)
—3J 119
Collins End. —3J 37
COLNBROOK. (SL3) —6E 48
COLTHROP. (RG18 & RG19)
—9M 81
COMBE. (RG17) —3D 116
COMPTON. (RG20) —1H 33
COOKHAM DEAN. (SL6) —9F 4
Cookham Rise. —8K 5
COOKHAM. (SL6) —8M 5
Cores End. —4N 5
Cornwall Coppice. —3J 61
Cowley Peachey. —7K 25
COWLEY. (UB8) —5K 25
Cox Green. —2M 43
Cranbourne. —6M 69
Crawley Hill. —4N 119
CRAZIES HILL. (RG10) —8L 17
Cricket Hill. —4B 118
CROCKHAM HEATH. (RG20)
—4C 100
Crooked Soley. —6E 50
CROOKHAM COMMON. (RG19)
—5G 102
CROOKHAM. (RG19) —5M 103
Crown Wood. —8A 92
CROWSLEY. (RG9) —1J 39
CROWTHORNE. (RG45)
—5G 112
CURRIDGE. (RG18) —7B 56

Darby Green. —3F 118
Datchet Common. —7M 47
DATCHET. (SL3) —6K 47
DEDWORTH. (SL4) —8A 46
DONNINGTON. (RG14) —5K 79
DORNEY REACH. (SL6) —2J 45
DORNEY. (SL4) —2M 45
Dowlesgreen. —4B 90
Dunsden Green. —6M 39

EARLEY. (RG6) —7N 63
East Burnham. —1C 22
EASTBURY. (RG17) —6M 27
EAST END. (RG20) —2M 117
Eastern Industrial Area,
Bracknell. —4A 92
EAST GARSTON. (RG17)
—7B 28
East Garston Woodlands.
—1N 53
Easthampstead. —7M 91
Eastheath. —9M 89
EAST ILSLEY. (RG20) —7B 12
EASTON. (RG20) —7N 53
EAST WOODHAY. (RG20)
—2L 117
EDDINGTON. (RG17) —4L 75
Egham Hythe. —9E 72
EGHAM. (TW20) —9B 72
Egham Wick. —2J 95

ELCOT. (RG20) —3J 77
Eling. —1H 57
Emmbrook. —2L 89
EMMER GREEN. (RG4) —7H 39
ENBORNE. (RG14 & RG20)
—2D 100
Enborne Row. —6F 100
Englefield Green. —1L 95
ENGLEFIELD. (RG7) —7C 60
ETON. (SL4) —5F 46
ETON WICK. (SL4) —4B 46
EVERSLEY. (RG27) —9F 110

FACCOMBE. (SP11) —8H 117
Fair Cross. —8D 108
FARLEY HILL. (RG7) —3A 110
Farley Wood. —4H 91
FARNBOROUGH. (OX12)
—6C 10
FARNHAM ROYAL. (SL2)
—3E 22
FAWLEY. (OX12) —7H 9
Fern. —2J 5
FIFIELD. (SL6) —7G 45
Finchampstead North. —3K 111
FINCHAMPSTEAD. (RG40)
—7K 111
Fishery. —8E 20
FLACKWELL HEATH. (HP10)
—1M 5
Forest Park. —8C 92
Foxhill. —5C 110
Fox Lane. —9J 119
Friary Island. —3L 71
FRILSHAM. (RG18) —5N 57
FRIMLEY. (GU16) —9N 119
Frogmore. —9M 47
(Windsor, Berks.)
FROGMORE. (GU17) —4G 118
(Camberley, Surrey)
FROXFIELD. (SN8) —7B 74
Furze Platt. —4A 20

GALLOWSTREE COMMON.
(RG4) —1C 38
Gardeners Green. —9C 90
GEORGE GREEN. (SL3)
—7M 23
Glanty. —8C 72
Goaters Hill. —3F 92
Goddard's Green. —9L 85
Goldfinch Bottom. —5F 102
Goose Green. —2H 27
Goose Hill. —7K 103
GORE END. (RG20) —6N 99
GORING HEATH. (RG8)
—2H 37
GORING. (RG8) —8L 15
GRAZELEY. (RG7) —9D 86
Great Hollands. —8K 91
Great Lea Common. —6G 86
GREAT SHEFFORD. (RG17)
—1F 52
Greenham Common. —5B 102
GREENHAM. (RG14 & RG20)
—2A 102

HALFWAY. (RG20) —6L 77
Ham Island. —1M 71
Ham Marsh. —8N 79
HAMPSTEAD NORREYS. (RG18)
—8J 33
HAM. (SN8) —7J 97
HAMSTEAD MARSHALL.
(RG20) —3M 99
Hanworth. —9L 91
(Bracknell, Berks.)
Hardings Green. —8G 5
HARE HATCH. (RG10) —5M 41
Harmanswater. —6B 92
HARMONDSWORTH. (UB7)
—5L 49
Harpsden Bottom. —8A 16
HARPSDEN. (RG9) —8D 16
Haughurst Hill. —9E 104
Hawley. —6J 119
Hawley Lane. —9M 119
Hawthorn Hill. —3A 68
HEADLEY. (RG19) —8G 103
HEAD'S HILL. (RG19) —6E 102
Heath End. —9H 105
HEATH END. (RG20) —9M 99
Hell Corner. —5F 98
HENLEY-ON-THAMES. (RG9)
—4C 16
HERMITAGE. (RG18) —5E 56
Highway. —8L 19
Hill Bottom. —2F 36

Hillfoot. —2C 82
Hillgreen. —7G 30
Hockley Hole. —2K 23
HOE BENHAM. (RG20) —3M 77
Hollingsworth. —8H 33
Hollington. —4N 117
Holloway. —9G 18
Holme Green. —8D 90
Holt, The. —4L 51
Holt, The. —4N 41
Holtwood. —5N 99
HOLYPORT. (SL6) —5E 44
Hopgood's Green. —3L 81
Horncastle. —7N 61
Hornhill. —1J 97
Horrid Hill. —7K 101
Horsemoor. —4M 55
HORTON. (SL3) —9B 48
(Slough)
Hungerford. —2C 66
Hungerford Newtown. —9A 52
HUNGERFORD. (RG17) —5K 75
Hunt's Green. —8A 16
HUNT'S GREEN. (RG20)
—2C 78
Hurley Bottom. —3D 18
HURLEY. (SL6) —2D 18
HURST. (RG10) —5L 65
Hyde End. —6A 104
Hythe End. —6C 72

Inhurst. —9E 104
INKPEN. (RG17) —5D 98
IVER HEATH. (SL0) —3E 24
IVER. (SL0) —7G 24

Jealott's Hill. —5M 67
Jennetts Hill. —9F 58

KIDMORE END. (RG4) —2E 38
KILN GREEN. (RG10) —3B 42
KINTBURY. (RG17) —9F 76
Knighton. —9A 50
Knowle Green. —9J 73
Knowle Hill. —9K 95
KNOWL HILL. (RG10) —1C 42

Lake End. —1M 45
LAMBOURN. (RG17) —3H 27
LAMBOURN WOODLANDS.
(RG17) —9F 26
Lambridge Hill. —1A 16
Langley Common. —9E 88
LANGLEY. (SL3) —2B 48
LECKHAMPSTEAD. (RG20)
—8D 30
Leckhampstead Thicket.
—7B 30
Lent. —5L 21
LENT RISE. (SL1) —7M 21
LEVERTON. (RG17) —2J 75
Liddiard's Green. —8C 10
LIGHTWATER. (GU18) —9K 113
Lilley. —2E 30
LINKENHOLT. (SP11) —8B 116
LITTLE BEDWYN. (SN8)
—2A 96
Little Britain. —7K 25
Little Heath. —4J 61
Little Hungerford. —4F 56
LITTLE MARLOW. (SL7) —2G 5
LITTLE SANDHURST. (GU17)
—9E 112
Littlestead Green. —6L 39
LITTLEWICK GREEN. (SL6)
—9F 18
Longford. —7J 49
(West Drayton)
Longfordmoor. —7H 49
Longlane. —8D 56
LOWER BASILDON. (RG8)
—3M 35
Lower Caversham. —3J 63
Lower Common. —9E 110
LOWER EARLEY. (RG6)
—2C 64
Lower Green. —5A 98
LOWER PADWORTH. (RG7)
—7M 83
Lower Pibworth. —3N 33
LOWER SHIPLAKE. (RG9)
—1G 40
Lynch Hill. —4A 22

Maidenhead Court. —3F 20
MAIDENHEAD. (SL6) —7C 20

MAIDEN'S GREEN. (RG42)
—7E 68
Malpas. —6F 60
Manor Farm Estate. —4M 71
MANOR PARK. (SL2) —6F 22
(Slough)
MAPLEDURHAM. (RG4)
—7M 37
Marlow Bottom. —2B 4
MARLOW. (SL7) —5B 4
Marridge Hill. —2A 50
MARSH BENHAM. (RG20)
—7B 78
Martin's Heron. —5C 92
Matthewsgreen. —3M 89
MEDMENHAM. (SL7) —1N 17
Mell Green. —5H 31
Membury. —2C 50
Merryhill Green. —9J 65
MIDDLE GREEN. (SL3) —9N 23
Midgham Green. —7D 82
MIDGHAM. (RG7) —8B 82
Mill Green. —8J 103
Minley. —8B 118
Moneyrow Green. —6D 44
Moor, The. —6E 72
Moor, The. —8L 5
MORTIMER. (RG7) —4H 107
MORTIMER WEST END. (RG7)
—6E 106
Moss End. —6M 67
Moulsford Bottom. —3G 14
MOULSFORD. (OX10) —2H 15
Mount, The. —7J 63
Myrke. —3H 47

Nash Grove. —1K 111
NETHERTON. (SP11) —9E 116
NEWBURY. (RG14 & RG20)
—8L 79
New Denham. —1J 25
Newell Green. —9A 68
Newtown. —7D 16
New Town. —5L 63
Newtown. —7C 96
New Town. —9M 35
NEWTOWN COMMON. (RG20)
—7L 101
NEWTOWN. (RG20) —6M 101
New Windsor. —9F 46
Nodmore. —6N 29
North Ascot. —3G 93
NORTH END. (RG20) —8L 99
North Street. —7E 60
NORTH SYDMONTON. (RG20)
—9D 102
North Town. —5C 20
NUPTOWN. (RG42) —5C 68

Oak Grove. —3J 119
OAKLEY GREEN. (SL4)
—8L 45
Oare. —4E 56
OLD WINDSOR. (SL4) —2J 71
OWLSMOOR. (GU15) —9J 113
OWNHAM. (RG20) —2A 78

PADWORTH. (RG7) —1N 105
Paley Street. —8M 43
PAMBER HEATH. (RG26)
—9N 105
PANGBOURNE. (RG8) —8D 36
PEASEMORE. (RG20) —6H 31
PENNYHILL PARK. (GU19)
—8E 114
PENWOOD. (RG20) —9E 100
Pield Heath. —6M 25
Pinewood. —3F 112
PINGEWOOD. (RG30) —4C 86
Pinkeys Green. —5K 19
Plastow Green. —9K 103
Play Hatch. —8N 39
Pooley Green. —9D 72
Popeswood. —3H 91
Poundgreen. —8C 86
POYLE. (SL3) —7F 48
Priestwood. —3L 91
PURLEY ON THAMES. (RG8)
—8L 37
Purton. —5A 32

Quick's Green. —8G 34

Ragnal. —4F 50
READING. (RG1 to RG8, RG10,
RG30 & RG31) —4H 63

Red Hill. —5A 100
Remenham Hill. —4H 17
REMENHAM. (RG9) —1F 16
RICHINGS PARK. (SL0)
—1G 49
RIDGES, THE. (RG40)
—6M 111
Ripley Springs. —1N 95
RISELEY. (RG7) —7J 109
Rivar. —9F 96
Rotten Row. —9H 59
Roundfield. —5L 81
Rounds Hill. —3K 91
Runnymede. —6M 71
RUSCOMBE. (RG10) —8L 41
RYEISH GREEN. (RG7) —8J 87

Salt Hill. —9E 22
SANDHURST. (GU15 & GU17)
—2F 118
Sandleford Park. —5L 101
Sanham Green. —9K 75
Schoolgreen. —7L 87
Scotland. —3C 82
SHALBOURNE. (SN8) —8E 96
Shaw Farm. —1G 70
SHAW. (RG14) —6M 79
Sheepdrove. —9L 7
SHEFFORD WOODLANDS.
(RG17) —5C 52
SHINFIELD. (RG2) —6L 87
SHIPLAKE. (RG9) —3B 40
Shiplake Row. —3B 40
Shreding Green. —7D 24
Shrubs Hill. —8E 94
SHURLOCK ROW. (RG10)
—3E 66
SILCHESTER. (RG7) —9C 106
SINDLESHAM. (RG41)
—3G 88
Sipson. —5N 49
Skimped Hill. —4M 91
Skinners Green. —2F 100
Slade, The. —2K 81
SLOUGH. (SL1 to SL3)
—1H 47
SONNING COMMON. (RG4)
—1F 38
SONNING EYE. (RG4) —8B 40
SONNING. (RG4) —9C 40
SOUTH ASCOT. (SL5) —8K 93
Southcote. —8B 62
South End. —1J 83
Southern Industrial Area,
Bracknell. —5J 91
SOUTH FAWLEY. (OX12)
—9H 9
Southlea. —8K 47
SOUTH STOKE. (RG8) —3K 15
SPEENHAMLAND. (RG14)
—7L 79
SPEEN. (RG14 & RG20)
—6H 79
SPENCERS WOOD. (RG7)
—9H 87
Spital. —9D 46
STAINES. (TW18 & TW19)
—8G 72
STANFORD DINGLEY. (RG7)
—8F 58
Stanford End. —7F 108
Stanmore. —3M 31
Stanwell Moor. —2H 73
STANWELL. (TW19) —3L 73
Stitchens. —2H 35
STOCKCROSS. (RG20) —5C 78
Stoke Green. —5K 23
STOKE POGES. (SL2) —1J 23
Stone Copse. —4B 80
Straight Soley. —7G 51
Stratfield Mortimer. —5L 107
STRATFIELD SAYE. (RG7)
—9A 108
STREATLEY. (RG8) —8J 15
Stroude. —5N 95
Stud Green. —6B 44
SULHAM. (RG8) —3F 60
SULHAMSTEAD ABBOTS. (RG7)
—7F 84
Sulhamstead Bannister
Upper End. —6E 84
SULHAMSTEAD. (RG7)
—5D 84
SUNNINGDALE. (SL5) —7C 94
SUNNINGHILL. (SL5) —7N 93
Sunnymeads. —1N 71
Sutton. —4D 48
(Slough)
SWALLOWFIELD. (RG7)
—4J 109

Areas covered by this Atlas

TADLEY. (RG26) —9L **105**
TAPLOW. (SL6) —5H **21**
Temple. —1G **18**
THATCHAM. (RG18 & RG19)
—8G **80**
THEALE. (RG7) —9F **60**
Thorney. —2J **49**
THREE MILE CROSS. (RG7)
—7H **87**
Tickleback Row. —6L **67**
TIDMARSH. (RG8) —2D **60**
TILEHURST. (RG30 & RG31)
—4L **61**
Tinker's Green. —4B **38**
Titcomb. —3E **98**
Tittle Row. —8L **19**
TOKERS GREEN. (RG4)
—6D **38**
Tot Hill. —9J **101**
Touchen End. —7A **44**
Trapshill. —7D **98**
Trash Green. —4J **85**
Trench Green. —5B **38**
Trumps Green. —8M **95**
Turner's Green. —4L **81**
TUTTS CLUMP. (RG7) —9H **59**

TWYFORD. (RG10) —9J **41**

Ufton Green. —6C **84**
UFTON NERVET. (RG7)
—8D **84**
UPPER BASILDON. (ARG8)
—8K **35**
UPPER BUCKLEBURY. (RG7)
—5M **81**
Upper Green. —6D **98**
UPPER LAMBOURN. (RG17)
—8E **6**
Upper Wargrave. —3K **41**
UPPER WOOLHAMPTON. (RG7)
—7F **82**
Upton. —2J **47**
(Slough)
Upton Park. —2H **47**
(Slough)
Uxbridge Moor. —3J **25**
UXBRIDGE. (UB8 to UB11)
—1K **25**

Village, The. —7C **70**

VIRGINIA WATER. (GU25)
—7N **95**

WALTHAM ST LAWRENCE.
(RG10) —7D **42**
Ward's Cross. —4L **65**
WARFIELD PARK. (RG42)
—1D **92**
WARFIELD. (RG42) —7B **68**
WARGRAVE. (RG10) —3J **41**
WARREN ROW. (RG10)
—8A **18**
Warren, The. —6C **92**
Wash Common. —5H **101**
WASH WATER. (RG20)
—7G **101**
Wasing. —5F **104**
WATER OAKLEY. (SL4)
—5J **45**
WELFORD. (RG20) —5M **53**
Well End. —2L **5**
Wellhouse. —7H **57**
Wentworth. —7G **95**
West Bedfont. —3N **73**
WESTBROOK. (RG20) —8B **54**

WEST DRAYTON. (UB7)
—1M **49**
West End. —9C **42**
West End. —9M **67**
(Bracknell, Berks.)
Western Industrial Area,
Bracknell. —4K **91**
West Fields. —9K **79**
WEST ILSLEY. (RG20) —5M **11**
WESTON. (RG20) —4J **53**
Westridge Green. —1D **34**
WEST WOODHAY. (RG20)
—7G **99**
WEXHAM COURT. (SL2)
—7L **23**
WEXHAM. (SL3) —5L **23**
Wexham Street. —2L **23**
WHISTLEY GREEN. (RG10)
—3K **65**
Whistley Park. —4J **65**
WHITCHURCH HILL. (RG8)
—3F **36**
WHITCHURCH ON THAMES.
(RG8) —6D **36**
WHITE WALTHAM. (SL6)
—6J **43**

Whitley. —1J **87**
Whitley Wood. —4J **87**
Whittonditch. —7A **50**
Wickham Green. —7J **53**
WICKHAM HEATH. (RG20)
—3N **77**
WICKHAM. (RG20) —8J **53**
WICK HILL. (RG40) —4M **111**
Wildridings. —6L **91**
WINDLESHAM. (GU20)
—6N **115**
Windsor Castle. —7G **46**
WINDSOR. (SL4) —7F **46**
WINKFIELD ROW. (RG42)
—9E **68**
WINKFIELD. (SL4) —7G **68**
Winkfield Street. —6F **68**
WINNERSH. (RG41) —1H **89**
WINTERBOURNE. (RG20)
—7H **55**
WOKINGHAM. (RG40 & RG41)
—5A **90**
Wokingham Without. —2D **112**
Wooburn. —3N **5**
Wood End. —1L **93**
(Windsor, Berks.)

Woodlands Park. —3K **43**
WOODLANDS ST MARY. (RG17)
—2J **51**
Woodley Airfield. —4H **65**
Woodley Green. —4F **64**
WOODLEY. (RG5 & RG6)
—5D **64**
Woodside. —9M **69**
(Windsor, Berks.)
WOODSPEEN. (RG20) —4F **78**
WOOLHAMPTON. (RG7)
—9E **82**
Woolley Green. —9K **19**
WOOLTON HILL. (RG20)
—9C **100**
Woose Hill. —5L **89**
World's End. —7A **32**
WRAYSBURY. (TW19) —3A **72**

YATELEY. (GU17) —3B **118**
YATTENDON. (RG18) —3A **58**
YIEWSLEY. (UB7) —9L **25**
York Town. —4L **119**